Econometric Society Monographs in Quantitative Economics

Instrumental variables

Econometric Society Publication No. 8

Books in both the Econometric Society Monographs in Pure Theory and the Econometric Society Monographs in Quantitative Economics are numbered in a single sequence for the purposes of the Econometric Society. A complete listing of books in the Econometric Society Monographs in Quantitative Economics is given on the following page.

Econometric Society Monographs in Quantitative Economics

Edited by
Angus Deaton, *Princeton University*
Charles Manski, *University of Wisconsin*
Hugo Sonnenschein, *Princeton University*

The Econometric Society is an international society for the advancement of economic theory in relation to statistics and mathematics. The Econometric Society Monographs in Quantitative Economics series is designed to promote the publication of original research contributions of high quality in mathematical economics and in theoretical and applied econometrics.

Other books in the series
Werner Hildenbrand *Advances in economic theory*
Werner Hildenbrand *Advances in econometrics*
G. S. Maddala *Limited-dependent and qualitative variables in econometrics*

Instrumental variables

ROGER J. BOWDEN *and*
DARRELL A. TURKINGTON
The University of Western Australia

CAMBRIDGE UNIVERSITY PRESS
Cambridge
London New York New Rochelle
Melbourne Sydney

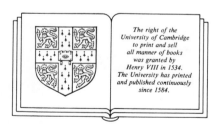

Published by the Press Syndicate of the University of Cambridge
The Pitt Building, Trumpington Street, Cambridge CB2 1RP
32 East 57th Street, New York, NY 10022, USA
10 Stamford Road, Oakleigh, Melbourne 3166, Australia

First published 1984

Printed in the United States of America

Library of Congress Cataloging in Publication Data

Bowden, Roger J. (Roger John), 1943–

Instrumental variables.

(Econometric Society monographs in quantitative economics)

1. Instrumental variables (Statistics)
I. Turkington, Darrell A. II. Title. III. Series.
HB139.B69 1984 519.5′35 84-7802
ISBN 0 521 26241 0

Contents

Preface

It has long been noted in textbooks of econometrics that the method of two-stage least squares is equivalent to an instrumental variables (IV) computation, even if the converse proposition, that every IV estimator is also a two-stage least-squares calculation, has not received the same exposure. More recently it has become realized that methods such as three-stage least squares and maximum likelihood applied to a system of stochastic equations can also be cast as instrumental variables estimators. In such cases, however, the interpretation is not in terms of the IV calculations that appear in the textbooks, but relies instead upon suitable generalizations of instrumental variables methods to models with nonspherical disturbance structures. Thus it is true that the methodology of instrumental variables may be regarded as a strong organizing principle with respect to estimation and hypothesis testing in econometrics. It is also true that the methodology itself needs some codifying in order to cope with the apparent range of IV-type estimators that have emerged in recent years. In the present book we have presented the methodology of instrumental variables in its most general form as a minimum-distance technique applied to either the original or a suitably transformed problem. We show how the resulting estimators can be used to organize the literature on a wide variety of estimation and hypothesis-testing problems in econometrics.

The project has been rather long in gestation, with work beginning in 1981 on the application of IV to nonspherical contexts and continuing until late 1983. In part, this reflects the personal movements and other preoccupations of the authors over this period. It has also something to do with the still unresolved status of some of the subject material. For instance, while we have shown that all serious (in efficiency terms) IV candidates can be reduced to one of two forms – what we have called the IV–OLS and IV–GLS analogs – we have not been able finally to resolve the circumstances under which one variant will perform better than the other. Likewise, the subject of hypothesis testing remains rather cloudy in some areas. But one has to call a halt at some point. We hope that what we have done represents a significant synthesis of many topics in econometrics that might hitherto have been regarded as "seemingly unrelated," in the jargon of estimation. The best compliment that a book of this type can attract is that, consciously or unconsciously, it conditions the way in which subsequent researchers and students approach its subject material, and so far we have felt quite encouraged in this respect by those who have read the manuscript. On a more humdrum level, the book contains some material previously rather inaccessible or known merely as part of an unwritten or unpublished body of econometric folklore. There is virtue in writing down such oral traditions as the role of instrument counting in identification or overidentification, if only because not all graduate or undergraduate students have equal access to such traditions.

We have been greatly helped by the readers for the series, under the stewardship of Angus Deaton as series coeditor. The referee of the penultimate draft, in particular, went over the manuscript in considerable detail and provided a series of useful comments some of which led to material improvements. We are grateful to authors who permitted us to quote from material from seminar papers or unpublished work, notably Tom Rothenberg with respect to material on second-order efficiency and Ray Byron on the IV interpretation of linear limited-information estimators. At Cambridge University Press, Rhona Johnson, in charge of manuscript development, noticed that our nebulous notation and numbering needed norming. Colin Day was always a source of encouragement. The manuscript must have been difficult for the copy editor, representing as it did a collage from four typists and at least five different typewriters. Michael Dauman Gnat also performed valiantly in this respect. As always, we owe a great debt for secretarial assistance to Marie Green at the University of Western Australia; Miriam Bailey at the World Bank in Washington, D.C., also rates honorable mention in this regard. Jane Bowerman at the university contributed a computer efficiency plot and drew the diagrams.

CHAPTER 1

Motivation

1.1 Introduction

The method of instrumental variables (IV) has traditionally been viewed as a response to a common problem in regression contexts, namely where one or more of the regressors on the right-hand side of the proposed equation are correlated with the equation disturbance. If this happens, the method of ordinary least squares suffers from consistency problems. The instrumental variables methods were developed to overcome these problems. It could legitimately be objected that the focus on consistency alone as a criterion of statistical effectiveness is misplaced. Thus it is often the case that estimators that are consistent possess inferior mean-square error properties to those that are not. Remarkably enough, however, the IV methodology can in many circumstances provide estimators that have superior efficiency properties all round. Indeed, it will be one of the themes of the later chapters of this book that the method of maximum likelihood may, in certain contexts of importance, itself be regarded as an instrumental variables estimator, so that IV estimators are asymptotically fully efficient. In the present chapter, however, we shall lower our sights a little and consider the motivation for instrumental variables as arising from requirements of statistical consistency.

On regressors and disturbances

Although the method of instrumental variables was not originally developed in the specific context of regression theory, it has since been viewed essentially as an adjunct to regression analysis. This is certainly the easiest way to motivate the method and is, by and large, the path toward its exposition followed throughout this book. Putting historical matters temporarily aside, let us begin by considering circumstances under which standard regression methods do not work.

Suppose that we are to fit the very simple regression model

$$y_i = \beta x_i + u_i, \qquad i = 1, \ldots, n, \tag{1.1}$$

where the u_i are disturbances that we shall suppose have zero expectation and common variance σ^2. We do not at this stage impose the assumption that successive disturbances are serially uncorrelated. Likewise, we shall not yet impose any particular specification or structure on the right-hand variables x_i. Now the least-squares estimator of the parameter β in equation (1.1) is

$$b = \sum y_i x_i / \sum x_i^2 = \beta + \sum x_i u_i / \sum x_i^2, \tag{1.2}$$

where we have utilized $y_i = \beta x_i + u_i$. If the x_i can be regarded as drawings from a distribution function of a random variable that is independent of the u_i, then the sum $(1/n) \sum x_i u_i$ tends in probability to zero and we assume that the sum $(1/n) \sum x_i^2$ tends in probability to a constant, say, σ_x^2. The same will be true, with reinterpretations as appropriate, if the x_i are regarded as fixed, that is, nonrandom variates that obey suitable regularity conditions. (At this point we shall not be explicit about what constitutes such conditions.) Under either of these circumstances, it will follow that the least-squares estimate b tends in probability to β; indeed, the convergence will be almost sure.[1]

Suppose, however, that the observations x_i are random variables that are correlated with the disturbances u_i, at least in the weak sense that $\operatorname{plim}(1/n) \sum x_i u_i \neq 0$. We shall tacitly assume that the limit in probability exists and is nonzero. It follows that the least squares estimate b does not tend in probability to the true value β; or more precisely, we cannot assert that it will. The term $\operatorname{plim}(1/n) \sum x_i u_i / \sigma_x^2$ represents the inconsistency of the estimator, namely $\operatorname{plim}(b - \beta)$.

The method of instrumental variables is basically a way of proceeding with remedial action in such situations, which possesses the merit of consistency, and which does so in a manner that preserves the regression framework, in a sense that will become clear as development proceeds. However, before turning to these methods, it is useful to review certain situations that do exhibit the problem of regressor–disturbance correlation. We do this for two reasons: first, because to do so now will save us some rather elementary exposition that would unduly interrupt the analysis at later stages, and second, to demonstrate that this particular problem occurs in a wide variety of models. Since these models are all amenable in varying degree to instrumental variables estimation, this will help to motivate the development of a general IV methodology.

All four applications are familiar to students of econometrics. We do suggest, however, that such readers take time out to look at the errors in variables material, which as a matter of interpretation improves on existing textbook discussions, and at the self-selection problem, which is discussed at length in Section 2.6.

Errors in variables and latent variables

Suppose that we have a bivariate data series x_i, y_i; $i=1,\ldots,n$, of mutually independent random variables with means χ_i, $\alpha+\beta\chi_i$ and variances ϕ^2, σ^2, respectively. An equivalent structural formulation is

$$x_i=\alpha+\beta\chi_i+u_i; \qquad \mathcal{E}u_i=0, \quad \mathcal{E}u_i^2=\sigma^2; \tag{1.3a}$$

$$x_i=\chi_i+\epsilon_i; \qquad \mathcal{E}\epsilon_i=0, \quad \mathcal{E}\epsilon_i^2=\phi^2; \tag{1.3b}$$

with in addition $\mathcal{E}u_i\epsilon_i=0$. This is the classic errors-in-variables model, the idea being that the true values of the variables are observed only with errors (u_i, ϵ_i). These "errors" may represent not only errors of observation but also a substantive hypothesis about the behavior of the agents concerned. The most celebrated of this latter class of theories is Friedman's (1957) permanent-income hypothesis. Here y_i would denote observed consumption and χ_i would be "permanent income," representing a smoothing by the household of temporary fluctuations in accordance with some desired pattern of lifetime consumption. Observed income differs from permanent income by a supposedly random disturbance ϵ_i. Although not a particularly convincing piece of consumption theory, models of this kind have been empirically fitted by Friedman and others.

Now the variates χ_i that appear in the errors in variables model (1.3) have the status of unknown parameters, even if of the nuisance or incidental variety, and it is readily apparent that the parameter space is potentially of infinite dimension. It is this fact that has led, over the years, to a voluminous statistical literature on an apparently very simple model. Only relatively recently has a fuller understanding of its properties been arrived at.

To start with, it has long been known that the method of maximum likelihood fails for this model. Some writers have labeled this failure an identifiability problem, but this is not really the case. To see this, denote by $\boldsymbol{\theta}$ the vector $(\beta, \sigma^2, \phi^2; \chi_i,\ i=1,\ldots,n)'$ of parameters and write the normal log-likelihood function (apart from a constant) in the form

$$\frac{1}{n}l(\boldsymbol{\theta})=-\left[\log(\sigma^2\phi^2)+\frac{1}{n\phi^2}\sum_i(x_i-\chi_i)^2+\frac{1}{n\sigma^2}\sum_i(y_i-\beta\chi_i)^2\right]. \tag{1.4}$$

For simplicity we have assumed $\alpha = 0$. The sample size is written as n, a convention that will be followed, except where otherwise indicated, throughout the book. Let us fix the sample size n and consider the identifiability of the parameters. Following the Kullback–Bowden information criterion for identification (Bowden 1973), let $\boldsymbol{\theta}_0$ denote the true parameter values and denote by $\mathcal{E}^0$ the operation of taking expectations, on the premise that the true parameter values are $\boldsymbol{\theta}_0$. By using decompositions such as $x_i - \chi_i = (x_i - \chi_i^0) + (\chi_i^0 - \chi_i)$, we derive

$$h(\boldsymbol{\theta};\boldsymbol{\theta}_0) = \mathcal{E}^0\left[\frac{1}{n} l(\boldsymbol{\theta})\right] = -\left[\log(\sigma^2\phi^2) + \frac{\phi_0^2}{\phi^2} + \frac{\sigma_0^2}{\sigma^2} + \frac{1}{n\phi^2}\sum_i (\chi_i - \chi_i^0)^2 + \frac{1}{n\sigma^2}\sum_i (\beta\chi_i - \beta_0\chi_i^0)^2\right]. \tag{1.5}$$

The parameter values $\boldsymbol{\theta}_0$ will be globally identified if and only if the function $h(\boldsymbol{\theta};\boldsymbol{\theta}_0)$ has an isolated global maximum at $\boldsymbol{\theta} = \boldsymbol{\theta}_0$. It is apparent by an inspection of expression (1.5) that such a global maximum is unique and is attained at $\boldsymbol{\theta} = \boldsymbol{\theta}_0$, a conclusion that can be verified by the usual methods of differential calculus.

There is therefore no lack of identification in the model, a fact that has been pointed out by previous commentators. Suppose, however, that one proceeds to maximize the likelihood function (1.4) as a problem in estimation. It turns out that there are two critical (stationary) points, according to the sign of β, and the value of the likelihood function is the same at each. Conventionally, one chooses the sign of β so that $\beta(\sum x_i y_i) > 0$. Apart from this problem of arbitrariness, however, further problems arise. By setting $\partial l/\partial \chi_i = 0$ one obtains (see Johnston 1963)

$$y_i - \hat{\beta}\chi_i = -\frac{\hat{\sigma}^2}{\hat{\beta}\hat{\phi}^2}(x_i - \chi_i).$$

Squaring and summing over i, one obtains

$$\hat{\beta}^2 = \hat{\sigma}^2/\hat{\phi}^2.$$

Clearly at least one of the maximum-likelihood estimates $\hat{\beta}^2, \hat{\sigma}^2, \hat{\phi}^2$ cannot be consistent.

Yet as we have seen, the model is identified. The resolution of this apparent paradox is that the likelihood function (1.4) is not a classical log likelihood based upon independent, identically distributed (i.i.d.) elements. It is instead a data density, constructed from probability elements that, because the means $(\chi_i, \beta\chi_i)$ differ, are independent but not identically distributed. Now if our observations took the form of independent replications of the entire vector $(\mathbf{x}', \mathbf{y}') = (x_1 ... x_n, y_1 ... y_n)$ for fixed n, no difficulty would arise. The problem is that we have only one replication. In other contexts, the stationarity assumptions often imply that one can derive ensemble properties from a single infinite realization. The presence of an infinite number of parameters χ_i precludes this convenient property in the errors-in-variables model.

As shown by Solari (1969) (see also Sprent 1970), the upshot is that the likelihood function – or better, the data density (1.5) – does not possess a proper maximum. The critical points noted above are in fact saddle points, with the main axis of the saddle oriented along a line in χ space joining the points $\mathbf{x}$ and $(1/\beta)\mathbf{y}$. Moreover, the likelihood function can be made to assume any value between $\pm\infty$ by appropriate parameter choices. The likelihood approach can be resurrected but needs some prior information, either of the "hard-and-fast" variety (say, assuming that the ratio $\lambda = \sigma^2/\phi^2$ is known) or else by specifying an informative prior for the Bayesian analysis of the problem (e.g., Lindley and El-Sayyad 1968).

The evident failure of the method of maximum likelihood does not by itself rule out an alternative methodology. Here again, however, a certain amount of caution is called for. In particular, the pitfalls of applying ordinary least squares (OLS) to the observable variables are well known. One may write the relationship between the observables as

$$y_i = \beta x_i + v_i,$$

where the new disturbance $v_i = u_i - \beta\epsilon_i$. Let us assume that the χ_i are bounded and that $\lim(1/n)\sum\chi^2 = s_\chi^2$, say. It is then easy to show that $\text{plim}(1/n)\sum x_i u_i = -\beta\sigma^2$ and that the asymptotic inconsistency of the estimator is $-\beta\phi^2/(s_\chi^2+\phi^2)$. This is directly related to the variance of the observation error on the dependent variable.

For the errors-in-variables model, therefore, the methods of maximum likelihood and ordinary least squares both fail, the one in absolute terms and the other in its inconsistency. No estimation method is known that satisfactorily handles this problem without introducing additional information in some way. It turns out that instrumental variables methods are available that are rather weak in their informational requirements. The application of such methods to this model is discussed in detail in Section 2.8.

More general models of the type (1.3) are now used extensively in the communications and control literature. In this context, the emphasis would be on time series ($i = t$) and the χ_i would represent an unobservable signal; the object is to filter out the "noise" – in this case the disturbances u_i, ϵ_i – to detect the signal sequence, which is usually specified as itself obeying some designated recursive relationship in time. The latter specification effectively helps to rid the model of the infinite-parameters drawback.

A somewhat different resolution to the problem of unobservable variates is followed in the literature on latent variables, the term indicating variables that are themselves unobservable or even simply imputations of some kind, but that determine, perhaps stochastically, variables that are measurable. An example is the "partial-expectations" model, studied by authors such as Duck et al. (1976), McDonald (1977), and Wickens (1982). This has the canonical form

$$\mathbf{y} = \beta \mathbf{z}^* + X\gamma + \boldsymbol{\epsilon},$$

$$\mathbf{z} = \mathbf{z}^* + \mathbf{v} = W\alpha + \mathbf{v},$$

where X and W are data matrices of observations on nonstochastic exogenous variables; $\boldsymbol{\epsilon}$ and $\mathbf{v}$ are independent, normally distributed random vectors with zero means and covariance matrices $\sigma_\epsilon^2 I$ and $\sigma_\mathbf{v}^2 I$, respectively. The vector $\mathbf{z}^*$ represents expectations held by economic agents as to the values of the economic variable z. The data matrix W contains observations on variables, considered exogenous, that are important in the formation of expectations; it is assumed that expectations are formed in unbiased fashion, giving rise to the above specification on the error $\mathbf{v}$. Related models have been considered in other contexts, where the latent variables may represent "desired" magnitudes, "true" values, or imputed equilibrium values depending upon the application.[2] All these models share the property that, unlike the pure errors-in-variables model, one is prepared to specify the generation of the latent variables in terms of observable magnitudes, even if some contamination with noise or error occurs. More or less conventional identification problems aside, the resulting parameter space is of finite dimension.

Most latent variable models can be handled by the use of instrumental variables techniques. Observe, for instance, that the above partial-expectation model may be rewritten in the following form:

$$\mathbf{y} = \beta \mathbf{z} + X\gamma + \boldsymbol{\epsilon} - \beta \mathbf{v} = H\boldsymbol{\delta} + \mathbf{u}, \tag{1.6a}$$

$$\mathbf{z} = W\alpha + \mathbf{v}, \tag{1.6b}$$

where $H = (\mathbf{z}\, X)$, $\boldsymbol{\delta} = (\beta\, \gamma')'$, and $\mathbf{u} = \boldsymbol{\epsilon} - \beta\mathbf{v}$. Since the elements of H and $\mathbf{u}$ are evidently correlated (both depend upon $\mathbf{v}$), we cannot simply apply OLS directly to equation (1.6a). However, it is always open to us to use the set (X, W) as instruments for H. In particular, if the elements of W include those of X, the model (1.6) constitutes a limited-information simultaneous model. The instrumental variables approach to such models is reviewed in detail in Section 4.3.

The self-selection problem

Suppose that we are trying to fit earnings functions that relate wages or earnings (y_i) of individual i to a set of individual characteristics represented by the vector of variables $\mathbf{x}_i$. We have observations on individuals in two sectors, say the factory sector (I) and the casual sector of employment (II), and we are interested in testing the hypothesis that the response of earnings to the variables $\mathbf{x}_i$ is the same in both sectors. We might set up the model

$$\begin{aligned} y_i &= \mathbf{x}_i'(\beta+\delta)+u_i \qquad &&\text{if } i \in \text{I}, \\ &= \mathbf{x}_i'\beta+u_i &&\text{if } i \in \text{II}. \end{aligned}$$

This can be expressed more compactly as

$$y_i = \mathbf{x}_i\beta + d_i\mathbf{x}_i'\delta + u_i, \qquad \begin{aligned} d_i &= 1 \qquad &&\text{if } i \in \text{I}, \\ &= 0 &&\text{otherwise}. \end{aligned} \tag{1.7}$$

We are interested in testing hypotheses on the elements of δ.

Suppose, however, that one of the sectors – the factory sector (I) – is viewed as being a more desirable work environment. Now the disturbance u_i represents unobservable variations in the individual's earning power that cannot be accounted for in terms of the observable variables $\mathbf{x}_i$. Given the more attractive workplace of sector I, it is rather more likely that an individual with $u_i \gg 0$ will choose sector I as his place of employment.

In terms of equation (1.7) we can interpret this preference as a positive correlation between the disturbance term u_i and the binary sector variable d_i. This means that an attempt to test hypotheses on δ with the use of ordinary least squares will fail, since these parameters are the coefficients of those variables most at risk from regressor–disturbance correlation. The use of IV methods for this problem is discussed at length in Section 2.6.

Self-selection problems are in fact quite pervasive in empirical work. To mention just one further example, studies that purport to measure the effect of unionization on wage rates typically contain (or in effect contain) a right-hand dummy variable indicating whether or not the individual belongs to a union. The application of OLS to such an equation would be valid (in the sense of consistency) only if unionized industries exhibited no tendency to pay more. Moreover, self-selection situations are by no means confined to representations like the model (1.7). The allocation of observations to excess demand or excess supply in simple disequilibrium models may be regarded[3] in the light of a self-selection procedure. Instrumental variables methods may also be applied to such problems, which are briefly considered in Section 5.2.

The simultaneous-equations model

Consider the following simple macroeconomic model of a closed economy, where the subscript t denotes time:

$$C_t = \beta_0 + \beta_1 Y_t + u_t, \qquad u_t \text{ i.i.d. with mean zero,} \tag{1.8a}$$

$$Y_t = C_t + I_t. \tag{1.8b}$$

The first equation is behavioral, to the effect that income Y_t determines consumption C_t. The second is definitional and says that consumption determines income, along with investment I_t, which is treated as exogenously determined outside the model. The evident circularity clearly renders void any assumption that Y_t is independent of the disturbance term u_t. Indeed, on solving for Y_t in terms of I_t and u_t we have

$$Y_t = \frac{\beta_0}{1-\beta_1} + \frac{I_t}{1-\beta_1} + \frac{u_t}{1-\beta_1},$$

from which it follows that

$$\operatorname{plim} \frac{1}{n} \sum Y_t u_t = \frac{1}{1-\beta_1} \operatorname{plim} \frac{1}{n} \sum u_t^2 = \frac{\sigma_u^2}{1-\beta_1} \neq 0.$$

In general, we can expect any model in which the right-hand variables are simultaneously determined along with the dependent or left-hand variables to create problems of regressor–disturbance correlation. Such circularity often arises from equilibrium considerations, in which a set of structural equations simultaneously determines equilibrium values. Thus a system comprising a demand equation and a supply equation for a certain good will have the equilibrium price and quantity transacted determined jointly by these equations. Or the population of lynxes may be determined by that of snowshoe hares, and the population of hares by that of lynxes, in a Volterra-type predator–prey nexus. Simultaneity bias may continue to apply even if the equilibrium values are not directly observable but are treated as moving targets, where the adjustment to equilibrium is not complete in every period. We note in passing, however, that there is a school of thought that maintains that structural relationships should always be specified in continuous rather than discrete time and that simultaneity may be an artifice that results from the necessity of measuring flows over some finite period of time (Bergstrom 1966). Whatever one's views on this, it is unavoidable as a matter of practice that in any system designed to determine an equilibrium or an adjustment to equilibrium, problems of regressor–disturbance correlation will arise.

The simultaneity effect may owe its genesis to individual decision problems as well as consideration of dynamic or market equilibrium of a more macro kind. For example, earlier work on the supply of labor assumed that the individual's supply of hours depended upon, in addition to nonlabor income and specific worker characteristics, the wage rate (where the latter could be treated as statistically exogenous). More recently, however, several authors (e.g., Rosen 1976, Hausman and Wise 1976, Burtless and Hausman 1978) have considered the wage rate to be endogenous. Because of the effects of progressive income tax rates, income-tested social security, and other welfare payments, the wage rate may in fact depend upon the supply of hours. Thus to simply regress hours worked upon the wage rates, together with other relevant individual characteristics, will result in problems of consistency, if not of specification and identification.

The existence of simultaneity is in fact pervasive in empirical work in economics. In some instances, one may be able to specify a complete model that accounts for all aspects of the simultaneity. Thus the multi-equation macroeconometric models typically aim to describe the joint probability distribution of every variable considered as endogenous. More often, however, one will be able to recognize that a given variable included among the right-hand regressors is in turn influenced by the left-hand or dependent variable, yet have no very precise model for the joint generation of the two variables concerned. In the parlance of stochastic simultaneous-equation theory, the latter is a "limited-information" situation. Since they are relatively robust with respect to specification error, IV methods are particularly suited to such incomplete-information contexts. Their application to both limited- and full-information models is considered in detail in Chapter 4, which deals with linear models, and Chapter 5, which concerns nonlinear models.

Time series problems

Consider the following distributed-lag model, which distributes or smoothes over time the effect of one variable (w_t) on a dependent variable:

$$y_t = \beta_0 + \beta_1(1-\lambda)(w_t + \lambda w_{t-1} + \lambda^2 w_{t-2} + \cdots) + u_t, \tag{1.9}$$

where $0 \leq \lambda < 1$ and the disturbances u_t have mean zero and are i.i.d. ("white noise," in the terminology), with variance σ^2. Thus investment plans may be determined in terms of an exponentially smoothed series of sales figures w_t. Equation (1.9) may be transformed by appropriate lag operations into

$$y_t = \lambda y_{t-1} + (1-\lambda)\beta_0 + (1-\lambda)\beta_1 w_t + v_t, \tag{1.10}$$

where in this autoregressive version the new disturbance is the moving average process $v_t = u_t - \lambda u_{t-1}$. As a regression formulation, equation (1.10) is plainly more convenient than the original. However, the effect of the transformation is that the regressor y_{t-1} and the new error v_t are correlated. Indeed,

$$\text{plim}\,\frac{1}{n}\sum y_{t-1} v_t = \text{plim}\,\frac{1}{n}\sum y_{t-1}(u_t - \lambda u_{t-1}) = -\lambda\sigma^2 \neq 0,$$

so that regressor and error in equation (1.10) are negatively correlated.

The above model provides an example of the transformation of a structural equation with a white-noise disturbance term into an estimating form in which the disturbance is no longer white noise. There are many examples of transformations of this type in the time series literature. As a general observation, it is satisfying to think that one is fitting an underlying structural model in which the disturbance term is purely random white noise, if only because this indicates that all sources of systematic variation, or information, are incorporated among the regressors. In many instances, however, it may be unduly restrictive to specify white-noise residuals, even if the researcher has no very precise theory as to why they should be serially correlated. Thus one should fit the structural model allowing for the presence of serially correlated residuals as a procedure in which the case of zero serial correlation can be appropriately nested. Given the widespread presence of lagged dependent variables arising from expectational or partial adjustment effects, this means that the estimation procedure should explicitly allow for the possibility of regressor–error correlation. The application of instrumental variable techniques to such models is considered in detail in Sections 3.3 and 3.4.

1.2 The instrumental variables estimator: a first approach

The models outlined in the previous sections may all be subsumed under the following forms:

(a) In the case of linear structures, a linear regression framework:

$$\mathbf{y} = X\beta + \mathbf{u}. \tag{1.11}$$

The structure of the data matrix X, the data vector $\mathbf{y}$, and the vector of disturbances $\mathbf{u}$ depends upon the dimensionality of the problem. If just one equation is concerned, we will assume that $\mathbf{y}$ is $n\times 1$; $\boldsymbol{\beta}$ is a $p\times 1$ vector of parameters; X is an $n\times p$ matrix of observations on right-hand variables (regressors) $x_1, \ldots, x_p$, possibly including the dummy intercept variable; and $\mathbf{u}$ is an $n\times 1$ vector of realizations on n disturbance variables u_i. If the context is multidimensional, as in the case of a system of simultaneous equations, the framework (1.11) can continue to apply, if we reinterpret $\mathbf{y}$ as a supervector of observations on the different dependent variables, stacked one on top of the other; X as possessing a block diagonal structure where each block represents the observations on each equation; and where $\boldsymbol{\beta}$ and $\mathbf{u}$ are also supervectors of parameters and disturbance realizations, respectively, for each equation stacked one on top of the other. In the present section, however, it will be simpler to confine attention to the single-equation context, reserving the simultaneous-equation model for detailed treatment in Chapter 4. The variables represented in the data matrix X may be either stochastic or nonstochastic. Some of the stochastic variables are assumed to be correlated with the disturbance variables. For expositional simplicity we assume that $\operatorname{plim}(1/n)X'\mathbf{u}$ exists but is not necessarily the null vector.

(b) If the model is nonlinear, we assume that it is of the additive disturbance type. A direct generalization of equation (1.11) is

$$\mathbf{y}=\mathbf{g}(x;\boldsymbol{\beta})+\mathbf{u}, \tag{1.12a}$$

where $\mathbf{g}$ is a vector of realizations on the function $g(\mathbf{x}_i;\, \boldsymbol{\beta})$ for observation i. A rather more general model would incorporate both y and $\mathbf{x}$ into a vector of variables $\mathbf{h}$, making no distinction between "subject" and "object" but treating all variables in a symmetric manner. The result is the implicit form

$$\mathbf{g}(h;\boldsymbol{\beta})=\mathbf{u}. \tag{1.12b}$$

A more detailed account of such representation may be found in Section 5.2. In either case, the elements y_i, $\mathbf{x}_i$, or $\mathbf{h}_i$ are all assumed to be possibly correlated with the disturbances u_i.

A common motivation of the IV estimator is as follows. Considering equation (1.11), let us suppose that the elements of X are *not* asymptotically correlated with the disturbances. Premultiplying both sides by X' and dividing by n, we have

$$\frac{1}{n}X'\mathbf{y}=\frac{1}{n}X'X\boldsymbol{\beta}+\frac{1}{n}X'\mathbf{u}.$$

Since $(1/n)X'\mathbf{u} \xrightarrow{p} \mathbf{0}$ ($\xrightarrow{p}$ means "tends in probability"), the vectors $(1/n)X'\mathbf{y}$ and $(1/n)X'X\boldsymbol{\beta}$ have the same limit in probability, motivating the estimator $(X'X)^{-1}X'\mathbf{y}$, which is, of course, just ordinary least squares. If, however, $(1/n)X'\mathbf{u}$ does not tend in probability to zero, this estimator will plainly be inconsistent. Suppose (i) that we have available a set of p variables comprising a data matrix Z, which are such that $(1/n)Z'\mathbf{u} \xrightarrow{p} \mathbf{0}$, that is, are asymptotically uncorrelated with the disturbances. Moreover, (ii) the matrix $(1/n)Z'X$ tends in probability to a nonsingular matrix of constants. Premultiplying equation (1.11) by Z', we have

$$\frac{1}{n}Z'\mathbf{y} = \frac{1}{n}Z'X\boldsymbol{\beta} + \frac{1}{n}Z'\mathbf{u}.$$

Properties (i) and (ii) motivate the estimator

$$\hat{\boldsymbol{\beta}} = (Z'X)^{-1}Z'\mathbf{y}, \tag{1.13}$$

which is clearly consistent.

Equation (1.13) is the estimator for the case where the number of instruments is equal to the number of regressors. If this is the case, then the matrix $Z'X$ is square and, under the nonsingularity assumption (ii) above, invertible at least asymptotically. Note that elements of the original data matrix X may be instruments for themselves if they are not "troublesome" (i.e., correlated with the disturbance). At this stage, however, we shall not comment further upon the choice of instruments.

It is not clear, however, how formula (1.13) generalizes to the case where the number of available instruments q differs from the number of regressors p. Clearly the case $q<p$ will lead to estimability problems, but the case $q>p$ is of very common occurrence in practice. Moreover formulas of type (1.13) do not extend to the nonlinear models (1.12). A second interpretation that overcomes these difficulties can be obtained by generalizing a method of moments interpretation originally due to Sargan (see Section 1.3) but recently elaborated by Hansen (1982). Let us suppose that we have available a set of variables z_r, $r=1, \ldots, q$, such that

$$\mathcal{E}u_i z_{ir} = 0, \qquad r = 1, \ldots, q. \tag{1.14}$$

Referring to equation (1.11), this implies that if we set

$$\boldsymbol{\delta}_i(\boldsymbol{\beta}) = \boldsymbol{\delta}(\boldsymbol{\beta}; y_i, \mathbf{x}_i, \mathbf{z}_i) = (y_i - \mathbf{x}_i'\boldsymbol{\beta})\mathbf{z}_i,$$

then at the true parameter value $\boldsymbol{\beta}_0$ we should have

$$\frac{1}{n}\sum_i \boldsymbol{\delta}_i(\boldsymbol{\beta}_0) \xrightarrow{p} \mathbf{0}.$$

This suggests that we estimate β_0 by choosing the value $\hat{\beta}_0$ that sets $(1/n)\sum \delta_i(\boldsymbol{\beta}; y_i, \mathbf{x}_i, \mathbf{z}_i)$ as close to zero as possible. This is the method-of-moments interpretation.

We can adapt this approach to the weaker requirements of the present context by replacing (1.14) by the corresponding limit in probability:

$$\operatorname{plim} \frac{1}{n} \sum_i u_i z_{ir} = 0, \qquad r = 1, \ldots, q. \tag{1.15}$$

Again we should like to choose $\boldsymbol{\beta}$ to have the sum $(1/n)\sum (y_i - \mathbf{x}_i'\boldsymbol{\beta})\mathbf{z}_i$ as small as possible. The notion of "smallness" can be made more precise by choosing a metric $d(\mathbf{a}, \mathbf{b}) = (\mathbf{a}-\mathbf{b})'W(\mathbf{a}-\mathbf{b})$, for any $\mathbf{a}, \mathbf{b} \in R_q$, where W is a suitably chosen positive definite matrix. Collecting the elements z_{ir} into a data matrix Z, we are to choose $\boldsymbol{\beta}$ to minimize $[(1/n)Z'\mathbf{u}]'W[(1/n)Z'\mathbf{u}]$, where $\mathbf{u}$ is set as $\mathbf{y} - X\boldsymbol{\beta}$. It turns out, however, to be more enlightening to arrange a minimand with a proper asymptotic distribution given $\boldsymbol{\beta} = \boldsymbol{\beta}_0$, the true value. If w is to be a constant matrix, we assume that $(1/\sqrt{n})Z'\mathbf{u}$ has an asymptotic distribution, and this suggests the minimand $(1/n)\mathbf{u}'ZWZ'\mathbf{u}$, where again $\mathbf{u} = \mathbf{y} - X\boldsymbol{\beta}$. For a given sample size n, the distinction is of course academic, and the criterion is simply to choose the estimate $\hat{\boldsymbol{\beta}}$ to minimize

$$\phi_w(\boldsymbol{\beta}) = (\mathbf{y} - X\boldsymbol{\beta})'ZWZ'(\mathbf{y} - X\boldsymbol{\beta}). \tag{1.16}$$

Carrying out the minimization,[4] the resulting estimate is

$$\hat{\boldsymbol{\beta}} = (X'P_w X)^{-1} X'P_w \mathbf{y}, \tag{1.17}$$

where $P_w = ZWZ'$. We note that the minimand remains defined for the nonlinear models (1.12). In the case of model (1.12b), it becomes

$$\phi_w(\boldsymbol{\beta}) = \mathbf{g}'(h; \boldsymbol{\beta})ZWZ'\mathbf{g}(h; \boldsymbol{\beta}). \tag{1.18}$$

However, an analytic solution such as expression (1.17) is not available, and the minimizing value $\hat{\boldsymbol{\beta}}$ must be achieved numerically.

It remains to discuss the choice of the weighting matrix W. The choice $W = I$ would yield the estimator $(X'ZZ'X)^{-1}X'ZZ'\mathbf{y}$. If the number of instruments $q = p$, the number of variables, then the matrices $X'Z$ and $Z'X$ are square and invertible and this estimator reduces to the basic form $(Z'X)^{-1}Z'\mathbf{y}$. In general, however, the choice $W = I$ is not optimal. A better idea is to drop the requirement that the weighting matrix is constant and allow it to depend upon the elements of Z (or even X) in such a way that the result nevertheless behaves asymptotically as a constant weighting matrix. A suitable choice is $W = (Z'Z/n)^{-1}$. For a given n, this gives the minimands

$$\text{(linear)} \quad \phi(\boldsymbol{\beta}) = (\mathbf{y} - X\boldsymbol{\beta})'Z(Z'Z)^{-1}Z'(\mathbf{y} - X\boldsymbol{\beta}), \tag{1.19a}$$

$$\text{(nonlinear)} \quad \phi(\boldsymbol{\beta}) = \mathbf{g}'(h; \boldsymbol{\beta})Z(Z'Z)^{-1}Z'\mathbf{g}(h; \boldsymbol{\beta}). \tag{1.19b}$$

Writing $P_z = Z(Z'Z)^{-1}Z'$, the estimator for the linear case is explicitly

$$\hat{\boldsymbol{\beta}} = (X'P_z X)^{-1}X'P_z\mathbf{y}. \tag{1.20}$$

We note that the minimand $\phi(\boldsymbol{\beta})$ has asymptotically the same behavior as $(1/n)(y - X\boldsymbol{\beta})'ZWZ'(\mathbf{y} - X\boldsymbol{\beta})$ with $W = \text{plim}(Z'Z/n)^{-1}$ as a matrix of constants. The estimator (1.20) is thus asymptotically of the class (1.17). We note again that if $p = q$, the estimator (1.19) reduces to the standard textbook form (1.13).

The choice of the weight matrix $(Z'Z)^{-1}$ may be intuitively rationalized as follows. The OLS minimand is $\mathbf{u}'\mathbf{u} = (\mathbf{y} - X\boldsymbol{\beta})'(\mathbf{y} - X\boldsymbol{\beta})$. For reasons of inconsistency, the resulting estimator is inapplicable as it stands. Let us try, however, to make the minimand (1.18) as close to the OLS minimand as possible. To do this let us write

$$ZWZ' \simeq I, \tag{1.21}$$

where the sign $\simeq$ means "as close as possible to," in some metric (see below). Now the matrix $(Z'Z)^{-1}Z'$ is a left generalized inverse for Z and the matrix $Z(Z'Z)^{-1}$ a right generalized inverse for Z'. Hence "solving" equation (1.21), we obtain

$$\begin{aligned} W &= (Z'Z)^{-1}Z'.Z(Z'Z)^{-1} \\ &= (Z'Z)^{-1}, \end{aligned}$$

giving $P_z = Z(Z'Z)^{-1}Z'$. A more rigorous interpretation of the resulting estimator is given in projective terms in Section 2.2.

The above estimator is particularly suitable for the case where $\mathcal{E}\mathbf{u}\mathbf{u}' = \sigma^2 I$, that is, where the disturbance is spherical. However, the necessity to apply IV techniques often arises from situations where this assumption is not met. Accordingly, let us assume that $\mathcal{E}\mathbf{u}'\mathbf{u} = \sigma^2\Omega$ for some matrix $\Omega \neq I$. The corresponding generalized least-squares minimand is

$$\text{(linear)} \quad \mathbf{u}'\Omega^{-1}\mathbf{u} = (\mathbf{y} - X\boldsymbol{\beta})'\Omega^{-1}(\mathbf{y} - X\boldsymbol{\beta}), \tag{1.22a}$$

$$\text{(nonlinear)} \quad \mathbf{u}'\Omega^{-1}\mathbf{u} = \mathbf{g}(h; \beta)'\Omega^{-1}\mathbf{g}(h; \beta), \tag{1.22b}$$

where the inverse Ω^{-1} may be replaced by a generalized inverse Ω^{-} if the covariance matrix is singular. Once again, we should like the IV minimands (1.19a) and (1.19b) to be as close as possible to (1.22a) and (1.22b), respectively. We can accomplish this by setting

$$ZWZ' \simeq \Omega^{-1}. \tag{1.23}$$

We can "solve" this problem by using (orthogonal) generalized inverse theory as follows. First we write $\Omega^{-1}=DD'$. The expression (1.23) can be transformed to

$$\tilde{Z}W\tilde{Z}' \simeq I, \tag{1.24}$$

where $\tilde{Z}=D^{-1}Z$. The problem (1.24) can now be solved along the same lines as the corresponding spherical problem (1.21). We obtain

$$\begin{aligned} W &= (\tilde{Z}'\tilde{Z})^{-1} = (Z'D'^{-1}D^{-1}Z)^{-1} \\ &= [Z'(DD')^{-1}Z]^{-1} = (Z'\Omega Z)^{-1}. \end{aligned}$$

The resulting minimand is

$$\text{(linear)} \quad (\mathbf{y}-X\boldsymbol{\beta})'Z(Z'\Omega Z)^{-1}Z'(\mathbf{y}-X\boldsymbol{\beta}), \tag{1.25a}$$

$$\text{(nonlinear)} \quad \mathbf{g}(h;\boldsymbol{\beta})'Z(Z'\Omega Z)^{-1}Z'g(h;\boldsymbol{\beta}). \tag{1.25b}$$

In the linear case, the minimizing $\boldsymbol{\beta}$ is

$$\hat{\boldsymbol{\beta}} = (X'PX)^{-1}X'P\mathbf{y}; \qquad P=Z(Z'\Omega Z)^{-1}Z'. \tag{1.26}$$

In the case $q=p$, equality of the number of instruments and regressors, the estimator (1.26) again reduces to the standard form (1.13). The latter is therefore invariant under different disturbance conditions. As remarked earlier, however, the case $q>p$ is the more usual in practice and the estimator (1.13) is not applicable. In this case the two estimators (1.20) and (1.26) differ if $\Omega \neq I$, and in fact it can be shown that the latter has superior efficiency properties. A more detailed approach to these matters is contained in Section 3.2, which also explores different alternatives for nonspherical IV estimators.

The process of "solving" the similarity or closeness relationships expressed by equations (1.21) and (1.23) seems a rather ill-defined sort of arrangement. However, the notion of closeness can be given a more precise meaning. Let us consider initially the spherical linear model. Recalling the discussion in connection with the approximate equation (1.21), we are to find W such that the distance based upon $\Delta = ZWZ'-I$ is minimized. Let us consider the norm

$$\operatorname{tr}\Delta'\Delta = \operatorname{tr}(ZWZ'-I)'(ZWZ'-I). \tag{1.27}$$

Differentiating this scalar function with respect to the matrix W, we obtain $W=(Z'Z)^{-1}$, as suggested. The proposed norm is equivalent to the sum of squares of all the elements of Δ, as can immediately be verified by writing $\mathbf{d}=\operatorname{vec}\Delta$ and establishing the equivalence of the proposed norm with the Euclidean distance $\mathbf{d}'\mathbf{d}$ (see Dhrymes 1978, p. 101). A feature of interest is that of all the generalized solutions of the equation

$$ZWZ' = I,$$

the solution $W = (Z'Z)^{-1}$ has itself a minimum norm on the above definition (i.e., tr $W'W$), so that the sum of squares of the elements of W is a minimum. We refer the reader to Rao and Mitra (1971, esp. Section 3.4.8) on such questions.

The argument becomes less intuitive when we extend it to the nonspherical model. As equation (1.23) indicates, we have to establish a natural norm for the difference $ZWZ' - \Omega^{-1}$ and show that the proposed choice of W does indeed minimize this norm. In the annex to this chapter it is shown that such a norm may be constructed as

$$\operatorname{tr}[\Omega(ZWZ' - \Omega^{-1})'(ZWZ' - \Omega^{-1})\Omega]. \tag{1.28}$$

This is the natural extension of the norm defined for the spherical case by expression (1.27) above. Minimizing expression (1.28) with respect to the matrix W yields $W = (Z'\Omega Z)^{-1}$, as suggested above in connection with the estimators (1.25).

There are other possible distance measures in addition to expression (1.28). However, the latter is well motivated, and it does indeed turn out in Section 3.2 that the estimator (1.25) with the corresponding choice of $W = (Z'\Omega Z)^{-1}$ has favorable efficiency properties. Nevertheless, the existence of several quite valid alternative IV estimators, for nonspherical contexts in particular, has led us to be cautious in ascribing any particular minimand or estimator as the official or canonical IV estimator for such contexts. Some of these alternative estimators are explored in detail in Section 3.2 and find applications throughout the remainder of the book.

1.3 Historical review

Until the valuable historical contribution by Goldberger (1972a), it was thought that the first systematic application of the methodology of instrumental variables took place in the context of errors-in-variables models or generalizations thereof.[5] As Goldberger pointed out, however, the method was of earlier genesis. These early contributions, which took place in the 1920s, are worked out as contributions to a rather different context, namely, the early development of the stochastic simultaneous-equations model. The model itself appears to have originated with the celebrated article of Working (1927), which discusses the simple equilibrium demand-and-supply model:

$$q^d = \alpha p + u, \tag{1.29a}$$

$$q^s = \beta p + v, \tag{1.29b}$$

$$q^d = q^s = q. \tag{1.29c}$$

The stochastic disturbance terms u and v were regarded by Working as random shocks that influence the market for the commodity, rather than, say, as incorporating errors of measurement. Working's graphical demonstration that the parameters of the model (1.29a) are not identified will be familiar to all students of econometrics. It includes the effects of adding further variables, uncorrelated with the equation disturbances, to equations (1.29a,b).

The use of instrumental variables as an adjunct to the estimation of the above model was considered soon afterward by Sewall Wright, working with his father, the economist P. G. Wright. In an appendix to his father's book *The Tariff on Animal and Vegetable Oils* (1928), Sewell Wright deals with the identification and estimation of the model (1.29). He assumes that observations are available on a variable z that has zero covariance with v:

$$C(z, v) = 0.$$

It follows that $C(z, q) = \beta C(z, p)$, so that

$$\beta = C(z, q)/C(z, p). \tag{1.30a}$$

Similarly, it is assumed that observations are available on a variable x that has zero covariance with u. Hence,

$$\alpha = C(x, q)/C(x, p). \tag{1.30b}$$

Estimators of the parameters α and β can be obtained by replacing the population covariances in (1.30a, b) with estimators of these covariances. If sample covariances are used, one obtains instrumental variables estimators for α and β.

As every student of econometrics knows, however, the model (1.29) as it stands is not identified. For the above methodology to work, it is necessary for the proposed instruments to be brought into a closer integration with the model structure. This defect was remedied along these lines by Sewell Wright, who in 1934 extended his analysis of supply and demand by considering the model

$$q^D = \alpha p + u \equiv \alpha p + \gamma z + u',$$

$$q^S = \beta p + v \equiv \beta p + \delta x + v',$$

$$q^S = q^D = q,$$

where $C(z, v) = 0$ and $C(x, u) = 0$. Wright noted that the seven estimable moments, namely $V(q)$, $V(p)$, $C(q, p)$, $C(z, q)$, $C(z, p)$, $C(x, q)$, and $C(x, p)$, suffice to determine estimates of the seven parameters, namely

α, β, γ, δ, $V(u')$, $V(v')$, and $C(u', v')$. As Goldberger (1972a) notes, this is a complete analysis of the instrumental variables approach for a model whose equations are just identified.

Turning now to the other strand of development, it was Olav Reiersol who coined the term *instrumental variables*. In his 1941 *Econometrica* article, he shows how his methodology of instrumental variables can be used to estimate the parameters of an economic model consisting of exact relationships, but whose variables are subject to random measurement errors. Suppose we have a random sample of size n on $2p-1$ variables that are divided into two sets:

$$\left.\begin{array}{ll} x_{it} & [i=1,2,\ldots,p] \\ z_{rt} & [r=1,2,\ldots,(p-1)] \end{array}\right\} \quad t=1,\ldots,n.$$

The x_{it} represent observations on the "investigation variables" and the z_{rt} represent observations on the "instrumental variables." Each variable in the latter set must be significantly correlated with at least one variable in the former set. The observations on the investigation variables are subject to random measurement errors, that is,

$$x_{it} = x_{it}^* + \epsilon_{it},$$

where x_{it}^* is the systematic part and ϵ_{it} is the random error or disturbance. Suppose that an exact relationship holds between the systematic parts, of the form

$$\sum_{i=1}^{p} \alpha_i x_{it}^* = c \qquad \text{for all } t, \tag{1.31}$$

where c is a constant and the α_i are parameters. We wish to obtain estimates of the $(p-1)$ coefficient ratios α_i/α_1. From (1.31) we have

$$\sum_i \alpha_i (x_{it}^* - \bar{x}_i^*) = 0,$$

where $\bar{x}_i^* = \Sigma_t\, x_{it}^*/n$. Multiplying by z_{rt} and taking sample averages, we obtain

$$\sum_i \alpha_i m_{ir}^* = 0, \qquad r=1,2,\ldots,(p-1), \tag{1.32}$$

where $m_{ir}^* = \Sigma_t\,(x_{it}^* - \bar{x}_i^*) z_{rt}/n$. The fact that the m_{ir}^* are unobservable prevents us from solving (1.32) for the ratios α_i/α_1. However, we do have available the sample moments:

$$m_{ir} = \sum_t (x_{it} - \bar{x}_i) z_{rt}.$$

Suppose we assume that the disturbances ϵ_{it} are independent of each other and of the systematic parts of the investigational variables, and, with respect to the instrumental variables, that their means are zero and their variances are finite. Under these assumptions, we may show[6] that the differences $m_{ir} - m^*_{ir}$ tend in probability to zero as the sample size n tends to infinity. Consider, then, the observable equations

$$\sum_i a_i m_{ir} = 0, \qquad r = 1, 2, \ldots, (p-1).$$

The solution ratios a_i/a_1 of these equations are continuous functions of the m_{ir}. Since the differences $m_{ir} - m^*_{ir}$ tend in probability to zero, the ratios a_i/a_1 will be asymptotically equivalent to the same functions of the m^*_{ir}. It follows that the instrumental variables estimators a_i/a_1 will be consistent estimators of the α_i/α_1.

One of the difficulties associated with Reiersol's method lay in obtaining a sufficient number of instrumental variables highly correlated with the investigational variables. Where the variables are economic time series, Reiersol suggested that lagged values of the investigational variables can be used as instrumental variables. Geary (1949) discusses models of the above form.

In January 1943, Trygve Haavelmo published an article, again in *Econometrica,* pointing to the need to formulate economic models in terms of stochastic equations rather than exact relationships. This article led to the birth of the linear simultaneous-equation model in econometrics as we understand it today. However, it was not until 1958 that Sargan adapted the method of instrumental variables to such models, although an earlier paper by Durbin (1954) applied similar methods to a simpler model. Instead of postulating exact linear relationships holding between the systematic parts of the investigational variables, Sargan writes an equation of the economic model as

$$\sum_{i=1}^{p} \alpha_i x^*_{it} = \eta_t,$$

where η_t is a random variable that is assumed to be independent of the systematic parts of all the previous observations. In terms of the observables, the equation is

$$\sum_i \alpha_i x_{it} = u_t, \tag{1.33}$$

where $u_t = \eta_t + \sum_i \alpha_i \epsilon_{it}$. The term u_t is called the *residual* of the system of linear simultaneous equations of which (1.33) is one equation. Suppose now that there are q instrumental variables available and the observations on these variables are given by z_{rt}. Then Reiersol's method amounts to postulating a zero sample covariance, at least asymptotically, between the residual and each instrumental variable. One therefore obtains the equations

$$\frac{1}{n}\sum_{t=1}^{n} u_t z_{rt} = 0, \qquad r = 1, \dots, q,$$

or

$$\sum_{i=1}^{p} \alpha_i \left(\frac{1}{n} \sum_{t=1}^{n} x_{it} z_{rt} \right) = 0, \qquad r = 1, \dots, q. \tag{1.34}$$

Equations (1.34) comprise q equations for the $p-1$ ratios of coefficients. If $q = p-1$, they can be solved to give the instrumental variables estimators of these ratios. Sargan goes on to obtain the limiting distribution of these estimators and their asymptotic covariance matrix. He also deals with the case where there are more instrumental variables available than the number of parameters to be estimated and comments on procedures for selecting instruments. Sargan gives an interesting canonical correlation interpretation of the estimated coefficients. Suppose that we take the variables x_{it}; $i = 1, \dots, p$ as one set of variables and the variables z_{rt}; $r = 1, \dots, q$ as the other. If there is actually a relationship between the variables x_{it} whose residual u_t is independent of the instruments, then this relationship should be obtainable as the canonical vector **a** associated with the smallest canonical correlation between the sets x_{it} and z_{rt}. This approach, which was also suggested by Bartlett (1949), is an interesting interpretation of the limited-information estimator. In general, the theories of the condensation of an instrument set and of the relationship between instrumental variables and canonical correlation theory have an important place in the present book, even if they are not necessarily approached in quite the same way. Sargan's paper was a brilliant and pathbreaking contribution to the estimation of structural relationships. Since its publication the literature has grown exponentially, and the method of instrumental variables as an adjunct to the estimation of structure has been applied to a wide variety of models in different contexts.

Annex

Choice of the weighting matrix W in nonspherical contexts

We are to seek a distance measure based upon the difference

$$\frac{1}{n}\mathbf{u}'(ZWZ' - \Omega^{-1})\mathbf{u}. \tag{i}$$

It would be desirable to choose W to minimize this expression, in some sense. Since the choice of W must be independent of the particular disturbance realization, we have to examine the limiting behavior of expression

(i) as $n \to \infty$. Considering first the expression $\phi_u = (1/n)\mathbf{u}'ZWZ'\mathbf{u}$, let us assume that the vector $(1/\sqrt{n})Z'\mathbf{u}$ tends in distribution to a random vector with mean zero and covariance matrix $\text{plim}(\sigma^2/n)Z'\Omega Z$, where $\sigma^2\Omega = \mathcal{E}\mathbf{uu}'$. Asymptotically, therefore, ϕ_u behaves as a random variable with expectation $\text{plim}(\sigma^2/n)\,\text{tr}\,WZ'\Omega Z = \text{plim}(\sigma^2/n)\,\text{tr}\,ZWZ'\Omega$. Likewise, the random variable $(1/n)\mathbf{u}'\Omega^{-1}\mathbf{u}$ has asymptotic expectation $(\sigma^2/n)\,\text{tr}\,I$ $(=\sigma^2)$. Now considering expression (i) above, we may write this as

$$\text{tr}\,\frac{1}{n}(ZWZ' - \Omega^{-1})\mathbf{uu}'. \tag{ii}$$

Thus to generate the limiting behavior of expression (i) we simply replace $\mathbf{uu}'$ in (ii) by its expectation Ω.

This suggests that, for a given sample size n, we can generate an appropriate norm in terms of the matrix $(ZWZ' - \Omega^{-1})\Omega = ZWZ'\Omega - I$. A fairly natural nonnegative norm is the sum of squares of the elements of this matrix, namely

$$\text{tr}(ZWZ'\Omega - I)'(ZWZ'\Omega - I) = \text{tr}[\Omega(ZWZ' - \Omega^{-1})'(ZWZ' - \Omega^{-1})\Omega], \tag{iii}$$

as suggested in the text.

Next we differentiate expression (iii) with respect to W. We write the left-hand side as

$$\text{tr}\,Z'\Omega ZWZ'\Omega ZW - 2\,\text{tr}\,Z'\Omega ZW + \text{tr}\,I.$$

Taking $\partial/\partial W$ (see Appendix A4) we obtain

$$(Z'\Omega Z)W(Z'\Omega Z) - Z'\Omega Z = \mathbf{O},$$

whence $W = (Z'\Omega Z)^{-1}$, which corresponds to a minimum. The value of the minimand at this "point" is $-\text{tr}\,I_q + \text{tr}\,I_n = n - q$.

CHAPTER 2

The spherical linear model

2.1 Introduction

We saw in Chapter 1 that many important applications involved a linear structure of the general form

$$\mathbf{y} = X\beta + \mathbf{u}, \tag{2.1}$$

where some of the regressors forming the data matrix X were stochastic and correlated with the disturbance vector $\mathbf{u}$, in the sense that $(1/n)X'\mathbf{u}$ did not tend in probability to the zero vector as the sample size $n \to \infty$. In this chapter we shall assume that the error distribution is spherical: $\mathcal{E}\mathbf{u} = \mathbf{0}$ and $\mathcal{E}\mathbf{uu}' = \sigma^2 I$, where I is the $n \times n$ identity matrix. This is undoubtedly a restrictive assumption, and it will be relaxed in due course. In the meantime, however, we can take advantage of its expositional convenience in order to establish some basic definitions and properties of the instrumental variables (IV) procedure.

A first approach to the motivation of the spherical IV estimator was presented in Section 1.2. We pointed out there that the conventional textbook formula

$$\hat{\beta} = (Z'X)^{-1}Z'\mathbf{y} \tag{2.2}$$

is unduly restrictive, for it gives no indication of how we might handle the situation where there are more instruments than regressors; nor does it extend to nonlinear models and the associated numerical minimization problems. However, a more general formulation could be derived, based upon a generalized minimum-distance idea. This is the point of departure for the discussion of Section 2.2. It is pointed out that the more general estimator has a projective interpretation. Various properties of the resulting estimator are established.

A group of topics concerned with the general subject of instrument efficiency or economy are investigated in sections 2.3–2.5. The notion that instruments should be highly correlated with regressors is formalized in Section 2.3, which exhibits the relationship of IV estimation with general multivariate theory. The idea of "minimal" instruments is introduced in Section 2.4, and computational matters are also touched on. We consider also estimability problems associated with an insufficient number of instruments. General efficiency considerations are summarized in Section 2.5.

We mark time, as it were, by turning in Section 2.6 to the first of our generic applications, where by "generic" we refer to the application of IV techniques to an entire class of models. It is shown that a class of self-selection problems can be handled by utilizing instruments constructed on the basis of a prior discriminant analysis. The development is illustrated with data from a labor market study.

Section 2.7 takes up a question that in a sense is logically prior to all the above matters, namely whether an instrumental variables approach is needed in the first place. Our concern here is with a context-free testing procedure for the existence of correlations between the independent variable and the disturbance. We consider also the problem of testing whether or not a set of instruments is admissible as such.

Section 2.8 illustrates some of the theoretical development with an account of IV approaches to the errors-in-variables problem. We show also that alternative estimators can be given an instrumental variables interpretation.

Instrumental variables estimation places heavy stress on consistency properties. This might be misplaced if the resulting estimator possesses a large finite sampling variance. Section 2.9 offers a preliminary excursion into estimators that result from combining OLS and IV minimands in, say, a convex combination. In Section 2.10 we consider the problem of testing against serial correlation – that is to say, whether the maintained hypothesis of spherical disturbances is justified. A summary concludes the chapter.

2.2 The minimand and the estimator

Geometric motivation

Since the IV estimator will be derived from projective considerations, it is helpful to begin by recalling the geometric interpretation of the

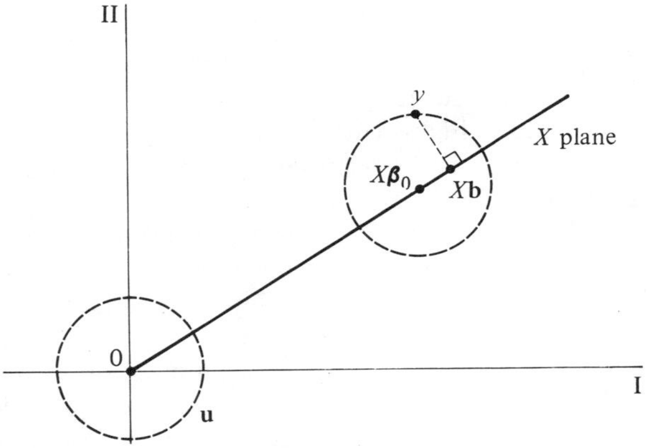

Figure 2.1

ordinary least-squares (OLS) estimator. For this purpose we shall temporarily assume that X is nonrandom, a design matrix fixed in repeated realizations of the system. The least-squares estimator minimand is $(\mathbf{y}-X\boldsymbol{\beta})'(y-X\boldsymbol{\beta})$, and the least-squares solution to the minimization problem is $\mathbf{b}=(X'X)^{-1}X'\mathbf{y}$. The fitted value of $\mathbf{y}$ is $\hat{\mathbf{y}}=P_x\mathbf{y}$, where $P_x=X(X'X)^{-1}X'$ is a projection matrix, that is, has the properties that $P_x^2=P_x$ (P_x is idempotent) and P_x is symmetric.

Figure 2.1 is a rather schematic geometric interpretation. The dotted circles are contours of the density of the disturbance vector $\mathbf{u}$. The location of the observed vector $\mathbf{y}$ is shown as a point on the contour centered around the mean vector $X\boldsymbol{\beta}_0$. The fitted value $\hat{\mathbf{y}}=X\mathbf{b}=P_x\mathbf{y}$ is obtained as an orthogonal projection upon the X plane, as indicated. Because of the sphericality of the u distribution, it is apparent that as the observed point $\mathbf{y}$ varies around a given contour, the fitted values – represented by the feet of the orthogonal projections – will center around the true value $X\boldsymbol{\beta}_0$. It will be apparent that this result is unchanged if we allow the data matrix X to be stochastic, provided that the conditional distribution of $\mathbf{u}$, given X, is independent of X.

Suppose, however, that this is not the case and that in particular $\mathcal{E}\mathbf{u}/X\neq\mathbf{0}$. A given contour for $\mathbf{y}$ is no longer centered at the point $X\boldsymbol{\beta}_0$. Figure 2.2 illustrates. The fitted values of ordinary least squares are no longer centered about the true value $X\boldsymbol{\beta}_0$. A better idea is to project orthogonally upon the plane Z for which $\mathcal{E}\mathbf{u}/Z=\mathbf{0}$. For such a plane the point given by $\mathcal{E}\mathbf{u}/X$ projects onto the point $\mathbf{0}$ in the Z plane, and the location of the Z plane in Figure 2.2 is thereby fixed as indicated. Denote the projections onto Z of X and $\mathbf{y}$ as $\hat{X}$, $\hat{\mathbf{y}}$ respectively. It will be apparent

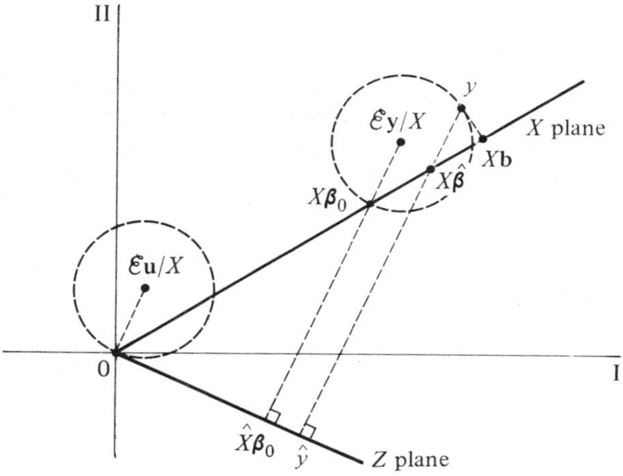

Figure 2.2

from Figure 2.2 that the estimates $\hat{\beta}$ defined by $\min_\beta(\hat{\mathbf{y}}-\hat{X}\beta)'(\hat{\mathbf{y}}-\hat{X}\beta)$ will, as $\mathbf{y}$ varies, be centered around the true value β_0.

Definitions

Like most geometric illustrations, the above treatment is somewhat heuristic, and it remains to provide a formal backing. Let X be an $n \times p$ data matrix and let Z be an associated data matrix of instruments of order $n \times q$. Both data matrices are of full-column rank.[1] Observe that we do not specify $q = p$, the number of regressors; however, we will specify $q \geq p$ as an identification requirement. The orthogonal projection referred to above is accomplished by the operations $\hat{\mathbf{y}} = P_z \mathbf{y}$ and $\hat{X} = P_z X$, where $P_z = Z(Z'Z)^{-1}Z'$ is the projection matrix associated with Z, that is, is symmetric and idempotent. The minimand is

$$(\hat{\mathbf{y}}-\hat{X}\beta)'(\hat{\mathbf{y}}-\hat{X}\beta) = (\mathbf{y}-X\beta)'P_z(\mathbf{y}-X\beta). \tag{2.3}$$

The IV estimator is therefore in the nature of a minimum-distance estimator with weighting matrix P_z, although we observe that P_z is singular. We may therefore set up the following:

Definition 2.1: The IV estimate is the value $\hat{\beta}$ that minimizes

$$(\mathbf{y}-X\beta)'P_z(\mathbf{y}-X\beta), \qquad \text{where} \quad P_z = Z(Z'Z)^{-1}Z'.$$

The basic results of IV estimation are set out in the following theorem.[2]

Theorem 2.2:

(a) $\hat{\beta} = (X'P_z X)^{-1} X'P_z \mathbf{y}$.

(b) *Suppose that* $(1/n)Z'\mathbf{u} \xrightarrow{p} \mathbf{0}$ *and that the moment matrices* $(1/n)Z'Z$ *and* $(1/n)Z'X$ *tend in probability to matrices of finite constants with full-column rank. Then the estimator* $\hat{\beta}$ *is consistent, that is,* $\hat{\beta} \xrightarrow{p} \beta_0$.

(c) *Suppose that the vector* $(1/\sqrt{n})Z'\mathbf{u}$ *tends in distribution to a normal vector with mean zero and covariance matrix* $\sigma^2 \operatorname{plim}(1/n)Z'Z$. *Then* $\sqrt{n}(\hat{\beta} - \beta_0)$ *is asymptotically normal with mean zero and covariance matrix* $\sigma^2 \operatorname{plim} n(X'P_z X)^{-1} = \sigma^2 [M_{xz} M_{zz}^{-1} M_{zx}]^{-1}$, *where* $M_{xz} = \operatorname{plim}(1/n)X'Z$, $M_{zz} = \operatorname{plim}(1/n)Z'Z$, *and* $M_{zx} = \operatorname{plim}(1/n)Z'X$.

Proof: Part (a) follows by direct differentiation of the minimand (2.3). Since all data matrices are assumed to have full-column rank and $p \leq q$, the matrix $X'P_z X$ is nonsingular and invertible.

For (b), substituting $\mathbf{y} = X\beta + \mathbf{u}$ in the IV estimator we derive

$$\hat{\beta} - \beta_0 = \left[\frac{X'Z}{n} \left(\frac{Z'Z}{n} \right)^{-1} \frac{Z'X}{n} \right]^{-1} \frac{X'Z}{n} \left(\frac{Z'Z}{n} \right)^{-1} \frac{Z'\mathbf{u}}{n}. \tag{2.4}$$

All matrices on the right-hand side except the last vector tend in probability to nonsingular matrices of finite constants. The vector $(1/n)Z'\mathbf{u}$ tends in probability to zero. Hence $\hat{\beta} \to \beta_0$ in probability.

(c)
$$\sqrt{n}(\hat{\beta} - \beta_0) = \left[\frac{X'Z}{n} \left(\frac{Z'Z}{n} \right)^{-1} \frac{Z'X}{n} \right]^{-1} \frac{X'Z}{n} \left(\frac{Z'Z}{n} \right)^{-1} \frac{Z'\mathbf{u}}{\sqrt{n}}. \tag{2.5}$$

As in (b), all matrices except the last vector tend in probability to the limiting matrices defined in part (c) of the theorem statement. By assumption the vector $(1/\sqrt{n})Z'\mathbf{u}$ tends in distribution to a $N(\mathbf{0}, \sigma^2 M_{ZZ})$ vector. It follows that $\sqrt{n}(\hat{\beta} - \beta_0)$ tends in distribution to a normal vector with mean zero and the covariance matrix indicated in part (c) of the theorem statement. ■

In proposing a given set of variables as instruments, one naturally wants to know whether they are valid for the purpose. This motivates the following definition:

Definition 2.3: A set Z of instruments will be referred to as *admissible* if it satisfies condition (b) of Theorem 2.2.

To be admissible, a given set of instruments have therefore to be asymptotically correlated with the regressors, to be asymptotically uncorrelated with the disturbances, and constitute a proper set, in the sense that the associated data matrix Z must have full rank, except possibly on a set of zero probability measure.

Several additional comments are in order regarding the scope of Theorem 2.2:

1. The theorem as it stands is necessarily somewhat vague since it is intended to cover a variety of contexts. Depending on the generation of the $\mathbf{x}_t$, $\mathbf{z}_t$, and u_t variables, its provisions may be considerably sharpened. Thus, if the sequence of random variables $\mathbf{v}_t = \{\mathbf{x}_t, \mathbf{z}_t, u_t\}$ can be regarded as independent drawings from a joint distribution $f(\mathbf{v}, \boldsymbol{\theta})$ whose sample moments converge almost surely to the corresponding distributional parameters for parameter values $\boldsymbol{\theta}$ in a compact set, then it can be shown that the convergence of $\hat{\boldsymbol{\beta}}$ to $\boldsymbol{\beta}_0$ is almost sure, rather than merely in probability. Essentially what is required is for the sequence of finite sample minima to converge to the minimum of the almost sure limit of expression (2.3); sufficient conditions for this are given in Appendix A3.

We remark that examination of such strong convergence properties is often facilitated if we can assume that the instruments z_{rt} and the disturbance u_t are uncorrelated in the sense that $\mathcal{E}z_{rt}u_t$ for all t and it is possible to construct a strong theory of instrumental variables on such a basis. In many instances, however, the instruments are constructed by some sort of prior regression process, and it may be that $\operatorname{plim}(1/n)Z'\mathbf{u} = \mathbf{0}$ but $\mathcal{E}z_{rt}u_t \neq 0$. It seems a virtue, therefore, to maintain an approach that, while perhaps weaker on occasion in terms of convergence properties, is stronger in terms of coverage.

2. One sometimes sees implicit claims that the consistency of IV estimation – meaning here the satisfaction of condition (b) of the theorem – implies an asymptotic normal distribution of the resulting estimator. It is not difficult to find counterexamples[3] to such a claim. Thus part (c) of the theorem has independent content. One would usually employ some version of the central limit theorem to show that the vector $(1/\sqrt{n})Z'\mathbf{u}$ has a limiting normal distribution, but the details will of course depend upon the nature of the $\mathbf{z}_t$ sequence and the higher-order moments of the u_t variables.

3. The distribution theory is asymptotic. In general, the finite sample distribution theory associated with IV estimators is difficult, although some progress has been made in recent years, particularly in connection with simultaneous stochastic models. This is reviewed in Chapter 4.

Constrained estimators and hypothesis testing

As with methods of ordinary least squares, constrained estimators may be derived. Thus, suppose that we wish to impose the set of s linear constraints $R\beta = \mathbf{r}$, where R is $s \times p$ of rank $s < p$. We may set up the Lagrangean

$$L = (\mathbf{y} - X\beta)'P_z(\mathbf{y} - X\beta) - 2\lambda'(R\beta - \mathbf{r}),$$

where λ is a vector of Lagrange multipliers. Let $\hat{\beta} = (X'P_zX)^{-1}X'P_z\mathbf{y}$ denote the unconstrained estimator. Then

$$\hat{\lambda} = -[R(X'P_zX)^{-1}R']^{-1}(R\hat{\beta} - \mathbf{r}), \tag{2.6}$$

and the constrained estimator is

$$\beta^* = \hat{\beta} - (X'P_zX)^{-1}R'[R(X'P_zX)^{-1}R']^{-1}(R\hat{\beta} - \mathbf{r}).$$

These are standard minimum-distance–type formulas.

Hypothesis testing is based upon the asymptotic normal distribution. We have

$$R\hat{\beta} = R\beta + R(X'P_zX)^{-1}X'P_z\mathbf{u}.$$

Thus under the null hypothesis $R\beta = \mathbf{r}$ we have

$$\sqrt{n}(R\hat{\beta} - \mathbf{r}) = \sqrt{n}R(X'P_zX)^{-1}X'P_z\mathbf{u}.$$

From considerations incorporated in the proof of Theorem 2.2, it follows that $\sqrt{n}(R\hat{\beta} - \mathbf{r})$ has an asymptotic normal distribution with mean zero and covariance matrix $\sigma^2 \operatorname{plim} nR(X'P_zX)^{-1}R'$. Under H_0, the statistic

$$(R\hat{\beta} - \mathbf{r})'[R(X'P_zX)^{-1}R']^{-1}(R\hat{\beta} - \mathbf{r})/\hat{\sigma}^2 \tag{2.7}$$

therefore tends in distribution to a χ^2 variable with s degrees of freedom. The consistent estimator $\hat{\sigma}^2$ may be obtained as $(1/n)(\mathbf{y} - X\hat{\beta})'(\mathbf{y} - X\hat{\beta})$. The rejection region would consist of large values of the Wald-type statistic (2.7).

Alternatively one can proceed with a Lagrange multiplier test derived directly from the above constrained minimization problem. If the null hypothesis H_0 were in fact true, then the marginal effect on the IV minimand of relaxing the vector of quantity constraints r should be zero. Now from expression (2.6) and the asymptotic distribution of $\sqrt{n}(R\hat{\beta} - \mathbf{r})$ it follows that under H_0, the dual variable $\hat{\lambda}/\sqrt{n}$ has asymptotically a multivariate normal distribution with mean zero and covariance matrix $\sigma^2 \operatorname{plim} n[R(X'P_zX)R']^{-1}$. Thus under H_0, the statistic $\hat{\lambda}R(X'P_zX)^{-1}R'\hat{\lambda}/\hat{\sigma}^2$ has a limiting χ_s^2 distribution. It is easy to verify that this test statistic is in fact the same as the expression (2.7) above. Thus the Wald and Lagrange multiplier tests are identical in the present context, just as they are for the corresponding ordinary least-squares model.

2.3 Instrumental variables and canonical correlations

One often comes across statements that the efficiency of an IV calculation depends upon the correlation between the regressors and their corresponding instruments. Expressed in such terms the idea is rather vague, but can nevertheless be given a more precise meaning by drawing on the theory of canonical correlations in multivariate analysis. Several consequences emerge that are both of intrinsic interest and useful for subsequent development.

We start by reviewing the basic elements of canonical correlations theory as they apply to the present context. Given the two data matrices X and Z, their canonical correlations are defined by the p (positive) solutions $r_1 \ldots r_p$ of the determinantal equations

$$\det[r^2 X'X - X'Z(Z'Z)^{-1}Z'X] = \det[X'(r^2 I - P_z)X] = 0.$$

If $q > p$, we may append $q-p$ zero correlations. Associated with each correlation r_j are canonical vectors $\mathbf{u}_j$ and $\mathbf{v}_j$. These may be collected into an $n \times p$ matrix U and an $n \times q$ matrix V with the properties $U'U = I$, $V'V = I$, and

$$U'V = (\Lambda_p \vdots \mathbf{O}),$$

where $\Lambda_p = \text{diag}(r_1 \ldots r_p)$ and the zero matrix is of order $p \times (q-p)$. In other words, the $\mathbf{u}_j$ and $\mathbf{v}_j$ are all pairwise orthogonal except that $\mathbf{u}'_j \mathbf{v}_j = r_j$. If we partition $V = (V_p \vdots V_{q-p})$, it will follow that $U'V_p = \Lambda_p$ and $U'V_{q-p} = \mathbf{0}$. We may indeed set up a regression model

$$U = V_p \Lambda_p + E_p, \tag{2.8}$$

where $E'_p V_p = \mathbf{O}$ and the variances of the error variables (the columns of E_p) are $1 - r_j^2$; $j = 1 \ldots p$. Finally, we note that we may transfer[4] to the new coordinate systems by nonsingular linear transformations $U = XA$, $V = ZB$.

Our first result expresses some useful IV projection matrices in terms of the canonical vectors.

Proposition 2.4:

(a) $P_z = VV'$.
(b) *If we define* $P_m = P_z X(X'P_z X)^{-1} X'P_z$, *then* $P_m = V_p V'_p$.
(c) $P_z - P_m = V_{q-p} V'_{q-p}$.

Proof:

(a) The result for P_z follows by the direct substitution $Z = VB^{-1}$ and the orthogonality of V.

(b) We may write

$$\begin{aligned}P_m &= P_z X(X'P_z X)^{-1}X'P_z \\ &= VV'UA^{-1}[A'^{-1}U'VV'UA^{-1}]^{-1}A'^{-1}U'VV' \\ &= (V_p \vdots V_{q-p})\begin{pmatrix}\Lambda_p \\ \cdots \\ \mathbf{O}\end{pmatrix}\left[(\Lambda_p \vdots \mathbf{O})\begin{pmatrix}\Lambda_p \\ \cdots \\ \mathbf{O}\end{pmatrix}\right]^{-1}(\Lambda_p \vdots \mathbf{O})\begin{pmatrix}V_p' \\ \cdots \\ V_{q-p}'\end{pmatrix} \\ &= V_p V_p'.\end{aligned}$$

(c) $P_z = VV' = V_p V_p' + V_{q-p}V_{q-p}' = P_m + V_{q-p}V_{q-p}'$. ■

This proposition will be utilized in Section 2.4. It essentially indicates that even if $q > p$, only p instruments are effectively employed. The meaning of the next proposition is perhaps more obvious at this juncture.

Proposition 2.5:

(a) *The IV estimator is given by*

$$\hat{\boldsymbol{\beta}} = (V_p'X)^{-1}V_p'\mathbf{y}. \tag{2.9}$$

(b) *Let* $\Sigma_{\hat{\beta}\hat{\beta}} = \sigma^2(X'P_z X)^{-1}$. *Then*

$$\det \Sigma_{\hat{\beta}\hat{\beta}} = 1/(\textstyle\prod_{j=1}^{p} r_j^2) \det \sigma^2(X'X)^{-1}. \tag{2.10}$$

Proof:

(a)
$$\begin{aligned}\hat{\boldsymbol{\beta}} &= (X'P_z X)^{-1}X'P_z\mathbf{y} \\ &= (A'^{-1}U'V_pV_p'X)^{-1}A'^{-1}U'V_pV_p'\mathbf{y} \\ &= (V_p'X)^{-1}\Lambda_p^{-1}\Lambda_pV_p'\mathbf{y} = (V_p'X)^{-1}V_p'\mathbf{y}.\end{aligned}$$

(b)
$$\begin{aligned}\Sigma_{\hat{\beta}\hat{\beta}} &= \sigma^2(X'P_z X)^{-1} = \sigma^2(X'V_pV_p'X)^{-1} \\ &= \sigma^2(A'^{-1}\Lambda_p^2A^{-1})^{-1}.\end{aligned}$$

Hence

$$\begin{aligned}\det \Sigma_{\hat{\beta}\hat{\beta}} &= \sigma^{2p} \det \Lambda_p^{-2} \det(AA') \\ &= 1/(\textstyle\prod_{j=1}^{p} r_j^2) \det \sigma^2(X'X)^{-1}.\end{aligned}$$ ■

Equation (2.9) reinforces an earlier remark that instruments of dimension just p are effectively used in forming the IV estimator $\hat{\boldsymbol{\beta}}$. We note that this equation exhibits the IV estimator in the form of equation (2.1), even if $q > p$. Part (b) of the proposition essentially refers to the limiting covariance matrix of the IV estimator $\hat{\boldsymbol{\beta}}$; for readability we have dropped the factor $1/n$ and explicit mention of limits in probability. It will be recognized that $\sigma^2(X'X)^{-1}$ refers to the (limiting) covariance matrix of the ordinary least-squares estimator on the supposition that regressor and disturbance are uncorrelated. The optimality properties of least squares under such ideal conditions are well known. Equation (2.10) indicates that so far as asymptotic efficiency is concerned we should try to use instruments for which all of the canonical correlations with the regressors X are maximized; this is our first point of contact with the topic of instrument efficiency.

Equation (2.10) also indicates that if all the canonical correlations approach unity, the IV estimator approaches the least-squares estimator. Indeed it is easy to show that

$$\hat{\beta} = A\Lambda_p^{-1}V_p'\mathbf{y} = AU'\mathbf{y} + A\Lambda_p^{-1}E_p'\mathbf{y},$$

from equation (2.8). Since $U = XA$, it follows that $AU' = (X'X)^{-1}X'$. Hence

$$\hat{\beta} = \mathbf{b} + A\Lambda_p^{-1}E_p'\mathbf{y},$$

where $\mathbf{b}$ is the ordinary least-squares estimate. Since $E_p'E_p = I - \Lambda_p^2$, we observe that $(E_p\Lambda_p^{-1})'E_p\Lambda_p^{-1} = \Lambda_p^{-2} - I$. Thus as $\Lambda_p \to I$ we have $\hat{\beta} \to \mathbf{b}$, for any sample size.

The canonical correlation interpretation formalizes the common conception that an instrument should be "correlated" with a regressor for which it is to serve. Note that from part (b) of the proof of Proposition 2.5 we may write

$$\Sigma_{\hat{\beta}\hat{\beta}} = \sigma^2 A\Lambda_p^{-2}A' = \sigma^2 \sum_j r_j^{-2}\mathbf{a}_j\mathbf{a}_j', \tag{2.11}$$

where $\mathbf{a}_j$ is the jth column of the loading matrix A. The asymptotic covariance matrix of the IV estimator is therefore expressible as a sum of one-dimensional matrices corresponding to the columns of the factor loading matrix A, weighted inversely by the corresponding (squared) canonical correlation. Suppose that one regressor variable – x_i, say – is not highly correlated with any or all of the variables in Z. One might anticipate that this lack of correlation should manifest itself in a small root r_j for some j; the corresponding loading a_{ij} will identify variable i as the specific problem. In such a circumstance, the variance contribution $(a_{ij}/r_j)^2$ will be appreciable and $\text{var}(\beta_j)$ may be large. In this way, a canonical correlation analysis can help in locating troublesome regressors. A convenient way of examining the importance of the various factor loadings (that is, to decide which variables influence a given canonical variable) is to form the matrix of correlation coefficients between the canonical variables (say, U) and the corresponding natural variables (X). Relevant formulas together with a useful practical discussion can be found in Cooley and Lohnes (1971) and guides to such computer packages as SSPS.

More often, however, the pattern of loadings (i.e., the elements of the matrix A) is more diffuse, so that a canonical correlation analysis will rarely indicate a complete pairing up of individual instruments with corresponding regressor variables. Thus the original notion of having to find a specific instrument for each regressor is neither necessary in itself nor an adequate description for purposes of efficiency analysis. As a practical matter, a complete canonical correlation analysis is a useful device in choosing or comparing different sets of instruments. Apart from this, we shall find the canonical correlation interpretation to be useful at various points in the ensuing discussion.

2.4 Minimal instruments

We have already observed that if the dimension of X is p, then even if the number of instruments q is greater than p, the dimensionality of the instrument set effectively used is just p. In the present subsection we shall explore the ramifications of this fact. Let us start by observing that we may write $P_z X = \hat{X}$, where $\hat{X} = X\hat{\Pi}$ and $\hat{\Pi} = (Z'Z)^{-1}Z'X$. In other words, we denote by $\hat{X}$ the fitted value in a multiequation least-squares regression of X upon Z. Then

$$\hat{\beta} = (X'P_z X)^{-1}X'P_z \mathbf{y} = (\hat{X}'X)^{-1}\hat{X}'\mathbf{y}. \tag{2.12}$$

This is of the form (2.1), and it is apparent that $\hat{X}$ is here playing the role of an instrument. Whereas we cannot invert $Z'X$, since it is not in general square, no such limitations apply to $\hat{X}'X$, which is of order $p \times p$.

We note, however, that the representation (2.2) is not unique. Indeed equation (2.9) of Proposition 2.5 exhibits another such representation with the canonical matrix V_p playing the role of the p-dimensional instrument. It turns out, however, that the associated projection matrices of all such *minimal instruments* are the same. Moreover, the minimand associated with these projection matrices has the same optimal value, namely zero, while the minimand associated with a nonminimal instrument set Z is greater than zero. The following development is designed to formalize these ideas.

Definition 2.6: Given $X_{n \times p}$ and an instrument set $Z_{n \times q}$ for which $q > p$, we define a *minimal instrument set* as a set of instruments with data matrix M of rank p such that

(a) $P_z P_m = P_m P_z = P_m$

and

(b) $P_m X = P_z X$,

where $P_m = M(M'M)^{-1}M'$ is the projection matrix associated with M.

Condition (a) ensures that the range space of M is contained within that of Z. Condition (b) requires that M capture all the information about X contained in Z. Our principal result concerning the relationship between minimal and nonminimal instrument sets is the following:

Theorem 2.7: *Let M be a minimal instrument set for Z in respect to X and suppose that $q>p$. Then*

(a) $\hat{\beta}_m=\hat{\beta}$.
(b) $(\mathbf{y}-X\hat{\beta})'P_m(\mathbf{y}-X\hat{\beta})=0$.
(c) $(\mathbf{y}-X\hat{\beta})'P_z(\mathbf{y}-X\hat{\beta})=\mathbf{y}'(P_z-P_m)\mathbf{y}\geq 0$.
(d) *P_m is unique; that is, if M_1 and M_2 are two minimal instrument sets, $P_{m1}=P_{m2}$. Its common value is $P_m=P_zX(X'P_zX)^{-1}X'P_z$.*

Proof:

(a)
$$\begin{aligned}\beta_m&=(M'X)^{-1}M'\mathbf{y}\\&=(X'P_mX)^{-1}X'P_m\mathbf{y}\\&=(X'P_zX)^{-1}X'P_z\mathbf{y}=\hat{\beta}.\end{aligned}$$

(b) $(\mathbf{y}-X\hat{\beta})'P_m(\mathbf{y}-X\hat{\beta})=(P_m\mathbf{y}-P_mX\hat{\beta})'(P_m\mathbf{y}-P_mX\hat{\beta})$.

Now

$$P_m\mathbf{y}-P_mX\hat{\beta}=P_m(\mathbf{y}-P_mX(M'X)^{-1}M'\mathbf{y}).$$

Since $P_m=M(M'M)^{-1}M'$, this is equal to $P_m(I-P_m)\mathbf{y}=\mathbf{0}$. Hence $(y-X\hat{\beta})'P_m(\mathbf{y}-X\hat{\beta})=0$.

(c), (d)

$$\begin{aligned}(\mathbf{y}-X\hat{\beta})'P_z(\mathbf{y}-X\hat{\beta})&=(P_z\mathbf{y}-P_mX\hat{\beta})'(P_z\mathbf{y}-P_mX\hat{\beta})\\&=(P_m\mathbf{y}+(P_z-P_m)\mathbf{y}-P_mX\hat{\beta})'(P_m\mathbf{y}+(P_z-P_m)\mathbf{y}-P_mX\hat{\beta})\\&=(P_m\mathbf{y}-P_mX\hat{\beta})'(P_m\mathbf{y}-P_mX\hat{\beta})-2\hat{\beta}'X'P_m(P_z-P_m)\mathbf{y}+\mathbf{y}'(P_z-P_m)\mathbf{y}\\&=(y-X\hat{\beta})'P_m(\mathbf{y}-X\hat{\beta})+\mathbf{y}'(P_z-P_m)\mathbf{y},\qquad\text{from Definition 2.6}\\&=\mathbf{y}'(P_z-P_m)\mathbf{y},\qquad\text{from part (b).}\end{aligned}$$

Suppose now that P_{m1} and P_{m2} are projection matrices for two minimal instrument sets M_1 and M_2. Then $0=(\mathbf{y}-X\hat{\beta})'P_{m1}(\mathbf{y}-X\hat{\beta})=\mathbf{y}'(P_{m1}-P_{m2})y$. Since $\mathbf{y}$ can be chosen at will, we must have $P_{m1}-P_{m2}=0$. It is easy to verify that $M=\hat{X}$ is a minimal instrument set. For this set we have $P_m=\hat{X}(\hat{X}'\hat{X}^{-1}\hat{X}=P_zX(X'P_zX)^{-1}X'P_z$. From Proposition 2.4 we then have

$$\mathbf{y}'(P_z-P_m)\mathbf{y}=\mathbf{y}'V_{q-p}V_{q-p}'\mathbf{y},$$

which, since $V_{q-p}'V_{q-p}=I$, represents the regression sum of squares in a regression of $\mathbf{y}$ upon V_{q-p}. Since Z has rank q, this is positive for almost all $\mathbf{y}$. ■

Some points of practical interest emerge from this discussion:

(a) We might think of choosing a set Z of instruments on the basis that it minimizes the "residual variance" $(\mathbf{y}-X\hat{\beta})'P_z(\mathbf{y}-X\hat{\beta})$. Such a decision rule is doomed to failure. To the extent that nonzero values for the minimand are obtained, this simply reflects differences in the amount of superfluous information contained in Z – in our terminology, the use of nonminimal instrument sets.

(b) A second point is computational. We saw that $\hat{X}$ is a minimal instrument for X and that

$$\hat{\beta}=(\hat{X}'X)^{-1}\hat{X}'\mathbf{y}. \tag{2.13}$$

Now $X'P_zX=X'P_zP_zX$, so that $\hat{X}'X=\hat{X}'\hat{X}$. Hence instead of (2.13) we could equally well employ the two-stage least-squares estimator

$$\hat{\beta}=(\hat{X}'\hat{X})^{-1}\hat{X}'\mathbf{y}. \tag{2.14}$$

That is, we run two least-squares programs, the first to regress X upon Z, the second to regress $\mathbf{y}$ upon the fitted value $\hat{X}$ so obtained. Thus from the computing point of view, an instrumental variables estimation can always be executed with a least-squares program. Even if $q=p$ so that equation (2.1) applies, there is room for argument as to which of the procedures is computationally more efficient. The strict IV formula needs only one inverse, $(Z'X)^{-1}$. The two-stage least-squares approach requires two inverse calculations. However, the inversions of the latter are of positive definite symmetric matrices, whereas the matrix $Z'X$ of equation (2.1) is in general form. Numerical routines for the inversion of positive definite matrices are in general considerably more efficient than general routines, less subject to rounding errors and problems with ill-conditioning. Our own preference is to compute IV estimates via the two-stage least-squares approach, utilizing computer routines for symmetric positive definite matrices.

A word of caution is in order. In the above description of the two-stage least-squares approach, the variables in X are all regressed upon the same set Z of exogenous variables, in order to obtain $\hat{X}$. What happens if, for economy or some other reason, one regresses the variables in X upon subsets of the Z variables, with the choice of subset differing according to the nature of the different variables in X? Thus consider the following simple model:

$$y_i=\beta_1x_{1i}+\beta_2x_{2i}+u_i, \tag{2.15}$$

where u_i is the disturbance. A data matrix $Z=[Z_1 \vdots Z_2]$ of instruments is available. Suppose that we regress x_1 upon Z_1, obtaining fitted values $\tilde{x}_1$; and x_2 upon Z_2, to obtain $\tilde{x}_2$. In the second stage we regress $\mathbf{y}$ upon $\hat{x}_1$ and $\hat{x}_2$.

This is clearly not the same estimator as the one that results from regressing x_1 upon the entire set Z to obtain $\hat{x}_1$, and x_2 upon Z to obtain $\hat{x}_2$, followed by a regression of y upon $\hat{x}_1$ and $\hat{x}_2$. The latter estimator corresponds to the estimator (2.14) above. But the estimator using $\tilde{x}_1$ and $\tilde{x}_2$ is not in general consistent. Indeed, let us write $\tilde{\mathbf{x}}_1 = P_{z_1}\mathbf{x}_1$ and $\tilde{\mathbf{x}}_2 = P_{z_2}\mathbf{x}_2$. Then the stage 2 estimation of equation (2.15) may be written in the form

$$y_i = \beta_1 \tilde{x}_{1i} + \beta_2 \tilde{x}_{2i} + \zeta_i, \tag{2.16}$$

where the disturbance vector ζ is defined by

$$\begin{aligned}\zeta &= \beta_1(x_1 - \tilde{x}_1) + \beta_2(x_2 - \tilde{x}_2) + \mathbf{u} \\ &= \beta_1(I - P_{z_1})\mathbf{x}_1 + \beta_2(I - P_{z_2})\mathbf{x}_2 + \mathbf{u}.\end{aligned}$$

Observe that since $P_{z_1}(I - P_{z_1}) = 0$,

$$\begin{aligned}\text{plim}\,\frac{1}{n}\zeta'\,\tilde{\mathbf{x}}_1 &= \text{plim}\,\frac{1}{n}\mathbf{x}_2'(I - P_{z_2})P_{z_1}\mathbf{x}_1 + \text{plim}\,\frac{1}{n}\mathbf{u}'P_{z_1}\mathbf{x}_1 \\ &= \text{plim}\,\frac{1}{n}\mathbf{x}_2'(I - P_{z_2})P_{z_1}\mathbf{x}_1.\end{aligned}$$

Similarly,

$$\text{plim}\,\frac{1}{n}\zeta'\tilde{\mathbf{x}}_2 = \text{plim}\,\frac{1}{n}\mathbf{x}'(I - P_{z_1})P_{z_2}\mathbf{x}_2.$$

It can now be seen that in the regression based upon equation (2.16) the regressors ($\tilde{x}_1$ and $\tilde{x}_2$) and disturbances will be asymptotically uncorrelated only if $P_{z_1} = P_{z_2}$, so that the columns of Z_1 and Z_2 span the same linear subspace. In all other cases, the two-stage procedure will yield inconsistent parameter estimates.

The same remark will also apply if, say, the full set Z is used for x_1 but a subset Z_2 is used for x_2, or for any other partition of instrument sets. One has therefore to be a little careful in executing a two-stage least-squares calculation, to ensure that the same basic instrument set Z is used to establish the fitted values for all regressors to be used in stage 2. The point has practical applicability in such topics as nonlinear two-stage least squares, where polynomials of different order in the exogenous variables are utilized as instruments. In this context, every right-hand function must be instrumentalized in terms of polynomials of the same order. We refer the reader ahead to Chapter 5 for a discussion of nonlinear IV methods.

Estimability failures

Earlier we mentioned the necessity of having at least as many instruments as regressors if the parameter vector β is to be estimable, or loosely speaking "identifiable," by means of IV techniques. We can make use of the interpretation of IV as a two-stage least-squares technique to throw some light on this problem of identification. Let $\boldsymbol{\beta}_0$ denote the true value of $\boldsymbol{\beta}$. Then $(1/n)$ times the IV minimand may be written

$$\frac{1}{n}(\mathbf{y}-X\boldsymbol{\beta})'P_z(\mathbf{y}-X\boldsymbol{\beta})$$

$$=\frac{1}{n}[\mathbf{y}-X\boldsymbol{\beta}_0-X(\boldsymbol{\beta}-\boldsymbol{\beta}_0)]'P_x[\mathbf{y}-X\boldsymbol{\beta}_0-X(\boldsymbol{\beta}-\boldsymbol{\beta}_0)]$$

$$=\frac{1}{n}\mathbf{u}'P_z\mathbf{u}-2(\boldsymbol{\beta}-\boldsymbol{\beta}_0')\frac{1}{n}X'P_z\mathbf{u}+(\boldsymbol{\beta}-\boldsymbol{\beta}_0)'\frac{X'P_zX}{n}(\boldsymbol{\beta}-\boldsymbol{\beta}_0),$$

where we have used $\mathbf{y}-X\boldsymbol{\beta}_0=\mathbf{u}$. Thus as $n\to\infty$, under suitable regularity conditions on the variables in X and Z, the almost sure (a.s.) limiting value of the minimand is $(\boldsymbol{\beta}-\boldsymbol{\beta}_0)'M(\boldsymbol{\beta}-\boldsymbol{\beta}_0)$, where M is the a.s. limit of $(1/n)X'P_zX$. If this expression can be zero for $\boldsymbol{\beta}\neq\boldsymbol{\beta}_0$, an identification problem evidently exists, for both $\boldsymbol{\beta}$ and $\boldsymbol{\beta}_0$ will attain the asymptotic IV minimum.

Now $X'P_zX=\hat{X}'\hat{X}$, where $\hat{X}$ is the fitted value in the regression of X upon Z. Thus if we disregard the deflating factor n, we have

$$(\boldsymbol{\beta}-\boldsymbol{\beta}_0)'X'P_zX(\boldsymbol{\beta}-\boldsymbol{\beta}_0)=(\boldsymbol{\beta}-\boldsymbol{\beta}_0)\hat{X}'\hat{X}(\boldsymbol{\beta}-\boldsymbol{\beta}_0).$$

Thus identification failures essentially arise from the possibility that

$$\hat{X}(\boldsymbol{\beta}-\boldsymbol{\beta}_0)=0$$

for $\boldsymbol{\beta}\neq\boldsymbol{\beta}_0$; that is to say, the second-stage regression matrix $\hat{X}$ in the two-stage least-squares interpretation of IV has less than full-column rank. Evidently we have reduced the problem of IV estimability to one of the existence of multicollinearity in the second-stage regression. Multicollinearity of this kind will arise when the number of instruments is less than the number of regressors. To see this, suppose that we have available just r instruments for the p regressors; $r<p$. Then

$$\operatorname{plim}(1/n)\hat{X}'\hat{X}=\Pi'\operatorname{plim}(Z'Z/n)\Pi,$$

where the $r\times p$ matrix Π is the limit in probability of $\hat{\Pi}=(Z'Z)^{-1}Z'X$, that is, $\hat{X}=Z\hat{\Pi}$. Assuming that $\operatorname{plim}(Z'Z/n)$ is nonsingular, we therefore have $(\boldsymbol{\beta}-\boldsymbol{\beta}_0)'M(\boldsymbol{\beta}-\boldsymbol{\beta}_0)=0$ if and only if

$$\Pi(\boldsymbol{\beta}-\boldsymbol{\beta}_0)=\mathbf{0},$$

which therefore defines the observationally equivalent subspace $\{\beta\}$. If $r\geq p$, this is the trivial singleton $\{\beta_0\}$ and no estimability problems exist. On the other hand, where $r<p$, we can only estimate linear combinations of the parameters $\boldsymbol{\beta}$.

The operational process of solving, or attempting to solve, for the $\hat{\beta}$ is facilitated by the following result:

Proposition 2.8: *If the number of instruments r is less than or equal to the number of regressors p, then the values β minimizing the IV minimand must satisfy the set of equations*

$$\hat{\Pi}\beta = \hat{\gamma}, \tag{2.17}$$

where $\hat{\Pi} = (Z'Z)^{-1}Z'X$ and $\hat{\gamma} = (Z'Z)^{-1}Z'\mathbf{y}$.

Proof: $P_z X = Z(Z'Z)^{-1}Z'X = Z\hat{\Pi}$ and $P_z y = Z\hat{\gamma}$. Thus the IV minimand is

$$V = (\mathbf{y} - X\beta)'P_z(\mathbf{y} - X\beta) = (P_z\mathbf{y} - P_zX\beta)'(P_z\mathbf{y} - P_zX\beta)$$
$$= (P_z\mathbf{y} - Z\hat{\Pi}\beta)'(P_z\mathbf{y} - Z\hat{\Pi}\beta).$$

Now let $\hat{\beta}$ be any value of β and suppose $\hat{\Pi}\hat{\beta} = \hat{\gamma} + \epsilon$. Then

$$V = (P_z y - Z\hat{\gamma} - Z\epsilon)'(P_z y - Z\hat{\gamma} - Z\epsilon)$$
$$= \epsilon' Z' Z\epsilon.$$

Since the matrix $Z'Z$ is positive definite [for $(Z'Z)^{-1}$ to exist], it follows that $\epsilon = \mathbf{0}$ for V to be a minimum. Thus any minimizing β must satisfy $\hat{\Pi}\beta = \hat{\gamma}$. ■

If $r = p$, the equations (2.17) reduce to $Z'X\beta = Z'\mathbf{y}$, with the unique solution $\hat{\beta} = (Z'X)^{-1}Z'\mathbf{y}$. However, if $r < p$, the insufficiency of instruments allows multiple solutions for β and the IV estimate cannot in general be said to exist. As with multicollinearity in classical regression we can only estimate linear combinations of the parameters. Of course, if we are prepared to specify some extraneous information about the coefficients, it is possible to bring the set of equations (2.17) up to full rank and thus uniquely identify all the β. In practice, too, it may be that the elements of one or more of the columns of $\hat{\Pi}$ are approximately zero, indicating that the corresponding regressors are not correlated with any of the instruments. It may still be possible to identify the coefficients of the remaining variables for which the instruments are effective. Thus the contingency of an insufficient number of instruments, while something that one wishes to avoid, is not altogether a lost cause.

2.5 The choice of instruments

Two related problems will concern us here. The first is the problem of choosing instruments that satisfy certain criteria of desirability in themselves. The second is the problem of economizing on a list of available instruments, all of which might look useful. Not all aspects of the latter problem, in particular, have been explored in the literature. Evidently it is a finite sample problem. With a very large sample we can add as many instruments as we please to the instrument set, knowing that we can do no worse by so doing. For small samples, however, creating $\hat{X}$ in terms of a large instrument set Z will lead to fewer degrees of freedom; it is the consequences of this loss of degrees of freedom that have not been fully explored. Some indications may be available from the finite sample theory of IV estimators in simultaneous equations contexts (see Section 4.8). Thus Nagar (1959) has shown that the bias to terms of order $1/n$ of the two-stage least-squares estimator increases as the instrument set is augmented in a manner corresponding to the difference $q-p$ in the present context. In general, we shall take it that a multiplicity of instruments is in itself undesirable and that some economization, in degree related to the available sample size, should be undertaken.

We have already mentioned one desirable attribute of a set of instruments – that they should be highly correlated, in the sense of Section 2.3, with the regressors. Thus, suppose that one is proposing to add another instrument to an existing list. The elements of the canonical loadings – the matrix B of Section 2.3 – should tell us whether this additional variable contributes importantly to the first p canonical variables, that is, those that will actually be used in the IV calculation. If it is associated more with one of the variables in V_{q-p}, then it is not worthwhile adding it to the instrument set.

An economization procedure that has been suggested by some authors is to perform a principal component analysis on the moment matrix $Z'Z$ and to choose (in our context) the first p principal components as the instruments. Thus let $Z'Z=\Theta D\Theta'$, where $D=\text{diag}(\lambda_1 \ldots \lambda_q)$ and Θ is orthogonal. Define the orthogonal components $W=Z\Theta$ and select the first p components corresponding to the largest eigenvalues λ_i, assembling these components into a data matrix W_p. The proposed IV estimator is $(W_p'X)^{-1}W_p'\mathbf{y}$. Such an estimator is mentioned in Section 4.4 in connection with simultaneous stochastic equations.

It is not difficult to show that the transformation to orthogonal components W leaves the canonical variables of Section 2.3 unchanged, that is, $V_w=V_z$. In the canonical variables approach we drop the last $q-p$ elements of V_w, which are associated with zero canonical correlations with the set of regressors X. With principal components we are to drop the last $q-p$ variables in W that are associated with the smallest eigenvalues λ_i of $Z'Z$. However, it is apparent that elements of W dropped according to this criterion could still be included according to the canonical correlation criterion which, as we have seen, is optimal. The principal component technique pays attention only to internal variation among the Z set rather than to the covariation between Z and X and in this sense "gets the metric wrong" in its selection of components to be excluded.

So far our discussion as to the choice of instrument has been confined to questions of covariance between the X and Z sets. It is the canonical correlations between these two sets of variables that determine the asymptotic efficiency of the technique. For finite samples, however, other consideration arise.

Thus, if we observe that

$$\hat{\beta}-\beta_0=(X'P_zX)^{-1}X'P_z\mathbf{u},$$

it follows that

$$\begin{aligned}(\hat{\beta}-\beta_0)'X'P_zX(\hat{\beta}-\beta_0)&=\mathbf{u}P_zX(X'P_zX)^{-1}X'P_z\mathbf{u}\\&=\mathbf{u}'P_m\mathbf{u},\end{aligned}\tag{2.18}$$

where P_m is the projection matrix of a minimal instrument set for Z. For finite n we can see that two things are desirable: First, the left-hand side of (2.18) indicates that we should like Z to be highly correlated with X, so that $X'P_zX$ should be as "large" as possible. It will indeed be recognized that apart from a factor $1/n$, the left-hand side is related to the concentration ellipsoid of $\hat{\beta}-\beta_0$ as $n\to\infty$. Secondly, we should like Z, or at least the associated minimal instrument set M, to have as small a covariance as possible with the equation error.

The latter point is of some importance. A great many instruments, especially in nonlinear context, are of the nature of fitted values, in which elements of X, or functions of the elements of X, are first regressed on a set of exogenous variables. We shall review some such instruments in the succeeding chapters. Fitted-value instruments may yield higher correlations with the X variables, but for finite sample sizes they may exhibit a relatively high correlation with the equation error. Of course, we have seen in the linear case that one particular fitted instrument, namely $\hat{X}$, is not subject to these difficulties. In more general contexts, however, there may be a trade-off between covariance with X and covariance with the equation error. Sampling experiments might give some guidance on the existence or importance of such a trade-off.

2.6 Applications: a self-selection problem

The problem we discuss in the present section not only illustrates some of the considerations of the preceding discussion but is a topic of considerable importance in its own right. The self-selection problem refers to the idea that properties of the disturbance term may lead to a classification of each individual into certain regimes and that if regressions are run on the basis of less than full sample coverage with respect to the generation of the underlying disturbances, then inconsistent and misleading parameter estimates may result. The particular model that we have selected for discussion has received exposure in the literature on testing earnings functions across certain designated groups - black versus white workers, for instance, or workers in different industrial sectors. After formulating a particular example of such a model, we shall suggest that an IV approach overcomes some of the drawbacks of solutions that have so far appeared, particularly in respect of robustness properties. In the ensuing discussion, this methodology is illustrated from a study of segmentation in a labor market.

The problem

The self-selection problem crops up in a wide variety of situations, so that no single universally applicable paradigm can really be said to exist (though see Heckman, 1976). We shall deal with a model that represents a subclass of general interest. To keep matters simple we shall initially imagine just two sectors. The model is

$$y_i = \mathbf{x}_i'(\boldsymbol{\beta}+\boldsymbol{\delta})+u_i \qquad \text{if } i \in \text{I} \tag{2.19a}$$

$$= \mathbf{x}_i'\boldsymbol{\beta}+u_i \qquad \text{if } i \in \text{II}. \tag{2.19b}$$

Thus we may be testing the hypothesis that earnings y are related to a set of variables such as age, education, work experience, and so on collectively denoted by $\mathbf{x}$. Response to these variables may differ between sectors, and one is interested in testing the hypothesis that $\boldsymbol{\delta}=\mathbf{0}$, with either individual or collective tests of significance. The disturbances u_i are spherical.

The two equations (2.19a, b) may be collapsed into the single equation

$$y_i = \mathbf{x}_i'\boldsymbol{\beta}+d_i\mathbf{x}_i'\boldsymbol{\delta}+u_i, \tag{2.20}$$

where the binary dummy variable d is defined by

$$d_i = 1 \qquad \text{if } i \in \text{I}$$

$$= 0 \qquad \text{if } i \in \text{II}.$$

Writing the equations in the structural version (2.20) is useful because it enables us to see the potential for self-selection bias in this type of model. Suppose that the regimes refer to industrial sectors and that one of the sectors is regarded as more desirable to work in than the other (as, say, the factory sector versus the informal sector in lesser developed countries). Then a higher realization u_i of the disturbance might tend to be associated with the realization $d_i = 1$. A person with some special characteristic not represented in the x_i might be more likely to choose employment in the more desirable of the two sectors. It is clear that the dummy variable d_i must be treated as a random variable and that this random variable may be correlated with the disturbance term u_i.

The consequence of this correlation is that we cannot write

$$\mathcal{E}(y_i \mid x_i, d_i) = \mathbf{x}_i \boldsymbol{\beta} + d_i \mathbf{x}_i' \boldsymbol{\delta}, \tag{2.21}$$

which in turn implies that simply running regressions on the observations, incorporating $\boldsymbol{\delta}$ according to whether or not the observation lies in regime I or II, will not do. The usual way out of this problem is to propose some explicit switching structure as an additional structural element in the model. Thus suppose that there exists a vector $\mathbf{w}_i$ of variables – usually treated as fixed rather than stochastic – such that

$$\begin{aligned} d_i &= 1 \qquad \text{if } \mathbf{w}_i'\boldsymbol{\gamma} \geq \epsilon_i \\ &= 0 \qquad \text{otherwise.} \end{aligned} \tag{2.22}$$

The term $\mathbf{w}_i'\boldsymbol{\gamma}$ is of the nature of a linear discriminant function and contains variates that hopefully enable us to predict which of the two sectors observation i will occupy. However, this discrimination is only probabilistic, and this latter element is handled with the spherical i.i.d. random variable ϵ_i. The variance of this disturbance term may be normalized as unity with no loss of generality. To allow for d_i and u_i to be correlated we assume the covariance structure

$$\text{Cov}(u_i, \epsilon_i) = \begin{bmatrix} \sigma_{\text{I}}^2 & \sigma_{1\epsilon} \\ \sigma_{1\epsilon} & 1 \end{bmatrix}.$$

It may then be shown that, for instance,

$$\mathcal{E}(u_i/d_i = 1) = -\sigma_{1\epsilon} \frac{n(\mathbf{w}_i'\boldsymbol{\gamma}; 0, 1)}{N(\mathbf{w}_i'\boldsymbol{\gamma}; 0, 1)},$$

where $n(\cdot\,; \mu, \sigma^2)$ denotes the normal density and $N(\cdot\,; \mu, \sigma^2)$ the distribution function. Hence the model in regime I can be written

$$y_i = \mathbf{x}_i'(\boldsymbol{\beta} + \boldsymbol{\delta}) - \sigma_{1\epsilon} \frac{n(\mathbf{w}'\boldsymbol{\gamma}; 0, 1)}{N(\mathbf{w}'\boldsymbol{\gamma}; 0, 1)} + \zeta_{\text{I}i}, \tag{2.23a}$$

where $\mathcal{E}(\zeta_{\text{I}i}/d_i = 1) = 0$, and it may also be shown that

$$\mathcal{E}(\zeta_{\text{I}i}^2/d_i = 1) = \sigma_{\text{I}}^2 - \sigma_{\text{I}\epsilon}^2 \mathbf{w}'\boldsymbol{\gamma} \frac{n(\mathbf{w}'\boldsymbol{\gamma}; 0, 1)}{N(\mathbf{w}'\boldsymbol{\gamma}; 0, 1)}. \tag{2.24}$$

A corresponding equation (2.23b), not reproduced here, holds for the restriction of the observations to sector II. We observe that equation (2.23a) is not the same as equation (2.19a).

To estimate the parameters of the model of equations (2.20) and (2.22) is reasonably straightforward. One may write out the likelihood function with little difficulty and proceed to a full iterative solution of a globally concave likelihood function. Or one may adopt a combined probit–OLS technique: Initial estimates of $\boldsymbol{\gamma}$ may be obtained from a probit analysis based on equation (2.22). The resulting value is substituted into equations (2.23a, b), followed by an OLS regression to obtain estimates $\hat{\boldsymbol{\beta}}$, $\hat{\boldsymbol{\delta}}$, and $\hat{\sigma}_{1\epsilon}$. Various improvements are possible on the latter technique; for example, we note from equation (2.24) the presence of heteroscedasticity of a tractable kind.

All this is standard but also, as a general technique, unsatisfactory. To begin with, the model as expressed by equations (2.19) or (2.20) and (2.22) is a completely specified structure, and both the likelihood or probit–OLS approaches depend upon an exact knowledge of that structure. On most occasions, however, we will not have a complete knowledge of all the systematic factors that might enter into the discriminating function $\mathbf{w}_i'\boldsymbol{\gamma}$. Moreover, the particular discriminating structure expressed by equation (2.22) is only a working hypothesis; it is difficult to imagine precisely why the world should be created in the likeness of a probit model. Finally it is very difficult, though not impossible, to extend the discriminating structure (2.22) to more than two regimes.

An IV approach

As an alternative to imposing an explicit discriminatory structure like equation (2.22), we propose to utilize a more standard discrimination analysis to construct instrumental variables for the direct estimation of the equation (2.20), combining the two sectors. As we have remarked, the source of the difficulty is the binary sector variable d_i. If we can find a proxy for this variable ($\mathbf{d}_i$, say) that at least asymptotically depends only upon exogenous variables, then we may utilize $\tilde{d}_i\mathbf{x}_i$ as instruments for the variables $d_i\mathbf{x}_i$.

Let us again suppose that we have a vector of exogenous variables $\mathbf{w}_i$ available to assist us in distinguishing the sectors. We shall no longer need to assume that there are just two sectors; the techniques to be described are readily applicable to any number of sectors. Recalling that the binary dummy d_i is essentially a classificatory variable, we can make use of standard packages for discrimination analysis that create such classifications. As a general procedure, we input all the data on the variables in **w**, together with the information as to which of the regimes each observation i belongs to. On the basis of this information, the program creates discriminant functions. Given now an observation $\mathbf{w}_i$ we predict, using these discriminant functions, which of the regimes the given observation will belong to. We set

$$\tilde{d}_i^j = 1 \quad \text{if observation } i \text{ is predicted to belong to regime } j$$
$$= 0 \quad \text{otherwise.}$$

Then $\tilde{d}_i^j$ (which, at least asymptotically, is a function of the exogenous variables **w**) should qualify as an instrument for the observed binary dummy variable d_i^j; for $j = 1 \ldots p$ sectors. We shall call $\tilde{d}_i^j$ the binary instrument, referring to its values of zero or one. An alternative procedure is to note that standard discrimination packages will also print out the computed probability that observation i belongs to regime j. Then we may define an instrument as

$$\check{d}_i^j = p_i^j,$$

where p_i^j is the above probability. We shall call this the probability instrument.

Before discussing further the admissibility or performance of the proposed instruments we shall briefly review the common procedures for discrimination and/or classification analysis. [For more practical detail, including a discussion of variants on these procedures, we refer the reader to Cooley and Lohnes (1971).]

(a) *The Anderson discriminant functions* (Anderson 1958, chap. 6). These assume that the variates $\mathbf{w}_i$ are random variables from one of p populations, corresponding to each regime. The variance–covariance matrix Σ is assumed to be the same across each regime (relaxations of this assumption are available but are hardly necessary for present purposes). However, the means μ_j are assumed to differ across the regimes. Assuming that the costs of misclassification are equal across sectors, define

$$u_{jk}(w) = \log[p_j(w)/p_k(w)] = [\mathbf{w} - \tfrac{1}{2}(\mu_j + \mu_k)]'\Sigma^{-1}[\mu_j - \mu_k]. \qquad (2.25)$$

In other words, the u_{jk} represent the relative probability of observation **w** being in either regime j or regime k. The rule is to classify observation i into regime j if $u_{jk}(\mathbf{w}_i) \geq 0$, for all $k \neq j$. That is, the discriminant function (2.25) indicates that observation i comes from regime j with maximal probability relative to other regimes.

(b) *R. A. Fisher's linear discriminant functions.* In the case of two groups, the (single) discriminant function maximizes the between-group sums of squares relative to the within-group sums of squares. The generalization to more than two groups is based upon a canonical correlation analysis with the set dual to the w set being interpreted as the set of binary dummy variables for each regime. As in Section 2.3, the canonical variates define a new coordinate system. The score of the given observation $\mathbf{w}_i$ is obtained on the rth canonical axis as $\mathbf{a}_r' \mathbf{w}_i$, where $\mathbf{a}_r$ is the rth column of the canonical loading matrix for the w set (cf. Section 2.3). Likewise the scores are obtained for each regime mean ("centroid") as $\mathbf{a}_r' \boldsymbol{\mu}_j$. Observation i is classified into the closest group, where the metric is defined as the Pythagorean distance between the observation w_i and the group centroid. If there are just two groups, the Fisher approach will yield a classification identical to the Anderson functions. This is, however, not necessarily true for more than two groups. We note also that the Fisher approach makes no assumptions about the distribution of the observation vectors $\mathbf{w}_i$; indeed, the discrimination remains meaningful if the $\mathbf{w}_i$ are interpreted as fixed variates or even dummy variables rather than true random variables. On the other hand, this is not as great an advantage in the present context as might appear since the Anderson procedure is generally considered not to be too sensitive to departures from the normality assumption.

Let us turn now to the question of the admissibility of the proposed instruments. At first sight, this might appear not to be a problem, since the proposed classification is to be based upon a set of variables ($\mathbf{w}$) that are considered to be exogenous. However, any sample discrimination analysis will reflect to some extent the influences of those disturbances or random errors that result in a given observation lying in one or another of the regimes. To see this, let us recall the particular example considered above. For a given realization of the w variables as $\mathbf{w}_i$, observation i will belong to regime I if $\epsilon_i \leq \mathbf{w}_i' \boldsymbol{\gamma}$. The random disturbance in this model essentially plays the role of a classificatory device. A given $\mathbf{w}_i$ may belong to either of the two groups. A large ϵ_i directs it to group II, a small ϵ_i to group I. Suppose now that the Anderson function is to be used. In order to use this, one must have sample estimates of the means μ_{I} and μ_{II} (and of the covariance matrix Σ). In terms of the allocation paradigm we have just outlined, such sample estimates will clearly depend upon the realization of the classificatory disturbances ϵ_i. In turn, the proposed instruments $\tilde{d}_i^j$ or $\check{d}_i^j$ may not therefore be strictly independent of the equation disturbances u_i, assuming ϵ_i and u_i to be correlated.

However, strict independence (in the sense, say, that $\mathcal{E}\tilde{d}_i^j u_i = 0$) is an unduly strong approach to IV estimation. As pointed out in Section 2.2, we require of any instrument z_{ir} only that

$$\operatorname{plim} \frac{1}{n} \sum_{i=1}^{n} z_{ir} u_i = 0$$

plus of course, nonzero instrument–regressor correlation, which we shall henceforth take as read. The proposed instruments $\tilde{d}_i^j$ or $\check{d}_i^j$ are special cases of constructed instruments of the form $z_{ir} = f(\hat{\theta}, w_i)$, where $\hat{\theta}$ represents estimates of some hypothesized of "constructed" parameters (see below). The function f is nonlinear and either continuous in $\hat{\theta}$ or such that its discontinuities form a set of measure zero. With regard to the meaning of $\hat{\theta}$, two cases of importance arise:

(a) The parameter vector $\hat{\theta}$ represents a sample estimate of a true underlying parameter θ_0. Then if $\hat{\theta}$ is strongly consistent, the sum $(1/n) \sum_i f(\hat{\theta}, w_i) u_i$ has the same asymptotic limit as $(1/n) \sum_i f(\theta_0, w_i) u_i$. If the variables w_i are independent of the equation disturbance u_i, then the latter sum will tend in probability to zero, so that the same property is true of $(1/n) \sum z_{ir} u_i$. A similar argument can be constructed if $\hat{\theta}$ is only weakly consistent, although care must be taken to ensure suitable regularity properties on f and its derivatives.[5]

(b) The vector $\hat{\theta}$ is not regarded as an estimate of a true parameter vector but is formally constructed in terms of sample means or sample variances and covariances. If these sample statistics converge strongly to vectors or matrices of constants, the limiting sums $(1/n) \sum f(\hat{\theta}, w_i) u_i$ will nevertheless continue to converge in probability to zero, under regularity conditions on the function f.

The implications of the above discussion for the present context are as follows. First, if the true discrimination structure is as assumed in the Anderson model – or is such that it generates naturally the Fisher-type procedure – then, since sample estimators of μ_j, μ_k, and Σ (or the canonical loadings $\mathbf{a}_r$) are strongly consistent, the proposed instruments $\tilde{d}_i^j$ or $\check{d}_i^j$ will be admissible. Second, the instruments will continue to be admissible even if the true discrimination structure is not correctly identified by the Anderson or Fisher procedures, provided only that the formal sample statistics ($\hat{\mu}_j$, $\hat{\mu}_k$, $\hat{\Sigma}$, etc.) converge strongly to vectors or matrices of constants.

This indeed highlights a feature of an IV calculation, namely that the instruments need not be optimal, in any sense, for the technique to remain consistent. In this sense, the IV calculation is not crucially dependent upon exact specification. It may be that the requirements for the Anderson or Fisherian discriminant functions are not met in all respects, or that certain discriminatory variables are not listed among the $\mathbf{w}$ variables, or yet again that the experimenter has no real knowledge of the underlying structure, which ultimately determines the classification. Under rather weak conditions, the IV estimators nevertheless remain consistent, and their efficiency can be examined empirically in terms of the canonical correlations between instrument and regressor. Thus an instrumental variables approach holds out promise of greater robustness, as well as ease of generalization to more than two groups.

Application

The results we quote are taken from a study by Bowden and Mazumdar (1983) of the Bombay labor market. There are three sector categories: the small business sector (I), the factory sector (II), and the casual or informal sector (III). The dependent variable is the logarithm of wages. The independent variables are of two types: (a) worker characteristics such as age, education, years of experience, migrant status, and marital status; and (b) sectoral characteristics specific to a sector such as factory size or whether the establishment is a movie theater or restaurant. In addition, binary sectoral dummies appear in order to test for a simple intercept earnings effect between sectors. In addition to the presence or absence of intercept effects one is interested in testing whether the coefficients of the worker characteristic variables differ across sectors, that is, in such propositions as whether or not the returns to experience or education differ between sectors. Some of the right-hand variables take the form of dummy variables. Educational levels are represented by five binary dummies, representing progressively higher levels of formal education accomplishment. For a fuller account of the context, methodology, and results of the study, we refer the reader to the original source.

Let us consider first the results of a discrimination analysis between the three sectors. The variables used for such purpose were the set of worker characteristics [set (a) above] also used in the regression equation. The procedure used is the DISCRIMINANT subprogram in the SSPS package. The basic classificatory procedure is based on the canonical discriminant function of the Fisher type; however, group probabilities are also calculated after the Anderson approach. (As remarked above, the latter assumes a multivariate normal distribution that is not applicable to some of the dummy variables appearing upon the discriminating variables; nevertheless, the probability instrument should retain its asymptotic validity.)

It turns out that of the two possible discriminant functions for the three groups, the first eigenvalue represents 93.48% of the variance existing in the discriminating variables, so that discrimination can very nearly be achieved along a single canonical axis. The classification results are shown in Table 2.1.

Table 2.1. *Classification results*

Actual group	Number of cases	Predicted group membership I	II	III
I	1,581	697 (44.1%)	705 (44.6%)	179 (11.3%)
II	2,464	285 (11.6%)	2,132 (86.5%)	47 (1.9%)
III	900	340 (37.8%)	338 (37.6%)	222 (24.7%)

Overall, the percentage of cases correctly classified was 61.7%. The reason for this rather low overall figure is apparent from Table 2.1. Group II members, the factory workers, are well differentiated, but the same is not true of groups I and III. This affects the likelihood of success attached to a full regression model. Thus consider the equation

$$y_i = \mathbf{x}'_{1i}\alpha + \mathbf{x}'_{2i}\beta + d_i^{\mathrm{II}}\mathbf{x}'_{2i}\delta_2 + d_i^{\mathrm{III}}\mathbf{x}'_{2i}\delta_3 + u_i. \tag{2.26}$$

Here $\mathbf{x}_1$ are the sector-specific (concomitant) variables and $\mathbf{x}_2$ are the worker characteristics (communal variables, as it were). The binary sector dummies are d_i^{II} and d_i^{III}; the parameters δ_2 and δ_3 represent the marginal effects of being in sectors II and III relative to sector I, which is taken as the base sector. Now the discriminant analysis reflected in Table 2.1 suggests that we could expect to construct a good instrument for the sector II binary d_i^{II}, but does not hold out much hope in respect of the sector III binary d_i^{III}.

However, the absence of almost any discrimination between sectors I and III suggests that an instrument is not really needed for the binary variable d_i^{III}. Assuming this to be the case, we will not do too much harm so far as the testing of $\delta_2 = \mathbf{0}$ is concerned by simply dropping the sector III observations and considering the model

$$y_i = \mathbf{x}'_{1i}\alpha + \mathbf{x}'_{2i}\beta + d_i^{\mathrm{II}}\mathbf{x}'_{2i}\delta_2 + u_i, \qquad i \in \mathrm{I, II}. \tag{2.27a}$$

This gives an estimate of the response differences of sector II with respect to sector I. We could also fit the model

$$y_i = \mathbf{x}'_{1i}\alpha + \mathbf{x}'_{2i}\beta + d_i^{\mathrm{II}}\mathbf{x}'_{2i}\delta_2 + u_i, \qquad i \in \mathrm{II, III}. \tag{2.27b}$$

This latter equation will yield the response differences of sector II with respect to sector III. It is, in any event, of interest to compare the OLS results from equation (2.27a) or (2.27b) with the IV results. For reasons of space we present only the results for the equation relating the factory to the small (informal) sector, with the latter as base.

Using the output from the discriminant analysis, the discrete and probability instruments $\tilde{d}_i^j$ and $\check{d}_i^j$ were calculated as outlined above. Considering equation (2.27a), we can write the regressor matrix as

$$X = [X_1 \vdots X_2 \vdots d_i^{\text{II}} X_2]$$

and the corresponding instrument matrices as

$$Z_d = [X_1 \vdots X_2 \vdots \tilde{d}_i^{\text{II}} X_2] \qquad \text{(discrete instrument)}$$

$$Z_p = [X_1 \vdots X_2 \vdots \check{d}_i^{\text{II}} X_2] \qquad \text{(probability instrument).}$$

The problem is now to choose between these alternative instrument sets. This was done by utilizing a canonical correlation between X and Z_d on the one hand, and X and Z_p on the other. In each case, 17 of the 28 canonical correlations were unity, reflecting the appearance of the common elements $X_1 \vdots X_2$ in both X and Z. We then computed the statistic $(\prod_{j=1}^{28} r_j^2)^{1/28}$, which can be taken as a geometric average measure attached to the magnitude of the (squared) correlation between the data sets X and Z. For the discrete version, the value was .3588, while its value for the probability instrument was .3822. This indicates a marginal preference for the probability instrument.

The results from an IV calculation utilizing this instrument are presented in Table 2.2, along with the corresponding OLS fit for purposes of comparison. In general it can be seen that there is quite a considerable difference, in signs as well as apparent significance levels, between the IV and OLS fits, and that these differences are by no means confined to the variables involving the sectoral dummy. So far as the sector-specific variables are concerned, there is a general reduction in apparent significance levels, with the shop and commercial establishment binaries losing their significance. With regard to the worker characteristics, the base education effects lose nearly all their significance and no marginal (sector III) differences are manifested. On the other hand, the marginal dummy for mastery of written and spoken English now appears significant, suggesting that there is an extra return in the factory sector to a worker with command of English. Clearly, an IV solution makes a great deal of difference to the conclusions that might be drawn on the basis of a straightforward least-squares regression.

2.7 Testing regressor–disturbance independence

Until now we have implicitly assumed that correlation between regressor and equation disturbance exists and is of sufficient magnitude to call for

Table 2.2. *The factory: small comparison*

	IV		OLS	
Variable	Value	(CV)	Value	(CV)
(α)				
Const.	3.942		3.73	
SIZE 1	−.354	(−9.55)	−.355	(−21.29)
SIZE 2	−.071	(−1.86)	−.067	(−3.87)
SIZE 3	−.0083	(.19)	.017	(.68)
SHOP	.040	(.27)	.250	(10.63)
CMESTAB	.036	(.24)	.232	(9.97)
RESTHTL	−.185	(−1.25)	.048	(.77)
THEATRE	.381	(2.11)	.692	(14.24)
(β)				
AGE	.063	(11.37)	.069	(14.77)
AGE 2	−.00050	(−6.99)	−.00077	(−3.82)
ED 1	.030	(.54)	.056	(1.91)
ED 2	.039	(.81)	.119	(4.96)
ED 3	.095	(1.54)	.150	(5.99)
ED 4	.288	(3.21)	.256	(8.44)
ED 5	.261	(1.62)	.378	(5.87)
MARRIED	.089	(1.18)	.051	(2.43)
MIGRANT	−.022	(−1.00)	−.101	(−.48)
ENGLISH	−.079	(−1.50)	.086	(3.75)
(δ)				
SECDUM 2	1.153	(6.45)	1.275	(11.04)
MIGRANT 2		([a])	−.123	(−.46)
AGE 2, 1	−.018	(−3.35)	−.022	(−3.33)
AGE 2, 2		([a])	.00029	(3.34)
ED 2, 1	.029	(.34)	−.011	(−.30)
ED 2, 2	.101	(1.42)	−.027	(−.88)
ED 2, 3	.098	(1.10)	−.011	(−.34)
ED 2, 4	−.108	(−.87)	−.067	(−1.71)
ED 2, 5	.278	(1.05)	.022	(.26)
ENGLISH 2	.294	(3.65)	.039	(1.32)
MARRIED 2	−.024	(−.19)	.027	(.92)
$\hat{\sigma}$		.3494		.3051

Note: Sample size $n = 4{,}045$; df $= 4{,}016$.

[a]Tolerance level not reached in a program for stepwise inclusion (SPSS) and can be taken to indicate that the effect of the variable in question is negligible.

an instrumental variables routine rather than a straightforward application of ordinary least squares. Ideally this is a proposition that one should like to test in advance, and this introduces the topic of formal tests of independence between regressors and disturbance. The power of such a test will naturally depend upon the particular context. For instance, if one thought that the equation under scrutiny was part of a simultaneous-equation system, an effective test of independence might utilize membership in such a system as an alternative hypothesis, so to speak. Likewise, if it is thought that possible regressor–disturbance correlation arises out of the combination of a lagged dependent variable with a serially correlated error, in the context of time series regressions, the test can be based upon the magnitude and significance of the key parameter of serial correlation. We shall consider such contexts in due course. For the present, however, it is useful to set out and discuss tests of regressor–disturbance independence that are relatively context-free, in accordance with the level of generality desired in the present chapter.

The Wu–Hausman tests

A family of such tests for independence was proposed by Wu (1973).[6] As one might expect, these tests are based upon the discrepancy between the IV and OLS estimators. Let us consider the model

$$\mathbf{y} = X\boldsymbol{\beta} + Z_2\boldsymbol{\gamma} + \mathbf{u} \tag{2.28}$$

where X is a data matrix of stochastic variables of order $n \times G$ and Z_2 is a data matrix of fixed (nonstochastic) variates of order $n \times K_2$. Since Z_2 is assumed fixed in repeated realizations, there is no question of correlation with the disturbance vector $\mathbf{u}$. On the other hand, the rows of X are assumed to be drawings from a multivariate normal distribution. Denoting by $\mathbf{x}_{t.}$ the tth row of X, we write $\mathrm{Cov}(\mathbf{x}_{t.}, u_t) = E(\mathbf{x}_{t.} - \boldsymbol{\mu}_{t.})u_t = \boldsymbol{\delta}'$, say, where $\boldsymbol{\mu}_{t.} = \mathcal{E}\mathbf{x}_{t.}$. The null hypothesis to be tested is that $\boldsymbol{\delta} = \mathbf{0}$, that is, the elements of X and $\mathbf{u}$ are uncorrelated.

It is assumed that a data matrix Z_1 of instruments for X, of order $K_1 \geq G$, is available. We may therefore employ $Z = [Z_1 \vdots Z_2]$ as an instrument matrix for the regressor data matrix $[X \vdots Z_2]$. By appropriate partitioning of the overall OLS and IV estimating equations, one can show that the estimates are given by

$$\text{(OLS)} \quad \mathbf{b} = [X'(I - P_{z_2})X]^{-1}X'(I - P_{z_2})\mathbf{y} \tag{2.29}$$

$$\text{(IV)} \quad \hat{\boldsymbol{\beta}} = [X'(P_z - P_{z_2})X]^{-1}X'(P_z - P_{z_2})\mathbf{y}, \tag{2.30}$$

where $P_z = Z(Z'Z)^{-1}Z'$ and $P_{z_2} = Z_2(Z_2'Z_2)^{-1}Z_2'$.

Consider now the difference $\mathbf{b} - \hat{\boldsymbol{\beta}}$ between the two estimates. It is straightforward to show from equations (2.28)–(2.30) that conditional upon X and under the null hypothesis ($\boldsymbol{\delta} = \mathbf{0}$),

$$\mathbf{b} - \hat{\boldsymbol{\beta}} \sim N(\mathbf{0}, \sigma^2 D),$$

where $D=[X'(P_z-P_{z_2})X]^{-1}-[X'(I-P_{z_2})X]^{-1}$ is positive definite.

Perhaps the most straightforward test statistic is then Wu's T_3, defined by

$$T_3=\frac{(\mathbf{b}-\hat{\boldsymbol{\beta}})'D^{-1}(\mathbf{b}-\hat{\boldsymbol{\beta}})}{\hat{\sigma}^2}, \tag{2.31}$$

where

$$\hat{\sigma}^2=\frac{(\mathbf{y}-X\hat{\boldsymbol{\beta}})'(I-P_{z_2})(\mathbf{y}-X\hat{\boldsymbol{\beta}})}{n-G-K_2}$$

is a consistent estimator of σ^2. Since $\hat{\sigma}^2 \xrightarrow{p} \sigma^2$, the statistic T_3 has the same limiting distribution as $(\mathbf{b}-\hat{\boldsymbol{\beta}})'D^{-1}(\mathbf{b}-\hat{\boldsymbol{\beta}})/\sigma^2$, which is chi-squared with G degrees of freedom. By considering the distribution of T_3 under the alternative hypothesis, Wu shows that the chi-squared test based upon T_3 is consistent, in the sense that the power function tends to unity if $\boldsymbol{\delta}\neq\mathbf{0}$ and to the critical probability α if $\boldsymbol{\delta}=\mathbf{0}$.

Two finite sample tests are also given by Wu, both of which are also consistent. The more useful of these appears to be

$$T_2=\frac{(\mathbf{b}-\hat{\boldsymbol{\beta}})'D^{-1}(\mathbf{b}-\hat{\boldsymbol{\beta}})/G}{Q/(n-K_2-2G)}, \tag{2.32}$$

where $Q=(\mathbf{y}-X\mathbf{b})'(I-P_{z_2})(\mathbf{y}-\mathbf{Xb})-(\mathbf{b}-\hat{\boldsymbol{\beta}})'D^{-1}(\mathbf{b}-\hat{\boldsymbol{\beta}})$. Conditional upon X and under the null hypothesis, it may be shown that T_2 is distributed as F with G and $n-K_2-2G$ degrees of freedom. Under the null hypothesis ($\boldsymbol{\delta}=\mathbf{0}$), the conditional distribution does not in fact depend upon X, so the F distribution is unconditional. The rejection region is defined by high values of T_2; that is, $T_2>C_\alpha$, where C_α is chosen to make the significance level equal to α.

The Wu tests may be regarded as particular examples of a general testing procedure later suggested by Hausman (1978). Consider the standard regression framework $\mathbf{y}=X\boldsymbol{\beta}+\mathbf{u}$ and suppose that we wish to test H_0: $\operatorname{plim}(1/n)X'\mathbf{u}=\mathbf{0}$. Under the null hypothesis, there will exist a consistent, asymptotically normal estimator that is efficient in the sense that it achieves the asymptotic Cramer–Rao lower bound. However, under the alternative hypothesis H_1: $\operatorname{plim} X'\mathbf{u}/n\neq\mathbf{0}$, this estimator will be biased and inconsistent. Call this estimator $\hat{\boldsymbol{\beta}}_0$. Suppose that we can find another estimator $\hat{\boldsymbol{\beta}}_1$ that is consistent both under H_0 and H_1 although not asymptotically efficient under H_0. Consider the difference between these two estimators, $\hat{\mathbf{q}}=\hat{\boldsymbol{\beta}}_1-\hat{\boldsymbol{\beta}}_0$. If H_0 is true, then, since $\hat{\boldsymbol{\beta}}_0$ and $\hat{\boldsymbol{\beta}}_1$ are both consistent under H_0, $\hat{\mathbf{q}}$ will have a probability limit equal to the null vector. If H_1 is true, then, since $\hat{\boldsymbol{\beta}}_0$ is inconsistent under H_1, $\operatorname{plim}\hat{\mathbf{q}}$ will not equal the null vector. A reasonable test statistic would be one that measures the distance of the vector $\hat{\mathbf{q}}$ from the null vector. That is, we could choose as our test statistic

$$n\hat{\mathbf{q}}'A\hat{\mathbf{q}},$$

where A is a positive definite matrix. A large observed value of $\hat{\mathbf{q}}'A\hat{\mathbf{q}}$ would be taken as evidence against H_0. The matrix A is chosen in such a way that we know the asymptotic distribution of our test statistic under H_0.

With suitable regularity assumptions, Hausman shows that if $\sqrt{n}(\hat{\boldsymbol{\beta}}_1 - \boldsymbol{\beta})$ has a limiting normal distribution under H_0, then asymptotically, $\sqrt{n}(\hat{\boldsymbol{\beta}}_0 - \boldsymbol{\beta})$ and $\sqrt{n}\hat{\mathbf{q}}$ have zero covariance. It follows that the covariance matrix $V(\hat{\mathbf{q}})$ of the difference $\hat{\mathbf{q}}$ is equal to $V(\hat{\beta}_1) - V(\hat{\beta}_0)$. Hence under H_0,

$$\sqrt{n}\hat{\mathbf{q}} \xrightarrow{d} N(\mathbf{0}, V(\hat{\mathbf{q}})), \tag{2.33}$$

and so $V(\hat{\mathbf{q}})^{-1}$ qualifies as an appropriate matrix A. Usually $V(\hat{\mathbf{q}})$ is unknown and will have to be replaced by a consistent estimator $\hat{V}$, but this should not affect the asymptotic results. The test statistic recommended by Hausman is then

$$n\hat{\mathbf{q}}'\hat{V}(\hat{\mathbf{q}})^{-1}\hat{\mathbf{q}}. \tag{2.34}$$

From (2.34) it follows that under H_0, this test statistic has a limiting central chi-squared distribution with p degrees of freedom, where p is the number of columns of X, that is, the dimension of $\boldsymbol{\beta}$. Hausman also investigated the distribution of the test statistic under the alternative hypothesis. Specifically, a sequence of local alternatives $H_1: \boldsymbol{\beta}_a = \boldsymbol{\beta} + \delta/\sqrt{n}$ is considered, a device that prevents the power of a consistent test from tending to unity as the sample size n increases (see Cox and Hinkley 1974). Under H_1, the test statistic has a limiting noncentral χ^2 distribution with K degrees of freedom and noncentrality parameter approximately equal to $\bar{\mathbf{q}}'M(\hat{\mathbf{q}})\bar{\mathbf{q}}$, where $\bar{\mathbf{q}} = \operatorname{plim}(\hat{\boldsymbol{\beta}}_1 - \hat{\boldsymbol{\beta}}_0)$ and $M(\hat{\mathbf{q}}) = (1/n) \operatorname{plim} \hat{V}(\hat{\mathbf{q}})$.

Further considerations

Let us consider the equation to be estimated:

$$y = X\boldsymbol{\beta} + \mathbf{u},$$

and suppose that we can write $\operatorname{plim}(1/n)X'\mathbf{u} = \boldsymbol{\theta}$, say. Now from the point of view of classical hypothesis testing, the test procedure described immediately above is something of an anomaly. The reasoning would run thus: We are interested in testing whether $\boldsymbol{\theta} = \mathbf{0}$, that is, the absence of regressor–error correlation. Yet to do this, we are (by comparing $\hat{\boldsymbol{\beta}}_1$

and $\hat{\beta}_0$) carrying out the test in terms of the sampling distribution of $\boldsymbol{\beta}$, which from the point of view of a test on $\boldsymbol{\theta}$ must be regarded as a nuisance parameter, in the sense that it is not of primary interest. It may be that tests on $\boldsymbol{\beta}$ may have limitations or qualifications if the primary object is a test on $\boldsymbol{\theta}$.

This point has been made by Holly (1982) and it will be useful, before discussing further the questions of principle involved, to review briefly his development. Holly works out his theory in the context of a maximum-likelihood estimation of two parameters: $\boldsymbol{\theta}$ the parameter of primary interest and $\boldsymbol{\gamma}$ (which corresponds to our $\boldsymbol{\beta}$) the nuisance parameter. Let $l(\boldsymbol{\theta}, \boldsymbol{\gamma})$ denote the log-likelihood function of the sample, where the parameter vectors $\boldsymbol{\theta} \in \Theta$ and $\boldsymbol{\gamma} \in \Gamma$ are of order r and s, respectively. We wish to test the null hypothesis that $\boldsymbol{\theta} = \boldsymbol{\theta}_0$, against the sequence of local alternatives $\boldsymbol{\theta} = \boldsymbol{\theta}_0 + \boldsymbol{\delta}/\sqrt{n}$. Let $(\hat{\boldsymbol{\theta}}, \hat{\boldsymbol{\gamma}})$ denote the unconstrained solutions (maximum-likelihood estimators) and let $(\boldsymbol{\theta}_0, \hat{\boldsymbol{\gamma}}_0)$ denote the constrained estimators; the latter are the solution to the problem

$$\max_{\theta = \theta_0,\ \gamma \in \Gamma} \quad l(\boldsymbol{\theta}_0, \boldsymbol{\gamma}).$$

Let

$$I = \begin{bmatrix} I_{\theta\theta} & I_{\theta\gamma} \\ I_{\gamma\theta} & I_{\gamma\gamma} \end{bmatrix}$$

denote the information matrix, evaluated at the true parameter values $(\boldsymbol{\theta}_0, \boldsymbol{\gamma}_0)$. [In other words,

$$I = -\operatorname{plim} \frac{1}{n} \frac{\partial^2 l}{\partial \boldsymbol{\phi}\, \partial \boldsymbol{\phi}'} (\boldsymbol{\theta}, \boldsymbol{\gamma})_0,$$

where $\boldsymbol{\phi}' = (\theta', \ \gamma')$.]

Holly shows that the test statistic resulting from Hausman's procedure is

$$n(\hat{\boldsymbol{\gamma}} - \hat{\boldsymbol{\gamma}}_0)'[(I_{\gamma\gamma} - I_{\gamma\theta} I_{\theta\theta}^{-1} I_{\theta\gamma})^{-1} - I_{\gamma\gamma}^{-1}](\hat{\boldsymbol{\gamma}} - \hat{\boldsymbol{\gamma}}_0). \tag{2.35}$$

With suitable regularity conditions and under H_1, the test statistic converges to a noncentral χ^2 distribution with s degrees of freedom and noncentrality parameter

$$\lambda^2 = \boldsymbol{\delta}' I_{\theta\gamma}[I_{\gamma\theta}(I_{\theta\theta} - I_{\theta\gamma} I_{\gamma\gamma}^{-1} I_{\gamma\theta})^{-1} I_{\theta\gamma}]^{-1} I_{\gamma\theta}\, \boldsymbol{\delta}. \tag{2.36}$$

Holly notes that this result assumes that the covariance matrix $(I_{\gamma\gamma} - I_{\gamma\theta} I_{\theta\theta} I_{\theta\gamma})^{-1} - I_{\gamma\gamma}^{-1}$ is positive definite. A necessary condition for this to be so is that the number of "nuisance" parameters s is less than or equal to r, the number of parameters under immediate test. The statistics (2.35) and (2.36) generalize to the case (of some importance in practice) where the asymptotic covariance matrix of $\sqrt{n}(\hat{\gamma}-\hat{\gamma}_0)$ is singular. In this case, the distribution under H_1 of the random variable

$$n(\hat{\gamma}-\hat{\gamma}_0)'[(I_{\gamma\gamma}-I_{\gamma\theta}I_{\theta\theta}^{-1}I_{\theta\gamma})^{-1}-I_{\gamma\gamma}^{-1}]^{-}(\hat{\gamma}-\hat{\gamma}_0)$$

converges to a noncentral χ^2 distribution with degrees of freedom equal to the rank of $I_{\gamma\theta}$ and noncentrality parameter

$$\lambda^2=\boldsymbol{\delta}'I_{\theta\gamma}I_{\gamma\gamma}^{-1}[I_{\gamma\gamma}^{-1}I_{\gamma\theta}(I_{\theta\theta}-I_{\theta\gamma}I_{\gamma\gamma}^{-1}I_{\gamma\theta})^{-1}I_{\theta\gamma}I_{\gamma\gamma}^{-1}]^{-}I_{\gamma\gamma}^{-1}I_{\gamma\theta}\boldsymbol{\delta}. \tag{2.37}$$

Now the noncentrality parameter defined by expression (2.36) arises from the fact that under the given sequence of alternatives, the vector $\sqrt{n}(\hat{\gamma}-\hat{\gamma}_0)$ converges in distribution to a normal distribution with mean vector $-I_{\gamma\gamma}^{-1}I_{\gamma\theta}\boldsymbol{\beta}$. This suggests that the null hypothesis actually tested in the Hausman procedure is

$$H_0^*: I_{\gamma\gamma}^{-1}I_{\gamma\theta}\boldsymbol{\delta}=\mathbf{0}. \tag{2.38}$$

H_0^* only reduces to $H_0: \boldsymbol{\delta}=\mathbf{0}$, when $s=r$ and rank $I_{\gamma\theta}=r$. For this special case it may be shown that the Hausman test is asymptotically equivalent to more conventional tests such as the Wald, likelihood ratio, or Rao tests, in the sense that all these test statistics have the same limiting distribution under H_0 and H_1.

At first sight, the above results are of limited applicability to the context of instrumental variables estimates. Indeed, we note that only rarely can we confidently specify the alternative hypothesis that $\text{plim}(1/n)X'\mathbf{u}=\boldsymbol{\theta}$, a constant. This being the case, a maximum-likelihood development is not applicable, for want of information about the precise generation of X. Rather, the Holly development points up some general principles. An apparent test of zero regressor–error correlation that is based upon the values of other nuisance or incidental parameters will not necessarily end up testing precisely the desired hypothesis. Thus if $\boldsymbol{\theta}=\mathbf{0}$ is the desired null hypothesis, equation (2.38) suggests that a Hausman-type procedure might really amount to testing the null hypothesis $D\boldsymbol{\theta}=\mathbf{0}$, where the matrix D ($\neq I$) depends upon the means used to estimate $\hat{\boldsymbol{\beta}}_0$ and $\hat{\boldsymbol{\beta}}_1$, that is, the two alternative estimation procedures. If the matrix D is of less than full-column rank, accepting $H_0: D\boldsymbol{\theta}=\mathbf{0}$ is not necessarily the same as accepting $H_0: \boldsymbol{\theta}=\mathbf{0}$.

On the other hand, one might remark that the object is not so much to test a specific hypothesis [e.g., $\text{plim}(1/n)X'\mathbf{u}=\boldsymbol{\theta}=\mathbf{0}$] as to test something about the relative properties of estimators of β; and for this purpose it is the regressor–error correlations that are incidental. If regressor–error correlations are zero, then the difference $\mathbf{b}-\hat{\boldsymbol{\beta}}_1$ between the OLS and IV estimators has asymptotically a central χ^2 distribution. If regressor–error correlations are nonzero, the difference has asymptotically a noncentral

χ^2. Suppose that the resulting noncentrality parameter depends upon $D\boldsymbol{\theta}$. Then all that matters is whether $D\boldsymbol{\theta}=\mathbf{0}$. If $\boldsymbol{\theta}\neq\mathbf{0}$, this is immaterial if $\boldsymbol{\theta}$ belongs to the null space of the matrix D. Thus the object is not really to test H_0: no regressor–disturbance correlation exists; but to test H_0: any form of correlation that may exist has no effect on the estimator $\hat{\boldsymbol{\beta}}_0$ (in this case, the OLS estimate $\mathbf{b}$).

Of course, the above cannot be regarded as a well-formulated or pure statistical hypothesis, and indeed the literature on the issue of precisely what is being tested by the Wu–Hausman methods remains unsettled, at best. Nevertheless, in the kind of situation, so common in practice, where a likelihood function cannot be written down for want of the necessary information, there remains no properly worked-out alternative procedure.

Testing instrument admissibility

In the discussion above, we were concerned with the problem of testing whether or not the regressor variables were correlated with the equation disturbance, and for this purpose we had available a set of variables (Z) that we knew in advance were admissible as instruments. In the present subsection we consider a rather different problem: We know, this time, that the regressor variables, or at least a designated subset thereof, are correlated with the equation disturbance. We have available a set of instruments Z_1 and a possible further set Z_2 that, if admissible, might improve efficiency. Are the second set admissible; or in terms of the slightly more limited framework of instrument–disturbance relationships, is it true that the variables of Z_2 are asymptotically uncorrelated with the disturbance term? The discussion of this problem that we outline below is due to Hausman and Taylor (1981).

We are given the equation

$$\mathbf{y}_1 = Y_1\boldsymbol{\beta} + X_1\boldsymbol{\gamma} + \mathbf{u}_1 = H_1\boldsymbol{\delta} + \mathbf{u}_1, \tag{2.39}$$

where $H_1=[Y_1 \vdots X_1]$ and $\boldsymbol{\delta}'=[\boldsymbol{\beta}' \vdots \boldsymbol{\gamma}')$. Here X_1 is an $n\times K_1$ matrix of observations on exogenous variables that are either fixed in repeated realizations or known to be independent of the disturbance terms. The variables that form the data matrix Y_1 are known to be correlated with the disturbance variable. [Equation (2.39) can be regarded as the first equation in a system of simultaneous equations; however, for present purposes we shall simply take the equation at face value, reserving a further understanding of the role of the remaining equations in the putative system for discussion in Chapter 4.] We have available an $n\times p_1$ data matrix of instruments Z_1 and an $n\times p_2$ data matrix of variables Z_2. The object is to test the null hypothesis

$$H_0\colon \operatorname{plim} \frac{1}{n} \mathbf{Z}_2' \mathbf{u}_1 = \mathbf{0}.$$

We assume that the columns of Z_1 span those of X_1, that is, $X_1 \in C(Z_1)$.

If H_0 is true and Z_2 is fully admissible, then we assume that the IV estimator

$$\hat{\boldsymbol{\delta}}_0 = (H_1' P_z H_1)^{-1} H_1 P_z \mathbf{y}_1 \tag{2.40}$$

is asymptotically efficient among the possible estimators of the equation (2.39), where $Z = [Z_1 \vdots Z_2]$ and P_z is the associated projection matrix. (At this stage we leave this as an assumption, but the conditions under which the efficiency claim is true will be apparent after reading Chapter 4.) However, if H_0 is not true, then the appropriate IV estimator is

$$\hat{\boldsymbol{\delta}}_1 = (H_1 P_{z_1} H_1)^{-1} H_1' P_{z_1} \mathbf{y}_1. \tag{2.41}$$

Hausman's test is based upon the difference between the estimators (2.40) and (2.41):

$$\hat{\mathbf{q}} = \hat{\boldsymbol{\delta}}_1 - \hat{\boldsymbol{\delta}}_0 = (H_1' P_{z_1} H_1)^{-1} \begin{bmatrix} Y_1' P_{z_1} (I - H_1 (H_1' P_z H_1)^{-1} H_1' P_z) \mathbf{y}_1 \\ X_1' P_{z_1} (I - H_1 (H_1' P_z H_1)^{-1} H_1' P_z) \mathbf{y}_1 \end{bmatrix}. \tag{2.42}$$

But $X_1' P_{z_1} = X_1'$, $P_{z_1} P_z = P_{z_1}$, and $X_1 \in C(Z)$. Hence we can write

$$\hat{\mathbf{q}} = (H_1' P_{z_1} H_1)^{-1} \begin{bmatrix} Y_1' P_{z_1} [I - P_z H_1 (H_1' P_z H_1)^{-1} H_1' P_z] \mathbf{y}_1 \\ \mathbf{O} \end{bmatrix}. \tag{2.43}$$

Using expression (2.43), we find that the covariance matrix of $\hat{q}$ is

$$V(\hat{q}) = (H_1' P_{z_1} H_1)^{-1} \begin{bmatrix} \sigma_1^2 Y_1' P_{z_1} M^* P_{z_1} Y_1 & \mathbf{O} \\ \mathbf{O} & \mathbf{O} \end{bmatrix} (H_1' P_{z_1} H_1)^{-1}, \tag{2.44}$$

where $M^* = I - P_z H_1 (H_1' P_z H_1)^{-1} H_1' P_z$. This covariance matrix is clearly singular with rank equal to that of $\sigma_1^2 Y_1' P_{z_1} M^* P_{z_1} Y_1$. The Hausman and Taylor exogeneity test statistic for known σ_1^2 is then

$$n \hat{\mathbf{q}}' V(\hat{\mathbf{q}})^- \hat{\mathbf{q}},$$

where $\hat{\mathbf{q}}$ and $V(\hat{\mathbf{q}})$ are given by expressions (2.43) and (2.44) and $(\ )^-$ signifies any generalized inverse. Since σ_1^2 will be unknown, it should be replaced by a consistent estimate. The test statistic then becomes

$$n \hat{\mathbf{q}}' \hat{V}(\hat{\mathbf{q}})^- \hat{\mathbf{q}}, \tag{2.45}$$

which under H_0 converges to the central chi-squared distribution with degrees of freedom equal to the rank of the matrix $Y_1' P_{z_1} M^* P_{z_1} Y_1$. Using properties of the generalized inverse, Hausman and Taylor show that the test statistic (2.45) is equal to

$$n(\hat{\beta}_0-\hat{\beta}_1)'V(\hat{\beta}_0-\hat{\beta}_1)^-(\hat{\beta}_0-\hat{\beta}_1).$$

The effect of this is that in forming a test for the admissibility of instruments, one need only take into account the coefficients of variables for which instruments are deemed necessary.

Pretest estimators

We have seen that the Wu–Hausman procedure is based upon the discrepancy between the OLS estimator **b** and the IV estimator $\hat{\beta}$. This immediately invokes the possibility of a *pretest estimator* $\tilde{\beta}$ defined by

$$\begin{aligned}\tilde{\beta}&=\hat{\beta} && \text{if the null hypothesis of independence is rejected}\\ &=\mathbf{b} && \text{otherwise.}\end{aligned}$$

It would be of interest to compare the finite sampling distribution of such a pretest estimator with that of $\tilde{\beta}$ or **b** alone.

A more structured pretest estimator has been advanced by Feldstein (1974) for a particular model, namely a simple errors-in-variables model (see Sections 1.1 and 2.8, below), in which an available instrument is assumed to be related to the unobservable by a theoretical regression with no intercept term. Feldstein suggests a weighted combination $\tilde{\beta}=\lambda\mathbf{b}+(1-\lambda)\hat{\beta}$, where the weight λ is chosen to minimize the asymptotic mean-square error of the combined estimator; the weighting factor λ may be calculated from preliminary OLS and IV estimates together with certain supplementary sample statistics.

Feldstein's weight λ is evidently specific to the particular model he considers, which even among errors-in-variables models is limited in applicability. However, his suggestions are ingenious, and it may be that similar weighted combinations of IV and OLS estimators have favorable mean-square error properties in more general contexts. As a general observation we may note that a strict application of the Wu–Hausman testing procedure leads to outright use of either IV or OLS, and the argument is essentially based upon the consistency properties, or lack thereof, of the two estimators. However, it may be that OLS is only mildly inconsistent; or in more traditional terms, its well-known favorable variance properties more than compensate even for a moderate level of inconsistency. Clearly the use of mean-square error as a distance criterion overcomes the distinctly unsatisfactory aspects of estimation choice based solely upon consistency. And by appropriately weighting the OLS and IV estimators one could in principle achieve a point on the trade-off between bias (or inconsistency) and variance that accords with the researcher's own preferences.

On the other hand, there are some difficulties with Feldstein-type procedures that should be noted. A trade-off between bias and variance makes complete sense only in the context of a finite sample size. Asymptotically, a consistent estimator with a limiting distribution will always achieve a minimum mean-square error relative to an inconsistent estimator. Indeed, Feldstein's own procedure essentially amounts to approximating a finite sample variance (of $\tilde{\beta}$) by $1/n$ times the variance of the asymptotic distribution (in the usual sense, namely of the variable $\sqrt{n}\tilde{\beta}$) and trading this off against the inconsistency, as a bias indicator. But clearly for n large enough for these approximations to be valid, the loss function for a consistent estimator $\hat{\beta}$ approaches zero, so that the problem simply disappears. The preferred solution is to work in terms of the exact finite sampling distribution of the estimator $\tilde{\beta}$. Unfortunately, this is difficult, even in the case where one has complete knowledge of the generation of the correlation between X and $\mathbf{u}$ and of the instruments Z.

Nevertheless, a further study of Feldstein-type estimators does seem to be a natural outgrowth of the recent literature on specification testing in IV contexts, and the general topic is worth pursuing further. We do not, in the present study, consider any further the properties of estimators $\tilde{\beta}=\lambda\mathbf{b}+(1-\lambda)\hat{\beta}$, that is, estimates that combine OLS and IV values. However, in Section 2.9 we do consider briefly a somewhat different way of combining OLS and IV methodology.

2.8 The errors-in-variables model

We recall from Section 1.1 that the simple errors-in-variables model may be represented[7] as follows:

$$y_i=\beta_0+\beta_1\chi_i+u_i, \qquad i=1\ldots n, \tag{2.46}$$

$$x_i=\chi_i+\epsilon_i. \tag{2.47}$$

These structural equations may be combined into a relationship between the observables y and x:

$$y_i=\beta_0+\beta_1 x_i+v_i; \qquad v_i=u_i-\beta\epsilon_i, \tag{2.48}$$

where the new disturbance term v_i is correlated with the observed regressor x_i. A substantial number of estimation techniques have been suggested in the literature on this model, and even among instrumental variables techniques several different approaches may be pursued, depending upon what is assumed about the error structure (ϵ_i, u_i) or about the generation of the unobserved variates χ_i.

To start with, no method is available that is completely information-free, in the sense that equations (2.46) and (2.47) generate all a priori and sample information. This said, some of the simpler approaches may not be too demanding in their informational requirements. Thus if the model is a time-series representation ($i=t$), it may be that the χ_i exhibit a certain degree of smoothness over time. If in addition the disturbances u_i and ϵ_i are serially uncorrelated, then x_{i-1} is uncorrelated with x_i. One can indeed utilize an instrument set $Z=(x_{i-1}\, x_{i-2} \dots x_{i-k})$ for x_i, for some truncation k chosen with such considerations in mind as the length of the available data series and the discussion of Section 2.3–2.5, above.

In some cases, genuine contemporaneous variables may be available as instruments. We mentioned in Section 1.1 an application of the errors-in-variables model to explain consumption in terms of "permanent" income. Although the latter variable is not directly observable, such proxies as house value or educational achievement may be available that are related to permanent income. One must be prepared to argue that these instruments are uncorrelated with the error (the "transitory" component) ϵ_i relating permanent to observed income. In this sense one cannot escape the necessity of assuming some sort of information extraneous to the model itself.

Grouping methods

Turning now to more systematic ways of constructing or using instruments, we may start with methods that involve grouping or ranking the observations. The seminal paper in this line of development is that of Wald (1940). Suppose that the observations (assumed even in number) are divided into two equal groups I and II and let $\bar{y}_{\mathrm{I}}$, $\bar{y}_{\mathrm{II}}$, $\bar{x}_{\mathrm{I}}$, and $\bar{x}_{\mathrm{II}}$ refer to group means. The basic Wald technique estimates β_1 as

$$\hat{\beta}_1 = \frac{\bar{y}_{\mathrm{II}} - \bar{y}_{\mathrm{I}}}{\bar{x}_{\mathrm{II}} - \bar{x}_{\mathrm{I}}}, \tag{2.49}$$

In other words, one regards the observations as being concentrated into just two points, corresponding to the group means.

As one might expect, however, we cannot simply divide the observations into groups at will. In order to understand the requirements in this respect – and to permit a generalization to models where more than two parameters are involved – it is useful to exhibit the above technique as an IV procedure. For a given partitioning, this is easily accomplished by introducing the dummy or categorical instruments

$$\begin{aligned} z_i &= -1 \qquad \text{if } i \in \mathrm{I} \\ &= +1 \qquad \text{if } i \in \mathrm{II}. \end{aligned}$$

The reader may verify that the estimate (2.49) corresponds to using z_i as an instrument for x_i.

Since the categorical instruments z_i must be uncorrelated with the observation errors, it is apparent that the Wald technique requires the grouping to be statistically independent of the observed x_i. And for the technique to be successful, the groups must discriminate between high and low values of the unobservable, in the sense that $\lim\inf|\bar{\chi}_{\mathrm{II}}-\bar{\chi}_{\mathrm{I}}|>0$. These are the criteria established by Wald, and they constitute genuine restrictions on the construction of groups. For instance, we cannot divide the observations into equal groups, one containing the high-value observations and the other with the lower values; such a division would violate the first requirement, that of statistical independence. Group construction should optimally be based upon some knowledge of the pattern of the underlying variation in χ_i.

The basic Wald technique has been extended in various ways. In the method of Nair and Shrivastava (1942) and Bartlett (1949), the data are divided into three groups on the basis of a presumed ranking of the χ_i. The slope estimator $\hat{\beta}_1$ is based on a formula similar to equation (2.49) applied to the difference between the means of the first and third groups, with observations from the middle group simply discarded. This method also has an IV interpretation, with a categorical instrument z_i taking, in addition to the values $+1$ (highest) and -1 (lowest), the value zero for the middle group.

A more or less logical extension of this line of attack is the method employed by Durbin (1954). If the complete ranking of the χ_i is known, then the natural numbers $1 \ldots n$ may be used as instruments for the x_i. In general, the ranking of the observed variables x_i may not be used for such a purpose. However, if it is known that the variance of the observation errors (u_i) is small and if it is observed that the observations x_i are well spread, then the use of rankings of the observed x_i for instrumental purposes may not entail serious error, although we are constrained to remark that in such a case not too much harm would result from the use of ordinary least squares.

On the practical plane, a grouping methodology has been employed by Friedman (1957) in a study of consumption behavior and permanent income. One might expect that a grouping by occupation should be linked to a ranking of permanent incomes. The associated categorical dummies should therefore constitute acceptable instruments for observed income, justifying Friedman's use of a slope estimator based on group means.

Attenuation estimators

On occasion, estimates may be available of the ratio of the measurement error variance to the total variance of the independent variables. Writing

$\lambda_i^2 = \sigma_{\epsilon_i}^2/\sigma_{x_i}^2$, the quantity $1-\lambda_i^2$ is referred to as the *reliability* of the variable x_i. The idea that one can correct estimated regression parameters (or other covariance-based estimates) for the reliability of the observations has a long, if on the whole informal, history in sociology and psychometrics. The resulting estimates are said to be corrected for attenuation. A formal analysis of attenuation in a regression context has been provided by Fuller and Hidiroglou (1978). Rather than directly following these authors, we shall note that the subject may be given a more convenient formulation in terms of an IV framework.

Consider the generalized form of equations (2.46) and (2.47), namely

$$\mathbf{y} = \chi\boldsymbol{\beta} + \mathbf{u}, \tag{2.50}$$

$$X = \chi + E, \tag{2.51}$$

where now $\mathbf{y}$ and X are $n \times 1$ and $n \times K$, χ is an $n \times K$ matrix of unknown variates, and E is an $n \times K$ matrix whose ith row $\epsilon_{i.}$ represents the ith realization of the measurement errors on the K variables in X. It is assumed that $\text{plim}(1/n)E'\mathbf{u} = \mathbf{0}$, so that measurement and equation errors are uncorrelated in this sense. For regularity purposes it is assumed that the matrix $(1/n)\chi'\chi$ tends to a nonsingular matrix of constants.

Suppose now that we apply IV estimation directly to equation (2.50), with the observable X used as an instrument for χ:

$$X'\chi\boldsymbol{\beta}^* = X'\mathbf{y}. \tag{2.52}$$

If we knew χ, such an IV estimation would clearly be valid (even if unnecessary!). The snag is, of course, that we do not have direct information on the unobservables χ. However, let us observe from (2.51) that

$$\text{plim}\,\frac{1}{n}X'E = \text{plim}\,\frac{1}{n}E'E.$$

Hence

$$\begin{aligned}\text{plim}\,\frac{1}{n}X'\chi &= \text{plim}\,\frac{1}{n}X'X - \text{plim}\,\frac{1}{n}X'E \\ &= \text{plim}\,\frac{1}{n}X'X - \text{plim}\,\frac{1}{n}E'E.\end{aligned}$$

Comparing this with equation (2.52), this suggests the general estimator $\hat{\boldsymbol{\beta}}$ defined by

$$(X'X - E'E)\hat{\boldsymbol{\beta}} = X'\mathbf{y}. \tag{2.53}$$

To make the estimator $\hat{\boldsymbol{\beta}}$ operational we need some assumption about the relationship of the measurement error variation to the observed X

variation. Denoting the expectation operator by $\mathcal{E}$, the usual specification is that $\mathcal{E}\epsilon_{ij}^2=\sigma_j^2$ and $\mathcal{E}\epsilon_{ij}\epsilon_{ij'}=0$ for $j\neq j'$; that is, the measurement errors for different variables are uncorrelated. Write $D_x=\operatorname{diag}(\Sigma x_1^2\ldots\Sigma x_k^2)$ and $\Lambda=\operatorname{diag}(\lambda_1\ldots\lambda_k)$. We observe that the matrices $(1/n)X'\chi$ and $(1/n)\times(X'X-\Lambda D_x\Lambda)$ have the same limit in probability. It follows that the estimator defined by

$$(X'X-\Lambda D_x\Lambda)\hat{\beta}=X'\mathbf{y} \tag{2.54}$$

has the same limiting distribution as β^*, the estimator defined by equation (2.52) in which we pretend that χ is known. Since the λ_i are assumed to be known, the estimator $\hat{\beta}$ is operational. Its asymptotic covariance matrix is given by the limit in probability of

$$\left[\frac{1}{n}(X'X-\Lambda D_x\Lambda)'\left(\frac{1}{n}X'X\right)^{-1}\frac{1}{n}(X'X-\Lambda D_x\Lambda)\right]^{-1},$$

which is positive definite.

We note that the estimator defined by equation (2.54) is not actually a finite sample IV estimator and that in particular the matrix $X'X-\Lambda D_x\Lambda$ may not be positive definite or may even be singular for some data sets. Correction techniques that will ensure invertibility are given by Fuller and Hidiroglou (1978). We note also that if the reliabilities are estimated, the sampling variation in the λ_i^2 will contribute to the covariance matrix of the estimate $\hat{\beta}$.

The effect of the correction for attenuation may be seen by writing

$$\hat{\beta}=[I-(X'X)^{-1}\Lambda D_x\Lambda]^{-1}\mathbf{b},$$

where $\mathbf{b}=(X'X)^{-1}X'\mathbf{y}$ is the least-squares estimator. In the simplest case $k=1$, $\hat{\beta}=b/(1-\lambda^2)$, where $1-\lambda^2$ is the reliability of the single regressor. The effect of the correction is therefore to sharpen the OLS estimate; the latter tends to "fudge" the slope estimates down toward zero.[8]

2.9 Mixed OLS and IV minimands: the k-class estimators

Earlier we observed that the choice of instrumental variables as an estimation technique implied a loss criterion in which unbiasedness or consistency was the overriding consideration. The potentially favorable variance properties of ordinary least squares were not considered. In Section 2.7 we considered the possibility (and the problems) of combining the OLS estimate $\mathbf{b}$ and the IV estimate $\hat{\beta}$ into a convex combination of the form $\tilde{\beta}=\lambda\mathbf{b}+(1-\lambda)\hat{\beta}$ that, with a suitable choice of λ, might achieve a more favorable mean-square error performance than either $\mathbf{b}$ or $\hat{\beta}$ by itself. In the present section we shall consider the somewhat different route of setting up convex combinations of the OLS and IV minimands, rather than the estimators themselves.

Consider, then, the following minimand:

$$\tilde{\phi} = (1-k)(y-X\beta)'(y-X\beta) + k(y-X\beta)'P_z(y-X\beta). \qquad (2.55)$$

The factor k may be either constant or itself stochastic. It will be convenient to think of k as lying in the range $0 \leq k \leq 1$, although this is not essential.[9] Evidently, by varying k in expression (2.55) we may give more or less weight to OLS or IV. Note that the minimand may be written as

$$\tilde{\phi} = (\mathbf{y}-X\beta)'[I-k(I-P_z)](\mathbf{y}-X\beta).$$

The corresponding estimator is

$$\tilde{\beta} = [X'P_k X]^{-1}X'P_k \mathbf{y}, \qquad (2.56)$$

where $P_k = I - k(I-P_z)$. Again, if $k=0$ we have OLS, and if $k=1$ we have IV.

The estimator (2.56) may be interpreted as follows. Write $\hat{V} = (I-P_z)X$ as the residual matrix in the regression of X upon Z. The estimator is then

$$\tilde{\beta} = (X'X - k\hat{V}'\hat{V})^{-1}(X-k\hat{V})'\mathbf{y}.$$

Those familiar with the theory of simultaneous stochastic equations will recognize this as Theil's k-class estimator applied to the problem considered in this chapter. We refer the reader forward to Section 4.3 for the application of k-class estimation to an equation that is part of a system of simultaneous equations. In this particular context, it is known that the estimator is fully efficient (best asymptotically normal) if k is such that plim $\sqrt{n}(k-1) = 0$, so that either $k=1$ or approaches 1 in probability very quickly. This suggests that it is not really necessary to consider supplementing IV estimation in the manner suggested above.

As remarked earlier, however, the potential benefit arises from considerations of the finite sampling distribution of the combined estimation. Thus it may be possible to choose $k = k(n)$ to minimize the mean-square error for a given sample size n. To be able to do this implies that we have some knowledge of the finite sample distribution of the k-class estimator for the problem in hand, or of suitable approximations to this distribution. So far as the present discussion is concerned, we are forced to leave this issue on the level of such generalities, having pointed up the general applicability and relevant interpretation of k-class estimators.

2.10 Testing against serial correlation

Tests analogous to certain standard tests for the presence of serial correlation in least-squares contexts can be developed or adapted for IV estimation. Some care, however, must be taken since on occasion the "obvious" adaptations do not in fact carry over directly. Thus Godfrey (1978a) has considered the problem of developing a test corresponding to Durbin's h test for serial correlation in the presence of lagged dependent variables. Godfrey sets up the following model:

$$y_t = \alpha y_{t-1} + \sum_i \delta_i w_{it} + u_t, \qquad u_t = \rho u_{t-1} + \epsilon_t, \tag{2.57}$$

where ϵ_t is a white-noise process with variance σ^2. The variables w_{it} may be correlated with the disturbance u_t. It is convenient to construct a data matrix $X = [\mathbf{y}_{-1} \vdots W]$ for the above regression. The problem is to test the null hypothesis $H_0 : \rho = 0$ against the alternative $\rho \neq 0$.

Given a matrix Z of instruments for X, let $\hat{\boldsymbol{\beta}}$ denote the IV estimate and let $\mathbf{e} = \mathbf{y} - X\boldsymbol{\beta}$ denote the residuals. One might think of defining a Durbin's h analog as

$$h = \frac{\sqrt{n}\hat{r}}{\sqrt{1 - nV(\hat{\alpha})}}, \tag{2.58}$$

where $\hat{r} = \Sigma e_t e_{t-1} / \Sigma e_{t-1}^2$ and $V(\hat{\alpha})$ is the estimated variance of $\hat{\alpha}$, that is, the first diagonal element of the estimated covariance matrix $s^2(X'P_z X)^{-1}$ under the null hypothesis.

In fact, however, the statistic (2.58) does not have an asymptotic $N(0,1)$ distribution under the null hypothesis. Godfrey shows that the asymptotic distribution of the residual autocorrelation coefficient $\hat{r}$ (more precisely, $\sqrt{n}\hat{r}$) has limiting variance:

$$G = 1 - 2\boldsymbol{\phi}'\boldsymbol{\psi} + \boldsymbol{\eta}'V(\hat{\beta})\boldsymbol{\eta}, \tag{2.59}$$

where
$$\boldsymbol{\phi} = \operatorname{plim}(Z'Z)^{-1}Z'X(X'P_z X)^{-1}X'\mathbf{u}_{-1},$$

$$\boldsymbol{\psi} = \frac{1}{\sigma^2} \operatorname{plim} \frac{1}{n} Z'\mathbf{u}_{-1},$$

$$V(\hat{\beta}) = \operatorname{plim} n(X'P_z X)^{-1}, \quad \text{and}$$

$$\boldsymbol{\eta} = \frac{1}{\sigma^2} \operatorname{plim} \frac{1}{n} X'\mathbf{u}_{-1}.$$

Comparing expressions (2.58) and (2.59), it is apparent that $G \neq 1 - nV(\hat{\alpha})$. For example, if $\operatorname{plim}(1/n)Z'\mathbf{u}_{-1} = \mathbf{0}$ so that $\boldsymbol{\psi} = \mathbf{0}$, we have $G = 1 + \boldsymbol{\eta}'V(\hat{\beta})\boldsymbol{\eta} > 1$, whereas the denominator of (2.58) is plainly < 1. It follows that the proposed h statistic (2.58) does not have the desired $N(0,1)$ distribution.

A suitable test statistic can be constructed as $H = \sqrt{n}\hat{r}/\hat{G}$, where $\hat{G}$ is a consistent estimate of G. The latter may be constructed in terms of expression (2.59) by replacing σ^2 with s^2 and terms such as $\text{plim}(1/n) \times X'\mathbf{u}_{-1}$ with $(1/n)X'\mathbf{e}_{-1}$, that is, employing computed residuals in place of the disturbance. Under $H_0: \rho = 0$, the statistic H has an asymptotic $N(0,1)$ distribution, which can in principle be used to test H_0 against $H_1: \rho \neq 0$. Note that the test can also be used when no lagged dependent variable occurs in equation (2.57).

However, where a lagged dependent variable exists, Durbin's h test, although it possesses a correct rejection region, has poor power properties, and we should not expect much (if any) improvement in generalizing the test to an IV context in the above manner. Even in ordinary least-squares contexts, testing for serial correlation is still not a fully understood problem; indeed, there is room for debate as to whether the problem has in the past been properly posed.[10] In the next chapter we take a rather more structured approach by postulating that the type of covariance structure of the disturbance process is known and considering how this affects problems of estimation and hypothesis testing.

2.11 Summary

In this chapter we have presented some of the themes that will run through the remainder of the book, even though variations on the basic IV estimator will appear in Chapter 3. The projective definition of the IV estimator as resulting from a minimization process is essential for the nonlinear contexts covered in Chapter 5. As in other nonlinear techniques, the IV estimator cannot be solved analytically in such contexts, and the minimand that is incorporated in Definition 2.1 will turn out to generalize very readily when it is needed for an iterative numerical approach. Moreover, the projective definition allows us to handle the case where more instruments are available than regressors and yields some insights into the case of a deficiency of instruments. In the linear context, the resulting insights have computational implications. From this point of view we observed that IV can always be viewed as a two-stage least-squares computation. One first regresses the X variables upon the instruments and then uses the fitted values in place of the original regressors in a second-stage regression. Econometricians will recognize such a procedure in the specific context of simultaneous-equations estimation, and the connection will be further explored in Chapter 4.

The asymptotic efficiency of the IV estimator can be analyzed with the help of canonical correlations theory, and this is indeed a point of contact with general multivariate theory. The idea that efficiency depends on the canonical correlations between the regressors and the proposed instruments makes it clear that regressors and instruments need not be "paired up." The commonly held notion that one thinks of an instrument for an offending regressor may therefore be unduly restrictive.

Applications of IV methodology should ideally be preceded by a test for whether it is needed in the first place. Suitable testing procedures are based upon the difference between the ordinary least-squares and IV estimators. This raises the possibility of pretest estimators, which could have efficiency and bias properties superior to those of either method by itself. A more systematic combination of OLS and IV methodology results from the interpretation of k-class estimation in terms of a weighted combination of OLS and IV minimands.

We have explored so far two "generic" applications of IV methodology. It was found that a certain class of self-selection problems, involving the problem of testing for sectoral differences in response parameters, could be handled by utilizing instruments constructed on the basis of a prior discriminant analysis. The IV methods were robust in respect of specification error as to the allocation of observations to different regimes. The second general application was to the well-known errors-in-variables problem. We observed that the construction of admissible instruments really involved some sort of extraneous information about the model being estimated. As pointed out in Section 1.1, all forms of estimation need additional information, and the virtue of the IV approach is that the extra information required may not be very demanding. A technique such as attenuation correction may also be given an interpretation in terms of instrumental variables.

In the final section of the chapter the problem of testing for serial correlation was briefly explored. Adopting standard tests such as Durbin's h statistic does not necessarily yield correct procedures. If serial correlation is likely to be present, this should affect one's approach to estimation and hypothesis testing. Accordingly, we move on in the next chapter to consider disturbance structures that are nonspherical.

CHAPTER 3

Instrumental variables and nonspherical disturbances

3.1 Introduction

In presenting the basic theory of instrumental variables estimation, we assumed that the error structure was spherical; that is, the disturbance terms u_t have a common distribution with variance σ^2 (homoscedasticity) and are also serially uncorrelated in the sense that $\mathcal{E}u_t u_{t-r} = 0$ for $r \neq 0$. Expository convenience aside, certain models do indeed fall into such a framework, and we discussed the errors-in-variables structure as an example. However, the sphericality assumption is less satisfactory in other contexts. Indeed, in some instances, the very necessity for an IV approach arises out of a nonspherical error structure. In the present chapter we shall explore some of the implications of nonsphericality in the disturbances, utilizing for the purpose models taken from time series analysis that involve serial correlation and a class of models exhibiting heteroscedasticity.

We commence with a general discussion of different definitions of the IV estimator where the error distribution is nonspherical; specifically, the covariance of the disturbance vector is a nondiagonal matrix of constants. We have already touched on this context in Section 1.2, where the estimator (1.26) associated with the minimand (1.25a) was suggested as appropriate for the nonspherical case. We shall, in the present chapter, further explore the nature and properties of this estimator. Initially, however, we shall find it profitable to take a rather different route to its derivation, for by doing so a second type of estimator is suggested. We are able to generate two generic kinds of estimator, the one interpretable as an ordinary least-squares analog, the other as an Aitken analog. The efficiency comparison of these two approaches is explored.

Following this general treatment, we turn to specific instances of nonsphericality. One of the leading examples is regression in a time series context where the error structure is nonspherical and a lagged dependent variable appears on the right-hand side of the proposed regression. Such models may arise naturally from transformation of distributed lag structures. A fairly full analysis of a representative model from this class is offered, which stresses the role of IV as providing an initial consistent estimator for second-round estimation by ordinary least squares or maximum likelihood. The properties of possible instruments are briefly explored, and a new instrument, the conditional expectation of the lagged dependent variable, is suggested as a "second-round" instrument.

The discussion of heteroscedasticity in Section 3.5 commences with a review of operational procedures in obtaining more efficient second-round estimators. In order to give the discussion of heteroscedastic error structures some added interest, we introduce in Section 3.5 a model of stochastic parameter estimation. This model possesses an additional degree of complexity in that the resulting error distribution depends upon the realization of the independent variables in addition to the original equation disturbance. Such a property turns out to profoundly affect the consistency of the alternative approaches to IV with nonspherical disturbances. The findings of the chapter are reviewed in Section 3.6.

3.2 IV and generalized least squares

Spherical IV as an Aitken-type estimator

Although we have motivated the IV estimator as resulting from a projective minimand, it is also helpful to think of it, even in spherical contexts, as a generalized least-squares estimator. Such an interpretation is often employed in connection with simultaneous stochastic models of the type to be discussed in Chapter 4. Consider the general form to be estimated:

$$\mathbf{y}=X\beta+\mathbf{u}, \tag{3.1}$$

where again it will be understood that the variables forming the data matrix X are correlated with the (spherical) disturbance term. Given an admissible instrument data matrix Z, we premultiply the above equation by Z':

$$Z'\mathbf{y}=Z'X\beta+Z'\mathbf{u}. \tag{3.2}$$

Assuming that it exists, the limiting covariance matrix of $1/\sqrt{n}$ times the new disturbance term is $\sigma^2 \operatorname{plim}(1/n)Z'Z$, where $\sigma^2=\operatorname{Var} u_t$.

Equation (3.2) can therefore be viewed as a regression relationship (with $q \geq p$ effective "observations") with a nonspherical disturbance covariance matrix given by $\hat{\Omega} = \sigma^2 Z'Z$. Applying the standard Aitken formula,[1] we obtain

$$\hat{\beta} = (X'Z\hat{\Omega}^{-1}Z'X)^{-1}X'Z\hat{\Omega}^{-1}\mathbf{y} = (X'P_z X)^{-1}X'P_z \mathbf{y},$$

where $P_z = Z(Z'Z)^{-1}Z'$. This will be recognized from Section 2.2 as the standard IV estimator.

Nonspherical equation disturbances

Suppose now that the original equation disturbances $\mathbf{u}$ are nonspherical – that is, that we can write $E\,\mathbf{uu}' = \Omega$, where $\Omega \neq \sigma^2 I$. For the purposes of the present section we shall assume that Ω is known. It turns out that there are several possible IV-type estimators, each of which may be consistent. As an elementary correspondence requirement, however, we should like our estimators to reduce to either ordinary least squares or generalized least squares with the substitution $Z = X$. Two generic varieties arise out of variants of the argument developed above for the interpretation of IV as a generalized least-squares (GLS) estimator.

(a) *The ordinary least-squares analog*

We start with equation (3.2) above and observe that with the nonspherical specification for $\mathbf{u}$ the indicated "estimate" of the covariance matrix of the new disturbance term is $Z'\Omega Z$. The suggested Aitken estimator is easily seen to be

$$\hat{\beta}_1 = [X'Z(Z'\Omega Z)^{-1}Z'X]^{-1}X'Z(Z'\Omega Z)^{-1}Z'\mathbf{y}. \tag{3.3}$$

If Z is an admissible instrument and if in addition the elements of the matrix $Z'\Omega Z/n$ are at least bounded in probability as $n \to \infty$, then the estimator $\hat{\beta}_1$ is consistent. Under regularity conditions that essentially correspond to those of Theorem 2.2 of Chapter 2, the asymptotic covariance matrix of $\sqrt{n}(\hat{\beta}_1 - \beta_0)$ is the limit in probability of

$$\left[\frac{X'Z}{n}\left(\frac{Z'\Omega Z}{n}\right)^{-1}\frac{Z'X}{n}\right]^{-1}. \tag{3.4}$$

The estimator (3.3) corresponds to the formula (1.26) derived in Chapter 1 as resulting from the minimand $(\mathbf{y} - X\beta)'P(\mathbf{y} - X\beta)$, where $P = Z(Z'\Omega Z)^{-1}Z'$. In turn, this minimand corresponds to the weighting matrix $W = (Z'\Omega Z)^{-1}$ employed in the generalized minimum-distance interpretation of IV established in Section 1.2. The resulting estimator may therefore be viewed as a direct generalization of the standard or spherical IV estimator discussed in Chapter 2. Indeed, if $p=q$, the estimator reduces to

$$\hat{\beta}_1=(Z'X)^{-1}Z'\mathbf{y}, \tag{3.5}$$

a familiar form. Also, if $Z=X$, the result is ordinary least squares. In the more general version (3.3), therefore, the appearance of Ω arises from the contingency $q>p$, that is, more instruments than regressors.

Finally, we note that the matrix $P=Z(Z'\Omega Z)^{-1}Z'$ is not an orthogonal projection matrix, since it is not idempotent; in fact, $P\Omega P=P$. However, the matrix $P\Omega$ is clearly idempotent, and as we shall shortly see, this property can be turned to advantage in a further useful interpretation of the resulting estimator.

(b) *The GLS analog*

Write the square-root factorization of Ω^{-1} as $\Omega^{-1}=D'D$. Premultiply the equation to be estimated by D:

$$D\mathbf{y}=DX\beta+D\mathbf{u}. \tag{3.6}$$

Since $ED\mathbf{u}\mathbf{u}'D'=\sigma^2 I$, it is evident that equation (3.6) is a transformed version of the original with a spherical disturbance. The transformed regressor is DX. This suggests that we use $Z_d=DZ$ as an instrument set. Accordingly, we may premultiply equation (3.6) by $Z_d'=Z'D'$ to obtain

$$Z'D'D\mathbf{y}=Z'D'D\beta+Z'D'D\mathbf{u}$$

or, in view of the definition of D:

$$Z'\Omega^{-1}\mathbf{y}=Z'\Omega^{-1}X\beta+Z'\Omega^{-1}\mathbf{u}. \tag{3.7}$$

The essential orthogonality condition for the instrument is that

$$\operatorname{plim}(1/n)Z'\Omega^{-1}\mathbf{u}=0.$$

This is equivalent to the requirement that DZ be asymptotically uncorrelated with $\boldsymbol{\epsilon}=D\mathbf{u}$.

Provided that the vector $(1/\sqrt{n})Z'\Omega^{-1}\mathbf{u}$ obeys suitable regularity conditions, the asymptotic covariance matrix of the disturbance in equation (3.7) is $\operatorname{plim}(1/n)Z'\Omega^{-1}Z$. The indicated Aitken estimator is therefore

$$\hat{\beta}_2=[X'\Omega^{-1}Z(Z'\Omega^{-1}Z)^{-1}Z'\Omega^{-1}X]^{-1}X'\Omega^{-1}Z(Z'\Omega^{-1}Z)^{-1}Z'\Omega^{-1}\mathbf{y}. \tag{3.8}$$

In terms of the generalized minimum-distance interpretation of Section 1.2, the weighting matrix W implied by the use of Z_d as instrument with equation (3.6) is $W=(Z_d'Z_d)^{-1}=(Z'\Omega^{-1}Z)^{-1}$. This would lead to the minimand

$$(Dy - DX\beta)'Z_d WZ_d'(Dy - DX\beta) = (y - X\beta)'P(y - X\beta),$$

where now $P = \Omega^{-1}Z(Z'\Omega^{-1}Z)^{-1}Z'\Omega^{-1}$. In turn, this yields the estimator (3.8) just obtained. We note again that P is not a projection matrix but that $P\Omega P = P$.

The estimate may be interpreted as follows. Write $\breve{X} = Z\breve{\Pi}$, where $\breve{\Pi} = (Z'\Omega^{-1}Z)^{-1}Z'\Omega^{-1}X$ is a generalized least-squares-type estimate for the multiequation fit of X on Z, with weighting matrix Ω^{-1}. The estimate $\hat{\beta}_2$ may then be written

$$\hat{\beta}_2 = (\breve{X}'\Omega^{-1}X)^{-1}\breve{X}'\Omega^{-1}\mathbf{y}. \tag{3.9}$$

If $q = p$ (equality of instrument and regressor dimensions), formula (3.9) reduces to

$$\hat{\beta} = (Z'\Omega^{-1}X)^{-1}Z'\Omega^{-1}\mathbf{y}. \tag{3.10}$$

Comparing this to the standard Aitken estimator $(X'\Omega^{-1}X)^{-1}X'\Omega^{-1}\mathbf{y}$, it is readily apparent that the estimators (3.9) and (3.10) can be regarded as IV analogs of generalized least squares.

An alternative approach to equation (3.6) is to use Z rather than DZ as instrument for DX. This yields the minimand $(D\mathbf{y} - DX\beta)'P_z(D\mathbf{y} - DX\beta)$, where P_z is the orthogonal projection matrix associated with Z. If we choose $D = \Omega^{-1/2}$, this minimand is of the form

$$(\mathbf{y} - X\beta)'\Omega^{-1/2}Z(Z'Z)^{-1}Z'\Omega^{-1/2}(\mathbf{y} - X\beta). \tag{3.11}$$

The implied estimator has been proposed in certain nonlinear contexts (see Section 5.5). However, because it is usually dominated in efficiency terms by one or both of the IV–OLS or IV–GLS analogs, we shall not consider it further in the present chapter.

Some efficiency comparisons

(a) *OLS versus GLS analogs*

We have just derived two different versions of an IV estimator applicable to regression models with nonspherical error structures. The first, represented in full generality by equation (3.3), reduces to the standard IV formula $(Z'X)^{-1}Z'\mathbf{y}$ if $p = q$, and this in turn may be viewed as an IV analog of ordinary least squares. The second, represented by equations (3.9) and (3.10), may be regarded as an Aitken analog.

We know that if the regressor matrix X independent of the (nonspherical) disturbances, Aitken estimation is more efficient than ordinary least squares. It is therefore of interest to ask whether a corresponding property carries over to the IV analogs. In exploring this question, we shall assume that a given instrument set (Z) is admissible for both estimators, and for simplicity we shall assume that $q=p$; that is, the number of instruments is the same as the number of regressors.

With the above assumptions, the asymptotic covariance matrices of the two estimators corresponding to equations (3.5) and (3.10) are

$$\Sigma_{\beta_1} = \operatorname{plim} n(Z'X)^{-1}Z'\Omega Z(X'Z)^{-1} \qquad \text{and}$$
$$\Sigma_{\beta_2} = \operatorname{plim} n(Z'\Omega^{-1}X)^{-1}Z'\Omega^{-1}Z(X'\Omega^{-1}Z)^{-1}.$$

The difference between these two covariance matrices may be written

$$\begin{aligned}
\Sigma_{\beta_1} - \Sigma_{\beta_2} &\\
&= (Z'X)^{-1}Z'\Omega Z(X'Z)^{-1} - (Z'\Omega^{-1}X)^{-1}Z'\Omega^{-1}Z(X'\Omega^{-1}Z)^{-1} \\
&= (Z'X)^{-1}Z'\Omega[\Omega^{-1} - \Omega^{-1}X(Z'\Omega^{-1}X)^{-1}Z'\Omega^{-1}Z(X'\Omega^{-1}Z)^{-1}X'\Omega^{-1}] \\
&\quad \times \Omega Z(X'Z)^{-1} \qquad (3.12)\\
&= (Z'X)^{-1}Z'(D'D)^{-1}D'[I - DX(Z'\Omega^{-1}X)^{-1}Z'\Omega^{-1}Z(X'\Omega^{-1}Z)^{-1}X'D'] \\
&\quad \times D(D'D)^{-1}Z(X'Z)^{-1},
\end{aligned}$$

where we recall that $\Omega^{-1} = D'D$. Consider now the term inside the square brackets of equation (3.12). Write $\tilde{X} = DX$ and $\tilde{Z} = DZ$. The term in question may then be written as

$$I - \tilde{X}(\tilde{Z}'\tilde{X})^{-1}\tilde{Z}'\tilde{Z}(\tilde{X}'\tilde{Z})^{-1}\tilde{X}' = I - \tilde{P}'\tilde{P}, \qquad (3.13)$$

say, where $\tilde{P} = \tilde{Z}(\tilde{X}'\tilde{Z})^{-1}\tilde{X}'$. Equation (3.12) may therefore be written

$$\Sigma_{\beta_1} - \Sigma_{\beta_2} = W'(I - \tilde{P}'\tilde{P})W,$$

where $W = D(D'D)^{-1}Z(X'Z)^{-1}$. Hence if the matrix $I - \tilde{P}'\tilde{P}$ defined by (3.13) is positive semidefinite, we can assert that $\Sigma_{\beta_1} > \Sigma_{\beta_2}$, in the usual sense that the difference is positive semidefinite.

Of course, if $\tilde{Z} = \tilde{X}$, the matrix $\tilde{P}$ is a projection matrix and $I - \tilde{P}'\tilde{P} = 1 - \tilde{P}$, which is positive semidefinite. In such a case $\Sigma_{\beta_1} > \Sigma_{\beta_2}$, in the sense already defined. This is simply a rather roundabout way of demonstrating the superiority of the classical Aitken estimator.

In our case, however, the data matrices $\tilde{Z}$ and $\tilde{X}$ do not coincide and the matrix $\tilde{P}$ is not symmetric, even though $\tilde{P}^2 = \tilde{P}$. It turns out that the resulting matrix $I - \tilde{P}'\tilde{P}$ is not in general positive semidefinite. To confirm this, consider the canonical correlations between the transformed data matrices $\tilde{X}$ and $\tilde{Z}$. These are (cf. Section 2.3) the solutions to the equation

$$\begin{aligned}
&\det[\tilde{r}^2\tilde{X}'\tilde{X} - \tilde{X}'\tilde{Z}(\tilde{Z}'\tilde{Z})^{-1}\tilde{Z}'\tilde{X}] \\
&\quad = \det[\tilde{r}^2X'\Omega^{-1}X - (X'\Omega^{-1}Z)(Z'\Omega^{-1}Z)^{-1}Z'\Omega^{-1}X] \\
&\quad = 0.
\end{aligned}$$

We note that the canonical correlations $\tilde{r}_i^2$ between the transformed variables $\tilde{X}=DX$ and $\tilde{Z}=DZ$ are not the same as the correlations r_i^2 between the original variables X and Z. Like the scalar coefficient of correlation, the canonical correlations are invariant to linear transformation, provided that only recombinations of variables are involved. In this case, however, the matrix D recombines rows, rather than columns, of the data matrices X and Z and the invariance no longer holds. Likewise, if we denote the corresponding canonical vectors by $\tilde{U}$ and $\tilde{V}$, it does not follow that $\tilde{U}=DU$ or $\tilde{V}=DV$.

Denote by $\tilde{\Lambda}$ the diagonal matrix containing the canonical correlations $\tilde{r}_i$; that is, $\tilde{\Lambda}=\text{diag}(\tilde{r}_1 \ldots \tilde{r}_p)$. Transferring to the new coordinate systems $\tilde{U}$, $\tilde{V}$ we may write

$$\begin{aligned} I-\tilde{P}'\tilde{P} &= I-\tilde{U}\tilde{\Lambda}^{-1}\tilde{V}'\tilde{V}\tilde{\Lambda}^{-1}\tilde{U}' \\ &= I-\tilde{U}\tilde{\Lambda}^{-2}\tilde{U}' \\ &= I-\tilde{U}\tilde{U}'-\tilde{U}(\tilde{\Lambda}^{-2}-I)\tilde{U}'. \end{aligned} \tag{3.14}$$

Denote by $P_{\tilde{x}}$ the projection matrix $\tilde{X}(\tilde{X}'\tilde{X})^{-1}\tilde{X}'$. In the new coordinate system $P_{\tilde{x}}=\tilde{U}\tilde{U}'$. Hence the matrix $I-\tilde{U}\tilde{U}'$ appearing on the right-hand side of equation (3.14) is certainly positive semidefinite.

The behavior of the matrix $I-\tilde{P}'\tilde{P}$ therefore hinges upon the magnitudes of the canonical correlations $\tilde{r}_i^2$ between DX and DZ. If these are all very close to unity, then the diagonal matrix $\Lambda^{-2}-I$ will have elements close to zero and the matrix $I-\tilde{P}'\tilde{P}$ is likely to be positive definite.[2] As a result the Aitken analog will be at least asymptotically superior to the OLS analog.

On the other hand, if one or more of the canonical correlations is small, the matrix $I-\tilde{P}'\tilde{P}$ in equation (3.14) will not be positive semidefinite. In this case very little can be said with any degree of confidence about the relative performance of the two IV estimators. One would anticipate that if the canonical correlations were low, the matrix $I-\tilde{P}'\tilde{P}$ would become negative semidefinite, leading to a corresponding property for the difference $\Sigma_{\beta_1}-\Sigma_{\beta_2}$. In this case the OLS analog would be superior to the Aitken analog.

(b) *The case $q>p$: minimal instruments*

A second efficiency comparison is between the conventional or "spherical" estimator $\hat{\boldsymbol{\beta}}=(X'P_zX)^{-1}X'P_z\mathbf{y}$ and the two estimators we have derived, namely the IV–OLS analog and the IV–GLS analog as appropriate for the nonspherical model. We have already remarked that if $q=p$, that is, the number of instruments is equal to the number of regressors, then the IV–OLS analog $\hat{\boldsymbol{\beta}}_1$ reduces to the conventional or spherical estimator $\hat{\beta}$. In many cases, however, we have available more instruments than regressors and it is therefore of interest to ask whether the efficiency of the IV–OLS analog $\hat{\beta}_1$ exceeds that of the spherical estimator. As we might expect from the above Aitken argument, the answer turns out to be affirmative. Indeed, we can put things more generally than this. We observed in Section 1.2 that all IV estimators in which a given matrix Z acted *directly* as instruments for X could be regarded as minimum-distance estimators, with the minimand

$$\phi(\beta) = (\mathbf{y} - X\beta)'ZWZ'(\mathbf{y} - X\beta). \tag{3.15}$$

Particular members of this class are the spherical estimator, where $W = (Z'Z)^{-1}$, and the IV–OLS analog, where $W = (Z'\Omega Z)^{-1}$. (On the other hand, the IV–GLS analog is not a member of this class, since for this estimator DZ is utilized as an instrument for the transformed data matrix DX.) We may now state the following analog to the generalized Gauss–Markov theorem:

Theorem 3.1: *Among all IV estimators of the type* (3.15) *for the nonspherical model, the choice* $W = (Z\Omega Z)^{-1}$ *yields the most efficient estimate, in the usual sense of differences in the asymptotic covariance matrix.*

Proof: The estimator corresponding to the minimand (3.15) is (cf. Chapter 1.2) $(Z'ZWZ'X)^{-1}X'ZWZ'\mathbf{y}$, with asymptotic covariance matrix $\sigma^2 \operatorname{plim} nA$, where

$$A = (X'ZWZ'X)^{-1}X'ZWZ'\Omega ZW'Z'X(X'ZWZ'X)^{-1}.$$

In particular, if $W = (Z'\Omega Z)^{-1}$, the general expression A reduces to

$$B = [X'Z(Z'\Omega Z)^{-1}Z'X]^{-1},$$

as noted in expression (3.4) above. For brevity, let us write $Z'X = C$. Now the difference

$$A - B = (C'WC)^{-1}C'W\{Z'\Omega Z - C[C'(Z'\Omega Z)^{-1}C]^{-1}C'\}W'C(C'WC)^{-1}. \tag{3.16}$$

Since the matrix $Z'\Omega Z$ is positive definite, there exists a nonsingular matrix P such that $Z'\Omega Z = P'P$. Writing $F = P'^{-1}C$, expression (3.16) becomes

$$A - B = (C'WC)^{-1}C'WP'\{I - F(F'F)^{-1}F'\}PW'C(C'WC)^{-1},$$

which is plainly positive semidefinite. Thus $A \geq B$ and the result follows by taking the appropriate limits in probability. ∎

Theorem 3.1 tells us that if the number of available instruments exceeds the number of regressors, we can in general do better than the standard or spherical IV technique by forming the minimal instruments in a different way. Consider again the estimator $\hat{\beta}_1 = (X'PX)^{-1}X'P\mathbf{y}$, with $P = Z(Z'\Omega Z)^{-1}Z'$. We may write

$$\hat{\beta}_1 = (X'PX)^{-1}X'P\mathbf{y} = (X'P\Omega PX)^{-1}X'P\Omega P\mathbf{y}$$
$$= (X'P\Omega.\Omega^{-1}\Omega PX)^{-1}X'P\Omega.\Omega^{-1}\Omega P\mathbf{y}.$$

Now define $X_0 = \Omega PX$, $\mathbf{y}_0 = \Omega P\mathbf{y}$. Then

$$\hat{\beta}_1 = (X_0'\Omega^{-1}X_0)^{-1}X_0'\Omega^{-1}\mathbf{y}_0. \tag{3.17}$$

Compare this with the standard IV estimator

$$\hat{\beta} = (\hat{X}'\hat{X})^{-1}\hat{X}'\mathbf{y},$$

where $\hat{X} = P_z X$. Evidently the minimal instruments are formed differently. In the case of the estimator (3.17), we form minimal instruments as $X_0 = \Omega PX$ instead of $\hat{X} = P_z X$, and apply GLS instead of OLS to these new variables and a redefined dependent variable $\mathbf{y}_0$. We note that the matrix ΩP is idempotent, since $(\Omega P)^2 = \Omega P\Omega P = \Omega P$, so that the transformation $X_0 = \Omega PX$ is rather similar to a least-squares-type fitted value; however since ΩP is not symmetric, the analogy is incomplete.

We may now summarize our efficiency discussion as follows:

(a) If $q = p$ (i.e., $\dim Z = \dim X$), the IV–OLS analog reduces to the standard spherical formula. The IV–GLS analog reduces to a form homologous with the Aitken estimate. No firm conclusions are available concerning the relative efficiency of these estimators. If one is uncertain about the strength of the correlations between Z and X, or about the effect of the linear transformation DZ, DX upon these correlations, it might be best to stick with the OLS analog as the more robust alternative. On the other hand, it is true that in some instances the linear transformations associated with the matrix D simply get rid of the necessity to use an IV approach; we shall see in what sense this is true in Section 3.3. Moreover, in the various models where the method of maximum likelihood can be shown to be equivalent to an iterative IV procedure, the estimator concerned is always the IV–GLS analog. Equivalences of this kind are explored in considerable detail in Chapters 4 and 5 and lend some support to the view of IV–GLS as optimal in a wide range of situations.

(b) If $q > p$, then the IV–OLS analog is superior to the standard, spherical formula. In effect, starting with an instrument set Z, one must recombine the variables of this set into a minimal instrument set by taking into account the elements of the covariance matrix Ω of residuals.

Operational matters

More often than not, one does not know the covariance matrix Ω of the disturbance process. An obvious two-step procedure is to estimate $\hat{\Omega}$ on the basis of a prior spherical-type IV estimation of the type considered in Chapter 2. Such a procedure is applicable when Ω depends on only a small number of parameters, as in many time series contexts. In such applications as heteroscedasticity, however, the matrix $\Omega = \operatorname{diag}(\sigma_t^2;\, t = 1, \ldots, n)$; and the variance parameters σ_t^2 cannot be estimated directly from a process of computed residuals $\hat{u}_t$. However, White (1980b, 1982) has pointed out that the requirement that the matrix Ω be estimated is unduly strong. In some circumstances it may be possible to derive consistent estimators of the matrix $Z'\Omega Z$, in the sense that if $V = \operatorname{plim}(1/n)Z'\Omega Z$, then an estimate $\hat{V}$ may be obtained which is such that $\operatorname{plim}(\hat{V} - V) = \mathbf{O}$. The operational version of the OLS analog would then be

$$\hat{\beta}_1 = (X'Z\hat{V}^{-1}Z'X)^{-1}X'Z\hat{V}^{-1}Z'\mathbf{y}. \tag{3.18}$$

The case of pure heteroscedasticity is a leading example where such a consistent estimator $\hat{V}$ is available; its derivation is illustrated in Section 3.5 below.

Hypothesis testing

Wald and Lagrange multiplier tests of the null hypothesis $R\boldsymbol{\beta} = \mathbf{r}$ may be obtained in a manner analogous to the derivation of Chapter 2 for the spherical case. Thus if $\hat{\boldsymbol{\beta}}_1$ is the IV–OLS analog, it is easy to verify that the statistic

$$W_1 = (R\hat{\boldsymbol{\beta}}_1 - \mathbf{r})'\{R[X'Z(Z'\Omega Z)^{-1}Z'X]^{-1}R'\}^{-1}(R\hat{\boldsymbol{\beta}}_1 - \mathbf{r})$$

has under H_0 a limiting chi-squared distribution with s degrees of freedom, where the restrictions matrix R has s rows. A similar statistic W_2 would be obtained with respect to the IV–GLS analog, making use of the covariance matrix of that estimator. The relative performance of the two tests has not been investigated.

Where Ω is unknown, a consistent estimate $\hat{\Omega}$ may be substituted without affecting the asymptotic distribution of the test statistic. Alternatively, in such situations as heteroscedasticity, White-type estimators $\hat{V}$ (see Section 3.5) may be employed to yield the statistic in the form

$$W_1 = n(\hat{R}\hat{\boldsymbol{\beta}}_1 - \mathbf{r})\left[R\left(\frac{X'Z}{n}\hat{V}^{-1}\frac{Z'X}{n}\right)^{-1}R'\right](R\hat{\boldsymbol{\beta}}_1 - \mathbf{r}),$$

where the two-step estimator $\hat{\boldsymbol{\beta}}_1$ is defined by expression (3.18) above.

3.3 IV and time series regressions

We remarked in Section 1.1 that the problem of correlation between regressor and disturbance often arises in time series models where a lagged value of the dependent variable is included among the right-hand variables and the disturbance term is serially correlated. Such models could arise from transformations of an original model containing a distributed lag expression, even where the original disturbance was spherical (in this context, "white noise"). However, this by no means exhausts the possibilities. Lagged dependent variables may appear among the regressors for a variety of reasons, representing such mechanisms as gradual adjustment of the dependent variable. And we may wish to allow for possible serial correlation in the disturbance simply because, in the words of Oscar Wilde, "the truth is rarely pure and never simple," and there remain more or less systematic influences of hopefully lesser importance that one can never hope to fully capture.

As a general observation, the method of instrumental variables is rarely used by itself in time series contexts. The method is seen in its most satisfactory light as an adjunct to methods that are computationally more demanding. Specifically, IV is often used to provide a starting up value for a "second-round" method such as maximum likelihood or – in a sense we shall later explore – least-squares methods. The particular value of the IV estimator when used in this way derives from the fact that it is itself consistent. This means that one feels confident that an initial value generated in this way is somewhere close to the mark (if the sample size is large). Moreover, methods such as maximum likelihood require only one further iteration for the second-round estimator to have the same asymptotic distribution as the full iterative solution to the likelihood problem. We shall elaborate on these points in due course. For the moment we note in addition to the above that IV has the advantage that not too much need be assumed about the precise structure of the error. Consider, for instance, the simple autoregressive model

$$y_t = \lambda y_{t-1} + \beta w_t + u_t, \tag{3.19}$$

where w_t is either nonstochastic or known to be independent of the error structure. We may not know, or we may not be prepared to specify, the structure of the disturbance process u_t, although we should certainly like to account for the possibility that it may exhibit serial correlation. However, if we assume that the resulting process (y_t) is stochastically stable, the influence of the distant past is likely to die off fairly quickly. Under such circumstances, it seems natural to construct an instrument set for the regressors y_{t-1}, w_t consisting of present and lagged values of the variables w_t; $Z = \{w_t, w_{t-1}, \ldots, w_{t-k}\}$, where the truncation point k might depend upon the length of the data series and one's prior beliefs about the damping of the system. An instrument set of this kind might work well if the variation in the exogenous variables w_t was large relative to that in the disturbance process u_t.

The drawback in this instance remains that since one is not prepared to specify the error process, it is not possible to work out even the asymptotic covariance of the IV estimators $\hat{\lambda}, \hat{\beta}$. We may, however, recall our earlier remarks on the subject of IV as an adjunct to more complete methods of estimation. The spectral regression methods associated with the name of Hannan are designed for such situations. It would take us too far afield to discuss such methods in detail. In essence, however, these methods applied to equation (3.19) would derive estimates for each band in the frequency domain and combine these band estimates by weighting inversely with estimates of the error spectrum evaluated at the corresponding band. One need not specify in parametric terms the precise process governing the disturbances. The required error spectrum is obtained by employing quasi-estimates of the disturbance, defined as

$$\hat{u}_t = y_t - \hat{\lambda} y_{t-1} - \hat{\beta} w_t,$$

where $\hat{\lambda}$ and $\hat{\beta}$ are initial consistent estimates. As already suggested, such estimates may be derived from IV considerations. For details of the complete method for this particular model we refer the reader to Hannan (1965, 1970).

If we are willing to specify an error mechanism, many more possibilities arise. Depending upon the precise instruments chosen, we may now be able derive the asymptotic covariance matrix of the IV estimators, which thereby become a more complete approach to estimation. Time and computational facilities permitting, however, it remains preferable to treat IV as a first-round estimator, with second (or subsequent) applications of such estimators as least squares or maximum likelihood.

It will be helpful to elaborate on these remarks with the use of a simple example, and for this purpose we shall add to the autoregression (3.19) the following moving-average error specification:

$$u_t = \epsilon_t - \rho \epsilon_{t-1}, \tag{3.20}$$

where the innovations process (ϵ_t) is white noise (spherical). The covariance matrix associated with the error process (3.20) is

$$\Omega = \begin{bmatrix} 1+\rho^2 & -\rho & 0 & \cdots & 0 \\ -\rho & 1+\rho^2 & -\rho & & \\ 0 & \ddots & \ddots & \ddots & \\ & & & & -\rho \\ 0 & & -\rho & & 1+\rho^2 \end{bmatrix}. \tag{3.21}$$

As regularity conditions we shall assume that $|\lambda|<1$ (ensuring stationarity) and $|\rho|<1$ (so that the moving-average process is invertible). The reader may recall from Chapter 1 that where $\rho=\lambda$, the model of (3.19) and (3.20) corresponds to the autoregressive transformation of an exponential distributed lag relationship between y and w. For the sake of a little useful generality, however, we shall assume ρ and λ to be distinct. Either way, we recall from our discussion of such models in Chapter 1 that the regressor y_{t-1} and the disturbance u_t in equation (3.19) are correlated, so that ordinary least squares will not yield consistent estimates of λ and β.

Let us consider first the application of basic or spherical IV to equation (3.19). Various approaches may be pursued with respect to finding suitable instruments for the lagged term y_{t-1}. Perhaps the simplest instrument was suggested by Liviatan (1963): w_{t-1} is used as an instrument for y_{t-1} and w_t as an instrument for itself, so that the instrument set is $Z=\{w_{t-1}, w_t\}$. Since this is our first real point of contact with the choice of instruments in a time series context, it will be useful to explore some of the issues involved with the help of this particular example. In doing so we shall initially assume that the parameter ρ of the error process is known.

In order for w_{t-1} to constitute a useful instrument we should like all of the following desiderata to be satisfied:

(a) The instrument w_{t-1} should be highly correlated with y_{t-1}.

(b) In order for the matrix $Z'X$ to be well conditioned for the necessary inversion, we should like w_{t-1} *not* to be highly correlated with w_t.

(c) The proposed instrument should not interact unfavorably with the error covariance matrix Ω; in terms of formula (3.4), the elements of $Z'\Omega Z$ should not be large.

Requirements (a) and (b) above may pose a bit of a problem in the time series context. Essentially what we should like is a substantial degree of independent variation between w_{t-1} and w_t. However, it may be difficult to "arrange" a high correlation between y_{t-1} and w_t unless there is a measure of smoothness in the w_t sequence, in which case we run the risk of violating requirement (b) above.

In order to investigate such questions, let us assume that the w_t series is generated by the following simple autoregressive scheme:

$$w_t = \theta w_{t-1} + \eta_t, \tag{3.22}$$

where η_t is a white-noise innovations process uncorrelated with ϵ_t. With such an assumption it is easy to show from equations (3.19)–(3.22) that

$$\text{plim}\,\frac{1}{T}X'Z = \sigma_w^2 \begin{bmatrix} \dfrac{\beta}{1-\lambda\theta} & \dfrac{\beta\theta}{1-\lambda\theta} \\ \theta & 1 \end{bmatrix}, \tag{3.23}$$

and

$$\text{plim}\,\frac{1}{T}Z'\Omega Z = \sigma_w^2(1+\rho^2-2\rho\theta)\begin{bmatrix} 1 & \theta \\ \theta & 1 \end{bmatrix}, \tag{3.24}$$

where $\sigma_w^2 = \mathcal{E}w_t^2$ is the variance of the w_t process. We may write $\sigma_w^2 = \sigma_\eta^2/(1-\theta^2)$, where σ_η^2 is the variance of the innovation process (η_t) defined by equation (3.22) above. From equations (3.23) and (3.24) it follows that the asymptotic variance of the Liviatan-type IV estimator under discussion is given by

$$\text{Var}\,\hat{\lambda} = \frac{\sigma^2}{\beta\sigma_\eta^2}(1+\theta)^2(1-\lambda\theta)(1+\rho^2-2\rho\theta). \tag{3.25}$$

As we should expect, the efficiency of the Liviatan instrument increases with β, since this parameter helps to determine the correlation of y_{t-1} with w_{t-1}. It also increases with the amount of "noise" (σ_η^2) in the exogenous process (w_t), for reasons which are identical with the corresponding phenomenon in ordinary least-squares estimation. The behavior with respect to the parameter θ, representing the autocorrelation in the exogenous process w_t, is less clear. Figure 3.1 shows some efficiency plots, where efficiency is taken as (the inverse of) the variance and we have ignored the factor $\sigma/\beta\sigma_\eta^2$ in formula (3.25). We have set $\rho = .7$, which indicates a healthy dose of serial correlation in the disturbance. It will be observed that efficiency, as a function of the autocorrelation parameter θ, depends upon the value of λ. For high values of λ efficiency increases steadily with θ. For lower values of λ, efficiency behavior is not monotonic, and values of θ at the lower or higher extremes of the allowable range are likely to correspond to more efficient estimation.

In terms of this example it appears that a measure of "smoothness" in the exogenous variables contributes to efficiency, in spite of the risk of ill-conditioning. However, the efficiency of a Liviatan-type instrument evidently does depend quite heavily upon the parameters to be estimated and their relationship to the parameters governing the exogenous process.

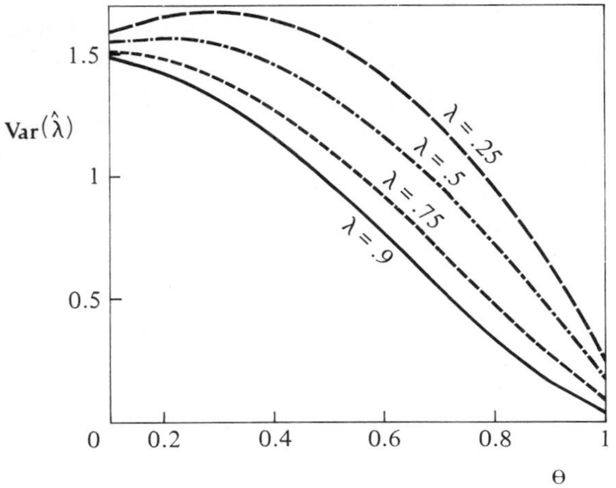

Figure 3.1 Plot of Var($\hat{\lambda}$) vs. θ.

As remarked above, there is nothing to stop one from using an extended instrument set of the form $Z = \{w_t, w_{t-1}, w_{t-2}, \ldots, w_{t-k}\}$ for some suitably chosen truncation point k. In terms of instrument correlation such a procedure can only improve upon the basic Liviatan technique, although the risk of ill-conditioning in the matrices Z and $Z'X$ arises afresh as an issue.

The procedure usually followed is to regress y_{t-1} upon the variables in Z and to employ its fitted value $\hat{y}_{t-1}$ as an instrument, so that the reduced instrument set $\hat{Z} = \{\hat{y}_{t-1}, w_t\}$ is employed for $X = \{y_{t-1}, w_t\}$. This clearly corresponds to an estimator $(X'P_z X)^{-1}X'P_z\mathbf{y}$ where $P_z = Z(Z'Z)^{-1}Z'$. As pointed in Section 3.2 above, a better estimator for the case $q > p$ is the estimator $(X'PX)^{-1}X'P\mathbf{y}$, with $P = Z(Z'\Omega Z)^{-1}Z'$. The latter estimate is the general form of what we have called the IV–OLS analog. In most circumstances one does not have available the disturbance covariance matrix Ω, so that one is forced to set $P = P_z$, as in the spherical case. However, the more general form can be employed as a second-round estimator, with the parameters of error covariance matrix Ω estimated from the first round, with the object of improving efficiency.

Conditional expectations as instruments

An alternative approach to seeking to expand the number of instruments is a two-stage IV calculation in which the object of the first stage is to "estimate" an instrument that is known to depend itself upon the parameters of the model. One class of such methods utilizes, as an instrument for the lagged dependent variable, its expectation conditioned upon the exogenous variables or more generally upon the set of all variables that are uncorrelated with the disturbance. Let us consider equations (3.19)–(3.21). We observe that the disturbance u_t is independent of innovation values up to ϵ_{t-2} and is therefore independent of $y_{t-2}, y_{t-3}, \ldots$, as well as of all the exogenous variables. Indeed, we may write

$$y_{t-1} = \lambda y_{t-2} + \beta w_{t-1} + (\epsilon_{t-1} - \rho\epsilon_{t-2}).$$

Consider the predictor

$$y_{t-1}^e = \lambda y_{t-2} + \beta w_{t-1} - \rho\epsilon_{t-2}. \tag{3.26}$$

The error of prediction is $y_{t-1} - y_{t-1}^e = \epsilon_{t-1}$. Since ϵ_{t-1} is independent of all information up to time $t-2$, we have $\mathcal{E}(y_{t-1} - y_{t-1}^e)/\ldots y_{t-2} = \mathcal{E}\epsilon_{t-1}/y_{t-2} = 0$, the unconditional expectation. Hence the predictor (3.26) is unbiased (or "rational" in the terminology of economists). Moreover, the (conditional) error variance is $\mathcal{E}(y_{t-1} - y_{t-1}^e)^2/\ldots y_{t-2} = \mathcal{E}\epsilon_{t-1}^2 = \sigma^2$, again equal to the unconditional variance of ϵ_{t-1}. The predictor (3.26) is the linear least-squares predictor of y_{t-1}. In general, to obtain such predictors we need only find the expectation of the variable to be predicted conditional upon the available information, and this in turn can usually be obtained by simply dropping the contribution from the current innovation. For a fuller account with operator methods we refer the reader to Whittle (1964).

As it stands, the predictor (3.26) is not directly operational since it contains the innovations variable ϵ_{t-2}. Observe, however, that $\epsilon_{t-2} = y_{t-2} - y_{t-2}^e$, the prediction error, which is observable. We may therefore write

$$y_{t-1}^e = \lambda y_{t-2} + \beta w_{t-1} - \rho(y_{t-2} - y_{t-2}^e), \tag{3.27}$$

which may be solved recursively for y_{t-1}^e given an initial value y_0^e. Now since y_{t-1}^e is equal to the conditional expectation of y_{t-1} given information up to time $t-2$, it will satisfy the two basic desiderata for instrument choice: (a) It is uncorrelated with $u_t = \epsilon_t - \rho\epsilon_{t-1}$; and (b) as the conditional expectation, it is likely to be highly correlated with y_{t-1}.

To form the conditional expectation instrument, we need prior estimates for the parameters λ, β, and ρ. There are various ways to tackle this problem. If one has a fairly good idea of what the parameters are likely to be, an initial "guesstimate" may be employed. The resulting IV estimates $\hat{\lambda}$, $\hat{\beta}$, and $\hat{\rho}$ may be reinserted into the prediction formula (3.27) to obtain a second-round instrument and the resulting estimation compared with the initial guesstimates for purposes of verification.

Alternatively, the parameters λ and β may be estimated by a preliminary use of Liviatan's instrument and the error process parameter ρ can be consistently estimated from the autocovariances of the residual process $\hat{u}_t = y_t - \hat{\lambda} y_{t-1} - \hat{\beta} w_t$. The following proposition will serve to demonstrate the consistency properties of the resulting instrument.

Proposition 3.2: *Suppose that initial consistent estimates $\hat{\lambda}$, $\hat{\beta}$, and $\hat{\rho}$ are available for the corresponding parameters. Let $y^e_{t-1}(\lambda, \beta, \rho)$ be the conditional expectation of y_{t-1}. Then $y^e_{t-1}(\hat{\lambda}, \hat{\beta}, \hat{\rho})$ is an admissible instrument.*

Proof: (a) We shall first show that $(1/n)\sum_t \hat{y}^e_{t-1} u_t \xrightarrow{p} 0$. Writing $\delta_{t-1} = \hat{y}^e_{t-1} - y^e_{t-1}$ and using equation (3.27) above, it follows that

$$\begin{aligned}\delta_{t-1} &= \hat{\rho}\delta_{t-2} + (\hat{\rho}-\rho) y^e_{t-2} + (\hat{\lambda}-\lambda) y_{t-2} + (\hat{\beta}-\beta) w_{t-1} - (\hat{\rho}-\rho) y_{t-2} \\ &= \hat{\rho}_n \delta_{t-2} + r_{tn},\end{aligned}$$

say, where we have emphasized the dependence of the estimates on the sample size n. Hence

$$\begin{aligned}\frac{1}{n}\sum_t \delta_{t-1} u_t &= \frac{1}{n}\sum_t \sum_{s=1}^{t-1} \hat{\rho}_n^s r_{t-s,n} u_t \\ &= \frac{1}{n}\sum_t a_{tn} u_t,\end{aligned} \tag{3.28}$$

say, where

$$a_{tn} = \sum_{s=1}^{t-1} \hat{\rho}_n^s r_{t-s,n}. \tag{3.29}$$

Consider now the elements $r_{t-s,n}$ appearing in equation (3.29). The last term in $r_{t-s,n}$ is $(\hat{\rho}_n - \rho) y_{t-s-2}$. Since y_{t-s-2} has a bounded variance, it follows from Tchebychev's theorem that $(\hat{\rho}_n - \rho) y_{t-s-2} \xrightarrow{p} 0$ as $t \to \infty$. Indeed, since the variance of y_{t-s-2} is independent of t and s, it follows that this convergence is uniform in t or s. Applying similar arguments to the first three elements of r_{tn}, it follows that $r_{tn} \xrightarrow{p} 0$, uniformly in t. Hence

$$|a_{tn}| \le \sum_{s=1}^{n-1} |\hat{\rho}_n^s|\,|r_{t-s,n}| \le b_n \sum_{s=1}^{n-1} |\hat{\rho}_n|^s,$$

where $b_n \xrightarrow{p} 0$. It follows that

$$|a_{tn}| \le b_n \frac{\hat{\rho}_n(1-\hat{\rho}_n^n)}{1-\hat{\rho}_n},$$

and the right-hand side plainly tends in probability to zero if $|\rho| < 1$, so that $a_{tn} \xrightarrow{p} 0$, uniformly in t.

Hence the sum $(1/n)\sum a_{tn}u_t \xrightarrow{p} 0$, so that in turn $(1/n)\sum \delta_{t-1}u_t$ as defined by equation (3.28) also tends to zero in probability. Now

$$\begin{aligned}\frac{1}{n}\sum_t \hat{y}^e_{t-1}u_t &= \frac{1}{n}\sum_t (y^e_{t-1}+\delta_{t-1})u_t \\ &= \frac{1}{n}\sum_t y^e_{t-1}u_t + \frac{1}{n}\sum_t \delta_{t-1}u_t.\end{aligned} \tag{3.30}$$

Since y^e_{t-1} is known to be an admissible instrument for y_{t-1}, the term $(1/n)\sum_t y^e_{t-1}u_t \xrightarrow{p} 0$. It follows that the estimate $\hat{y}^e_{t-1}$ is asymptotically uncorrelated with the disturbance u_t.

(b) We now show that $\operatorname{plim}(1/n)\sum \hat{y}^e_{t-1}y_{t-1} \neq 0$. Considering first the sum $(1/n)\sum y^e_{t-1}y_{t-1}$, we have

$$\begin{aligned}\frac{1}{n}\sum_t y^e_{t-1}y_{t-1} &= \frac{1}{n}\sum_t (y_{t-1}-\epsilon_{t-1})y_{t-1} \\ &= \frac{1}{n}\sum_t y^2_{t-1} - \frac{1}{n}\sum_t \epsilon_{t-1}y_{t-1}.\end{aligned}$$

It follows that $\operatorname{plim}(1/n)\sum_t y^e_{t-1}y_{t-1} = \sigma^2_y - \sigma^2$, where $\sigma^2_y = \mathcal{E}y^2_{t-1}$. It is easy to show[3] that $\sigma^2_y > \sigma^2$ for $\beta \neq 0$. Thus $\operatorname{plim}(1/n)\sum y^e_{t-1}y_{t-1}$ exists and is nonzero. Now

$$\frac{1}{n}\sum \hat{y}^e_{t-1}y_{t-1} = \frac{1}{n}\sum y^e_{t-1}y_{t-1} + \frac{1}{n}\sum \delta_{t-1}y_{t-1},$$

where the definition $\delta_t = \hat{y}^e_t - y^e_t$ will be recalled from part (a). One can reproduce the argument used there to show now that $(1/n)\sum \delta_{t-1}y_{t-1} = (1/n)\sum a_{tn}y_{t-1} \xrightarrow{p} 0$. Thus $\operatorname{plim}(1/n)\sum \hat{y}^e_{t-1}y_{t-1} = \sigma^2_y - \sigma^2$, a positive constant.

Combining the results of parts (a) and (b) above, the instrument $\hat{y}^e_{t-1}$ is admissible as an instrument for y_{t-1}. ■

With regard to distributional problems, it is straightforward if rather tedious to demonstrate that terms such as $(1/\sqrt{n})\sum_t (\epsilon_t - \rho\epsilon_{t-1})y^e_{t-1}(\lambda, \beta, \rho)$ have a limiting normal distribution. Hence the resulting IV estimator also is asymptotically normal. It is less clear that this property is true if consistent estimators $\hat{\lambda}, \hat{\beta}, \hat{\rho}$ are employed to construct the conditional expectation instrument; this evidently depends upon the estimation process used to derive the initial consistent estimators, and no results are available.

One can expect the above result to generalize to any model where the conditional expectations instrument is available. If the initial estimates of the parameters used to form these expectations are reasonably precise, one would expect the constructed instruments to be more efficient. To be reliable, however, the initial estimates should themselves be provided by an IV or similar consistent technique. The result is a two-stage method in which an inefficient instrument is used to construct an efficient one. It would be of interest to explore the gain in efficiency resulting from use of the second-round instrument.

Finally, we remark that the conditional expectation instrument is not applicable to all types of model. Suppose that instead of a moving-average structure we had specified an autoregressive error structure of the form $u_t = \rho u_{t-1} + \epsilon_t$. In this case it is clear that the conditional expectation of y_{t-1} given the past information is no longer independent of the disturbance term. The conditional expectation instrument may indeed be viewed as a specific instance of the general proposition that the choice of effective instruments is best approached in a rather ad hoc manner, using what is known about the structural properties of the particular model being fitted.

The generalized least-squares analog

Up to this point we have discussed the application of the basic, or the OLS analog, version of instrumental variables to the time series problem. It is therefore of interest to ask whether the GLS analog derived in Section 3.2 is likely to provide a useful alternative. In a stationary time series context the answer is likely to be in the negative, and it is not difficult to see why. We recall from Section 3.2 that the IV–GLS analog is derived by a linear operation (premultiplying by the matrix D) that effectively "sphericalizes" the error. If the original error structure constitutes a regular stationary stochastic process that is invertible[4] to an autoregressive form, the right-hand variables of the transformed structure will now be uncorrelated with the error. Hence an IV approach to the transformed model is no longer necessary.

Consider, for instance, the model used above:

$$y_t = \lambda y_{t-1} + \beta w_t + u_t; \qquad u_t = \epsilon_t - \rho \epsilon_{t-1}. \tag{3.31}$$

If the observations are ordered naturally in time, the covariance matrix Ω given by expression (3.21) above is reduced to approximate sphericality by the linear transformation

$$D = \begin{bmatrix} 1 & 0 & \cdots\cdots & & 0 \\ \rho & 1 & \ddots & & \\ \vdots & & \ddots & \ddots & \\ \rho^{T-1} & \rho^{T-2} & \cdots & 1 & 0 \\ \rho^{T} & \rho^{T-1} & \cdots & \rho & 1 \end{bmatrix}. \tag{3.32}$$

This corresponds to transformed variables in which, for example, y_t is replaced by $(y_t+\rho y_{t-1}+\cdots+\rho^{t-1}y_1)$. The transformed version of the original equation (3.31) reads as follows:

$$\begin{aligned} y_t &= (\lambda-\rho)(y_{t-1}+\rho y_{t-2}+\cdots+\rho^{t-2}y_1) \\ &\quad +\beta(w_t+\rho w_{t-1}+\cdots+\rho^{t-1}w_1)+\epsilon_t \\ &= (\lambda-\rho)Y_{t-1}(\rho)+\beta W_t(\rho)+\epsilon_t, \end{aligned} \tag{3.33}$$

say, where the definition of $Y(\rho)$ and $W(\rho)$ will be clear from the context.

It is apparent from equation (3.33) that the transformed right-hand variables do not suffer from problems of correlation with the (spherical) error term ϵ_t. Of course, equation (3.33) is not by itself operative as an estimating equation since ρ is in general unknown. But the example will serve to point up the general rule that in regression in a pure time series context, the problem of regressor–disturbance correlations arises simply because[5] the error structure is not white noise. A transformation that creates white-noise residuals from the original disturbances gets rid of that problem. The fresh complications that arise are best dealt with in the next section, which deals with the combination of first-round IV estimates with appropriate second-stage methods.

3.4 Second-round estimators

We have emphasized the role of IV estimators as initial conditions, as it were, for more powerful estimation routines. It remains to elaborate on these remarks. To begin with, although one can usually write down a likelihood function for the model to be estimated, it is only rarely that analytic solutions are available for the maximizing parameters (at least if the maximum-likelihood approach is to be useful at all). One is accordingly forced to devise iterative methods for the maximization, and for such purposes it obviously helps to have a reasonable initial estimate as the starting-up value.

What makes the IV estimate particularly useful for such purposes is its consistency properties. Indeed, if the IV estimator $\hat{\theta}$ is such that $\sqrt{n}(\hat{\theta}-\theta)$ has a limiting distribution – which we should usually hope – then as $n\to\infty$, $\hat{\theta}=\theta+0(1/\sqrt{n})$, where the latter expression denotes that the discrepancy is of order $1/\sqrt{n}$ or less in probability. Under these circumstances we may use a simplified version of the likelihood solution. Let $\ln L$ denote the log-likelihood function and denote by $\partial \ln L/\partial\theta\,\partial\theta'$ its Hessian (matrix of second-order partial derivatives). Then the "scoring" estimator defined by

$$\theta^* = \hat{\theta} - \left[\frac{\partial^2 \ln L}{\partial\theta\,\partial\theta'}\right]_{\theta=\hat{\theta}} \left(\frac{\partial \ln L}{\partial\theta}\right)_{\theta=\hat{\theta}} \tag{3.34}$$

has the same limiting distribution as the full maximum-likelihood estimator. Those familiar with numerical maximization techniques will recognize the estimator (3.34) as the first iteration, starting from $\hat{\theta}$, of a basic, or unpowered, Newton–Raphson optimization of $\ln L(\theta)$. The essence of the scoring estimator is that, starting with the IV estimator, only one iteration is needed in order for the second-round estimator to have the same asymptotic distribution as the full iterative solution to the likelihood maximization problem. Moreover, the Hessian in equation (3.34) can be replaced, without asymptotic loss, by $n\times$, the sample covariance matrix of the gradient, that is by

$$\frac{1}{n}\sum_t \left[\frac{\partial}{\partial\theta}\ln f(y_t,\theta)\frac{\partial}{\partial\theta'}\ln f(y_t,\theta)\right].$$

This enables considerable savings both in labor and in possibilities for error. To be sure, the scoring estimator requires appropriate regularity conditions on the structure of the model and the generation of its independent variables. This is an important caveat in time series contexts, where one is usually dealing with a data density rather than the classical independent-element likelihood functions considered by authors (e.g., Rothenberg and Leenders 1964) who have studied the scoring technique. However, if the underlying structure is stochastically stable, one would expect the scoring method to work well.

On occasion, further simplification is available, and the resulting estimator again has an asymptotic distribution equal to that of the full maximum-likelihood estimator. One such method is a technique due to Amemiya and Fuller (1967), which essentially combines an initial IV estimator with ordinary least squares as a second-round estimator applied to a suitably transformed model. We shall outline the technique in the context of the model employed for the purpose by Amemiya and Fuller, although it is of more general applicability. The problem is to estimate an exponential distributed lag model (cf. Section 1.1) where the equation disturbance may obey a first-order Markov process. The model is

$$y_t=\alpha\sum_{j=0}^{t}\lambda^j w_{t-j}+\alpha\lambda^t\eta_0+u_t;\qquad t=1,\dots,n \tag{3.35}$$

$$u_t=\rho u_{t-1}+\epsilon_t;\qquad |\lambda|,|\rho|<1 \tag{3.36}$$

$$\mathcal{E}\epsilon\epsilon'=\sigma^2 I.$$

One has observations $w_0, w_1, \dots, w_n$ on the exogenous variables, which are assumed to follow a stationary stochastic process or, if regarded as nonrandom, to possess a limiting sample variance. The parameter η_0 is introduced as an artifice to represent the unobserved terms $w_{-1}, w_{-2}, \dots,$ which in theory contribute also to the distributed lag:

$$\eta_0 = w_{-1} + \lambda w_{-2} + \lambda^2 w_{-3} + \cdots.$$

The following notation will be useful:

$$W_t = W_t(\lambda) = \sum_{j=0}^{\infty} \lambda^j w_{t-j} = \sum_{j=0}^{t} \lambda^j w_{t-j} + \lambda^t \eta_0 \tag{3.37}$$

$$W_t^d = W_t^d(\lambda, \rho) = W_t - \rho W_{t-1}. \tag{3.38}$$

Thus W_t refers to the distributed lag term and W_t^d to its "quasi-difference" with parameter ρ.

Observe from equation (3.35) that we may write the autoregressive form

$$y_t = \lambda y_{t-1} + \alpha w_t + v_t, \tag{3.39}$$

where $v_t = u_t - \lambda u_{t-1}$. Initial consistent estimates $\hat{\lambda}$ and $\hat{\alpha}$ may be derived by the use of (say) Liviatan's instrument set $Z = (w_{t-1}, w_t)$. Since these estimates possess a limiting distribution, their sampling error is of order $1/\sqrt{n}$ in probability. Returning to equation (3.35), we may estimate the "initial condition" η_0 as

$$\hat{\eta}_0 = \frac{\sum_{t=0}^{n} \hat{\lambda}^t (y_t - \hat{\alpha} \sum_{j=0}^{t} \hat{\lambda}^j w_{t-j})}{\hat{\alpha} \sum_{j=0}^{n} \hat{\lambda}^2 j}. \tag{3.40}$$

In fact, consistent estimators of η_0 do not exist (Dhrymes 1971). However, for large sample sizes, the influence of the initial condition on the final estimates for α, λ, and ρ becomes very small, and subsequent development indeed confirms this. Thus the precise choice of $\hat{\eta}_0$ is not crucial. Finally, an initial consistent estimator for ρ can be obtained as

$$\hat{\rho} = \sum_{t=1}^{n} \hat{u}_t \hat{u}_{t-1} \Big/ \sum_{t=0}^{n} \hat{u}_t^2, \tag{3.41}$$

where the computed residual is based on equation (3.35):

$$\hat{u}_t = y_t - \hat{\alpha} W_t(\hat{\lambda}).$$

Consider now a second round of estimation, which we shall set up as follows. Write equation (3.35) with a white-noise disturbance term as

$$y_t = \rho y_{t-1} + \alpha (W_t(\lambda) - \rho W_{t-1}(\lambda)) + \epsilon_t. \tag{3.42}$$

Define

$$S_t(\lambda) = \frac{\partial}{\partial \lambda} W_t(\lambda) = \sum_{j=0}^{n} j \lambda^{j-1} w_{t-j} + t \lambda^{t-1} \eta_0$$

and let $S_t^d = S_t - \rho S_{t-1} = (\partial / \partial \lambda) W_t^d$. Expanding the right-hand side of equation (3.42) about the point $\hat{\alpha}$, $\hat{\lambda}$, $\hat{\rho}$, and $\hat{\eta}_0$, we obtain

$$y_t = \hat{\rho} y_{t-1} + \alpha \hat{W}_t^d + (\lambda - \hat{\lambda}) \hat{S}_t^d + (\rho - \hat{\rho}) \hat{u}_{t-1}$$
$$+ \hat{\alpha} \hat{\lambda}^t (\hat{\lambda} - \hat{\rho})(\eta_0 - \hat{\eta}_0) + \epsilon_t + 0_p(1/n), \tag{3.43}$$

where, for instance, $\hat{W}_t^d = W_t^d(\hat{\lambda}, \hat{\rho}, \hat{\eta})$. The remainder terms consist in products of, for example, $(\hat{\alpha} - \alpha)^2$ with random variables of finite variance and are therefore of order $1/n$ in probability, as indicated. Note also that the term in $(\eta_0 - \hat{\eta}_0)$ is likely to be small in magnitude for all but very low values of t and that we may therefore safely disregard it.

Equation (3.43) therefore suggests a second-round ordinary least-squares estimation of the parameters α, λ, and ρ:

$$\begin{bmatrix} \alpha^* \\ \lambda^* \\ \rho^* \end{bmatrix} = \begin{bmatrix} 0 \\ \hat{\lambda} \\ \hat{\rho} \end{bmatrix} + \left[\begin{bmatrix} \hat{W}_t^{d'} \\ \hat{S}_t^{d'} \\ \hat{u}_{t-1}' \end{bmatrix} (\hat{W}_t^d, \hat{S}_t^d, \hat{u}_{t-1}) \right]^{-1} \begin{bmatrix} \hat{W}_t^{d'} \\ \hat{S}^{d'} \\ \hat{u}_{t-1}' \end{bmatrix} (y_t - \hat{\rho} y_{t-1}) \tag{3.44}$$

in a notation that should be clear from the OLS estimation implied. Amemiya and Fuller show that the estimates as obtained have the same asymptotic distribution as the full maximum-likelihood estimator. This proposition is established from a comparison of the limiting covariance matrix of the estimator (3.44) with the asymptotic covariance matrix of the full maximum-likelihood estimation that may be based either on equation (3.42) or on the autoregressive transform (3.39) that has an autoregressive moving average (ARMA) (1, 1) disturbance. The common limiting covariance matrix is

$$\sigma^2 \begin{bmatrix} \operatorname{plim} \frac{1}{n} W_t^{d'} W_t^d & \operatorname{plim} \frac{1}{n} W_t^{d'} S_t^d & 0 \\ \operatorname{plim} \frac{1}{n} S_t^{d'} W_t^d & \operatorname{plim} \frac{1}{n} S_t^{d'} S_t^d & 0 \\ 0 & 0 & \sigma_u^2 \end{bmatrix}^{-1} .$$

This is, of course, just what an OLS program based upon equation (3.44) would output, so far as the calculations are concerned.

A multistage methodology is applicable to other models. Hatanaka (1974) considers the following model:

$$y_t = \lambda y_{t-1} + \beta w_t + u_t \tag{3.45a}$$

$$u_t = \rho u_{t-1} + \epsilon_t . \tag{3.45b}$$

Consistent estimates $\tilde{\lambda}, \tilde{\beta}$ may be derived in terms of an IV calculation based upon present and past values of the exogenous sequence w_t; the latter variables are assumed to follow suitable regularity conditions.

Forming $\tilde{u}_t = y_t - \tilde{\lambda} y_{t-1} - \tilde{\beta} w_t$, a consistent estimate $\tilde{\rho}$ may be obtained as $\tilde{\rho} = \Sigma \tilde{u}_t \tilde{u}_{t-1} / \Sigma \tilde{u}_{t-1}^2$. Lagging equation (3.45a) and multiplying by $\tilde{\rho}$, the second-stage model may be written as

$$y_t - \tilde{\rho} y_{t-1} = \lambda(y_{t-1} - \tilde{\rho} y_{t-2}) + \beta(w_t - \tilde{\rho} w_{t-1}) + (\rho - \tilde{\rho})\tilde{u}_{t-1} + \zeta_t, \tag{3.46}$$

where the residual $\zeta_t = \epsilon_t + (\rho - \tilde{\rho})(u_{t-1} - \tilde{u}_{t-1})$. The dependent variable in the new regression is $y_t^d(\tilde{\rho}) = y_t - \tilde{\rho} y_{t-1}$. The right-hand variables are $y_{t-1}^d(\tilde{\rho})$, $w_t^d(\tilde{\rho})$, and $\tilde{u}_{t-1}$.

Hatanaka shows that the resulting second-round estimates $\hat{\lambda}$, $\hat{\beta}$, and $\hat{\rho}$ (the latter is defined as $\widehat{\rho - \tilde{\rho}} + \tilde{\rho}$) are asymptotically efficient, that is, have the same limiting distribution as the full maximum-likelihood estimator. An alternative two-stage procedure developed earlier by Wallis (1967) is to utilize the first-round estimates $\tilde{\rho}$ to construct $\tilde{\Omega} = \Omega(\tilde{\rho})$, the estimated covariance matrix of the disturbance vector $\mathbf{u}$. The second stage consists of an application of generalized least squares with this estimated covariance matrix. Unlike the Hatanaka procedure, however, this latter technique is not asymptotically efficient.

The Amemiya–Fuller and Hatanaka two-stage techniques constitute ingenious applications of the initial IV estimators that are applicable to more general models of the classes considered. Even for simple models, a numerical maximum-likelihood solution of a theoretically concave log-likelihood function can sometimes go badly astray, and because of the "black box" nature of most packaged routines one very often has little idea of just what has gone wrong. In addition to their simplicity, the advantage of two-stage techniques of the kind we have just described is that the source of ill-conditioning (if this is the problem) is often immediately apparent, and one can proceed directly to remedial action.

3.5 Heteroscedasticity

The polar case of heteroscedasticity is where the disturbance variances σ_t^2; $t = 1, \ldots, n$ may not be equal but the off-diagonal elements of the covariance matrix Ω are zero. Traditional approaches to estimation and hypothesis testing for regression models with such disturbances usually postulated some additional structure on the σ_t^2, the effect of which was to limit the number of unknown parameters to fewer than n. Thus one could assume that σ_t^2 was proportional to one or more of the regressors or simple functions thereof. Such approaches are obviously less useful where the regressors themselves are stochastic. However in a pathbreaking article, White (1980b) suggested that if one's primary interest lay in the coefficients β rather than the precise magnitude of the σ_t^2, it was not necessary to specify and estimate the generating mechanisms for the σ_t^2.

Instead, consistent estimates of the coefficients $\hat{\beta}$ could be obtained by a two-pass procedure, in which the object was the estimation, not of Ω itself, but of certain weighted sums involving both the X elements and the elements of the matrix Ω; it was these weighted sums that appeared in the formula for $\boldsymbol{\beta}$ and its covariance matrix. In a later article, White (1982) extended these ideas to the IV context.[6] Referring to the IV–OLS estimator, the essential task is to estimate the matrix $V = \text{plim}(1/n)Z'\Omega Z$. Given an estimate $\hat{V}$, we have the estimator $\hat{\boldsymbol{\beta}}_1 = (X'Z\hat{V}^{-1}Z'X)^{-1}X'Z\hat{V}^{-1}Z'\mathbf{y}$.

Suppose that we apply ordinary (spherical) IV to obtain a residual process $\hat{\mathbf{u}} = \mathbf{y} - X\hat{\boldsymbol{\beta}}$, where $\hat{\boldsymbol{\beta}} = (X'P_z X)^{-1}X'P_z\mathbf{y}$. Then writing $\mathbf{z}_t'$ as the tth row of Z, the suggested estimator for V is

$$\hat{V}_n = \frac{1}{n}\sum_{t=1}^{n} \hat{u}_t^2 \mathbf{z}_t \mathbf{z}_t' = \frac{1}{n} Z'\tilde{\Omega}Z, \tag{3.47}$$

where $\tilde{\Omega} = \text{diag}(\hat{u}_t^2; t = 1, \ldots, n)$. In investigating the (weak) asymptotic behavior of the estimator (3.47), we note that $\hat{\mathbf{u}} = \mathbf{u} - X(X'P_z X)^{-1}X'P_z\mathbf{u}$, so that $\hat{u}_t = u_t - \mathbf{x}_t'\boldsymbol{\delta}_n$, where $\text{plim}\,\boldsymbol{\delta}_n = 0$. Hence $\hat{u}_t$ differs from u_t by a random variable that approaches zero in probability, uniformly in t. It is then easy to show that $\hat{V}_n$ has the same limiting behavior as $(1/n)\sum u_t^2 \mathbf{z}_t \mathbf{z}_t'$. Thus the weak consistency of $\hat{V}_n$ can be established in terms of the moments of independent but nonidentically distributed (i.n.i.d.) random variables involving u_t and the instruments z_{it}, z_{jt}. If the z_{it} are bounded nonstochastic constants, there is no essential difficulty in showing that

$$\text{plim}\left(\frac{1}{n}\sum u_t^2 \mathbf{z}_t \mathbf{z}_t' - \frac{1}{n}\sum \sigma_t^2 \mathbf{z}_t \mathbf{z}_t'\right) = \mathbf{O}. \tag{3.48}$$

Likewise, the z_{it} could be proper random variables, independent over t and such that (a) $\mathcal{E} z_{it} u_t = 0$ for all i and t; and (b) the moments $\mathcal{E}|z_{it} u_t|^{1+\delta}$ and $\mathcal{E}|z_{it} z_{jt} u_t|^{1+\delta}$ are uniformly bounded in t for some $\delta > 0$. Under these conditions one can apply the law of large numbers for i.n.i.d. random variables to show that the result (3.48) is again true. Indeed, one suspects that this result is valid under appropriate regularity conditions even in cases where the z_{it} are not independent, but are constructed in terms of some prior and possibly nonlinear estimation procedure.

The random parameter case

Heteroscedasticity is usually taken to refer to the case where the disturbance variances are not equal. In many instances, however, this phenomenon is accompanied by nonzero off-diagonal elements in the covariance matrix of the errors, so that one has to consider simultaneously the effects of both heteroscedasticity in the strict sense just mentioned and serial correlation. One such instance arises in random parameter models, and it is of interest to look at some of the problems that arise when the random parameter is compounded with the regressor–disturbance correlation problem. The resulting model is by no means fanciful; indeed, it could well be held that a random parameter assumption should be the norm rather than the exception in some contexts.

The particular model we shall consider is very simple, but the insights gained with its help will extend to more comprehensive specifications. Let us suppose two dimensions of sample variation, subscripted by t ("time," say) and j ("countries," to take a common context). Thus we could be fitting a relationship between aggregate consumption and national income; for each country we have a time series of length T and there are N countries in the sample. The model is specified as

$$y_{jt} = X_{jt}\mu_j + u_{jt}; \qquad t = 1, \dots, T, \quad j = 1, \dots, N.$$

Initially we shall suppose just one independent variable X_{jt} and the regression is to have no intercept. The slope parameter μ_j is random, and the distribution of μ_j for country j has mean μ and variance σ^2, so that all countries exhibit the same distribution for the random parameter. The random parameters μ_j are independent of each other and are independent of the additive equation disturbances u_{jt}. These latter errors are independent across j and are spherical for a given j, with variance parameter σ_j^2, which may differ across countries.

With regard to the independent variables X_{jt}, we shall assume that these have mean M_{jt}; the simplest case would be where the X_{jt} are drawings from a process with constant mean. We denote by $\mathbf{M}_j$ the vector of means M_{jt}, $t = 1, \dots, T$. It is assumed that the X_{jt} are correlated with the equation disturbances in the sense that $\text{plim}(1/T)\sum_t X_{jt}u_{jt}$ exists and is nonzero. Apart from these specifications on the independent variables, the model we have described is a simple example of the structures considered extensively by Swamy (1970, 1971).

Write $\mathbf{X}_j$ as the column vector of time series observations for country j; and write $\mathbf{y}_j, \mathbf{u}_j$ as vectors of dependent-variable observations and equation disturbances, respectively. We may write the model as

$$\mathbf{y}_j = \mathbf{X}_j\mu_j + \mathbf{u}_j; \qquad j = 1, \dots, N, \tag{3.49}$$

with $\mathcal{E}\mathbf{u}_j\mathbf{u}_j' = \sigma_j^2 I$. Indeed, we can write $\mu_j = \mu + \epsilon_j$ with $\mathcal{E}\epsilon_j^2 = \sigma^2$, so that the model (3.49) can be written

$$\mathbf{y}_j = \mathbf{X}_j\mu + \mathbf{v}_j; \qquad \mathbf{v}_j = \mathbf{u}_j + \mathbf{X}_j\epsilon_j. \tag{3.50}$$

The new compound disturbance term has covariance matrix

$$\Omega_j = \mathcal{E}\mathbf{v}_j\mathbf{v}_j' = \sigma^2(w_j I + \mathbf{M}_j\mathbf{M}_j') \tag{3.51}$$

where $w_j = \sigma_j^2/\sigma^2$.

We assume that a set of instruments Z_j is available, one for each country, which are correlated with X_j but asymptotically uncorrelated with the compound disturbances $\mathbf{v}_j$. Notice that the latter will in most circumstances amount to independence of the Z_j from both ϵ_j and u_j; that is, the instruments must be chosen to be asymptotically uncorrelated with both equation and parameter disturbances. For expositional simplicity we assume that just one instrument is employed for the single variable X_{jt}.

We can assemble the set of equations (3.50) by stacking the $\mathbf{y}_j$ on top of each other to form a supervector $\mathbf{y}$ and doing the same with the regressors, instruments, and disturbances to obtain $\mathbf{X}$, $\mathbf{Z}$, and $\mathbf{v}$, respectively. The system may therefore be represented in the form

$$\mathbf{y} = \mathbf{X}\mu + \mathbf{v}. \tag{3.52}$$

We note that the covariance matrix of the system disturbance $\mathbf{v}$ is $\Omega = \operatorname{diag}(\Omega_1, \Omega_2, \ldots, \Omega_N)$, where the notation indicates a block diagonal matrix. We shall now examine the formation and consistency properties of the two estimators IV–OLS and IV–GLS.

(a) *IV–OLS*

Since the dimensionality of instrument and regressor sets are equal (namely, unity), the IV–OLS estimator is

$$\hat{\mu}_1 = (\mathbf{Z}'\mathbf{X})^{-1}\mathbf{Z}'\mathbf{y} = \left(\sum_{j=1}^{N}\mathbf{Z}_j'\mathbf{X}_j\right)^{-1}\sum_{j=1}^{N}\mathbf{Z}_j'\mathbf{y}_j. \tag{3.53}$$

It is easy to verify that this estimator is consistent as $T \to \infty$, for any N. The asymptotic covariance matrix for fixed N is the limit in probability of

$$\left[\left(\sum_j \frac{\mathbf{X}_j'\mathbf{Z}_j}{T}\right)\left(\sum_j \frac{\mathbf{Z}_j'\Omega_j\mathbf{Z}_j}{T}\right)\left(\sum_j \frac{\mathbf{Z}_j'\mathbf{X}_j}{T}\right)\right]^{-1}. \tag{3.54}$$

Notice that this formula requires estimates of the σ_j^2 and of σ^2. Such estimates may be derived from the process of estimation at country level. Thus the IV–OLS analog estimator for country j is $\hat{\mu}_j = (\mathbf{Z}_j'\mathbf{X}_j)^{-1}\mathbf{Z}_j'\mathbf{y}_j$. Consider the estimated residual vector

$$\begin{aligned}\hat{\mathbf{v}}_j &= \mathbf{y}_j - \mathbf{X}_j\mu_j\\ &= (I - \mathbf{X}_j(\mathbf{Z}_j'\mathbf{X}_j)^{-1}\mathbf{Z}_j')(\mathbf{u}_j + \mathbf{X}_j\epsilon_j)\\ &= (I - \mathbf{X}_j(\mathbf{Z}_j'\mathbf{X}_j)^{-1}\mathbf{Z}_j')\mathbf{u}_j.\end{aligned}$$

It will be observed that the random parameter component of the error (ϵ_j) has been eliminated from the residual. It is now straightforward to demonstrate that $\text{plim}(1/T)\mathbf{v}_j'\mathbf{v}_j=\sigma_j^2$. Thus consistent estimates of the variances of the additive disturbance components may be obtained in terms of the residual variances from the IV estimation at a country level.

Let us turn to the estimation of σ^2, the variance of the random parameter. We may write

$$\begin{aligned}\hat{\mu}_j &= \mu+(\mathbf{Z}_j'\mathbf{X}_j)^{-1}\mathbf{Z}_j'(\mathbf{u}_j+\mathbf{X}_j\epsilon_j)\\ &= \mu+\epsilon_j+\left(\frac{\mathbf{Z}_j'\mathbf{X}_j}{T}\right)^{-1}\frac{1}{T}\mathbf{Z}_j'\mathbf{u}_j.\end{aligned} \tag{3.55}$$

It follows from equation (3.55) that $(1/N)\sum_{j=1}^{N}\hat{\mu}_j\xrightarrow{p}\mu$ as $N\to\infty$; that is, the sample mean (across countries) of the country estimators $\hat{\mu}_j$ is a consistent estimate of the overall expectation μ. Consider, therefore, the variance estimator

$$\hat{\sigma}^2=\frac{1}{N}\sum_{j=1}^{N}(\hat{\mu}_j-\bar{\hat{\mu}}_j)^2 \tag{3.56}$$

Since $\bar{\hat{\mu}}_j\xrightarrow{p}\mu$, it is easy to show that $\hat{\sigma}^2$ has the same limiting behavior in probability as the quasi-estimate $(1/N)\sum(\hat{\mu}_j-\mu)^2$. The latter can be written [from equation (3.55)] as

$$\frac{1}{N}\sum_j\left[\epsilon_j+\left(\frac{\mathbf{Z}_j'\mathbf{X}_j}{T}\right)^{-1}\frac{1}{T}\mathbf{Z}'\mathbf{u}_j\right]^2,$$

which tends in probability to σ^2. The sample variance defined by equation (3.56) above therefore yields a consistent estimate of the random parameter variance σ^2 as the number of countries $N\to\infty$. The estimates of σ^2 and σ_j^2, $j=1,\dots,N$, may now be substituted into the expression (3.51) above to obtain estimates for the Ω_j and hence estimates of the asymptotic covariance matrix (3.54) for the IV–OLS estimator. We remark in conclusion that the consistency properties of the IV–OLS estimator continue to hold when the model is generalized to incorporate additional regressors.

(b) *IV–GLS*

Interestingly enough, a rather different story holds for the IV–GLS estimator. The indicated IV–GLS estimator is:

$$\hat{\mu}_2=(\mathbf{Z}'\Omega^{-1}\mathbf{X})^{-1}\mathbf{Z}'\Omega^{-1}\mathbf{y} \tag{3.57a}$$

$$=\mu+(\mathbf{Z}'\Omega^{-1}\mathbf{X})^{-1}\mathbf{Z}'\Omega^{-1}\mathbf{v}. \tag{3.57b}$$

Consider now the constituent parts of the product on the right-hand side of equation (3.57b). We have

$$\frac{1}{T}\mathbf{Z}'\Omega^{-1}\mathbf{v} = \sum_{j=1}^{N} \mathbf{Z}_j'\Omega_j^{-1}\mathbf{v}_j/T.$$

Now $\Omega_j = \sigma^2(w_j I + \mathbf{M}_j \mathbf{M}_j')$. Hence

$$\Omega_j^{-1} = \frac{1}{\theta_j}[I - \mathbf{M}_j \mathbf{M}_j'/(\theta_j + \mathbf{M}_j' \mathbf{M}_j)] \tag{3.58}$$

where $\theta_j = \sigma^2 w_j$. Thus apart from the constant θ_j,

$$\mathbf{Z}_j'\Omega_j^{-1}\mathbf{v}_j/T = \frac{\mathbf{Z}_j'\mathbf{v}_j}{T} - \frac{\mathbf{Z}_j'\mathbf{M}_j}{T}\,\frac{\mathbf{M}_j'\mathbf{v}_j}{T}\bigg/\left(\frac{\theta_j}{T} + \frac{\mathbf{M}_j'\mathbf{M}_j}{T}\right).$$

It follows from this decomposition that provided the limit $\mathbf{M}_j'\mathbf{M}_j/T$ exists, $(1/T)\mathbf{Z}_j'\Omega_j^{-1}\mathbf{v}_j \xrightarrow{p} 0$ as $T \to \infty$. Thus the instrument and disturbance are correlated in the general sense required for IV–GLS admissibility.

Consider, however, the first term of the product in equation (3.57a), namely

$$\mathbf{Z}'\Omega^{-1}\mathbf{X} = \sum_{j=1}^{N} Z_j'\Omega_j^{-1}X_j.$$

Utilizing the inverse (3.58), we have

$$\frac{1}{T}\mathbf{Z}_j'\Omega_j^{-1}\mathbf{X}_j = \frac{1}{\theta_j}\left[\frac{1}{T}\mathbf{Z}_j'\mathbf{X}_j - \frac{\mathbf{Z}_j'\mathbf{M}_j}{T}\,\frac{\mathbf{M}_j'\mathbf{X}_j}{T}\bigg/\left(\frac{\theta_j}{T} + \frac{\mathbf{M}_j'\mathbf{M}_j}{T}\right)\right]. \tag{3.59}$$

Now under fairly general conditions, the terms $\mathbf{M}_j'\mathbf{X}_j/T$, $\mathbf{M}_j'\mathbf{M}_j/T$ have the same limiting value, the first as a limit in probability, the second as an ordinary limit. Now suppose that the instruments $\mathbf{Z}_j$ are nonstochastic. Write $\mathbf{X}_j = \mathbf{M}_j + \eta_j$, where $\mathcal{E}\eta_j = \mathbf{0}$. Then

$$\mathbf{Z}_j'\mathbf{X}_j/T = \mathbf{Z}_j'\mathbf{M}_j/T + \mathbf{Z}_j'\eta_j/T.$$

Again under suitable regularity conditions, the second term on the right-hand side of this equation tends in probability to zero. Thus considering the behavior of all the terms in expression (3.59), it is apparent that at least in the case where the instruments are nonstochastic,

$$\operatorname{plim} \frac{1}{T}\mathbf{Z}_j'\Omega_j^{-1}\mathbf{X}_j = 0.$$

It follows that the estimator defined by equation (3.57) has an indeterminate limiting behavior. The problem is not one of nonzero instrument–disturbance correlation, but of the asymptotically zero generalized covariance $\mathbf{Z}'\Omega^{-1}\mathbf{X}/T$ between the instrument and regressor. This is a rather striking example of the necessity to check both requirements for admissibility of an instrument set or an IV procedure. It is also a singular example of the failure of the IV–GLS technique, which must therefore be viewed as less robust than IV–OLS in its application to a variety of situations.

3.6 Summary

Applications of instrumental variables techniques to models with nonspherical errors are sometimes criticized on the grounds that the estimation ignores the structure of the equation disturbance. It is therefore natural to examine the properties of an IV estimator that takes into account the nonsphericality properties of the disturbance. The resulting estimator is what we have called the IV–GLS analog, since it represents the most direct adaptation of the method of generalized least squares to an IV format. We have seen that this estimator must be treated with a certain amount of caution. Essentially it amounts to transforming both regressor and instrument data matrices to achieve a spherical disturbance. However, if the canonical correlations were not uniformly high between the transformed regressor and instrument, the IV–GLS estimator could be dominated in efficiency by another IV estimator, the IV–OLS analog. Moreover, in certain circumstances the IV–GLS may fail as a determinate estimator; this was illustrated in the random parameter discussion of Section 3.5.

Nevertheless, the IV–GLS has some very important efficiency properties. We shall show in Chapters 4 and 5 that in a variety of simultaneous-equation contexts, with and without serially correlated disturbances, linear and nonlinear, the method of maximum likelihood has an interpretation as an iterated IV estimator. And whenever this is the case, it is the IV–GLS form that provides this interpretation. For certain kinds of noniterative procedures, the IV–OLS and the IV–GLS estimators collapse to the same estimator. Where this is not possible, it is the latter estimator that is applicable.

Moreover, the distinction between estimators that do and do not make use of the error structure of the model is not as sharp as one might think. It was pointed out in Section 3.2 that the estimator that we have called the IV–OLS analog does in fact incorporate the disturbance covariance matrix if the number of available instruments exceeds the number of regressors. We remarked on this again in discussing instruments for time series regressions, where the prescription suggested by the IV–OLS analog differed from that in common use. Likewise, the choice of instrument in a time series context may be improved by a knowledge of the structure of the disturbance process. Thus in the particular model considered in Section 3.3, a second-round instrument could be constructed by employing the conditional expectation of the offending regressor. The latter can be formed using knowledge of both systematic and unsystematic components of the proposed regression equation.

The particular usefulness of the IV estimator in single-equation nonspherical contexts derives from its flexibility as an initial or first-round estimation process, to be input into second-round calculations such as those based upon maximum-likelihood methods or techniques or spectral regression in the frequency domain. One's approach to this initial estimation need assume very little about the structure of the process, so that the same initial estimate may serve as a first round for more structured techniques applied to several specifications of the error process. On the other hand, if one is fairly confident of the complete model, a more structured approach to the derivation of instruments may be employed. Finally, the special usefulness of the IV estimator as a first-round estimator derives from its consistency properties. As we saw in Section 3.4, this means that a favorable maximum-likelihood approach needs only one iteration if the initial value is itself a consistent estimator. In practice, too, one often has available a plethora of possible instruments, and under such circumstances the resulting IV estimate may be fairly precise, even for small samples. Such a property is obviously extremely useful for a second-round estimation. In the case of maximum-likelihood methods, it means that the Hessian of the likelihood function, evaluated at the initial value, may be approximated by the covariance matrix of the gradient. Such a property often enables considerable simplification and savings in time and accuracy so far as a full iterative solution of the likelihood function is concerned.

CHAPTER 4

Linear simultaneous equations

4.1 Introduction

The topic of simultaneous stochastic equations will be familiar to readers who have some acquaintance with empirical economics, for it is in econometrics that this methodology has been worked out most fully. On the other hand, one can conceive of situations where variables are jointly determined as the solution to simultaneous equations in other contexts. In population dynamics, for example, the number of predators (lynxes, say) may depend upon the number of prey (snowshoe hares), and likewise the number of hares will depend upon the number of lynxes; and although such a dependence will unquestionably have dynamic elements, it is nevertheless essentially simultaneous. In view of the historical development of simultaneous stochastic equation theory, however, it is perhaps inevitable that an economic flavor creeps into the discussion. For this reason, it will be as well to commence with a very brief and simple outline of the essential problems involved in the simultaneous context. The reader who can understand these examples should have no difficulty with the remainder of the chapter. Indeed, it will be found that the methodology of instrumental variables, as it has appeared in previous chapters, offers a relatively painless approach to the topic for the reader whose statistical numeracy outruns his economic literacy. On the other hand, the econometrician may like to skip directly from this point to Section 4.2, perhaps pausing to look at the chapter outline at the end of the present section.

Motivation

In Section 1.1, it was pointed out that the methodology of ordinary least squares was not entirely suitable in a simultaneous-equation context, and to show this we employed a simple macromodel of income determination. The latter model, however, is not adequate to exhibit the full range of problems associated with the estimation of structural equations. Let us consider here the following model of supply and demand for a commodity.[1] It contains two equations. The first represents a demand function for an (imaginary) agricultural commodity, cast in terms of price p and income Y. The second represents a supply function, again containing price with a contribution from a rainfall variable R. In both cases q represents the amount sold. The model is

$$\text{(demand)} \quad q = a_1 + b_1 p + c_1 Y + u_1 \tag{4.1}$$

$$\text{(supply)} \quad q = a_2 + b_2 p + c_2 R + u_2, \tag{4.2}$$

where u_1 and u_2 are disturbances that are assumed to be serially uncorrelated, although we may have $\mathcal{E} u_1 u_2 = \sigma_{12} \neq 0$.

A question prior to estimating the parameters of such a model concerns the identifiability of those parameters. As it stands, the model determines simultaneously the values of p and q, which are called the endogenous variables. The variables Y and R are not determined by the model. In the terminology, the latter variables are "exogenous"; in the way this term is used in the present chapter, a variable is exogenous if it is statistically independent of the disturbance terms u_1 and u_2. Now suppose that it is known that $c_1 = c_2 = 0$, so that the model is now

$$q = a_1 + b_1 p + u_1 \tag{4.1$'$}$$

$$q = a_2 + b_2 p + u_2. \tag{4.2$'$}$$

Consider a weighted combination of the above two equations with given weights $w, 1-w$:

$$q = a_1^* + b_1^* p + u_1^*, \tag{4.3}$$

where $a_1^* = wa_1 + (1-w)a_2$, $b_1^* = wb_1 + (1-w)b_2$, $u^* = wu_1 + (1-w)u_2$.

Consider now the system formed by the two equations (4.2′) and (4.3). Inspection of this pair relative to the original pair (4.1′) and (4.2′) reveals immediately that there is nothing statistically unique about the parameters a_1 and b_1; in estimating the first equation of the system, we could be estimating (a_1, b_1) or (a_1^*, b_1^*) or an infinite number of alternatives. The same complaint holds in respect of the parameters a_2, b_2. This is a rather extreme example of an identifiability problem. It turns out that adding additional exogenous variables to either equation will help to solve such identification problems. In geometric terms, the reader can verify that the points (p, q) that satisfy simultaneously the pair (4.1′) and (4.2′) form an undifferentiated mass of points – a "glob" – around the intersection of the two lines $q = a_1 + b_1 p$ and $q = a_2 + b_2 p$ (assuming that $b_1 < 0$, such an intersection should exist). The addition of an exogenous variable such as R to the supply equation produces a more determinate pattern of observations that in fact now enables us to identify the parameters a_1 and b_1 of the demand equation.

Returning to the more general model (4.1) and (4.2), we may solve for the endogenous variables in terms of the exogenous variables and the disturbance, as follows:

$$q = \pi_{11} + \pi_{12} Y + \pi_{13} R + v_1 \tag{4.4}$$

$$p = \pi_{21} + \pi_{22} Y + \pi_{23} R + v_2, \tag{4.5}$$

where

$$\begin{aligned} \pi_{11} &= \frac{a_1 b_2 - a_2 b_1}{b_2 - b_1}; & \pi_{12} &= \frac{c_1 b_2}{b_2 - b_1}; & \pi_{13} &= \frac{-c_2 b_1}{b_2 - b_1}; \\ \pi_{21} &= \frac{a_1 - a_2}{b_2 - b_1}; & \pi_{22} &= \frac{c_1}{b_2 - b_1}; & \pi_{23} &= \frac{-c_2}{b_2 - b_1}. \end{aligned} \tag{4.6}$$

The new disturbances v_1 and v_2 are also linear combinations of the original disturbances u_1 and u_2. The model (4.4) and (4.5) is called the *reduced form* of the original model (4.1) and (4.2); the latter is referred to as the *structural form,* since it is presumed to reflect basic structural hypotheses.

Statistically speaking, there is no essential difficulty about the identification of the reduced-form parameters (π_{ij}) in equations (4.4) and (4.5), which individually satisfy classical Gauss–Markov assumptions. Thus we might cast the structural identification problem as one of uniquely deriving the structural parameters, given the reduced-form parameters. It will be apparent that one can certainly solve for all the parameters $a_1 \dots c_2$ appearing in the structural form (4.1) and (4.2) in terms of the π_{ij} by utilizing the set of equations (4.6) above. Thus we can assert that the relevant structural form is identified. Clearly, however, this is a laborious process, and one needs to develop criteria that are more readily applicable. Such criteria, as we shall see, can be presented in terms of an instrument-counting approach.

Turning now to estimation, we might think of applying least squares directly to the structural form, say to equation (4.1). The difficulty is that the estimates of a, b, and c will not in general exhibit desirable bias or consistency properties, and it is not difficult to see why. Since p [on the right-hand side of equation (4.1)] is itself endogenous, it is influenced by the disturbances u_1 and u_2, as indeed the reduced-form equation (4.5) tells us. Hence a regressor, namely p, is correlated with the equation disturbance, namely u_1.

If direct estimation of the structural form fails, we could try a least-squares estimation of the parameters π_{ij} in the reduced-form equations (4.4) and (4.5), subsequently recovering the structural parameters from equations (4.6). The implied estimation technique, which is called indirect least squares, is indeed consistent, but there may be difficulties with efficiency. Suppose that instead of equations (4.1) and (4.2) we had specified

$$\text{(demand)} \quad q = a_1 + b_1 P + c_1 Y + d_1 R \tag{4.7}$$

$$\text{(supply)} \quad q = a_2 + b_2 P. \tag{4.8}$$

(Thus the commodity in question might be ice cream or beer.) The reduced form is (formally) the same as equations (4.4) and (4.5). It may be verified, however, that

$$b_2 = \pi_{12}/\pi_{22} = \pi_{13}/\pi_{23}. \tag{4.9}$$

If we now estimate the reduced-form parameters π_{ij} by OLS applied to equations (4.4) and (4.5), there is no reason why we should obtain $\hat{\pi}_{12}/\hat{\pi}_{22} = \hat{\pi}_{13}/\hat{\pi}_{23}$, at least for a finite sample size. This leaves the corresponding estimator b_2 undetermined. Perhaps more to the point, least squares applied to the reduced form takes no account of the theoretical constraint $\pi_{12}/\pi_{22} = \pi_{13}/\pi_{23}$. Models that exhibit such constraints are said to be *overidentified,* and the indirect least-squares estimation of such models will, since it ignores the reduced-form constraints, be inefficient. Since overidentification is a very common phenomenon in practice, most of the estimation techniques developed for the structural form do not proceed by first estimating the reduced form.

Synopsis

With the above as a sketch of the background considerations, we are now ready for the more general models established in Section 4.2. A natural division for purposes of exposition is between "limited"-information and "full"-information estimation. In many practical settings, attention may focus on just one particular equation, although the investigator may be well aware that this equation is imbedded in a larger system. Thus one may be estimating a demand for money function, with income (Y) as a right-hand variable. It is realized that the demand for money function is really part of a large macroeconomic model in which income (Y) is endogenous; yet one may not be prepared to specify fully the equations of the rest of the system, content merely to recognize the necessity to develop special techniques that will recognize the endogeneity of Y. Such contexts are called *limited information,* and the idea is formalized and investigated in its estimation aspects in Section 4.3. So far as full-information techniques are concerned, the emphasis is somewhat different. We may again be interested specifically in the demand for money function, but it may be that known restrictions (such as certain coefficients being zero) in equations elsewhere in the system will enable us to estimate more efficiently the parameters of the demand for money equation. In other words, full efficiency requires the use of all equations jointly. Such full-information estimation techniques are discussed in Section 4.4. Our concern in both Sections 4.3 and 4.4 is to find estimators that efficiently use all the information incorporated in their respective views of the world (whether limited or full information). The notion of best, asymptotically normal (BAN) estimators is employed as an efficiency criterion, and this, together with the interpretation of the proposed estimators as IV methods, provides a unifying thread for the discussion of estimation. As we shall see, several estimators qualify as BAN, and it is therefore natural to investigate whether they differ in their efficiency to terms of a higher order in $1/\sqrt{n}$. The notion of second-order efficiency has been utilized for such purposes, and Section 4.5 is concerned with the application of such ideas, largely to limited-information estimators. Section 4.6 covers general criteria for identification and overidentification. Logically, a discussion of this kind should precede questions of estimation, and this is indeed the path followed in most textbooks. However, in demonstrating certain propositions in this section we find it useful to have already covered the estimation techniques, and this is why we have reversed the normal order of exposition. In Section 4.7 we turn away from primary emphasis on estimation and identification of the structural form to discuss briefly the efficient estimation of the reduced form. Section 4.8 is a brief account of an expanding literature on finite sample properties of some of the limited-information estimators considered earlier in the chapter. Simultaneous models with serially correlated errors are considered in Section 4.9. A short summary as Section 4.10 concludes the chapter.

4.2 Formalization and notation

We can represent the structural form of a linear simultaneous stochastic model as

$$\begin{aligned}\mathbf{y}_1 &= Y_1\beta_1 + X_1\gamma_1 + \mathbf{u}_1 = H_1\delta_1 + \mathbf{u}_1\\ \mathbf{y}_2 &= Y_2\beta_2 + X_2\gamma_2 + \mathbf{u}_2 = H_2\delta_2 + \mathbf{u}_2\\ &\vdots\\ \mathbf{y}_G &= Y_G\beta_G + X_G\gamma_G + \mathbf{u}_G = H_G\delta_G + \mathbf{u}_G.\end{aligned} \tag{4.10}$$

Here we assume that all definitional equations have been "solved out" of the model and that the resultant behavioral equations have been normalized so one endogenous variable can be isolated on the left-hand side of each equation. Then for $i=1,\ldots,G$, $\mathbf{y}_i$ is an $n\times 1$ vector of observations on the ith such endogenous variable, Y_i is an $n\times G_i$ matrix of observations on the other G_i endogenous variables in the ith equation, X_i is an $n\times K_i$ matrix of observations on the K_i exogenous variables in this equation ("predetermined" if lagged endogenous variables are present in the model) and $\mathbf{u}_i$ is an $n\times 1$ vector of random variables. Finally, H_i is the $n\times(G_i+K_i)$ matrix $[Y_i \;\; X_i]$ and $\boldsymbol{\delta}_i$ is the $(G_i+K_i)\times 1$ vector $(\beta_i' \;\; \gamma_i')'$. In the whole system of equations we assume there are G endogenous variables and K exogenous variables. The observations on the K exogenous variables are given by an $n\times K$ matrix X.

Except in Section 4.9, we place the following simplifying assumptions on the random terms of the model:

(i) The expectation of the random vector $\mathbf{u}_i$ is $\mathbf{0}$, $i=1,\ldots,G$.

(ii) Errors are contemporaneously correlated. That is,

$$\begin{aligned}\mathcal{E}(u_{si}u_{tj}) &= 0, && s\neq t,\\ &= \sigma_{ij}, && s=t, \quad \forall i,j=1,\ldots,G,\end{aligned}$$

or, alternatively, $\mathcal{E}(\mathbf{u}_i\mathbf{u}_j') = \sigma_{ij}I_n$.

(iii) Each random vector $\mathbf{u}_i$ has a multivariate normal distribution with mean 0 and covariance matrix $\sigma_{ii}I$.

We can write the model and the assumptions more succinctly as

$$\begin{aligned}&\mathbf{y} = H\boldsymbol{\delta} + \mathbf{u}, && \mathcal{E}(\mathbf{u}) = \mathbf{0},\\ &V(\mathbf{u}) = \Sigma\otimes I, && \mathbf{u}\sim N(0,\Sigma\otimes I),\end{aligned} \tag{4.11}$$

where $\mathbf{y}=(\mathbf{y}_1'\ldots\mathbf{y}_G')'$, $\mathbf{u}=(\mathbf{u}_1'\ldots\mathbf{u}_G')'$, $\boldsymbol{\delta}=(\boldsymbol{\delta}_1'\ldots\boldsymbol{\delta}_G')'$, H is the block diagonal matrix

$$\begin{bmatrix} H_1 & & \mathbf{0}\\ & \ddots & \\ \mathbf{0} & & H_G\end{bmatrix},$$

and Σ is the symmetric matrix, assumed to be positive definite, whose i,jth element is σ_{ij}. The statistical model (4.11) is known as the *linear simultaneous-equation model* or the full-information model.

Sometimes it is more convenient to assemble the equations differently and write the model as

$$YB + X\Gamma = U, \tag{4.12}$$

where Y is an $n \times G$ matrix of observations on the G endogenous variables, X is a $n \times K$ matrix of observations on the K predetermined variables,[2] B is a $G \times G$ matrix of the coefficients of the endogenous variables in our equations, Γ is a $K \times G$ matrix of the coefficients of the predetermined variables in our equations, and u is the $n \times G$ matrix $(\mathbf{u}_1 \dots \mathbf{u}_G)$. It follows that some of the elements of B are known a priori to be equal to 1 or 0, since $\mathbf{y}_i$ has a coefficient of 1 in the ith equation and some endogenous variables are excluded from certain equations. Similarly, some of the elements of Γ are known a priori to be 0 as some of the predetermined variables are excluded from each equation. Finally, the assumptions of (4.11) imply that the rows of U are independent random vectors normally distributed with expectation $\mathbf{0}$ and covariance matrix Σ.

In order for our model to have a reduced form, we assume that B is a nonsingular matrix. The reduced form is then given by

$$Y = -X\Gamma B^{-1} + UB^{-1} = X\Pi + V. \tag{4.13}$$

From our assumptions it follows also that the rows of V are independent random vectors normally distributed with expectation $\mathbf{0}$ and covariance matrix $\Omega = B^{-1\prime}\Sigma B^{-1}$. Finally taking[3] the vec of both sides of (4.13) we can write the reduced form as

$$\mathbf{y} = (I \otimes X)\boldsymbol{\pi} + \mathbf{v},$$

where $\boldsymbol{\pi} = \operatorname{vec} \Pi$, $\mathbf{v} = \operatorname{vec} V$. Clearly $\mathbf{v}$ has a normal distribution with expectation $\mathbf{0}$ and covariance matrix $\Omega \otimes I$.

Sometimes our interest is in making statistical inference about only one of the equations in our model, say the first one. It may even be the case that we do not know the exact form of the other equations in the model. All we have specified is this first equation (hereafter "equation 1") and the reduced form of the right-hand endogenous variables of this equation. That is, we have the following equations:

$$\mathbf{y}_1 = Y_1 \boldsymbol{\beta}_1 + X_1 \boldsymbol{\gamma}_1 + \mathbf{u}_1 = H_1 \boldsymbol{\delta}_1 + \mathbf{u}_1$$

$$Y_1 = X\Pi_1 + V_1,$$

where Π_1 is the appropriate submatrix of Π, V_1 the appropriate submatrix of V. This system of equations is often known as the *limited-information model,* limited because we do not impose the complete specification of all the equations in our model. If all the equations of the structural form of our model are completely specified and utilized, we say we have the *full-information model.*

In both the limited-information case and the full-information case the statistical assumptions made differ drastically from those made in the linear regression model. The implication of the differences in assumptions is that unlike the linear regression model, best linear unbiased estimators are not available to us for simultaneous-equation models. In fact, the best we can hope for are consistent estimators that are asymptotically efficient. As we shall see, instrumental variables estimation is a general method of obtaining estimators for our model that have these properties.

4.3 The limited-information model

Introduction

As mentioned above, the limited-information model arises when the economist is interested in making statistical inference about the parameters of a single equation of his model. We assume that this equation has been specified, but the other structural-form equations still remain unspecified. The only additional information the economist has is the reduced-form equations of the right-hand endogenous variables of the equation of interest. We write the model as

$$\mathbf{y}_1 = Y_1 \boldsymbol{\beta}_1 + X_1 \boldsymbol{\gamma}_1 + \mathbf{u}_1 = H_1 \boldsymbol{\delta}_1 + \mathbf{u}_1$$

$$Y_1 = X\Pi_1 + V_1,$$

where Y_1 is an $n \times G_1$ matrix of observations of the right-hand endogenous variables, X_1 is an $n \times K_1$ matrix of observations of the exogenous variables appearing in the equation, X is the $n \times K$ matrix of observations on all the exogenous variables appearing in the system, $H_1 = [Y_1 \;\; X_1]$ and $\boldsymbol{\delta}_1 = (\boldsymbol{\beta}_1' \;\; \boldsymbol{\gamma}_1')'$. The second equation $Y_1 = X\Pi_1 + V_1$ is the reduced-form equation for Y_1.

We assume that the rows of $(\mathbf{u}_1, V_1)$ are statistically independent, identically normally distributed random vectors with mean 0 and covariance matrix

$$\Sigma = \begin{bmatrix} \sigma^2 & \boldsymbol{\phi}' \\ \boldsymbol{\phi} & \Omega_1 \end{bmatrix}.$$

For the purposes of developing our asymptotic theory we assume that $X'X/n$ tends to a positive definite matrix M as n tends to infinity.

Properties of ordinary least squares

The fact that $\phi \neq 0$ implies that Y_1 is correlated with $\mathbf{u}_1$ in the first equation. In turn, this means that the ordinary least-squares estimators (OLSEs) of $\boldsymbol{\delta}_1$ are biased and inconsistent. The OLSEs of $\boldsymbol{\delta}_1$ are

$$\hat{\boldsymbol{\delta}}_1 = (H_1'H_1)^{-1}H_1'\mathbf{y}_1 = \boldsymbol{\delta}_1 + (H_1'H_1)^{-1}H_1'\mathbf{u}_1.$$

Therefore, $\mathcal{E}(\hat{\boldsymbol{\delta}}_1) = \boldsymbol{\delta}_1 + \mathcal{E}(H_1'H_1)^{-1}H_1'\mathbf{u}_1$. The expectation of the right-hand side is not the null vector and thus $\mathcal{E}(\hat{\boldsymbol{\delta}}_1) \neq \boldsymbol{\delta}_1$. Moreover,

$$\hat{\boldsymbol{\delta}}_1 = \boldsymbol{\delta}_1 + \left(\frac{H_1'H_1}{n}\right)^{-1} \frac{H_1'\mathbf{u}_1}{n},$$

where

$$\frac{H_1'H_1}{n} = \begin{bmatrix} Y_1'Y_1/n & Y_1'X_1/n \\ X_1'Y_1/n & X_1'X_1/n \end{bmatrix} \quad \text{and} \quad \frac{H_1'\mathbf{u}_1}{n} = \begin{bmatrix} Y_1'\mathbf{u}_1/n \\ X_1'\mathbf{u}_1/n \end{bmatrix}.$$

Now

$$\frac{Y_1'Y_1}{n} = \frac{\Pi_1X'X\Pi_1}{n} + \frac{\Pi_1'X'V_1}{n} + \frac{V_1'X\Pi}{n} + \frac{V_1'V_1}{n}$$

$$\frac{Y_1'X_1}{n} = \frac{\Pi_1'X'X_1}{n} + \frac{V_1'X_1}{n}.$$

It follows that

$$Y_1'Y_1/n \xrightarrow{p} \Pi_1'M\Pi_1 + \Omega_1,$$

$$Y_1'X_1/n \xrightarrow{p} \Pi_1'M_1$$

where $M_1 = \lim X'X_1/n$, and thus

$$\operatorname{plim} \frac{H_1'H_1}{n} = \begin{bmatrix} \Pi_1'M\Pi_1 + \Omega_1 & \Pi_1'M_1 \\ M_1'\Pi_1 & M_{11} \end{bmatrix},$$

where $M_{11} = \lim X_1'X_1/n$, a submatrix of M. Similarly $Y_1'\mathbf{u}_1/n \xrightarrow{p} \boldsymbol{\phi}$ and $X_1'\mathbf{u}_1/n \xrightarrow{p} \mathbf{0}$. Hence

$$\hat{\boldsymbol{\delta}}_1 - \boldsymbol{\delta}_1 \xrightarrow{p} \begin{bmatrix} \Pi_1'M\Pi_1 + \Omega_1 & \Pi_1'M_1 \\ M_1'\Pi_1 & M_{11} \end{bmatrix}^{-1} \begin{bmatrix} \boldsymbol{\phi} \\ \mathbf{0} \end{bmatrix},$$

$$\neq \mathbf{0}.$$

In general, therefore, the OLS estimates are not consistent.

Instrumental variables estimation and the Cramer–Rao bound

The inconsistency of the OLSE of $\boldsymbol{\delta}_1$ arises from the fact that the correlation between Y_1 and $\mathbf{u}_1$ implies that $\operatorname{plim} H_1'\mathbf{u}_1/n \neq \mathbf{0}$. In order to obtain a consistent estimator of δ_1 we need a set of instruments for H_1. From the equation $Y_1 = X\Pi_1 + V_1$ we see that the matrix of exogenous variables X is correlated with the vectors of Y_1 and therefore with H_1. Moreover, $\text{plim}\, X'\mathbf{u}_1/n = \mathbf{0}$. It follows that a set of instruments can be obtained from X. Although it will by no means exhaust the list of potential instruments, it will be useful to consider in the first instance instruments Z that are linear combinations of the exogenous variables, that is,

$$Z = XA,$$

where A is a $K \times (G_1 + K_1)$ matrix of rank $G_1 + K_1$. We assume that $K \geq G_1 + K_1$ for the time being. The opposite case will be considered in Section 4.6 on identification.

We shall choose A in such a way that the resultant IV estimator $\bar{\delta}_1$ is a best, asymptotically normal (BAN) estimator. That is, A is chosen so the asymptotic covariance matrix of $\bar{\delta}_1$ attains the (asymptotic) Cramer–Rao lower bound. We shall now work out this bound.

Write the limited-information model as

$$\mathbf{y}_1 = Y_1 \boldsymbol{\beta}_1 + X_1 \boldsymbol{\gamma}_1 + \mathbf{u}_1 = H_1 \boldsymbol{\delta}_1 + \mathbf{u}_1$$

$$\mathbf{y}_2 = (I \otimes X)\boldsymbol{\pi}_1 + \mathbf{v}_1,$$

where $\mathbf{y}_2 = \text{vec}\, Y_1$, $\boldsymbol{\pi}_1 = \text{vec}\, \Pi_1$, and $\mathbf{v}_1 = \text{vec}\, V_1$. With this notation we can write the model more succinctly as

$$\mathbf{y} = H\boldsymbol{\delta} + \mathbf{u}, \tag{4.14}$$

where $\mathbf{y} = (\mathbf{y}_1' \;\; \mathbf{y}_2')'$, $\mathbf{u} = (\mathbf{u}_1' \;\; \mathbf{v}_1')'$, $\boldsymbol{\delta} = (\boldsymbol{\delta}_1' \;\; \boldsymbol{\pi}_1')'$, and

$$H = \begin{pmatrix} H_1 & \mathbf{O} \\ \mathbf{O} & I \otimes X \end{pmatrix}.$$

By our assumptions $\mathbf{u}$ has a multivariate normal distribution with mean $\mathbf{0}$ and covariance matrix $\psi = \Sigma \otimes I$, where in this context

$$\Sigma = \begin{pmatrix} \sigma^2 & \boldsymbol{\phi}' \\ \boldsymbol{\phi} & \Omega_1 \end{pmatrix}.$$

From (4.14), the probability density function of $\mathbf{u}$ is

$$f(\mathbf{u}) = (2\pi)^{-n} \det \psi^{-1/2} \exp(-\tfrac{1}{2}\mathbf{u}'\psi^{-1}\mathbf{u}).$$

But $\det \psi = \det(\Sigma \otimes I) = (\det \Sigma)^n$. Hence

$$f(\mathbf{u}) = (2\pi)^{-n} (\det \Sigma)^{-n/2} \exp(-\tfrac{1}{2}\mathbf{u}'\psi^{-1}\mathbf{u}).$$

It follows that the probability density function of $\mathbf{y}$ is

$$g(\mathbf{y}) = |J|(2\pi)^{-n}(\det \Sigma)^{-n/2} \exp[-\tfrac{1}{2}(\mathbf{y} - H\boldsymbol{\delta})'\psi^{-1}(\mathbf{y} - H\boldsymbol{\delta})],$$

where $|J|$ is the absolute value of the Jacobian of the transformation from the $\mathbf{u}$ elements to the $\mathbf{y}$ elements. But J is the determinant of an upper triangular matrix with 1's in the main diagonal elements, and so $|J|$ is 1. Thus the log-likelihood function is

$$l(\delta, \Sigma; \mathbf{y}) = k + \frac{n}{2} \log \det \Sigma^{-1} - \frac{1}{2}(\mathbf{y} - H\delta)'\psi^{-1}(\mathbf{y} - H\delta), \quad (4.15)$$

where k is a constant.

Finally noting that $\operatorname{tr} ABC = (\operatorname{vec} C')'(B' \otimes I) \operatorname{vec} A$, it follows that $\mathbf{u}'(\Sigma^{-1} \otimes I)\mathbf{u} = \operatorname{tr} \Sigma^{-1}U'U$, where $U \equiv (\mathbf{u}_1 \ V_1)$, and hence we can write the log-likelihood function as

$$l = k + \frac{n}{2} \log \det \Sigma^{-1} - \frac{1}{2} \operatorname{tr} \Sigma^{-1}U'U. \quad (4.16)$$

Using the results $\partial \log \det A/\partial A = (A')^{-1}$ and $(\partial/\partial A) \operatorname{tr} AB = B'$, we maximize this first with respect to Σ^{-1} to obtain the necessary condition

$$\frac{\partial l}{\partial \Sigma^{-1}} = \frac{n}{2}\Sigma = \frac{1}{2}U'U = \mathbf{O}.$$

Solving gives $\Sigma = U'U/n \equiv S$, and substituting this in (4.16) gives the concentrated log-likelihood function

$$l^{**} = k - \frac{n}{2} \log \det S - \frac{1}{2}\mathbf{u}'(S^{-1} \otimes I)\mathbf{u}.$$

But $\mathbf{u}'(S^{-1} \otimes I)\mathbf{u} = \operatorname{tr} S^{-1}U'U = 2/n$. Thus

$$l^{**} = k^{**} - \frac{n}{2} \log \det S,$$

where k^{**} is a constant.

Maximizing l^{**} with respect to Π_1 gives a value of Π_1 equal to $(X'M_{\mathbf{u}}X)^{-1}X'M_{\mathbf{u}}Y_1$, where $M_{\mathbf{u}} = I - \mathbf{u}_1(\mathbf{u}_1'\mathbf{u}_1')^{-1}\mathbf{u}_1'$. Substituting this value into S gives

$$\det S^* = \frac{\mathbf{u}'\mathbf{u}}{n}\left|\frac{Y_1'M_{\mathbf{u}}[I - M_{\mathbf{u}}X(X'M_{\mathbf{u}}X)^{-1}X'M_{\mathbf{u}}]M_{\mathbf{u}}Y_1}{n}\right|.$$

Imagine now a regression of Y_1 on X and $\mathbf{u}_1$. Write $M = I - X(X'X)^{-1}X'$. Considering alternative stepwise fitting procedures, it will be apparent that the residual sum of squares in the regression of $M_{\mathbf{u}}Y_1$ on $M_{\mathbf{u}}X$ is equal to the residual sum of squares in the regression of MY_1 on $M\mathbf{u}$. It follows that

$$|Y_1'M_u[I-M_uX(X'M_uX)^{-1}X'M_u]M_uY_1|$$
$$=|Y_1'M[I-M\mathbf{u}_1(\mathbf{u}_1'M\mathbf{u}_1)^{-1}\mathbf{u}_1'M]MY_1|$$
$$=\left|Y_1'MY_1-\frac{Y_1'M\mathbf{u}_1\mathbf{u}_1'MY_1}{\mathbf{u}_1'M\mathbf{u}_1}\right|.$$

Using the partitioned determinant,[4] the last determinant is equal to

$$\frac{1}{\mathbf{u}_1'M\mathbf{u}_1}\begin{vmatrix}\mathbf{u}_1'M\mathbf{u}_1 & \mathbf{u}_1'MY_1\\ Y_1'M\mathbf{u}_1 & Y_1'MY_1\end{vmatrix}=\frac{1}{\mathbf{u}_1'M\mathbf{u}_1}|(Y_1\ \ \mathbf{u}_1)'M(Y_1\ \ \mathbf{u}_1)|.$$

Thus we can write

$$\det S^*=\frac{\mathbf{u}_1'\mathbf{u}_1}{\mathbf{u}_1'M\mathbf{u}_1}|(Y_1\ \ \mathbf{u}_1)'M(Y_1\ \ \mathbf{u}_1)|.$$

Furthermore,

$$(Y_1\ \ \mathbf{u}_1)'M(Y_1\ \ \mathbf{u}_1)=\begin{pmatrix}I & -\beta_1\\ \mathbf{0}' & 1\end{pmatrix}'(Y_1\ \ \mathbf{y}_1)'M(Y_1\ \ \mathbf{y}_1)\begin{pmatrix}I & -\beta_1\\ \mathbf{0}' & 1\end{pmatrix},$$

where the first partitioned matrix on the right-hand side has a determinant equal to 1. Therefore,

$$|(Y_1\ \ \mathbf{u}_1)'M(Y_1\ \ \mathbf{u}_1)|=|(Y_1\ \ \mathbf{y}_1)'M(Y_1\ \ \mathbf{y}_1)|,$$

which does not depend on $\boldsymbol{\delta}_1$. Thus the log-likelihood function, concentrated in $\boldsymbol{\delta}_1$, is

$$l^*=k^*+\frac{n}{2}\log\frac{\mathbf{u}_1'M\mathbf{u}_1}{\mathbf{u}_1'\mathbf{u}_1}, \tag{4.17}$$

where k^* is a constant not dependent on $\boldsymbol{\delta}_1$.

The asymptotic Cramer–Rao lower bound is

$$-\operatorname{plim}\frac{1}{n}\begin{bmatrix}\dfrac{\partial^2 l}{\partial\boldsymbol{\delta}_1\,\partial\boldsymbol{\delta}_1'} & \dfrac{\partial^2 l}{\partial\boldsymbol{\delta}_1\,\partial\boldsymbol{\theta}'}\\ \dfrac{\partial^2 l}{\partial\boldsymbol{\theta}\,\partial\boldsymbol{\delta}_1'} & \dfrac{\partial^2 l}{\partial\boldsymbol{\theta}\,\partial\boldsymbol{\theta}'}\end{bmatrix}^{-1}=\begin{bmatrix}\bar{R}_1 & \bar{R}_2\\ \bar{R}_2 & \bar{R}_3\end{bmatrix}^{-1}=\bar{R}^{-1},$$

where $\boldsymbol{\theta}=(\operatorname{vec}\Pi_1'\ \operatorname{vec}\Sigma')'$. We are interested in the lower bound for $\boldsymbol{\delta}_1$ only, that is, in the submatrix of $\bar{R}^{-1}$ corresponding to $\bar{R}_1$. Denoting this submatrix by R^{-1}, we note that

$$R^{-1}=(\bar{R}_1-\bar{R}_2\bar{R}_3^{-1}\bar{R}_2')^{-1}.$$

In the case where Σ is unrestricted it can be proved (see, for example, Anderson and Rubin 1949, pp. 46–63) that

$$R^{-1} = -\text{plim}\,\frac{1}{n}\left[\frac{\partial^2 l^*}{\partial \boldsymbol{\delta}_1\,\partial \boldsymbol{\delta}_1'}\right]^{-1}.$$

Now from expression (4.17),

$$\frac{\partial l^*}{\partial \boldsymbol{\delta}_1} = n\left(\frac{H_1'\mathbf{u}_1}{\mathbf{u}_1'\mathbf{u}_1} - \frac{H_1'M\mathbf{u}_1}{\mathbf{u}_1'M\mathbf{u}_1}\right),$$

and

$$\frac{\partial l^*}{\partial \boldsymbol{\delta}_1\,\partial \boldsymbol{\delta}_1'} = 2n\left[\frac{(H_1'\mathbf{u}_1)^2}{(\mathbf{u}_1'\mathbf{u}_1)^2} - \frac{(H_1'M\mathbf{u}_1)^2}{(\mathbf{u}_1'M\mathbf{u}_1)^2}\right] + n\left[\frac{H_1'MH_1}{\mathbf{u}_1'M\mathbf{u}_1} - \frac{H_1'H_1}{\mathbf{u}_1'\mathbf{u}_1}\right],$$

$$= A + B,$$

say. Then clearly $\text{plim}(A/n) = \mathbf{O}$ and

$$\text{plim}\,\frac{B}{n} = \frac{1}{\sigma^2}\,\text{plim}\,\frac{1}{n}\begin{bmatrix} \Pi_1'X'X\Pi_1 & \Pi_1'X'X_1 \\ X_1'X\Pi_1 & X_1'X_1 \end{bmatrix}$$

$$= \frac{1}{\sigma^2}\,\text{plim}\left(\frac{H_1'NH_1}{n}\right),$$

where $N = X(X'X)^{-1}X'$. Thus the Cramer–Rao lower bound for a consistent estimator of $\boldsymbol{\delta}_1$ is

$$\sigma^2\,\text{plim}(H_1'NH_1/n)^{-1}.$$

Instrumental variables estimators that achieve the asymptotic Cramer–Rao lower bound

Several estimators of $\boldsymbol{\delta}_1$ achieve the asymptotic Cramer–Rao lower bound, and all these have an IV estimation interpretation (although this may not have been the original motivation behind the estimator). We deal with each of these in turn.

(a) *The two-stage least-squares estimator $\hat{\boldsymbol{\delta}}_1$*

The two-stage least-squares estimator (2SLSE) represents a straightforward application of the projective estimator discussed in Section 2.2. The instrument set (Z) is simply the set X of all the exogenous or predetermined variables, and the associated projection matrix (P_Z) is $N = X(X'X)^{-1}X'$. The 2SLSE is then

$$\hat{\boldsymbol{\delta}}_1 = (H_1'NH_1)^{-1}H_1'N\mathbf{y}_1,$$

and

$$\sqrt{n}(\hat{\boldsymbol{\delta}}_1 - \boldsymbol{\delta}_1) \xrightarrow{d} N(\mathbf{0}, V),$$

where $V = \text{plim}(H_1'NH_1/n)^{-1}$. It follows that the 2SLSE is a best asymptotically normal estimator.

Writing $\hat{H}_1 = X(X'X)^{-1}X'H_1 = NH_1$, it will be apparent that $\hat{H}_1$ is being utilized as an instrument for H_1, so that in terms of the categorization employed above, $\hat{H}_1 = XA$, where $A = (X'X)^{-1}X'H_1$. In terms of the argument of Section 2.4, the method may be interpreted as follows: First regress H_1 on X to obtain $\hat{H}_1$, and then regress $\mathbf{y}_1$ on $\hat{H}_1$. In other words, one utilizes the structural form with Y_1 replaced by its fitted value $\hat{Y}_1$. The resulting estimate $\hat{\boldsymbol{\delta}}_1$ is the two-stage least-squares estimator. This was indeed the original line of attack on the problem by the originators (Theil 1953a, b and Basmann 1957), from which the name is derived. We recall from Chapter 2, however, that the two-stage least-squares interpretation is of wide applicability as a computational device associated with instrumental variables methods.

(b) *Limited maximum-likelihood estimators* $\tilde{\boldsymbol{\delta}}_1$

The limited maximum-likelihood estimators (MLEs) are obtained by maximizing the likelihood function with respect to the parameters $\boldsymbol{\delta}_1$, Π_1, and

$$\Sigma = \begin{bmatrix} \sigma^2 & \boldsymbol{\phi}' \\ \boldsymbol{\phi} & \Omega \end{bmatrix}.$$

This can be carried out in a stepwise fashion. First we maximize the log-likelihood function l with respect to Σ and form the concentrated log-likelihood function l^*. Next we maximize l^* with respect to $\boldsymbol{\delta} = (\boldsymbol{\delta}_1' \ \text{vec}\, \Pi_1')'$. The maximum-likelihood estimators of $\boldsymbol{\delta}_1$ and Π_1 are thus obtained by solving the following system of nonlinear equations arising from the first-order conditions:

$$\frac{\partial l^{**}}{\partial \boldsymbol{\delta}} = H'(S^{-1} \otimes I)\mathbf{u} = \mathbf{0}.$$

It is well known that maximum-likelihood estimators are consistent and asymptotically efficient in the sense that their asymptotic covariance matrix attains the Cramer–Rao lower bound. Hausman (1975) and Byron (1978) show that the limited maximum-likelihood estimator of $\boldsymbol{\delta}_1$ has an IV interpretation. Byron arrives at this interpretation of the limited-information maximum-likelihood (LIML) estimators by forming the likelihood function of the reduced-form parameters. We can write the reduced form of the limited-information model as

$$\mathbf{y}_1 = X\boldsymbol{\pi}_1 + \mathbf{v}_1 \qquad Y_1 = X\Pi_1 + V_1$$

or more succinctly as

$$Y^* = X\Pi^* + V^*, \tag{4.18}$$

where $Y^* = [\mathbf{y}_1 \ \ Y_1]$, $\Pi^* = [\pi_1 \ \ \Pi_1]$, $V^* = [\mathbf{v}_1 \ \ V_1]$, and X is the partitioned matrix $[X_1 \ \ X_2]$.

Forming the likelihood function and maximizing this with respect to the covariance matrix of vec V^* gives the concentrated reduced-form log-likelihood

$$l^* = -\frac{n}{2} \log \det \Omega^*, \tag{4.19}$$

where $\Omega^* = V^{*\prime}V^*/n$ and $V^* = Y^* - X\Pi^*$. The MLEs of the reduced-form parameters must take account of the overidentification restrictions (Section 4.6). These restrictions may be obtained by postmultiplying (4.18) by $\boldsymbol{\beta}^* = [1, -\boldsymbol{\beta}']'$ to get

$$X_1\gamma_1 + \mathbf{u}_1 = X\Pi^*\boldsymbol{\beta}^* + V^*\boldsymbol{\beta}^*.$$

This equation implies that we must place the following restrictions on the reduced-form parameters Π^*:

$$\Pi^*\boldsymbol{\beta}^* = \begin{pmatrix} \gamma_1 \\ \mathbf{0} \end{pmatrix} \qquad \text{or} \qquad \Pi^*\boldsymbol{\beta}^* + R\boldsymbol{\gamma}_1 = \mathbf{0}, \tag{4.20}$$

where $R' = [I \ \ \mathbf{0}']$. Maximum-likelihood estimation for the reduced-form parameters involved maximizing (4.19) subject to the restrictions (4.20). The Lagrangian function is

$$\mathfrak{L} = -\frac{n}{2} \log \det \Omega^* - \boldsymbol{\mu}'(\Pi^*\boldsymbol{\beta}^* + R\boldsymbol{\gamma}_1).$$

The first-order conditions are

$$\frac{\partial \mathfrak{L}}{\partial \Pi^*} = X'\tilde{V}^*\tilde{\Omega}^{*-1} - \tilde{\boldsymbol{\mu}}\tilde{\boldsymbol{\beta}}^{*\prime} = \mathbf{O} \tag{4.21}$$

$$\frac{\partial \mathfrak{L}}{\partial \boldsymbol{\beta}_1} = \tilde{\Pi}'\tilde{\boldsymbol{\mu}} = \mathbf{0} \tag{4.22}$$

$$\frac{\partial \mathfrak{L}}{\partial \boldsymbol{\gamma}_1} = R'\tilde{\boldsymbol{\mu}} = \mathbf{0} \tag{4.23}$$

$$\frac{\partial \mathfrak{L}}{\partial \boldsymbol{\mu}} = \tilde{\Pi}^*\tilde{\boldsymbol{\beta}}^* + R\tilde{\boldsymbol{\gamma}}_1 = \mathbf{0}, \tag{4.24}$$

where the tilde ($\tilde{}$) signifies constrained estimates.

From (4.21) we get

$$\tilde{\boldsymbol{\mu}} = X'\tilde{V}^*\tilde{\boldsymbol{\beta}}^*/\tilde{\sigma}_{\mathbf{u}}^2$$

where $\tilde{\sigma}_{\mathbf{u}}^2 = \tilde{\beta}^{*\prime}\tilde{\Omega}^*\tilde{\beta}^*$. Using the overidentifying restrictions (4.20) we can rewrite this as

$$\tilde{\mu} = X'H^*\tilde{\delta}^*/\tilde{\sigma}_{\mathbf{u}}^2, \tag{4.25}$$

where $H^* = [Y^*, X_1]$ and $\tilde{\delta}^{*\prime} = [\tilde{\beta}^{*\prime}\tilde{\gamma}_1']$.

Substituting (4.25) in the first-order conditions for β_1 and γ_1 we get

$$\tilde{\Pi}_1'X'H^*\tilde{\delta}^* = \mathbf{0}, \qquad X_1'H^*\tilde{\delta}^* = \mathbf{0}.$$

But as $H^*\tilde{\delta}^* = -\mathbf{y} + H_1\tilde{\delta}_1$, where $\tilde{\delta}_1$ is the MLE of δ_1, we have, letting $\tilde{Y}_1 = X\tilde{\Pi}_1$,

$$\tilde{Y}_1'\mathbf{y}_1 = \tilde{Y}_1'H_1\tilde{\delta}_1, \qquad X_1'\mathbf{y}_1 = X_1'H_1\tilde{\delta}_1.$$

We have therefore shown that the MLE of $\tilde{\delta}_1$ can be written as the IV estimator

$$\tilde{\delta}_1 = (\tilde{H}_1'H_1)^{-1}\tilde{H}_1'\mathbf{y}_1,$$

with the matrix of instruments $\tilde{H}_1 = [\tilde{Y}_1, X_1]$.

(c) *Theil's k-class estimators $\tilde{\delta}_1^k$*

For H_1 in the equation $\mathbf{y}_1 = H_1\delta_1 + \mathbf{u}_1$, the k-class estimators (Theil 1961) use $\hat{H}_1 = [Y_1 - k\hat{V}_1 X_1]$ as instruments, where $\hat{V}_1$ is the residual matrix from the regression of Y_1 on X (i.e., $\hat{V}_1 = MY_1$) and k is a scalar that is possibly random. The k-class estimators are given by

$$\tilde{\delta}_1^k = (\hat{H}_1'H_1)^{-1}\hat{H}_1'y_1.$$

Setting $k=0$ clearly gives the OLSE, and setting $k=1$ gives the 2SLSE. The probability limit of this estimator is

$$\operatorname{plim}\tilde{\delta}_1^k = \delta_1 + (\operatorname{plim}\bar{H}_1'H_1/n)^{-1}\begin{bmatrix}\operatorname{plim}Y_1'\mathbf{u}_1/n - \operatorname{plim}k\operatorname{plim}V_1'M\mathbf{u}_1/n \\ \mathbf{0}\end{bmatrix}.$$

But $\operatorname{plim}Y_1'\mathbf{u}_1/n = \operatorname{plim}V_1'M\mathbf{u}_1/n$ and $\operatorname{plim}\hat{H}_1'H_1/n \neq \mathbf{O}$. Thus for the k-class estimator to be a valid IV estimator we require $\operatorname{plim}k = 1$. However, to have the same asymptotic distribution as the optimal IVEs, k must satisfy the stricter condition $\operatorname{plim}\sqrt{n}(k-1) = 0$. To see this, assume $\operatorname{plim}k = 1$ and consider

$$\operatorname{plim}\sqrt{n}(\tilde{\delta}_1^k - \hat{\delta}_1).$$

As $\operatorname{plim}k = 1$, we can write

$$\operatorname{plim}\sqrt{n}(\tilde{\delta}_1^k - \hat{\delta}_1) = (\operatorname{plim}\hat{H}_1'H_1/n)^{-1}\begin{bmatrix}\operatorname{plim}\sqrt{n}(k-1)\operatorname{plim}V_1'M\mathbf{u}_1/n \\ \mathbf{0}\end{bmatrix}.$$

It follows that $\tilde{\delta}_1^k$ and $\hat{\delta}_1$ have the same limiting distribution only if $\text{plim}\sqrt{n}(k-1)=0$ as $\text{plim}\, V_1' M\mathbf{u}_1/n \neq \mathbf{0}$. The class of estimators with $\text{plim}\sqrt{n}(k-1)=0$ is further characterized in the discussion on second-order efficiency in Section 4.7.

Testing for simultaneity

So far we have simply assumed the need for an IV approach rather than a more straightforward OLS calculation. Ideally one should test for a significant simultaneity effect in advance. It is in fact convenient to do this by means of a comparison of OLS and 2SLS estimators, so that the results from the estimation technique chosen on the strength of the test are immediately on hand. A suitable procedure is based upon the Wu–Hausman methodology described in Section 2.6. We give an example that is a more or less straightforward application of the Hausman test.

Consider the following limited-information model:

$$\mathbf{y}_1 = Y_2 \boldsymbol{\alpha} + \mathbf{u} \tag{4.26a}$$

$$Y_2 = X\Pi + V. \tag{4.26b}$$

We specify that each row of the disturbance terms $(\mathbf{u}, V)$ is i.i.d. with mean zero and covariance matrix

$$\Sigma = \begin{bmatrix} \sigma^2 & \boldsymbol{\phi}' \\ \boldsymbol{\phi} & \Sigma_{\mathbf{v}} \end{bmatrix}.$$

It is desired to test the null hypothesis $H_0: \boldsymbol{\phi} = \mathbf{0}$ against the alternative $H_1: \boldsymbol{\phi} \neq \mathbf{0}$.

If H_0 is true, then the best asymptotically normal estimator of $\boldsymbol{\alpha}$ is the ordinary least-squares estimator $\hat{\boldsymbol{\alpha}}_0 = (Y_2' Y_2)^{-1} Y_2' \mathbf{y}_1$. Under H_1, however, this estimator is inconsistent. The two-stage least-squares estimator $\hat{\boldsymbol{\alpha}}_1 = (Y_2' N Y_2)^{-1} Y_2' N \mathbf{y}_1$, where $N = X(X'X)^{-1}X'$, is a BAN estimator under H_1, and is also consistent under H_0. Hausman's test statistic is based, then, on

$$\sqrt{n}\hat{\mathbf{q}} = \sqrt{n}(\hat{\boldsymbol{\alpha}}_0 - \hat{\boldsymbol{\alpha}}_1) = \sqrt{n}((Y_2' Y_2)^{-1} Y_2' \mathbf{u} - (Y_2' N Y_2)^{-1} Y_2' N \mathbf{u}). \tag{4.27}$$

The right-hand side of (4.27) is asymptotically equivalent to

$$[B^{-1} \;\; B^{-1} - A^{-1}] \begin{bmatrix} V'\mathbf{u}/\sqrt{n} \\ \Pi' X' \mathbf{u}/\sqrt{n} \end{bmatrix},$$

where $B = \text{plim}\, Y_2' Y_2/n = \Pi' M \Pi + \Sigma_{\mathbf{v}}$ and $A = \text{plim}\, Y_2' N Y_2/n = \Pi' M \Pi$. Applying a multivariate version of the central limit theorem, we find that under the null hypothesis, $\sqrt{n}\hat{\mathbf{q}}$ tends in distribution to a multivariate normal random vector with mean $\mathbf{0}$ and covariance matrix $V(\hat{\mathbf{q}}) = \sigma^2(A^{-1} - B^{-1})$. In forming a practical test statistic we need a consistent estimator of $V(\hat{\mathbf{q}})$. The obvious one to use is

$$\hat{V}(\hat{\mathbf{q}}) = \hat{\sigma}^2\left[\left(\frac{Y_2'NY_2}{n}\right)^{-1} - \left(\frac{Y_2'Y_2}{n}\right)^{-1}\right], \tag{4.28}$$

where $\hat{\sigma}^2 = \hat{\mathbf{u}}'\hat{\mathbf{u}}/n$ and $\hat{\mathbf{u}} = \mathbf{y}_1 - Y_2\hat{\alpha}_1$ is the two-stage least-squares residual vector. The Hausman test statistic is obtained by substituting (4.27) and (4.28) into the expression $n\hat{\mathbf{q}}'\hat{V}(\hat{\mathbf{q}})^{-1}\hat{\mathbf{q}}$. Under H_0 this test statistic has a limiting central chi-squared distribution, with G degrees of freedom.

The above development can easily be modified to allow for the presence of exogenous variables in the equation under test [e.g., equation (4.26a) above]. We recall from Section 2.6 that in such a test one need only take into account the estimated coefficients on the endogenous variables. The test statistic resulting from a slightly more general model with exogenous variables in the equation under test will therefore have the form of the expression $n\hat{\mathbf{q}}'\hat{V}(\hat{\mathbf{q}})^{-1}\hat{\mathbf{q}}$.

4.4 The full-information model

In many instances one will have available not only the specification of the structural-form equation under active consideration but also the specification of all the other structural-form equations of the model. If this is the case, this additional information should give rise to estimators of the parameters of any single equation that are more efficient asymptotically than the optimal estimators derived from the limited-information model. We now consider the structural form of the complete model:

$$\begin{aligned}
\mathbf{y}_1 &= Y_1\beta_1 + X_1\gamma_1 + \mathbf{u}_1 = H_1\delta_1 + \mathbf{u}_1\\
\mathbf{y}_2 &= Y_2\beta_2 + X_2\gamma_2 + \mathbf{u}_2 = H_2\delta_2 + \mathbf{u}_2\\
&\ \vdots\\
\mathbf{y}_G &= Y_G\beta_G + X_G\gamma_G + \mathbf{u}_G = H_G\delta_G + \mathbf{u}_G,
\end{aligned}$$

or more compactly,

$$\mathbf{y} = H\boldsymbol{\delta} + \mathbf{u}.$$

As mentioned above, the statistical assumptions of the full-information model are

$$\mathcal{E}(\mathbf{u}) = \mathbf{0}, \qquad V(\mathbf{u}) = \Sigma \otimes I, \qquad \mathbf{u} \sim N(\mathbf{0}, \Sigma \otimes I),$$

where the notation is given in Section 4.2. The corresponding reduced form is

$$\mathbf{y} = (I \otimes X)\pi + \mathbf{v},$$

where we assume $\mathcal{E}(\mathbf{v}) = \mathbf{0}$, $V(\mathbf{v}) = \Omega \otimes I$, and $\mathbf{v} \sim N(\mathbf{0}, \Omega \otimes I)$.

Since the H_i contain current endogenous variables, it follows that plim $H_i' \mathbf{u}_i / n \neq \mathbf{0}$ and plim $H' \mathbf{u}/n \neq \mathbf{0}$. Thus consistent estimation requires that we find a set of instruments for H in the equation $\mathbf{y} = H\delta + \mathbf{u}$. The reduced form tells us that $I \otimes X$ is available to us for this purpose. As we shall see, this by no means exhausts the list of possible instruments. Before considering such matters, however, it will be helpful to begin by writing down the full-information likelihood function and stating a result concerning the Cramer–Rao lower bound.

The likelihood function and the Cramer–Rao lower bound for the full-information model

To obtain the likelihood function for the full-information model, it is convenient to write the structural form as

$$YB + X\Gamma = U$$

or

$$B'\mathbf{y}_t + \Gamma'\mathbf{x}_t = \mathbf{u}_t, \qquad t = 1, \ldots, n,$$

where $\mathbf{y}_t$ is the column vector containing the tth observations on all the current endogenous variables, and so forth. Then the reduced form can be written as

$$\mathbf{y}_t = \Pi'\mathbf{x}_t + \mathbf{v}_t$$

where $\Pi' = -B^{-1\prime}\Gamma'$, $\mathbf{v}_t = B^{-1\prime}\mathbf{u}_t$. From our assumptions it follows that $\mathbf{y}_t \sim N(\Pi'\mathbf{x}_t, \Omega)$, where $\Omega = B^{-1\prime}\Sigma B^{-1}$. Hence the probability density function of $\mathbf{y}_t$ is

$$f(\mathbf{y}_t) = k(\det \Omega)^{-1/2} \exp[-\tfrac{1}{2}(\mathbf{y}_t - \Pi'\mathbf{x}_t)'\Omega^{-1}(\mathbf{y}_t - \Pi'\mathbf{x}_t)],$$

with k a constant, and the likelihood function is

$$L(\Pi, \Omega; \mathbf{y}_t) = k^n (\det \Omega)^{-n/2} \exp\left[-\tfrac{1}{2}\sum_t (\mathbf{y}_t - \Pi'\mathbf{x}_t)'\Omega^{-1}(\mathbf{y}_t - \Pi'\mathbf{x}_t)\right].$$

But

$$\sum_t (\mathbf{y}_t - \Pi'\mathbf{x}_t)'\Omega^{-1}(\mathbf{y}_t - \Pi'\mathbf{x}_t) = \operatorname{tr} \sum_t \mathbf{v}_t'\Omega^{-1}\mathbf{v}_t = \operatorname{tr} \Omega^{-1} \sum_t \mathbf{v}_t \mathbf{v}_t' = \operatorname{tr} \Omega^{-1} V'V.$$

So the log-likelihood function is given by

$$l(\Pi, \Omega; \mathbf{y}_t) = k^* + \frac{n}{2} \log \det \Omega^{-1} - \frac{1}{2} \operatorname{tr} \Omega^{-1}(Y - X\Pi)'(Y - X\Pi). \qquad (4.29)$$

To get the log-likelihood function in terms of structural-form parameters we substitute $\Pi = -\Gamma B^{-1}$ and $\Omega = B^{-1\prime}\Sigma B^{-1}$ in (4.29) to get

$$l(\Gamma, B, \Sigma; \mathbf{y}_t) = k^* + \frac{n}{2} \log \det \Sigma^{-1} + n \log|\det B|$$

$$-\frac{1}{2} \operatorname{tr} \Sigma^{-1}(YB + X\Gamma)'(YB - X\Gamma).$$

Alternatively, noting that $\operatorname{tr} \Sigma^{-1}U'U = \mathbf{u}'(\Sigma^{-1} \otimes I)\mathbf{u}$, we can write this as

$$l(\boldsymbol{\delta}, \Sigma; \mathbf{y}_t) = k^* + \frac{n}{2} \log \det \Sigma^{-1} + n \log|\det B|$$

$$-\frac{1}{2}(\mathbf{y} - H\boldsymbol{\delta})'(\Sigma^{-1} \otimes I)(\mathbf{y} - H\boldsymbol{\delta}).$$

This is the version of the likelihood function used by Rothenberg and Leenders (1964) to obtain the Cramer–Rao lower bound for a consistent estimator of $\boldsymbol{\delta}$. The actual derivation is lengthy and the reader is referred to the original source for details. Here we merely present their result in the form of a theorem, without proof.

Theorem 4.1: *The asymptotic Cramer–Rao lower bound for a consistent estimator of* $\boldsymbol{\delta}$ *is*

$$\operatorname{plim} n[H'(\Sigma^{-1} \otimes N)H]^{-1},$$

where $N = X(X'X)^{-1}X'$.

We turn now to investigate methods that achieve this lower bound.

Instrumental variables estimators that achieve the Cramer–Rao lower bound

As in the limited-information model, there are several full-information estimators of $\boldsymbol{\delta}$ that achieve the asymptotic Cramer–Rao lower bound, and all of these have an IV interpretation. These estimators are studied in detail below.

(a) *The three-stage least-squares estimator* $\hat{\boldsymbol{\delta}}$

The three-stage least-squares estimator (3SLSE) can be motivated by assuming initially that Σ is known and applying the ideas of Section 3.2 concerning IV estimators in nonspherical contexts. Thus we are to consider the model

$$\mathbf{y} = H\boldsymbol{\delta} + \mathbf{u},$$

with $V(\mathbf{u}) = \Sigma \otimes I$. Let us employ as instrument matrix the Kronecker product $I \otimes X$. We may now state the following.

Proposition 4.2:

(a) *The minimum-distance matrices* (P) *associated with the IV–OLS analog and IV–GLS analog are identical, with common value* $P = \Sigma^{-1} \otimes N$, *where* $N = X(X'X)^{-1}X'$.

(b) *The IV estimator so defined is given by*

$$\delta^* = [H'(\Sigma^{-1} \otimes N)H]^{-1} H'(\Sigma^{-1} \otimes N)\mathbf{y}. \tag{4.30}$$

(c) *This estimator attains the Cramer–Rao lower bound, with asymptotic covariance matrix*

$$\operatorname{plim} n[H'(\Sigma^{-1} \otimes N)H]^{-1}. \tag{4.31}$$

Proof: (The reader may like to refer to Appendix A4 for the various properties of Kronecker products used in this proof.)

(a) It will be recalled from Section 3.2 that, in general notation, the minimum-distance matrix for the IV–OLS analog is $P_1 = Z(Z'\Omega Z)^{-1}Z'$ and that for the IV–GLS analog $P_2 = \Omega^{-1}Z(Z'\Omega^{-1}Z)^{-1}Z'\Omega^{-1}$. We need only verify that setting $Z = I \otimes X$, $\Omega = \Sigma \otimes I$ yields the desired results. Considering first the IV–OLS analog, we have

$$\begin{aligned} P_1 &= (I \otimes X)[(I \otimes X')(\Sigma \otimes I)(I \otimes X)]^{-1}(I \otimes X'), \\ &= (I \otimes X)[\Sigma \otimes (X'X)]^{-1}(I \otimes X'), \\ &= (I \otimes X)[\Sigma^{-1} \otimes (X'X)^{-1}](I \otimes X'), \\ &= \Sigma^{-1} \otimes N. \end{aligned}$$

Similarly,

$$\begin{aligned} P_2 &= (\Sigma^{-1} \otimes I)(I \otimes X)[(I \otimes X')(\Sigma^{-1} \otimes I)(I \otimes X)]^{-1}(I \otimes X')(\Sigma^{-1} \otimes I), \\ &= (\Sigma^{-1} \otimes X)[\Sigma \otimes (X'X)^{-1}](\Sigma^{-1} \otimes X'), \\ &= \Sigma^{-1} \otimes N, \\ &= P_1. \end{aligned}$$

(b) Writing $P_1 = P_2 = P$, the estimator is defined by

$$\begin{aligned} \delta^* &= (H'PH)^{-1}H'P\mathbf{y}, \\ &= [H'(\Sigma^{-1} \otimes N)H]^{-1}H'(\Sigma^{-1} \otimes N)\mathbf{y}, \end{aligned}$$

as desired.

(c) From Section 3.2, the asymptotic covariance matrix of the IV–OLS analog is $\operatorname{plim} n(H'PH)^{-1} = \operatorname{plim} n[H'(\Sigma^{-1} \otimes N)H]^{-1}$. The result follows from comparison with Theorem 4.1. ■

Usually we cannot form the estimator $\boldsymbol{\delta}^*$ because the covariance matrix Σ is unknown. The operational 3SLSE replaces Σ in expressions (4.30) and (4.31) by a consistent estimator $\hat{\Sigma}$ obtained in the following manner. First, run 2SLS on each of the equations and obtain the 2SLS residual vectors $\hat{\mathbf{u}}_i$, say. Second, estimate Σ by $\hat{\Sigma}=\{\hat{\sigma}_{ij}\}$, where $\hat{\sigma}_{ij}=\hat{\mathbf{u}}_i'\hat{\mathbf{u}}_j/n$. Substituting $\hat{\Sigma}$ for the unknown Σ, the 3SLSE is given by

$$\hat{\boldsymbol{\delta}}=(H'(\hat{\Sigma}^{-1}\otimes N)H)^{-1}H'(\hat{\Sigma}^{-1}\otimes N)\mathbf{y}.$$

It is easily seen that

$$\sqrt{n}(\hat{\boldsymbol{\delta}}-\boldsymbol{\delta})\xrightarrow{d}N\left(\mathbf{0},\ \text{plim}\,\frac{1}{n}[H'(\Sigma^{-1}\otimes N)H]^{-1}\right)$$

and thus the 3SLSE is an instrumental variables estimator that achieves the Cramer–Rao lower bound.

(b) *Full-information maximum-likelihood estimators* $\tilde{\boldsymbol{\delta}}$

The full-information maximum-likelihood (FIML) estimators are found by maximizing the log-likelihood function,

$$\begin{aligned} l(\Gamma,B,\Sigma,\mathbf{y}_t)=k^*+\frac{n}{2}\log\det\Sigma^{-1}+n\log|\det B| \\ -\frac{1}{2}(\mathbf{y}-H\boldsymbol{\delta})'(\Sigma^{-1}\otimes I)(\mathbf{y}-H\boldsymbol{\delta}), \end{aligned} \tag{4.32}$$

with respect to Σ and the unknown elements of B and Γ. We assume that there are no restrictions on the elements of Σ.

We shall now show that the FIML estimator may itself be regarded as an IV estimator, with the instrument involved being updated at each iteration in a numerical maximization of the likelihood function (4.32). This was first pointed out by Hausman (1975); however, we shall follow a different path to the derivation of this result, which has the merit of a closer relationship with the kind of system representation we employ. The maximization of expression (4.32) may be carried out in a stepwise fashion. First we differentiate with respect to the elements of $\Sigma^{-1}=\{\sigma^{ij}\}$ to obtain

$$\frac{\partial l}{\partial\sigma^{ij}}=\sigma_{ij}-\frac{1}{n}(\mathbf{y}_i-H_i\boldsymbol{\delta}_i)'(\mathbf{y}_j-H_j\boldsymbol{\delta}_j)=0.$$

Solving for σ_{ij} gives

$$\hat{\sigma}_{ij}=\frac{1}{n}(\mathbf{y}_i-H_i\boldsymbol{\delta}_i)'(\mathbf{y}_j-H_j\boldsymbol{\delta}_j)\equiv s_{ij}. \tag{4.33}$$

Substituting expression (4.33) into (4.32) gives the concentrated log-likelihood function

$$l^*(\Gamma, B) = k^* - \frac{n}{2}\log\det S + n\log|\det B| - \frac{1}{2}\mathbf{u}'(S^{-1}\otimes I)\mathbf{u},$$

where $S = \{s_{ij}\} = U'U/n$. But $\mathbf{u}'(S^{-1}\otimes I)\mathbf{u} = \operatorname{tr} S^{-1}U'U = nG$. Hence the concentrated likelihood function becomes

$$l^* = k^* - \frac{n}{2}\log\det S + n\log|\det B|.$$

The maximum-likelihood estimator of $\boldsymbol{\delta}_i$ is found by maximizing this function with respect to $\boldsymbol{\delta}_i$. Let

$$\mathbf{p}(\boldsymbol{\delta}_i) \equiv \frac{\partial\log|\det B|}{\partial\boldsymbol{\delta}_i}, \qquad \mathbf{q}(\boldsymbol{\delta}_i) \equiv -\frac{1}{2}\frac{\partial\log\det S}{\partial\boldsymbol{\delta}_i}.$$

Then the first-order conditions are given by

$$\mathbf{p}(\boldsymbol{\delta}_i) + \mathbf{q}(\boldsymbol{\delta}_i) = \mathbf{0}, \qquad i = 1, \dots, G.$$

The first derivative may be written as

$$\mathbf{p}(\boldsymbol{\delta}_i) = -\begin{pmatrix} R_i'(B^{-1'})_i \\ \mathbf{0} \end{pmatrix} = -R_i'\begin{pmatrix} (B^{-1'})_i \\ \mathbf{0} \end{pmatrix}$$

where $(\quad)_i$ signifies the ith column of the matrix in the brackets and R_i is a selection matrix with the property $YR_i = Y_i$, the matrix of endogenous variables on the right-hand side of the ith equation. Also:

$$\begin{aligned}
\mathbf{q}(\boldsymbol{\delta}_i) &= -\frac{1}{2}\sum_{k=1}^{G}\sum_{j=1}^{G}\frac{\partial\log\det S}{\partial S_{kj}}\frac{\partial S_{kj}}{\partial\boldsymbol{\delta}_i} \\
&= \frac{n}{2}\left(\sum_{k=1}^{G} S^{ik}H_i'\mathbf{u}_k + \sum_{j=1}^{G} S^{ji}H_i'\mathbf{u}_j\right) \\
&= \frac{1}{n}\sum_{k=1}^{G} S^{ki}H_i'\mathbf{u}_k = H_i'U(U'U)_i^{-1}.
\end{aligned}$$

Thus the first-order conditions can be written as

$$\left[H_i' - R_i'\begin{pmatrix} B^{-1\prime} \\ \mathbf{O} \end{pmatrix}U'\right]U(U'U)_i^{-1} = \mathbf{0}, \qquad i = 1, \dots, G. \tag{4.34}$$

Let

$$\tilde{H}_i' = H_i' - R_i'\begin{pmatrix} B^{-1\prime} \\ \mathbf{O} \end{pmatrix}U'.$$

As we have written it, $\tilde{H}_i$ looks unwieldy. However, substituting for U' gives

$$\tilde{H}_i' = \begin{bmatrix} R_i'Y' \\ X_i' \end{bmatrix} - R_i'\begin{bmatrix} Y' + B^{-1\prime}\Gamma'X' \\ \mathbf{O} \end{bmatrix} = \begin{pmatrix} \Pi_i'X' \\ X_i' \end{pmatrix},$$

where we write the reduced form of the endogenous variables on the right-hand side of the ith equation as $Y_i = X\Pi_i + V_i$. Thus we see that $\tilde{H}_i$ gives the systematic part of the matrix of right-hand variables of the ith equation (i.e., of $H_i = [Y_i \; X_i]$).

The first-order conditions (4.34) may now be written as

$$\tilde{H}_i' U(U'U/n)_i^{-1} = \mathbf{0}, \qquad i = 1, \ldots, G. \tag{4.35}$$

Aggregating, let $\tilde{H}'$ be the block diagonal matrix with $\tilde{H}_i'$ as the matrix in the ith block diagonal position. Noting that

$$\operatorname{vec} U(U'U/n)^{-1} = \begin{bmatrix} U(U'U/n)_1^{-1} \\ \vdots \\ U(U'U/n)_G^{-1} \end{bmatrix},$$

we can write (4.35) as

$$\tilde{H}' \operatorname{vec} US^{-1} = \mathbf{0}.$$

But $\operatorname{vec} US^{-1} = (S^{-1} \otimes I)\mathbf{u}$. Hence we can write the first-order conditions as

$$\tilde{H}'(S^{-1} \otimes I)(\mathbf{y} - H\boldsymbol{\delta}) = \mathbf{0}. \tag{4.36}$$

Equation (4.36) yields the IV interpretation of FIML:

$$\tilde{\boldsymbol{\delta}} = (\tilde{H}'(S^{-1} \otimes I)H)^{-1}\tilde{H}'(S^{-1} \otimes I)\mathbf{y}. \tag{4.37}$$

Referring back to formula (3.9) of Chapter 3, it will be seen that $\tilde{\boldsymbol{\delta}}$ can be viewed as an IV–GLS-type estimator, although not identical to the one described in that chapter since $\tilde{H}$ is formed in a different manner. Equation (4.37) is nonlinear, since $\tilde{H}$ contains elements of $\tilde{\boldsymbol{\delta}}$ (as, implicitly, does S). Hausman (1975) recommends the application of Durbin's iterative method (see Malinvaud 1970, p. 686). Given a value $\tilde{\boldsymbol{\delta}}_{r-1}$ at the $(r-1)$st iteration, we form $\tilde{H}_{r-1}$ and S_{r-1} in a manner apparent from the definitions given above for these matrices. The rth iteration is then

$$\tilde{\boldsymbol{\delta}}_r = [\tilde{H}_{r-1}'(S_{r-1}^{-1} \otimes I)H]^{-1}\tilde{H}_{r-1}'(S_{r-1}^{-1} \otimes I)\mathbf{y},$$

and the process is continued until convergence is obtained. Like other maximum-likelihood estimators, assuming the appropriate regularity conditions hold, the FIML estimators achieve the Cramer–Rao lower bound and are BAN estimators.

(c) *System k-class estimators* $\hat{\boldsymbol{\delta}}^k$

The concept of k-class estimators for a single equation has been generalized for a system of equations by Srivastava (1971) and Savin (1973). Instruments $Z = (\hat{\Sigma}^{-1} \otimes (I - kM))H$ are used, where $\hat{\Sigma}$ is a consistent estimator of Σ, and M is the idempotent matrix $I-N=I-X(X'X)^{-1}X'$. The system k-class estimator is then given by

$$\hat{\delta}^k=(H'(\hat{\Sigma}^{-1}\otimes(I-kM))H)^{-1}H'(\hat{\Sigma}^{-1}\otimes(I-kM))\mathbf{y}.$$

As with the single-equation k-class estimator, consistency requires plim $k=1$ and asymptotic efficiency requires plim $\sqrt{n}(k-1)=0$.

Condensing the instrument set

Both 3SLS and 2SLS estimation require that the sample size n be greater than the number of predetermined variables in the system K. But some economic models involve large numbers of exogenous variables, and this condition is violated. Brundy and Jorgenson (1971) propose an iterated IV estimator that only requires that $n>G_i+K_i$ for $i=1,\ldots,G$. First they obtain estimators $\hat{\delta}_i$ by applying some IV estimation procedure to each equation i separately. These estimators although consistent will not be efficient as use is not made of all the a priori restrictions. Next they use the $\hat{\delta}_i$ terms to form consistent estimators $\hat{\Sigma}$ of Σ and of $[(\Gamma B^{-1})_i]^u$, where the u signifies that the latter incorporates all the a priori restrictions. Finally, they form the IV estimator

$$\hat{\hat{\delta}}=(\hat{H}'(\hat{\Sigma}^{-1}\otimes I)H)^{-1}\hat{H}'(\hat{\Sigma}^{-1}\otimes I)\mathbf{y}$$

where

$$\hat{H}=\operatorname{diag}(\hat{H}_1,\ldots,\hat{H}_G) \quad \text{and} \quad \hat{H}_i=(X(\hat{\Gamma}\hat{B}^{-1})_i^u\ X_i). \tag{4.38}$$

Comparing (4.38) with the FIML estimator (4.37), we see that $\hat{\hat{\delta}}$ must be asymptotically efficient as $\hat{H},\hat{\Sigma}$ are asymptotically equivalent to the maximum-likelihood estimators $\tilde{H},\tilde{\Sigma}$.

An alternative procedure was suggested by Kloek and Mennes (1960). Instead of using $X=[X_1 \vdots X_2]$ as the instrument set, where the $n\times K_2$ matrix X_2 denotes the predetermined variables excluded from the first equation, they propose a principal component analysis on the X_2 variables. The first p principal components are chosen, so that K_1+p is less than n.

This suggestion has the merit of compacting the information in the data matrix X_2. However, we have already commented in Section 2.5 on its drawbacks. A better procedure would be to perform a canonical correlation analysis between the set of included endogenous variables (e.g., Y_1 for the first equation) and as many variables of X_2 as are feasible. Usually only a few of the canonical variables so defined will contain the bulk of the variance, and these variables are chosen in place of the full set X_2.

A rather more structural approach to the problem of instrument economy was elaborated by Fisher (1965). Suppose that each behavioral equation of our structural form has been normalized in such a way that the right-hand-side variables provide a causal explanation of the left-hand-side endogenous variable. Then we can use this a priori information contained in the structural form to get a causal ordering of instruments as follows. In the equation explaining $\mathbf{y}_i$ the predetermined variables are said to be of first causal order (with respect to $\mathbf{y}_i$). Now consider the equations explaining the right-hand endogenous variables in this equation; the predetermined variables from these equations are of second causal order. This procedure is continued until no new right-hand endogenous variables are encountered. The result is a list of possible instruments for $\mathbf{y}_i$ that are ranked according to their causal order number. Predetermined variables of first causal order are known to have a direct causal influence on $\mathbf{y}_i$, predetermined variables of second causal order affect $\mathbf{y}_i$ indirectly through having a direct causal effect on the right-hand endogenous variables of $\mathbf{y}_i$, and so forth. This list of possible instruments for $\mathbf{y}_i$ is now pruned using the a posteriori information contained in the sample in the following manner. Suppose there are n observations in the sample. Regress $\mathbf{y}_i$ on the *first* $n-2$ possible instruments, then drop the instrument appearing at the end of the list from the regression. If the multiple correlation of the regression drops significantly, then the $(n-2)$nd instrument contributes significantly to the causal explanation of $\mathbf{y}_i$ and should be retained. If the multiple correlation of the regressions does not drop significantly, the "instrument" adds nothing and should be dropped from the list. Now consider the $(n-3)$rd instrument in the same way [retaining the $(n-2)$nd instrument if it has qualified]. See whether omitting it reduces the multiple correlation significantly. If so, retain it; otherwise omit it and proceed to the next-lower-numbered instrument. When all possible instruments have been tested in this way, those remaining are the ones that should be used to form instrumental variable estimators of the coefficients of the ith equation. In a later article Mitchell and Fisher (1970) deal with problems that can arise in this procedure such as how to handle identities and rankings where ties appear. The reader is referred to this article for details.

In general, the Fisher procedure makes a sensible use of the causal structure of the model for the purpose of instrument choice. However, it suffers from the defect that whether an instrument is a first-, second-, or third-round endogenous variable does not have any necessary relationship with its efficacy as an instrument for that variable; it is quite possible, depending upon the magnitude of the reduced-form parameters, for a third-round instrument to be more effective than a first-round instrument. Although therefore unavoidably ad hoc, the Fisher approach remains useful as a suggestive device for the choice of instruments.

4.5 Second-order efficiency of estimators

We saw in Sections 4.3 and 4.4 that for simultaneous-equations models several IV estimators exist that are BAN (best, asymptotic normal) estimators.[5] That is, for both the limited-information model and the full-information model there are several IV estimators that tend in distribution to a normal random vector and whose asymptotic covariance matrix is the Cramer–Rao lower bound. These estimators are first-order asymptotic equivalent. The question may be asked whether we can distinguish between these estimators by carrying the asymptotic approximation to higher orders. Such higher-order approximations can sometimes be obtained by expanding the distribution function of the estimator in an Edgeworth expansion. In our treatment of the subject, we begin by outlining the general idea of second-order efficiency. Following this, some results are given for the limited-information model. Few results have been obtained for the full-information model.

Second-order efficiency in general

Suppose we have a random sample of size n from a population whose distribution is described by a continuous probability density function $f(x,\theta)$, where θ is an unknown parameter. Let $\hat{\theta}$ be a BAN estimator of θ and let $X_n=\sqrt{n}(\hat{\theta}-\theta)/\sigma(\theta)$ be the standardized estimator, where $\sigma(\theta)$ is the Cramer–Rao lower bound. Let $F_n(x)=P(X_n\leq x)$ be the distribution function of X_n. We restrict ourselves to the class C of BAN estimators that admit an Edgeworth expansion to order n^{-1}. That is, if $\hat{\theta}$ belongs to C, we can write

$$F_n(x)=F(x)+0(n^{-1}),$$

where

$$F(x)=\Phi(x)+\frac{A(x)}{\sqrt{n}}+\frac{B(x)}{n}. \tag{4.39}$$

In (4.39) $\Phi(x)$ is the standard normal distribution function, and $A(x)$ and $B(x)$ are integrable functions, usually polynomials, times the normal probability density function $\phi(x)$.

The first-order asymptotic approximation to $F_n(x)$ is $\Phi(x)$, whereas $F(x)$ is the "second-order" approximation. The mean and variance of $\Phi(x)$ are considered as first-order approximations to the mean and variance of X_n, whereas second-order approximations can be obtained using the first and second moments of $F(x)$.

Define the second-order bias and variance of the standardized estimator X_n as

$$b(\hat{\theta}) = \int_{-\infty}^{\infty} x f(x)\, dx$$

$$V(\hat{\theta}) = \int_{-\infty}^{\infty} x^2 f(x)\, dx - b^2(\theta),$$

where $f(x) = F'(x)$.

For each $\hat{\theta} \in C$, let $\hat{\theta}^* = \hat{\theta} - b(\hat{\theta})\sigma(\hat{\theta})/\sqrt{n}$ be its bias-corrected variant. Second-order efficiency involves comparing estimators $\hat{\theta} \in C$ by looking at the second-order variances of the $\hat{\theta}^*$. The results obtained are discussed by Efron (1975) and can be summarized in the following proposition.

Proposition 4.3: *Let $\hat{\theta}_{\text{ML}}$ be the maximum-likelihood estimator and let $\hat{\theta}^*_{\text{ML}}$ be its bias-corrected variant. Then under rather general conditions, $\hat{\theta}^*_{\text{ML}}$ is second-order efficient in the sense that its second-order variance is at least as small as that of any other bias-corrected estimator in C. In other words, $\hat{\theta}_{\text{ML}}$ has second-order variance at least as small as that of any other estimator in C having the same second-order bias.*

Second-order efficiency and the limited-information model

Consider the limited-information model

$$\mathbf{y}_1 = Y_1 \boldsymbol{\beta}_1 + X_1 \boldsymbol{\gamma}_1 + \mathbf{u}_1 = H_1 \boldsymbol{\delta}_1 + \mathbf{u}_1$$

$$Y_1 = X\Pi_1 + V_1,$$

where the notation is that of Section 4.3. In Section 4.3 we showed that several IVEs were BAN estimators, namely 2SLSE, LIMLE, and the k-class estimators, with suitable restrictions placed on k. In fact, all these estimators can be regarded as special cases of Theil's "k-class" estimators.

We define the following projection matrices:

$$N = X(X'X)^{-1}X', \qquad N_1 = X_1(X_1'X_1)^{-1}X_1',$$

$$M = I - N, \qquad \bar{N} = N - N_1.$$

Let $\bar{K} = K - K_1$. Then we can write Theil's "k-class" estimators as

$$\hat{\boldsymbol{\delta}}_1^k = (H_1'(I - kM)H_1)^{-1} H_1'(I - kM)\mathbf{y}_1 \tag{4.40}$$

and we restrict k by

$$k = \frac{1 + a\lambda - b}{n - \bar{K}} \tag{4.41}$$

with a and b fixed constants, and λ being the smallest root of the equation

$$\left|(\mathbf{y}_1\ Y_1)'\left(\bar{N}-\frac{\lambda M}{n-\bar{K}}\right)(\mathbf{y}_1\ Y_1)\right|=0.$$

Anderson and Rubin (1950) proved that λ has a limiting chi-squared distribution. Thus $\sqrt{n}(k-1)$ converges in probability to 0 and so the k-class estimators $\hat{\boldsymbol{\delta}}^k$ with k restricted by (4.41) are all BAN estimators. Letting $a=b=0$, $\hat{\boldsymbol{\delta}}^k$ becomes the 2SLSE. Moreover, it can be shown (see Koopmans and Hood 1953, p. 167, and Theil 1971, p. 504), that when $a=1$ and $b=0$, $\hat{\boldsymbol{\delta}}^k$ becomes the LIML estimator.

The following proposition concerning the second-order efficiency of such k-class estimators can be derived from the results of Fuller (1977).

Proposition 4.4: *For the k-class estimators defined by* (4.40) *and* (4.41) *second-order efficiency requires* $a=1$.

Comment: It follows from this proposition that the LIML estimators are second-order efficient, whereas 2SLS and other members of the k-class estimators are not.

4.6 Identification

In previous sections we implicitly assumed that instrumental variables could be formed for the equation whose parameters we were trying to estimate. These instrumental variables were obtained using the predetermined variables excluded from the right-hand side of the equation in hand. Nowhere did we explicitly concern ourselves with the question of what happens when there is an insufficient number of excluded predetermined variables to form the required number of instruments. This question is now studied in detail.

Write the full-information model as

$$B'\mathbf{y}_t+\Gamma'\mathbf{x}_t=\mathbf{u}_t,$$

where $\mathbf{y}_t$ is a $G\times 1$ vector containing the tth observations on the current endogenous variables, $\mathbf{x}_t$ is a $K\times 1$ vector containing the tth observations, and the predetermined variables B' and Γ' are $G\times G$ and $G\times K$ matrices of parameters, respectively. For convenience we list the assumptions of the model again:

(i) The $\mathbf{u}_t$ terms are independent, identically distributed random vectors with mean $\mathbf{0}$ and covariance matrix Σ.

(ii) The matrix B is nonsingular.

The reduced form of the model is

$$\mathbf{y}_t = -B'^{-1}\Gamma'\mathbf{x}_t + B'^{-1}\mathbf{u}_t = \Pi'\mathbf{x}_t + \mathbf{v}_t. \tag{4.42}$$

Sometimes we assume that $\mathbf{u}_t$ is normally distributed.

It follows from our assumptions and (4.42) and $\mathbf{y}_t$ is a random vector with mean $\Pi'\mathbf{x}_t$ and covariance matrix $\Omega = B'^{-1}\Sigma B^{-1}$. Any statistical inference about the structural-form parameters $S = (B' \ \Gamma' \ \Sigma)$ is made on the basis of the probability distribution of $\mathbf{y}_t$. Identification concerns itself with the problem of whether knowledge of the probability distribution of $\mathbf{y}_t$ allows statistical inference to be made about the unknown parameters S. Clearly, if two sets of structural-form parameters $S_0 = (B_0' \ \Gamma_0' \ \Sigma_0)$ and $S_1 = (B_1' \ \Gamma_1' \ \Sigma_1)$ give rise to the same probability distribution of $\mathbf{y}_t$, then knowledge of the latter will not help one in making statistical inference about the former, and we say that the structural form parameters are *unidentified or underidentified.*

Identification may be defined formally as follows.

Definition 4.5: *Let $\mathcal{S}$ be the set of allowable structural-form parameters. Then the structural-form parameters are identified if $S_0 \in \mathcal{S}$ implies that there does not exist another $S_1 \in \mathcal{S}$ that gives rise to the same probability distribution of $\mathbf{y}_t$.*

Comment: For normal distributions, the probability distribution of $\mathbf{y}_t$ is completely characterized by its mean $\Pi' x_t$ and its covariance matrix Ω; identification requires that no two $S_1, S_2 \in \mathcal{S}$ give rise to the same Π' and Ω.

Identification arises from a priori knowledge about some of the elements of B, Γ, and Σ. If there is no a priori knowledge of the structural-form parameters, then there is no identification:

Proposition 4.6: If no restrictions are placed on the set S, then the structural-form parameters are unidentified.

Proof: Suppose we fix Π to equal Π_0 and Ω to equal Ω_0 and that $S_0 = (B_0' \ \Gamma_0' \ \Sigma_0)$ gave rise to these reduced-form parameters. Then

$$B_0'\Pi_0' + \Gamma_0' = \mathbf{O} \qquad \text{and} \qquad \Omega_0 = B_0'^{-1}\Sigma_0 B_0^{-1}. \tag{4.43}$$

Let $B_1 = B_0 D$, $\Gamma_1 = \Gamma_0 D$, and $\Sigma_1 = D'\Sigma_0 D$, where D is an arbitrary $G \times G$ nonsingular matrix. Then

$$B_1'\Pi_0' + \Gamma_1' = \mathbf{O} \qquad \text{and} \qquad \Omega_0 = B_1'^{-1}\Sigma_1 B_1^{-1}. \qquad \blacksquare$$

Fortunately we have some a priori knowledge of the structural form parameters, and so the set $\mathcal{S}$ is subject to restrictions. We know, for example, that for the ith structural-form equation certain predetermined variables and endogenous variables are excluded, and we assume that the coefficient of $\mathbf{y}_i$ is 1. We may also have some knowledge of the elements of the covariance matrix Σ. The question we must answer is: When is this a priori knowledge sufficient to ensure identification?

We shall consider initially the case where we have a priori knowledge of some of the elements of $A=(B' \ \Gamma')$ only. (This assumption is relaxed below.) We restrict $\mathcal{S}$ to the following set:

$$\mathcal{S}=\{(A \ \ \Sigma): \ B \text{ is nonsingular, } \Sigma \text{ is positive definite, and certain elements of } A \text{ are subject to known linear restrictions}\}.$$

Let $\boldsymbol{\alpha}_i$ be the elements of the ith row of A written as a $(G+K)\times 1$ column vector. We write the linear restrictions on the elements of A as

$$\begin{aligned} \Phi_1 \boldsymbol{\alpha}_1 &= \boldsymbol{\varphi}_1 \\ &\vdots \\ \Phi_G \boldsymbol{\alpha}_G &= \boldsymbol{\varphi}_G, \end{aligned} \tag{4.44}$$

where Φ_i is a known $r_i \times (G+K)$ matrix and $\boldsymbol{\varphi}_i$ is a known $r_i \times 1$ vector. We ask when restrictions (4.44) combined with

$$B'\Pi_0'+\Gamma'=\mathbf{O}, \qquad \Omega_0=B'^{-1}\Sigma B^{-1} \tag{4.45}$$

will give rise to a unique solution $S_0=(B_0' \ \Gamma_0' \ \Sigma_0')$. Note that as the elements of Σ are assumed to be completely unrestricted (4.45) places no restrictions on our set $\mathcal{S}$. Hence we need only consider when restrictions (4.44) combined with

$$A\begin{pmatrix} \Pi_0' \\ I \end{pmatrix}=\mathbf{O} \tag{4.46}$$

give rise to a unique solution S_1.

Note also that identification can be studied one equation at a time. Taking the ith row of A in (4.46) gives

$$\boldsymbol{\alpha}_i'\begin{pmatrix} \Pi_0' \\ I \end{pmatrix}=\mathbf{0}.$$

Thus we can ask if the equations

$$\begin{bmatrix} \Pi_0 & I \\ & \Phi_i \end{bmatrix}\alpha_i=\begin{bmatrix} \mathbf{0} \\ \varphi_i \end{bmatrix} \tag{4.47}$$

give a unique solution for $\boldsymbol{\alpha}_i$. If they do, then statistical inference can be made about the parameters of the ith equation of the structural-form model. A necessary and sufficient condition is

$$\operatorname{rank}\begin{bmatrix} \Pi_0 & I \\ & \Phi_i \end{bmatrix} = G+K. \tag{4.48}$$

Equation (4.48) is known as the *rank condition* for identification. A necessary condition, often called the order condition, is that $r_i \geq G$.

A more convenient way of stating the rank condition is obtained by considering the identity

$$\begin{bmatrix} \Pi_0 & I_K \\ & \Phi_i \end{bmatrix}\begin{bmatrix} \mathbf{O} & B_0 \\ I_K & \Gamma_0 \end{bmatrix} \equiv \begin{bmatrix} I_K & \mathbf{O} \\ \Phi_i\begin{pmatrix} 0 \\ I_K \end{pmatrix} & \Phi_i A_0' \end{bmatrix}.$$

The matrix

$$\begin{bmatrix} \mathbf{O} & B_0 \\ I_K & \Gamma_0 \end{bmatrix}$$

is nonsingular and so

$$\operatorname{rank}\begin{bmatrix} \Pi_0 & I \\ & \Phi_i \end{bmatrix} \equiv \operatorname{rank}\begin{bmatrix} I_K & \mathbf{O} \\ \Phi_i\begin{pmatrix} 0 \\ I_K \end{pmatrix} & \Phi_i A_0' \end{bmatrix}.$$

But the matrix on the right-hand side has rank $G+K$ if and only if

$$\operatorname{rank}(\Phi_i A_0') = G,$$

the required condition.

The rank condition and availability of instrumental variables

The rank condition of identification can be interpreted as a requirement that ensures the existence of sufficient instrumental variables needed for consistent estimation. Consider the first equation in our model,

$$\mathbf{y}_1 = Y_1\beta_1 + X_1\gamma_1 + \mathbf{u}_1 = H_1\delta_1 + \mathbf{u}_1.$$

Consistent estimation requires that we find instrumental variables for the right-hand endogenous variables Y_1, and these are obtained from excluded predetermined variables that enter the reduced-form equations of Y_1. These variables will be correlated with the variables in Y_1 but uncorrelated with the error terms. Write the reduced form $Y = X\Pi + V$ as

$$(\mathbf{y}_1 \; Y_1 \; Y_2) = X(\boldsymbol{\pi}_1 \; \Pi_1 \; \Pi_2) + V,$$

where Y is partitioned into the left-hand current endogenous variable $\mathbf{y}_1$, the included right-hand current endogenous variables Y_1, and the excluded endogenous variables Y_2. Π is partitioned likewise. Then

$$\begin{bmatrix} \Pi & I_K \\ & \Phi_1 \end{bmatrix} = \left[\begin{array}{cccc:cc} \pi_1 & \Pi_1 & \Pi_2 & & I_K & \\ 1 & \mathbf{0}' & \mathbf{0}' & \mathbf{0}' & & \mathbf{0}' \\ \mathbf{0} & \mathbf{O} & I_{G_2} & \mathbf{O} & & \mathbf{O} \\ \mathbf{0} & \mathbf{O} & \mathbf{O} & \mathbf{O} & & I_{K_2} \end{array}\right], \tag{4.49}$$

with $G_2 =$ number of excluded current endogenous variables, and $K_2 =$ number of excluded predetermined variables. Under this notation $G = G_1 + G_2 + 1$ and $K = K_1 + K_2$.

The right-hand-side matrix of (4.49) is row-equivalent to

$$\left[\begin{array}{ccc:cc} 0 & \Pi_1 & \mathbf{0} & I_K & \\ 1 & \mathbf{0}' & \mathbf{0}' & \mathbf{0}' & \mathbf{0}' \\ \mathbf{0} & \mathbf{O} & I_{G_2} & \mathbf{O} & \mathbf{O} \\ \mathbf{0} & \mathbf{O} & \mathbf{O} & \mathbf{O} & I_{K_2} \end{array}\right]. \tag{4.50}$$

Now partition X into $(X_1\ X_2)$, where X_2 are the excluded predetermined variables, and likewise partition Π_1 into $[\Pi_{11}'\ \Pi_{21}']'$. Then (4.50) is row-and-column-equivalent to

$$\left[\begin{array}{cc:ccc} 1 & \mathbf{0}' & \mathbf{0}' & \mathbf{0}' & \mathbf{0}' \\ \mathbf{0} & \Pi_{21} & \mathbf{O} & \mathbf{O} & \mathbf{O} \\ \mathbf{0} & \mathbf{O} & & I_{K+G_2} & \end{array}\right].$$

Hence

$$\operatorname{rank}\begin{bmatrix} \Pi & I_K \\ & \Phi_1 \end{bmatrix} = K + G$$

if and only if

$$\operatorname{rank}(\Pi_{21}) = G_1.$$

That is, one must be able to form G_1 linearly independent "instrumental variables" from the predetermined variables excluded from the right-hand side of the first equation but entering the reduced form of the included right-hand endogenous variables. A necessary condition for this is that there exists at least as many predetermined variables excluded from the equation as current endogenous variables included on the right-hand side.

Exact identification and overidentification

It may be that we have more a priori knowledge about the structural-form parameters than we need to obtain identification. For example, suppose we cross out a row of Φ_1 to give Φ_1^1 and that

$$\operatorname{rank}\begin{bmatrix} \Pi & I_K \\ & \Phi_1^1 \end{bmatrix} = K + G.$$

This implies that the restriction corresponding to the crossed-out row was not needed to give identification. We would then say that equation 1 is overidentified. If, on the other hand,

$$\operatorname{rank}\begin{bmatrix} \Pi & I_K \\ & \Phi_1^1 \end{bmatrix} \neq K+G,$$

then we say equation 1 is exactly or just identified; all a priori knowledge is needed to obtain identification in this case.

If an equation is overidentified, then the number of excluded predetermined variables that qualify as instrumental variables is greater than the number of right-hand current endogenous variables. If an equation is exactly identified, then the number of excluded predetermined variables that qualify as instrumental variables is equal to the number of right-hand current endogenous variables.

Considerable simplification takes place if all the equations in our model are just identified. Then 3SLSEs, 2SLSEs, FIML, and LIML all collapse to the same basic IV estimator, namely, the one that uses the excluded predetermined variables as instruments for the right-hand endogenous variables. To prove this consider the 2SLSE of the first equation

$$\hat{\delta}_1 = (H_1'X(X'X)^{-1}X'H_1)^{-1}H_1'X(X'X)^{-1}X'\mathbf{y}_1.$$

With exact identification $H_1'X$ is square and nonsingular. Using this fact, the 2SLSE becomes

$$\hat{\delta}_1 = (X'H_1)^{-1}X'\mathbf{y}_1. \tag{4.51}$$

Similarly, we can write the 3SLSE as

$$\begin{aligned}\hat{\boldsymbol{\delta}} = {} & (H'(I\otimes X)(\hat{\Sigma}^{-1}\otimes(X'X)^{-1})(I\otimes X')H)^{-1} \\ & \times H'(I\otimes X)(\hat{\Sigma}^{-1}\otimes(X'X)^{-1})(I\otimes X')\mathbf{y}.\end{aligned} \tag{4.52}$$

If each equation is exactly identified, $H'(I\otimes X)$ is nonsingular and (4.52) becomes

$$\hat{\boldsymbol{\delta}} = ((I\otimes X')H)^{-1}(I\otimes X')\mathbf{y}. \tag{4.53}$$

For δ_1, (4.53) gives the estimator $\hat{\delta}_1 = (X'H_1)^{-1}X'\mathbf{y}_1$.

To prove the result for the maximum-likelihood estimators requires a bit more work. Write the reduced form as

$$\mathbf{y} = (I\otimes X)\pi + \mathbf{v}, \tag{4.54}$$

where the covariance matrix of $\mathbf{v}$ is $V(\mathbf{v}) = \Omega\otimes I$. Since Ω is symmetric and positive semidefinite, so is Ω^{-1}. Hence there exists a nonsingular matrix P such that $P'P = \Omega^{-1}$. Consider

$$(P\otimes I)\mathbf{y} = (P\otimes X)\pi + (P\otimes I)\mathbf{v}. \tag{4.55}$$

Now $V[(P\otimes I)\mathbf{v}]=I\otimes I$, so (4.55) satisfies the Gauss–Markov assumptions. It follows that the MLE of π is obtained by applying OLS to (4.54). But this gives

$$\tilde{\boldsymbol{\pi}}=(I\otimes(X'X)^{-1}X')\mathbf{y},$$

which is the OLSE from equation (4.54).

Alternatively, if we write the reduced form as $Y=X\Pi+V$, the MLE of Π is

$$\tilde{\Pi}=(X'X)^{-1}X'Y.$$

As MLEs are invariant, we can find the MLEs for the structural-form parameters from $\tilde{\Pi}$ if we can solve the equations

$$\tilde{\Pi}=-\tilde{\Gamma}\tilde{B}^{-1},$$

for $\tilde{\Gamma}$ and $\tilde{B}$. This is possible if all the equations in the structural form are exactly identified. To obtain the solution for $\tilde{\boldsymbol{\delta}}_1$, partition the reduced form as

$$(\mathbf{y}_1\ Y_1\ Y_2)=(X_1\ X_2)\begin{pmatrix}\pi_{11} & \Pi_{11} & \Pi_{12}\\ \pi_{21} & \Pi_{21} & \Pi_{22}\end{pmatrix}+V.$$

The relationship between the structural-form parameters and the reduced-form parameters is

$$\Pi B=-\Gamma. \tag{4.56}$$

In particular, for the first equation we have

$$\begin{pmatrix}\pi_{11} & \Pi_{11} & \Pi_{12}\\ \pi_{21} & \Pi_{21} & \Pi_{22}\end{pmatrix}\begin{pmatrix}-1\\ \boldsymbol{\beta}_1\\ \mathbf{0}\end{pmatrix}=-\begin{pmatrix}\boldsymbol{\gamma}_1\\ \mathbf{0}\end{pmatrix}.$$

Hence, the MLEs for $\boldsymbol{\beta}_1$ and $\boldsymbol{\gamma}_1$ can be obtained by solving

$$-\tilde{\boldsymbol{\pi}}_{11}+\tilde{\Pi}_{11}\tilde{\boldsymbol{\beta}}_1=-\tilde{\boldsymbol{\gamma}}_1,\qquad -\tilde{\boldsymbol{\pi}}_{21}+\tilde{\Pi}_{21}\tilde{\boldsymbol{\beta}}_1=\mathbf{0}. \tag{4.57}$$

If the first equation is exactly identified, Π_{21} is square, the rank condition of identification ensures that it is nonsingular, and (4.67) can be solved for $\tilde{\boldsymbol{\beta}}_1$ and $\tilde{\boldsymbol{\gamma}}_1$. The solution is

$$\tilde{\boldsymbol{\beta}}_1=\tilde{\Pi}_{21}^{-1}\tilde{\boldsymbol{\pi}}_{21},\qquad \tilde{\boldsymbol{\gamma}}_1=\tilde{\boldsymbol{\pi}}_{11}-\tilde{\Pi}_{11}\tilde{\Pi}_{21}^{-1}\tilde{\boldsymbol{\pi}}_{21}. \tag{4.58}$$

Now

$$\tilde{\Pi}_1=\begin{pmatrix}\tilde{\Pi}_{11}\\ \tilde{\Pi}_{21}\end{pmatrix}=(X'X)^{-1}X'Y_1\qquad\text{and}\qquad \tilde{\boldsymbol{\pi}}_1=\begin{pmatrix}\tilde{\boldsymbol{\pi}}_{11}\\ \tilde{\boldsymbol{\pi}}_{21}\end{pmatrix}=(X'X)^{-1}X'\mathbf{y}_1.$$

Using the inverse of a partitioned matrix (see Theil 1971, pp. 17, 18), we get

$$\begin{aligned}\tilde{\Pi}_{21} &= (X_2' M_1 X_2)^{-1} X_2' M_1 Y_1 \\ \tilde{\Pi}_{11} &= (X_1' X_1)^{-1} X_1' (Y_1 - X_2 \tilde{\Pi}_{21}) \\ \tilde{\boldsymbol{\pi}}_{21} &= (X_2' M_1 X_2)^{-1} X_2' M_1 \mathbf{y}_1 \\ \tilde{\boldsymbol{\pi}}_{11} &= (X_1' X_1)^{-1} X_1' (\mathbf{y}_1 - X_2 \tilde{\boldsymbol{\pi}}_{21}),\end{aligned} \tag{4.59}$$

where $M_1 = I - X_1(X_1'X_1)^{-1}X_1'$. Substituting (4.59) into (4.58) gives

$$\begin{aligned}\tilde{\boldsymbol{\beta}}_1 &= (X_2' M_1 Y_1)^{-1} X_2' M_1 \mathbf{y}_1 \\ \tilde{\boldsymbol{\gamma}}_1 &= (X_1' X_1)^{-1} X_1' (\mathbf{y}_1 - Y_1 \tilde{\boldsymbol{\beta}}_1).\end{aligned} \tag{4.60}$$

Again using the inverse of a partitioned matrix, we can write (4.60) as

$$\tilde{\boldsymbol{\delta}}_1 = \begin{pmatrix} \tilde{\boldsymbol{\beta}}_1 \\ \tilde{\boldsymbol{\gamma}}_1 \end{pmatrix} = (X'H_1)^{-1} X' \mathbf{y}_1.$$

The same result applies for LIML, as LIML can be regarded as FIML applied to the limited-information model.

Another interesting result pertaining to exact identification is the following proposition, proved by Narayan (1969) and Court (1973).

Proposition 4.7: *Suppose that some equations are overidentified while others are just identified. The 3SLSEs of the parameters of the overidentified equations may be obtained by applying 3SLS to a system made up only of the overidentified equations.*

The proof of this proposition is rather lengthy and is not given here. But a useful application is as follows. Consider the limited-information model

$$\begin{aligned}\mathbf{y}_1 &= Y_1 \boldsymbol{\beta}_1 + X_1 \boldsymbol{\gamma}_1 + \mathbf{u}_1 = H_1 \boldsymbol{\delta}_1 + \mathbf{u}_1 \\ Y_1 &= X \Pi_1 + V_1.\end{aligned}$$

Suppose we decide to apply 3SLS to the model as a whole. The equation $Y_1 = X\Pi_1 + V_1$ is trivially just identified. So by the proposition the 3SLSE of $\boldsymbol{\delta}_1$ is obtained by applying 3SLS to the equation $\mathbf{y}_1 = H_1 \boldsymbol{\delta}_1 + \mathbf{u}_1$ by itself. But 3SLS applied to a single equation is just 2SLS.

Restrictions on the covariance matrix

We have seen that one of the necessary conditions for a variable Z_i to qualify as a predetermined variable for the jth equation is that plim $Z_i'\mathbf{u}_j/n$ must be zero. Such a requirement will usually preclude the endogenous variables from acting as predetermined variables. For the endogenous variables Y satisfy

$$Y' = -(B')^{-1}\Gamma'X' + (B')^{-1}U' = \Pi'X' + V',$$

so that

$$\begin{aligned}\text{plim}(Y'U/n) &= \Pi' \,\text{plim}(X'U/n) + \text{plim}(V'U/n)\\ &= \text{plim}(V'U/n) = (B')^{-1}\Sigma.\end{aligned}$$

In general the matrix $(B')^{-1}\Sigma$ has no zero elements. But suppose that the i, jth element of $(B')^{-1}\Sigma$ is known to be zero. Then this means that the ith endogenous variable is known to be asymptotically uncorrelated with the disturbance term of the jth equation, and the former may therefore qualify as an instrument for that equation. (An additional requirement is that plim $\mathbf{y}_i' H_j/n \neq \mathbf{0}$.) If this is the case, then such knowledge must help in the identification and estimation of the jth equation.

Zero elements in the matrix $(B')^{-1}\Sigma$ arise as a result of known restrictions on the matrix of coefficients B and on the covariance matrix Σ. A common example in the literature is when B is known to be triangular and Σ is known to be diagonal. In this case $(B')^{-1}\Sigma$ will be triangular, the equations will be (exactly) identified, and ordinary least squares is the appropriate estimation procedure. A system that satisfies such restrictions is known as a *recursive system*. If the restrictions on B and Σ are such that $[(B')^{-1}\Sigma]_{ij} = 0$, then following Hausman and Taylor (1980) we say that equations (j, i) are *relatively recursive*. The left-hand variable of the ith equation $\mathbf{y}_i$ can then be considered as a predetermined variable in the estimation of the jth equation. Hausman and Taylor derive a set of necessary conditions for equations (j, i) to be relatively recursive in terms of chain products of the jth row and ith column of B. They also extend the order condition and rank condition for identification to the case where, together with linear restrictions on (B, Γ), we have zero restrictions (i.e., certain elements known to be zero) on (B, Σ). We give their results for the first equation. Suppose as before that the a priori linear restrictions of the parameters of the first equation are given by

$$\Phi_1 \alpha_1 = \phi_1,$$

α_1' being the first row of $A = (B_1' \;\; \Gamma')$. Along with these linear restrictions we have zero restrictions, which we write as

$$\psi(B')^{-1}\Sigma_1 = \mathbf{0},$$

where Σ_1 is the first column of Σ and ψ is an appropriate selection matrix. Since $\Omega = B'^{-1}\Sigma B^{-1}$ we can write the second set of restrictions as

$$\psi\Omega B_1 = \mathbf{0},$$

where B_1 is the first column of B. Hausman and Taylor prove that a necessary and sufficient condition for the identification of the first equation is

$$\text{rank}\begin{bmatrix} \Pi & \vdots & I \\ & \Phi & \\ \psi\Omega & \vdots & 0 \end{bmatrix} = G+K.$$

Their order condition is that the number of unconstrained coefficients of $(B_1\ \Gamma_1\ \Sigma_1)$ must not exceed the number of instrumental variables, which include all the predetermined variables for the first equation. The rank and order conditions for *local* identification in the most general case where we have restrictions on *all* the elements of $(B\ \Gamma\ \Sigma)$ have been derived by Rothenberg (1973).

Knowledge that the elements of Σ are subject to a priori restrictions should help us obtain more efficient estimators of B and Γ. In fact, one can show that such knowledge lowers the asymptotic Cramer–Rao lower bound (see Rothenberg 1973). It follows that the IV estimators such as 3SLS discussed in Section 4.4 are asymptotically inefficient when Σ is constrained. Their asymptotic covariance matrices remain unchanged, whereas the asymptotic covariance matrix bound decreases. Of course, by definition the likelihood function incorporates all the known restrictions, and so FIML remains asymptotically efficient.

4.7 Estimation of the reduced form

Up to this point we have concentrated on the estimation of the structural-form parameters. Now we briefly consider the estimation of the reduced-form parameters. In the preceding section we saw that the reduced-form parameters are linked to the structural-form parameters of the first equation by

$$-\pi_{11}+\Pi_{11}\beta_1=-\gamma_1 \qquad \text{and} \qquad -\pi_{21}+\Pi_{21}\beta_1=\mathbf{0}. \tag{4.61}$$

The rank condition of identification requires that the $K_2\times G_1$ matrix Π_{21} has rank G_1. If equation 1 is just identified, then $K_2=G_1$ and Π_{21} is square and nonsingular. Here equation (4.61) implies no real constraint on the reduced-form parameters. But if equation 1 is overidentified, then $K_2>G_1$ and the rows of Π_{21} are linearly dependent, so that equation (4.61) implies restrictions on the reduced-form parameters. We have the following proposition:

Proposition 4.8: *If each equation in the structural form is exactly identified, then the a priori knowledge leading to identification places no restrictions on the reduced-form parameters. If, however, one or more of the equations in the structural form is overidentified, then the a priori knowledge leading to identification places restrictions on the reduced-form parameters. The number of these restrictions equals the degree of system overidentification* $\Sigma_i\,(K-K_i)$.

Turning to questions of estimation, we remark that if each equation in the structural form is exactly identified, then the analysis of Section 4.6 (exact identification) applies. The equation

$$(P \otimes I)\mathbf{y} = (P \otimes I)(I \otimes X)\boldsymbol{\pi} + (P \otimes I)\mathbf{v} \tag{4.62}$$

satisfies the Gauss–Markov assumptions, where $P'P = \Omega^{-1}$. Thus the best linear unbiased estimators (BLUEs) and the MLEs are found by applying OLS to the equation. But this gives

$$\hat{\boldsymbol{\pi}} = (I \otimes (X'X)^{-1}X')\mathbf{y},$$

which is the estimator of $\boldsymbol{\pi}$ we would obtain by applying OLS directly to the reduced-form equation $\mathbf{y} = (I \otimes X)\boldsymbol{\pi} + \mathbf{v}$.

If, on the other hand, some of the equations in the structural form are overidentified, then equation (4.62) no longer satisfies the Gauss–Markov assumptions, as there are now restriction on $\boldsymbol{\pi}$. Efficient estimation must take these restrictions into account. Two methods that do this are the following:

(i) Apply some asymptotically efficient method of estimation to the structural form to obtain estimators $\hat{B}$ and $\hat{\Gamma}$. Obtain estimators of the reduced-form parameters by $\hat{\Pi} = -\hat{\Gamma}\hat{B}^{-1}$.

(ii) Use the constrained MLE. Maximize the likelihood function, expressed in terms of the reduced-form parameters subject to the implied restrictions on the reduced-form parameters.

It can be shown that the estimators obtained by these methods are asymptotically equivalent (see, for example, Rothenberg 1973, chap. 4).

Partially restricted reduced forms

Both methods (i) and (ii) above of estimating the reduced form of an overidentified model are subject to drawbacks. First, obtaining all the structural parameters $\hat{\boldsymbol{\beta}}$ and $\hat{\Gamma}$ is a tedious business, particularly if one is only really interested in the estimation of the parameters of a single reduced form. Similar remarks apply to a full, constrained maximum-likelihood solution. Instead Amemiya (1966) and Kakwani and Court (1972) originally proposed the following procedure, which is called partially restricted reduced-form estimation.

Consider one of the equations of the structural form, say the first one:

$$\mathbf{y}_1 = Y_1\boldsymbol{\beta}_1 + X_1\boldsymbol{\gamma}_1 + \mathbf{u}_1 = H_1\boldsymbol{\delta}_1 + \mathbf{u}_1.$$

The reduced-form equations corresponding to $\mathbf{y}_1$ and Y_1 may be written as

$$\mathbf{y}_1 = X_1\boldsymbol{\pi}_{11} + X_2\boldsymbol{\pi}_{21} + \mathbf{v} \qquad \text{and} \qquad Y_1 = X_1\Pi_{11} + X_2\Pi_{21} + V.$$

We saw above that our parameters must satisfy the relationships

$$-\pi_{11}+\Pi_{11}\beta_1=-\gamma_1 \qquad \text{and} \qquad \pi_{21}+\Pi_{21}\beta_1=\mathbf{0}$$

or

$$\pi_1=\begin{pmatrix}\pi_{11}\\ \pi_{21}\end{pmatrix}=\begin{pmatrix}\Pi_{11} & I\\ \Pi_{21} & \mathbf{O}\end{pmatrix}\begin{pmatrix}\beta_1\\ \gamma_1\end{pmatrix}=\begin{pmatrix}\Pi_1 & \begin{matrix} I\\ \mathbf{O}\end{matrix}\end{pmatrix}\delta_1. \tag{4.63}$$

The partially restricted reduced-form estimator $\tilde{\pi}_1$ of π_1 involves estimating Π_1 by ordinary least squares and δ_1 by some k-class estimator. If two-stage least squares is the k-class estimator used, then the partially restricted reduced estimator of π_1 would be

$$\tilde{\pi}_1=\begin{pmatrix}\hat{\Pi}_1 & \begin{matrix} I\\ \mathbf{O}\end{matrix}\end{pmatrix}\hat{\delta}_1,$$

with $\hat{\Pi}_1=(X'X)^{-1}X'Y_1$ and $\hat{\delta}_1=(H_1'NH_1)^{-1}H_1'N\mathbf{y}_1$.

The partially restricted reduced-form estimator coincides with the unrestricted reduced-form estimator in the case where the structural-form equation is just identified. If, however, the structural-form equations are overidentified, the partially restricted reduced-form estimators are asymptotically less efficient than the restricted reduced-form estimators, although computationally more convenient. The known small sample properties of the partially restricted reduced-form estimators are given in Section 4.8.

4.8 Small-sample theory

The IV estimators studied in the previous sections were motivated by large-sample considerations. Consistency, asymptotic normality, asymptotic efficiency as given by the Cramer–Rao lower bound, and second-order efficiency are all large-sample concepts. However, it is quite evident that in many situations the economist has not the luxury of a large sample but instead must base his statistical inference on a relatively small number of sample observations. In such cases the large-sample properties are academic, and the choice of the appropriate estimation technique to use should be based on small-sample considerations.

Since Nagar's seminal article (Nagar 1959), theoretical results have been derived for small sample properties of estimators used in simultaneous-equation models (see, e.g., Basmann 1961, 1963, 1974; Mariano 1972, 1973a, b, 1974, 1977; Phillips 1980; Richardson 1968; Sargan 1976; and Sawa 1969). These properties have been obtained using two basic approaches. The first of these is that of Nagar, who derived approximations to the small-sample moments of an estimator by taking a power series approximation of the estimator and then obtaining the moments by taking expectations of an appropriate number of terms in this series approximation. The second approach, that of Richardson, Sawa, Mariano, and others, involves using properties of the Wishart distribution to derive expressions for the exact probability distribution of the estimator. Although the analytic form of this distribution is often not very revealing, it can be used to obtain various small-sample properties of the estimator such as the existence of moments and the symmetry of the distribution.

Below we briefly illustrate the two methods for some of the estimators associated with the simplest limited-information model:

$$\mathbf{y}_1 = \alpha\mathbf{y}_2 + \mathbf{u}, \qquad \mathbf{y}_2 = X\boldsymbol{\pi} + \mathbf{v}. \tag{4.64}$$

This is followed by a listing of the known small-sample properties of simultaneous-equation estimators in the limited-information context.

Nagar's approach

Consider the simple limited-information model (4.64), where the usual assumptions are made about the error vectors **u** and **v** with the additional assumption that they are jointly normally distributed. Then the 2SLSE of α is given by

$$\hat{\alpha} = \frac{\mathbf{y}_1' N \mathbf{y}_2}{\mathbf{y}_2' N \mathbf{y}_2} = \alpha + \frac{\mathbf{u}' N (X\boldsymbol{\pi} + \mathbf{v})}{(X\boldsymbol{\pi} + \mathbf{v})' N (X\boldsymbol{\pi} + \mathbf{v})}$$

where we recall that $N = X(X'X)^{-1}X'$. It follows that

$$\hat{\alpha} - \alpha = \frac{\mathbf{u}'X\boldsymbol{\pi} + \mathbf{u}'N\mathbf{v}}{\boldsymbol{\pi}'X'X\boldsymbol{\pi}} \left[1 \Big/ \left(1 + \frac{\mathbf{v}'N\mathbf{v} + 2\boldsymbol{\pi}'X'\mathbf{v}}{\boldsymbol{\pi}'X'X\boldsymbol{\pi}} \right) \right]. \tag{4.65}$$

Notice that the $\boldsymbol{\pi}'X'X\boldsymbol{\pi}$ is of order n, whereas all the other terms in (4.65) are of smaller order. Using a power series expansion for the term in the square brackets of (4.65), ignoring terms of order n^{-2} and smaller we can write

$$\hat{\alpha} - \alpha \approx \frac{\mathbf{u}'X\boldsymbol{\pi} + \mathbf{u}'N\mathbf{v}}{\boldsymbol{\pi}'X'X\boldsymbol{\pi}} \left[1 - \frac{\mathbf{v}'N\mathbf{v} + 2\boldsymbol{\pi}'X'\mathbf{v}}{\boldsymbol{\pi}'X'X\boldsymbol{\pi}} \right]. \tag{4.66}$$

An approximation to the small-sample bias of the 2SLSE can then be found by taking the expectation of the right-hand side of (4.66). In doing this we note that as **u** and **v** are normally distributed, all odd moments have zero expectation and thus $\mathcal{E}(\boldsymbol{\pi}'X'\mathbf{u}\mathbf{v}'N\mathbf{v}) = 0$ and $\mathcal{E}(\mathbf{v}'N\mathbf{u}\boldsymbol{\pi}'X'\mathbf{v}) = 0$. Clearly,

$$\mathcal{E}(\boldsymbol{\pi}'X'\mathbf{u}\mathbf{v}'X\boldsymbol{\pi}) = \boldsymbol{\pi}'X'\mathcal{E}(\mathbf{u}\mathbf{v}')X\boldsymbol{\pi} = \sigma_{uv}\boldsymbol{\pi}'X'X\boldsymbol{\pi}.$$

For the rest of the terms it is useful to make the transformation $\tilde{\mathbf{v}} = P\mathbf{v}$ and $\tilde{\mathbf{u}} = P\mathbf{u}$, where P is the orthogonal matrix such that $P'NP$ is equal to

$$\begin{pmatrix} I_K & \mathbf{O} \\ \mathbf{O} & \mathbf{O} \end{pmatrix}.$$

Such a transformation exists as N is a projection matrix of rank K. Moreover, $(\tilde{\mathbf{u}}' \ \tilde{\mathbf{v}}')'$ is normal and

$$\mathbf{u}'N\mathbf{u} = \sum_{i=1}^{K} \tilde{v}_i \tilde{u}_i \qquad \text{and} \qquad \mathbf{v}'N\mathbf{v} = \sum_{j=1}^{K} \tilde{v}_j^2.$$

Hence,

$$\mathcal{E}(\mathbf{v}'N\mathbf{u}) = \mathcal{E}\left(\sum_{i=1}^{K} \tilde{v}_i \tilde{u}_i \right) = K\sigma_{uv},$$

and

$$\begin{aligned} \mathcal{E}(\mathbf{v}'N\mathbf{u}\mathbf{v}'N\mathbf{v}) &= \mathcal{E}\left(\sum_{ij}^{K}\sum \tilde{v}_i \tilde{u}_i \tilde{v}_j^2 \right) = \mathcal{E}\left(\sum_{i \neq j}^{K}\sum \tilde{v}_i \tilde{u}_i \tilde{v}_j^2 + \sum_{i=1}^{K} \tilde{u}_i \tilde{v}_i^3 \right) \\ &= \sigma_{uv}\sigma_v^2(K^2 - K) + 3K\sigma_{uv}\sigma_v^2 \\ &= \sigma_{uv}\sigma_v^2(K^2 + 2K). \end{aligned}$$

Using (4.66) and these expectations we obtain

$$\mathcal{E}(\hat{\alpha} - \alpha) \approx \frac{\sigma_{uv}}{\pi' X' X \pi}(K-2) - \frac{\sigma_{uv}\sigma_v^2(K^2 + 2K)}{(\pi' X' X \pi)^2}. \tag{4.67}$$

The second term of the right-hand side of (4.65) is of order n^{-2}, so if we ignore this term we have to order n^{-1}:

$$\mathcal{E}(\hat{\alpha} - \alpha) \approx \frac{\sigma_{uv}}{\pi' X' X \pi}(K-2). \tag{4.68}$$

Notice that whereas asymptotic theory gave the result that the 2SLSE is (asymptotically) unbiased, small-sample theory indicates that it is in fact biased. From (4.68), this bias decreases as the sample size n increases but increases as K, the number of excluded exogenous variables, increases.

In this approach it is not altogether clear why terms whose order are smaller than n^{-2} can be safely ignored, given that n is not large in small samples and that the ignored terms are moments of a multivariate normal distribution and may be quite large in themselves. [See Hatanaka (1973) and Sargan (1976) on the validity of Nagar-type expansions.]

Expressions for the moments of other estimators of the k-class family associated with the limited-information model can be obtained similarly. We refer the reader to Nagar's seminal article (1959) for details.

The approach based on the Wishart distribution

Suppose that $\mathbf{z}$ is a random vector having a multivariate normal distribution with mean $\boldsymbol{\mu}$ and covariance matrix $\sigma^2 I$ and let A and B be symmetric idempotent matrices of constants. Then it is well known that $\mathbf{z}'\mathbf{z}/\sigma^2$ has a noncentral chi-squared distribution with noncentrality parameter $\boldsymbol{\mu}'\boldsymbol{\mu}/\sigma^2$. Similarly, $\mathbf{z}'A\mathbf{z}/\sigma^2$ and $\mathbf{z}'B\mathbf{z}/\sigma^2$ have noncentral chi-squared distribution with degrees of freedom equal to tr A and tr B, respectively, and noncentrality parameters $\boldsymbol{\mu}'A\boldsymbol{\mu}/\sigma^2$ and $\boldsymbol{\mu}'B\boldsymbol{\mu}/\sigma^2$, respectively. Moreover, $\mathbf{z}'A\mathbf{z}$ is independent of $\mathbf{z}'B\mathbf{z}$ if and only if $AB = \mathbf{O}$.

The Wishart distribution is a matrix generalization of the noncentral chi-squared distribution. Consider the random $n \times p$ matrix

$$Z = \begin{pmatrix} \mathbf{z}_1' \\ \vdots \\ \mathbf{z}_n' \end{pmatrix} = (\mathbf{z}^{(1)}, \mathbf{z}^{(2)}, \ldots, \mathbf{z}^{(p)}),$$

where we assume that the $\mathbf{z}_i$ terms are independent normal random vectors with mean $\boldsymbol{\mu}_i$ and covariance matrix Σ. It follows that the columns $\mathbf{z}^{(j)}$ are normally distributed with mean $\boldsymbol{\mu}^{(j)}$, say, and covariance matrix $\sigma_{jj} I$. Let $W = Z'Z = \sum_{i=1}^n \mathbf{z}_i \mathbf{z}_i'$. The (i, j)th element of W is $\mathbf{z}^{(i)'}\mathbf{z}^{(j)}$. Then W is said to be a Wishart matrix, and the elements of W have a noncentral Wishart distribution of order p, with n degrees of freedom, covariance matrix Σ, and "means sigma" $M = \sum_{i=1}^n \boldsymbol{\mu}_i \boldsymbol{\mu}_i'$. We denote this by

$$W \sim W_p(n, \Sigma, M).$$

The distribution is said to be central if $M = \mathbf{O}$. The joint probability density function of a noncentral Wishart distribution is rather complicated, involving both Bessel functions and gamma functions [see Johnson and Kotz (1972), sec. 38 for details], but the Wishart distribution has properties similar to that of the noncentral chi-squared distribution. For example, if A and B are symmetric idempotent matrices, then $Z'AZ \sim W_p[q, \Sigma, \mathcal{E}(Z)'A\mathcal{E}(Z)]$, where q is the rank of A, and $Z'AZ$ and $Z'BZ$ have independent Wishart distributions if and only if $AB = 0$.

Returning now to the simple limited-information model of (4.64), we write the reduced form of this model as

$$\mathbf{y}_1 = \alpha X \pi - \alpha \mathbf{v} + \mathbf{u} = X\boldsymbol{\pi}_1 + \mathbf{w}$$

$$\mathbf{y}_2 = X\boldsymbol{\pi} + \mathbf{v},$$

where $\mathcal{E}(\mathbf{w}\mathbf{w}') = \sigma_w^2 I$ and $\mathcal{E}(\mathbf{w}\mathbf{v}') = \sigma_{wv} I$, say. Clearly, $\mathbf{y}_1 \sim N(X\boldsymbol{\pi}_1, \sigma_w^2 I)$ and $\mathbf{y}_2 \sim N(X\boldsymbol{\pi}, \sigma_v^2 I)$. Let $Y = (\mathbf{y}_1 \;\; \mathbf{y}_2)$ so the tth row of Y, (y_{t1}, y_{t2}) written as a column vector has a bivariate normal distribution with mean vector

$$\mu_t = \begin{pmatrix} \mathbf{X}_{t.} & \pi_1 \\ \mathbf{X}_{t.} & \pi \end{pmatrix},$$

and covariance matrix

$$\Omega = \begin{pmatrix} \sigma_w^2 & \sigma_{wv} \\ \sigma_{wv} & \sigma_v^2 \end{pmatrix}.$$

It follows that

$$W = Y'Y = \begin{pmatrix} \mathbf{y}_1'\mathbf{y}_1 & \mathbf{y}_1'\mathbf{y}_2 \\ \mathbf{y}_2'\mathbf{y}_1 & \mathbf{y}_2'\mathbf{y}_2 \end{pmatrix} = \{\omega_{ij}\}$$

has a noncentral Wishart distribution of order 2, with n degrees of freedom, covariance matrix Ω, and means sigma matrix

$$M = \boldsymbol{\pi}'X'X\boldsymbol{\pi}\begin{pmatrix} \alpha^2 & \alpha \\ \alpha & 1 \end{pmatrix}.$$

That is, $W \sim W_2(n, \Omega, M)$. Moreover the OLSE of α is given by

$$a = \frac{\mathbf{y}_1'\mathbf{y}_2}{\mathbf{y}_2'\mathbf{y}_2} = \frac{\omega_{12}}{\omega_{22}}.$$

Thus starting with the Wishart joint density function of the ω_{ij} and making suitable transformations one can eventually derive the exact density function of the OLSE α [see Sawa (1969) for details].

Consider now

$$H = Y'NY = \begin{pmatrix} \mathbf{y}_1'N\mathbf{y}_1 & \mathbf{y}_1'N\mathbf{y}_2 \\ \mathbf{y}_2'N\mathbf{y}_1 & \mathbf{y}_2'N\mathbf{y}_2 \end{pmatrix} = \{h_{ij}\},$$

where N is the symmetric idempotent matrix $X(X'X)^{-1}X'$. Then

$$H \sim W_2(K, \Omega, M),$$

and the 2SLSE of α is given by

$$\hat{\alpha} = \frac{h_{12}}{h_{22}}.$$

It follows that the distribution of the 2SLSE is essentially the same as that of the OLSE estimator, as it is based on a Wishart distribution with exactly the same parameters except that the degrees of freedom for 2SLSE are K, whereas for the OLSE the degrees of freedom are n.

The distributions of other members of the family of instrumental variables estimators for the limited-information model can be similarly derived, starting off with an underlying Wishart matrix [see Mariano (1973a, b, 1977), Sargan (1976), and Phillips (1980) for details]. From these exact distributions small-sample properties can be derived for the various estimators. A selection of the better known of these properties is given below.

Some results from small-sample theory

Consider the limited-information model

$$\mathbf{y} = Y_1 \beta_1 + X_1 \gamma_1 + \mathbf{u}_1 = H_1 \delta_1 + \mathbf{u}_1$$

$$Y_1 = X\Pi_1 + V_1,$$

where we assume that the errors are normally distributed. Then the following results have been derived from small-sample theory.

R.1 (Nagar 1959): Consider the subset of k-class estimators of $\boldsymbol{\delta}_1$ defined in Section 4.3, where k can be written as

$$k = 1 + x/n,$$

x being a real number independent of n. (The 2SLSE belongs to this set, for example, and is obtained by setting x equal to 0.) Then the *bias* of such a k-class estimator to order n^{-1} is given by

$$\mathcal{E}(\mathbf{e}_k) = \mathcal{E}(\tilde{\boldsymbol{\delta}}_1^k - \boldsymbol{\delta}_1) \approx [-x + L - 1]Q\mathbf{q},$$

where

$$Q = \begin{bmatrix} \Pi_1' X'X\Pi_1 & \Pi_1' X'X_1 \\ X'X\Pi_1 & X_1' X_1 \end{bmatrix}^{-1}, \qquad \mathbf{q} = \mathcal{E}\begin{pmatrix} V'\mathbf{u}/n \\ \mathbf{0} \end{pmatrix}$$

and L is the degree of overidentification; that is, $L = K - K_1 - G_1$.

R.2: Because the elements of V and $\mathbf{u}$ are normally distributed, we can write $V = \mathbf{u}\boldsymbol{\pi}' + W$, say. Let $C = \mathcal{E}(V'V/n) = \sigma^2 \boldsymbol{\pi}\boldsymbol{\pi}' + \mathcal{E}(W'W/n) = C_1 + C_2$. Then the moment matrix to order n^{-2} of the above k-class estimators around $\boldsymbol{\delta}_1$ is given by

$$\mathcal{E}(\mathbf{e}_k \mathbf{e}_k') \approx \sigma^2 Q(I + A^*),$$

where

$$A^* = [(2x - 2L + 3)\operatorname{tr}(C_1 Q) + \operatorname{tr}(C_2 Q)]I$$
$$+ \{(x - L + 2)^2 + 2(x+1)\}C_1 Q + (2x - L + 2)C_2 Q.$$

R.3 (Mariano 1972, Hatanaka 1973): The necessary and sufficient conditions for the 2SLSE to have finite moments is that the order of the moments must be less than or equal to the degree of overidentification $L = K - K_1 - G_1$.

The necessary and sufficient conditions for the OLSE to have finite moments is that the order of the moments must be less than or equal to $n-K_1-G_1$.

For the special case where the equation to be estimated has two endogenous variables, the limited-information model can be written as

$$\mathbf{y}_1 = \alpha \mathbf{y}_2 + X_1 \gamma + \mathbf{u}$$

$$\mathbf{y}_2 = X\pi + \mathbf{v} = X_1 \pi_1 + X_2 \pi_2 + \mathbf{v}.$$

Let $\rho = \sigma_{uv}/\sqrt{\sigma_u^2 \sigma_v^2}$ be the correlation coefficient between y_{2t} and u_t, and μ^2 be the concentration parameter defined by

$$\mu_2 = \pi_2' X_2' (N - N_1) X_2 \pi_2 / \sigma_v^2,$$

where N and N_1 are the idempotent matrices $X(X'X)^{-1}X'$ and $X_1(X_1'X_1)^{-1}X_1'$, respectively.

Then for this special case we have the following results.

R.4 (Sawa 1969)**:** The exact distributions of the OLSE and 2SLSE of α are highly sensitive to ρ, the distribution of the 2SLSE being considerably asymmetric while that of the OLSE is almost symmetric. Both the OLSE and 2SLSE are biased in the same direction, the numerical values of the biases being monotonically increasing functions of $|\rho|$. If the 2SLS bias is finite, it is less than the OLS bias.

R.5 (Sawa 1969)**:** The OLS and 2SLS mean-squared errors are both monotonically increasing functions of $|\rho|$ and monotonically decreasing functions of the concentration parameter μ.

R.6 (Mariano and Sawa 1972, Sawa 1972)**:** The moments of the limited-information estimator of $\boldsymbol{\alpha}$ of order greater than or equal to 1 do not exist. The moments of the k-class estimators with k nonstochastic do not exist for $k > 1$.

Some authors [see, for example, Mariano (1974), Sawa (1972)], have derived small-sample properties based on asymptotic expansions of the distribution functions of the estimators, the asymptotics being conducted by holding the sample size n constant and allowing the concentration parameter μ^2 to tend to infinity. The following result is based on such asymptotic expansions for the special case of one right-hand endogenous variable.

R.7: Up to terms of order $1/\mu$, the distributions of both the 2SLSE and LIML estimators of α are skewed to the left if ρ is positive and skewed to the right if ρ is negative. Up to terms of order $1/\mu^2$, the median of the

LIML estimator is the true parameter value, while for 2SLS the median is α only if the equation is just identified or $\rho = 0$. In terms of probabilities of absolute deviations around α, small ρ^2 favors 2SLS while a high degree of overidentification favors LIML.

Finally, some small-sample properties have been obtained for the partially restricted reduced-form estimators defined in Section 4.7. Nagar and Sahay (1978) derive the exact bias and mean-squared error of forecasts based on these estimators when the structural-form equation under consideration has only two endogenous variables. The following result concerns the existence of moments of these estimators.

R.8 (McCarthy 1981, Swamy and Mehta 1981): Suppose that the partially restricted reduced-form estimators are formed using the k-class estimators with fixed k and $0 \leq k \leq 1$, and that X has full-column rank. Then if $\mathcal{E}(\mathbf{y}_1'\mathbf{y}_1)^r$ is finite, the partially restricted reduced-form estimators possess moments up to the order $2r$.

Note that if we assume that the disturbance terms are normally distributed, then $\mathcal{E}(\mathbf{y}_1'\mathbf{y}_1)^r$ exists for finite r and the partially restricted reduced-form estimators possess all moments (see Knight 1977).

4.9 Serially correlated disturbance structures

Up to this point, all our discussion has specified the disturbance structure of the simultaneous system to be well behaved, certainly in the sense that no serial correlation exists. As one might expect, devising maximum-likelihood estimators becomes unwieldy very quickly when we drop this assumption. However, it turns out that one can obtain the first-order conditions for the case where the disturbance obeys a general first-order vector autoregressive process. These optimizing conditions are remarkably enough of rather simple form, and it is possible to show that, just as in the analysis of Section 4.4, these conditions may be interpreted as an iterative IV estimator of the IV–GLS variety. This result extends more or less immediately to autoregressive processes of higher order and motivates also a 3SLS estimator. However, before presenting this work, which occupies the bulk of this section, we shall look first at more traditional IV methods applied to a limited-information context.

Two-stage least-squares methods

The 2SLS techniques extend very readily to certain simple nonindependent disturbance specifications, and indeed one can use the IV formulation to generate a variety of different estimators. Consider the following model in which the disturbance term of the chosen equation (the first one, say) obeys a first-order Markov process:

$$\mathbf{y}_1 = Y_1\beta_1 + X_1\gamma_1 + \mathbf{u}_1$$

$$\mathbf{u}_1 = \rho\mathbf{u}_{1,-1} + \epsilon_1, \qquad 0 \leq \rho < 1,$$

where the subscript minus-one (-1) indicates the lagged value and ϵ_{1t} is an i.i.d. (white-noise) disturbance term with variance σ_1^2. By an appropriate lagging and subtraction operation, we may transform this model to

$$\mathbf{y}_1 = \rho\mathbf{y}_{1,-1} + (Y_1 - \rho\mathbf{Y}_{1,-1})\beta_1 + (X_1 - \rho X_{1,-1})\gamma_1 + \epsilon_1. \tag{4.69}$$

Equation (4.69) now has a white-noise residual; however, the regressor element Y_1 remains possibly correlated with ϵ_1.

Given an arbitrary matrix Z of instruments, we form the IV minimand:

$$\phi = [\mathbf{y}_1 - \rho\mathbf{y}_{1,-1} - (Y_1 - \rho Y_{1,-1})\beta_1 - (X_1 - \rho X_{1,-1})\gamma_1]'$$
$$\times P_z[\mathbf{y}_1 - \rho\mathbf{y}_{1,-1} - (Y_1 - \rho Y_{1,-1})\beta - (X_1 - \rho X_{1,-1})\gamma_1].$$

Suppose now that the columns of Z span the exogenous and lagged variables $\mathbf{y}_{1,-1}, Y_{1,-1}, X_1$, and $X_{1,-1}$. Write $\hat{Y}_1 = P_z Y_1$, the fitted value in a regression of Y_1, the included right-hand endogenous variables upon Z. By writing $P_z y_1 = \mathbf{y}_1 - (I - P_z)\mathbf{y}_1$ and recalling that P_z is a projection matrix, it is now easy to show that

$$\phi = \phi_1 - \mathbf{y}_1'(I - P_z)\mathbf{y}_1,$$

where

$$\phi_1 = [\mathbf{y}_1 - \rho\mathbf{y}_{1,-1} - (\hat{Y}_1 - \rho Y_{1,-1})\beta_1 - (X_1 - \rho X_{1,-1})\gamma_1]'$$
$$\times [\mathbf{y}_1 - \rho\mathbf{y}_{1,-1} - (\hat{Y}_1 - \rho Y_{1,-1})\beta_1 - (X_1 - \rho X_{1,-1})\gamma_1]. \tag{4.70}$$

Minimizing ϕ with respect to the desired parameters ρ, β_1, and γ_1 is evidently equivalent to minimizing ϕ_1 defined by expression (4.70) with respect to these parameters. The latter is formally a nonlinear least-squares-type minimand. However, the problem can be solved by a one-dimensional iteration on the Markovian parameter ρ. For a given ρ, fit a linear regression of $\mathbf{y}_1 - \rho\mathbf{y}_{1,-1}$ on $\hat{Y}_1 - \rho Y_{1,-1}$ and $X_1 - \rho X_{1,-1}$, obtaining the residual sum of squares RSS(ρ). The value of ρ is chosen that minimizes RSS(ρ). This technique was suggested by Fair (1970), although not originally put in the above terms. The asymptotic covariance matrix is given by

$$A\,\mathrm{Cov}(\hat{\rho}, \hat{\beta}_1, \hat{\gamma}_1)$$
$$= \sigma_1^2 \operatorname{plim} n[(\mathbf{y}_{1,-1} - \mathbf{Y}_{1,-1}\beta_1 - X_{1,-1}\gamma_1 \vdots \hat{Y}_1 - \rho Y_{1,-1} \vdots X_1 - \rho X_{1,-1})'$$
$$\times (\mathbf{y}_{1,-1} - Y_{1,-1}\beta_1 - X_{1,-1}\gamma_1 \vdots \hat{Y}_1 - \rho Y_{1,-1} \vdots X_1 - \rho X_{1,-1})]^{-1}. \tag{4.71}$$

We refer the reader forward to Section 5.2, which derives this formula from considerations of nonlinear theory.

The principal operational difficulty lies in the choice of the matrix Z of instruments. As indicated above, it is desirable to include among the columns of this matrix the variables $\mathbf{y}_{1,-1}$, $Y_{1,-1}$, X_1, and $X_{1,-1}$. In general we should also want to include elements of the exogenous or predetermined variables that are not included in equation 1. However, we may note that, corresponding to equation (4.69), the reduced-form expressions for the elements of Y_1 will depend upon lagged values of the exogenous variables, and one should like to add such terms to the instrument set Z. At this point, the dimensionality of the instrument set becomes troublesome. Fair (1970) suggests ways to overcome this problem. We refer the reader to the discussion in Section 4.4 of the present chapter, which deals with a similar problem in a full-information context.

A final point concerns the efficiency of 2SLS estimators in this context. Unlike the corresponding 2SLS estimator for the standard simultaneous model, the estimator defined by the minimization (4.70) is no longer efficient; that is, it does not in general attain the Cramer–Rao lower bound. Accordingly, we turn next to consider the maximum-likelihood approach to the estimation of simultaneous models with autoregressive disturbances.

Maximum-likelihood estimation

Our strategy in presenting the maximum-likelihood estimator and its IV interpretation is to consider first the full-information problem and to follow this with some remarks on the limited-information estimator. We write the full-information model as

$$B'\mathbf{y}_t + \Gamma'\mathbf{x}_t = \mathbf{u}_t, \qquad t = 1 \ldots n. \tag{4.72}$$

As before, $\mathbf{y}_t$ is the column vector containing the tth observations on the current endogenous variables. The vector $\mathbf{x}_t$ may include lagged endogenous as well as true exogenous variables. With regard to the disturbances, we assume that $\mathbf{u}_t$ is generated by a vector autoregressive process of the form

$$\mathbf{u}_t = R\mathbf{u}_{t-1} + \mathbf{e}_t, \tag{4.73}$$

where R is a $G \times G$ matrix of parameters and the $\mathbf{e}_t$ are independent normal random vectors with zero mean and covariance matrix Σ (vector "white noise"). In order to ensure that the various moment matrices exist we shall assume that the characteristic roots of the matrix R lie within the unit circle. (This is not strictly a necessary assumption, but it would take us too far afield to detail more embracing conditions.)

Let $U' = (\mathbf{u}_1 \ldots \mathbf{u}_n)$ and $E' = (\mathbf{e}_1 \ldots \mathbf{e}_n)$. Then (4.73) can be written as

$$U' = RU'_{-1} + E', \tag{4.74}$$

where the subscript -1 denotes the lagged value of the matrix in question.

Let $\mathbf{d}_t = (\mathbf{y}_t' x_t')'$, $D' = (\mathbf{d}_1 \ldots \mathbf{d}_n)$, and $A = (B' \vdots \Gamma')$. The system (4.72) and (4.73) may then be written in data matrix form as

$$AD' - RAD'_{-1} = E'.$$

An alternative representation in stacked form will also be useful. Define $\mathbf{u} = \operatorname{vec} U$ and $\mathbf{e} = \operatorname{vec} E$. Then using the properties of vec( ), equation (4.74) may be written

$$\mathbf{u} = (R \otimes I)\mathbf{u}_{-1} + \mathbf{e}. \tag{4.75}$$

Now recall our earlier notation $H_i = (Y_i \; X_i)$ for the data matrix of the ith equation with $\boldsymbol{\delta}_i = (\beta_i' \gamma_i')'$. Combining all the equations as in Section 4.4 above, we have

$$\mathbf{y} = H\boldsymbol{\delta} + \mathbf{u},$$

where H is the block diagonal matrix with H_i in the ith block. Now define the quasi-differences:

$$\mathbf{y}^d = \mathbf{y} - (R \otimes I)\mathbf{y}_{-1} \tag{4.76a}$$

$$H^d = H - (R \otimes I)H_{-1}. \tag{4.76b}$$

Utilizing equation (4.75), we obtain a transformed system with white-noise disturbances:

$$\mathbf{y}^d = H^d \boldsymbol{\delta} + \mathbf{e}. \tag{4.77}$$

Suppose for the moment that R was known. Evidently the quasi-differencing eliminates the serial correlation. However, since H remains correlated with $\mathbf{e}$, we cannot apply OLS to equation (4.77). But if we define $\tilde{H}^d = \hat{H} - (R \otimes I)H_1$, where $\hat{H}$ is a suitable instrument for H, we can overcome this problem. Note that $\operatorname{Cov}(\mathbf{e}) = \Sigma \otimes I$, so that one of the generalized IV estimators will be appropriate. Thus we could try the IV–GLS version:

$$\tilde{\boldsymbol{\delta}} = [\tilde{H}^d(\Sigma^{-1} \otimes I)H^d]^{-1} \tilde{H}^d(\Sigma^{-1} \otimes I)y^d. \tag{4.78}$$

The fact that Σ is unknown is no real problem, since we can replace it by a consistent estimate S. Recall, however, that we have also assumed that R is unknown. We might think of simply replacing R by an estimate $\hat{R}$. Thus forming

$$\hat{\tilde{H}}^d = \hat{H} - (\hat{R} \otimes I)H_{-1} \tag{4.79a}$$

$$\hat{H}^d = H - (\hat{R} \otimes I)H_{-1} \tag{4.79b}$$

$$\hat{\mathbf{y}}^d = \mathbf{y} - (\hat{R} \otimes I)\mathbf{y}_{-1}, \tag{4.79c}$$

we try the estimator

$$\hat{\boldsymbol{\delta}} = [\hat{\hat{H}}^{d\prime}(S^{-1} \otimes I)\hat{H}^d]^{-1}\hat{\hat{H}}^{d\prime}(S^{-1} \otimes I)\hat{\mathbf{y}}^d. \tag{4.80}$$

Of course, we should not be too sanguine about the consistency of such a method in general, even if "extraneous" consistent estimates of R, Σ, and appropriate instruments $\hat{H}$ are available. Remarkably enough, however, the estimator (4.80) emerges in a natural way from the first-order optimizing conditions for the system maximum-likelihood estimator. With suitable interpretations of $\hat{R}$, S, and $\hat{H}$, it is in fact the maximum-likelihood estimator. This result is worth stating formally.

Theorem 4.9: *The first-order conditions for the maximization of the system likelihood function may be written in the form of the IV–GLS estimator* (4.80), *where the matrices* $\hat{\hat{H}}^d$ *and* $\hat{H}^d$ *and the supervector* $\hat{\mathbf{y}}^d$ *are defined by equations* (4.79a–c) *and in addition:*

(a) $\hat{E}' = \hat{A}D' - \hat{R}\hat{A}D'_{-1}$, $\quad S = \hat{E}'\hat{E}/n$,

(b) $\hat{U} = \hat{A}D'$, $\quad \hat{R}' = (\hat{U}'_{-1}\hat{U}_{-1})^{-1}\hat{U}'_{-1}\hat{U}$,

(c) $\hat{H}_i = \begin{pmatrix} \hat{\Pi}_i' X' \\ X_i' \end{pmatrix}$,

where Π_i *is the portion of the reduced form referring to the included right-hand variables* Y_i *in the ith equation.*

Proof: Under the assumption of normality, the probability density of $\mathbf{e}_t$ is

$$(2\pi)^{-n/2} \det \Sigma^{-1/2} \sum_{t=1}^{n} \exp(-\tfrac{1}{2}\mathbf{e}_t'\Sigma^{-1}\mathbf{e}_t).$$

It follows that the log-likelihood function for the model is

$$l = k + n \log|\det B| - \frac{n}{2}\log\det\Sigma - \frac{1}{2}\operatorname{tr}\Sigma^{-1}E'E. \tag{4.81}$$

We assume that the elements of both Σ and R are unrestricted. Thus the first-order conditions when we maximize (4.81) with respect to Σ^{-1} and R are

$$\frac{\partial l}{\partial \Sigma^{-1}} = \mathbf{O}, \qquad \text{which yields} \quad \hat{\Sigma} = E'E/n$$

and

$$\frac{\partial l}{\partial R} = \mathbf{O}, \qquad \text{which yields} \quad \hat{R} = U'U_{-1}(U'_{-1}U_{-1})^{-1}.$$

Substituting these into (4.81) gives the form of the concentrated log-likelihood function as obtained by Sargan (1961) and Hendry (1971):

$$l^* = \text{const.} + n \log|\det B| - \frac{n}{2} \log \det S,$$

where $S = \hat{E}'\hat{E}/n$ and $\hat{E} = U - U_{-1}\hat{R}'$. The maximum-likelihood estimator of $\boldsymbol{\delta}_i$ is found by maximizing this function with respect to $\boldsymbol{\delta}_i$. This is done in a similar fashion to the procedure given in Section 4.4. Let

$$\mathbf{p}(\boldsymbol{\delta}_i) = \frac{\partial \log|\det B|}{\partial \boldsymbol{\delta}_i}, \qquad \mathbf{q}(\boldsymbol{\delta}_i) = -\frac{1}{2} \frac{\partial \log \det S}{\partial \boldsymbol{\delta}_i}.$$

Then the first-order conditions are given by

$$\mathbf{p}(\boldsymbol{\delta}_i) + \mathbf{q}(\boldsymbol{\delta}_i) = \mathbf{0}.$$

As in the previous analysis, the first derivative may be written as

$$\mathbf{p}(\boldsymbol{\delta}_i) = -\begin{bmatrix} W_i'(B^{-1'})_i \\ \mathbf{0} \end{bmatrix} = -W_i' \begin{bmatrix} (B^{-1'})_i \\ \mathbf{0} \end{bmatrix}, \tag{4.82}$$

where $(\quad)_i$ signifies the ith column of the matrix in brackets and W_i is a selection matrix with the property that $YW_i = Y_i$, the matrix of endogenous variables on the right-hand side of the ith equation.

The second derivation requires considerable effort to obtain. The details are given in the annex to this chapter, where we show that

$$\mathbf{q}(\boldsymbol{\delta}_i) = H_i'\hat{E}(\hat{E}'\hat{E})_i^{-1} - H_{i,-1}'\hat{E}(\hat{E}'\hat{E})^{-1}\hat{R}_i, \tag{4.83}$$

where $\hat{R}_i$ is the ith column of $\hat{R}$.

Combining (4.82) and (4.83), we see that the first-order derivatives can be written as

$$\left(H_i' - W_i'\begin{pmatrix} B^{-1'} \\ \mathbf{O} \end{pmatrix}\hat{E}'\right)\hat{E}(\hat{E}'\hat{E})_i - H_{i,-1}'\hat{E}(\hat{E}'\hat{E})^{-1}\hat{R}_i. \tag{4.84}$$

Now

$$H_i' - W_i'\begin{pmatrix} B^{-1'} \\ \mathbf{O} \end{pmatrix}\hat{E}' = \begin{bmatrix} W_i'Y' \\ X_i' \end{bmatrix} - W_i'\begin{bmatrix} B^{-1'}(BY' + \Gamma X' - \hat{R}U_{-1}') \\ \mathbf{O} \end{bmatrix}$$
$$= \hat{H}_i + W_i'\begin{bmatrix} B^{-1'}\hat{R}'U_{-1}' \\ \mathbf{O} \end{bmatrix},$$

where

$$\hat{H}_i = \begin{pmatrix} \Pi_i'X' \\ X_i' \end{pmatrix}$$

is the systematic part of H_i. The first-order conditions (4.84) may now be written as

$$\hat{H}_i'\hat{E}(\hat{E}'\hat{E})_i^{-1} - H_{i,-1}'\hat{E}(\hat{E}'\hat{E})^{-1}\hat{R}_i + W_i'\begin{bmatrix} B^{-1'}\hat{R}U_{-1}' \\ \mathbf{O} \end{bmatrix}\hat{E}(\hat{E}'\hat{E})_i^{-1} = \mathbf{0}. \tag{4.85}$$

But $\hat{R}U_{-1}' = U'P$, where $P = U_{-1}(U_{-1}'U_{-1})^{-1}U_{-1}'$, and $\hat{E} = QU$, where $Q = I - P$. Since $QP = \mathbf{O}$, it follows that $\hat{R}U_{-1}'\hat{E} = \mathbf{O}$ and hence that the last matrix of the left-hand side of (4.85) is $\mathbf{O}$. We have therefore reduced the first-order derivatives to the form

$$\hat{H}_i'\hat{E}(\hat{E}'\hat{E})_i^{-1} - H_{i,-1}'\hat{E}(\hat{E}'\hat{E})^{-1}\hat{R}_i, \qquad i = 1\ldots G. \tag{4.86}$$

We shall now proceed to "stack" this expression.

Let $\hat{H}'$ be the block diagonal matrix with $\hat{H}_i'$ in the ith block diagonal position and H_{-1}' be the block diagonal matrix with $H_{i,-1}'$ in the ith block diagonal position. Then the first-order conditions (4.86) taken together can be written as

$$\hat{H}' \operatorname{vec} \hat{E}S^{-1} - H_{-1}' \operatorname{vec} \hat{E}S^{-1}\hat{R} = \mathbf{0}.$$

Using the properties of vec( ) listed in Appendix A4, we have

$$[\hat{H} - H_{-1}'(\hat{R}' \otimes I)](S^{-1} \otimes I)\hat{\mathbf{e}} = \mathbf{0}.$$

But $\hat{\mathbf{e}} = \operatorname{vec} \hat{E} = (I \otimes Q)\mathbf{u}$, so we can write this as

$$[\hat{H}' - H_{-1}'(\hat{R}' \otimes I)](I \otimes Q)(S^{-1} \otimes I)(\mathbf{y} - H\boldsymbol{\delta}) = \mathbf{0}. \tag{4.87}$$

Now $(I \otimes Q)(S^{-1} \otimes I) = (S^{-1} \otimes I)(I \otimes Q)$, from the properties of Kronecker products. And

$$\begin{aligned}(I \otimes Q)(\mathbf{y} - H\boldsymbol{\delta}) &= (I \otimes Q)\mathbf{u} = (I \otimes (I - P))\mathbf{u} \\ &= \mathbf{u} - \hat{\mathbf{u}} = \mathbf{u} - (\hat{R} \otimes I)\mathbf{u}_{-1} \\ &= \mathbf{y} - H\boldsymbol{\delta} - (\hat{R} \otimes I)(\mathbf{y}_{-1} - H_{-1}\boldsymbol{\delta}) \\ &= \mathbf{y} - (\hat{R} \otimes I)y_{-1} - [H - (\hat{R} \otimes I)H_{-1}]\boldsymbol{\delta} \\ &= \hat{\mathbf{y}}^d - \hat{H}^d\boldsymbol{\delta}.\end{aligned}$$

Hence the first-order conditions (4.87) become the IV normal equations

$$\hat{\hat{H}}^d(S^{-1} \otimes I)(\hat{\mathbf{y}}^d - \hat{H}^d\boldsymbol{\delta}) = \mathbf{0},$$

from which the result follows by solving for $\boldsymbol{\delta}$. ■

As with the IV interpretation of the maximum-likelihood estimator for the standard model, a potential exists for an iterative interpretation. Thus given estimates at stage $(r-1)$ of $\boldsymbol{\delta}_{r-1}$, we obtain corresponding estimates Π_{r-1}, S_{r-1}, and R_{r-1} as defined in the statement of Theorem

4.9. These matrices are used to update the estimate given by equation (4.80), to obtain $\boldsymbol{\delta}_r$. The process continues, hopefully to convergence. Of course, even if we do not choose to follow this particular procedure, formula (4.80) and those appearing in the statement of the theorem nevertheless will suffice to obtain an analytic gradient vector for a maximization by Gauss–Newton or other gradient-based numerical techniques.

Although the derivation has formally been carried out for the case of a first-order disturbance process, it is apparent that by an appropriate redefinition of the state vector **u**, second and higher orders can be accommodated. The underlying rationale is the same. One first converts the model to a white-noise disturbance, in the obvious generalization of equation (4.77) above, leading to a redefinition of H^d to incorporate the higher-order lags. Estimates of the autoregressive matrices $\hat{R}_i$ are obtained and the matrices $\hat{H}^d$, $\hat{\hat{H}}^d$ are constructed. The IV–GLS estimator $\boldsymbol{\delta}$ is formed just as in equation (4.80). An autoregressive process of any finite order can be handled in this way.

The above development can in principle be specialized to handle a limited-information model. In doing so, a degree of arbitrariness arises in deciding precisely what is to correspond to the limited-information model of Section 4.3. Consider the equation system

$$\mathbf{y}_1 = Y_1\boldsymbol{\beta}_1 + X_1\boldsymbol{\gamma}_1 + \mathbf{u}_1; \qquad \mathbf{u}_1 = \rho\mathbf{u}_{1,-1} + \boldsymbol{\epsilon}_1 \tag{4.88a}$$

$$Y_1 = X\Pi_1 + V_1. \tag{4.88b}$$

The regressor–error correlation in the structural equation (4.88a) presumably arises because of the reverse causation implied by simultaneity. Since at least some of the variables in Y_1 depend upon $\mathbf{y}_1$, which exhibits serial correlation, we should therefore expect the disturbance $\mathbf{v}_t$ in equation (4.88b) to exhibit serial correlation. This suggests that we should add to the equations the disturbance specification of the form

$$(\mathbf{u}_1 \;\; V_1)' = \Lambda(\mathbf{u}_1 \;\; V_1)'_{-1} + E, \tag{4.89}$$

where the rows $\mathbf{e}'_t$ of E constitute a vector white-noise process and the top left-hand element of Λ is the parameter ρ of equation (4.88a). Under this interpretation, the limited-information model would amount to the determination of $\boldsymbol{\beta}_1$, $\boldsymbol{\gamma}_1$, Π_1, Λ, and Θ as the covariance matrix of $\mathbf{e}_t$. Equations (4.88) and (4.89) evidently constitute a special case of the full-information model considered in detail above, so that one can in principle derive the limited-information estimators $\hat{\boldsymbol{\beta}}_1, \hat{\boldsymbol{\gamma}}_1$ by an appropriate partitioning of the full-information estimator.

4.10 Summary

We have now given a fairly complete account of IV estimation and related matters in respect of the linear simultaneous stochastic model. In order to keep an already long discussion within manageable proportions there remain areas such as hypothesis testing that we have barely touched on. Even with respect to estimation we have not covered in detail the literature on the estimation of dynamic models with serially correlated disturbance terms, although we hope that Section 4.9 contributes to the literature in this respect.

As a general proposition we hope to have demonstrated that the IV approach provides useful insights into the identification and estimation of the standard linear stochastic model. With respect to the former, we noted that the well-known rank condition of identification could be interpreted in terms of the existence of a sufficient number of excluded predetermined variables to act as instruments for the included endogenous variables, a property highly useful not only for interpretive purposes but as a simple mnemonic for the harassed student!

Turning to estimation, we showed that IV estimators could be applied to both limited- and full-information contexts. In both contexts, an appropriate IV estimator of the structural form was asymptotically efficient. Thus in the limited-information model the two-stage least-squares method and in the full-information model the three-stage least-squares method both attain the Cramer–Rao lower bound. On the other hand, it was remarked in Section 4.5 that the two-stage least-squares estimator is not second-order-efficient.

It was also shown that the methods of maximum likelihood, both in their limited- and full-information contexts, could be regarded as an iterative application of instrumental variables, in which the instruments were updated at each iteration. We remark also that these estimates have the property that starting from an initial consistent estimation, only one iteration is required for the second-round result to be asymptotically efficient. There is indeed a close connection between such a foreshortened version of maximum likelihood and the method of three-stage least squares. We shall observe in the next chapter that such convenient properties do not automatically extend to nonlinear systems.

Annex: the derivative $\mathbf{q}(\delta_i)$

This annex refers to the proof of Theorem 4.9, and the notation is as employed in Section 4.9, except where stated variations occur.

$$\textit{The derivative } \mathbf{q}(\delta_i) \equiv -\frac{1}{2}\frac{\partial \log \det S}{\partial \delta_i}$$

In evaluating this derivative use is made of the following standard matrix differentiation results:

Lemma MD: *Let $A = \{a_{ij}\}$ be a nonsingular matrix with inverse $A^{-1} = \{a^{ij}\}$, whose elements a_{ij} are functions of a vector $\boldsymbol{\theta}$. Then*

$$\frac{\partial \log|\det A|}{\partial a_{ij}} = a^{ji}$$

and

$$\frac{\partial a^{ij}}{\partial \boldsymbol{\theta}} = -\sum_{hm} a^{ih}\frac{\partial a_{hm}}{\partial \boldsymbol{\theta}} a^{mj}.$$

We have

$$\mathbf{q}(\delta_i) = -\frac{1}{2}\sum_k \sum_j \frac{\partial \log \det S}{\partial S_{kj}} \frac{\partial S_{kj}}{\partial \delta_i}.$$

Applying Lemma MD, we obtain

$$\mathbf{q}(\delta_i) = -\frac{1}{2}\sum_k \sum_j S^{jk}\frac{\partial S_{kj}}{\partial \delta_i}. \qquad \text{(i)}$$

Thus we need to evaluate the derivative $\partial S_{kj}/\partial \delta_i$, where

$$S = \frac{\hat{E}'\hat{E}}{n} = \frac{U'U}{n} - \frac{U'PU}{n},$$

and $P = I - U_{-1}(U_{-1}'U_{-1})^{-1}U_{-1}'$. So $S_{kj} = (1/n)(\mathbf{u}_k'\mathbf{u}_j - \mathbf{u}_k'P\mathbf{u}_j)$, where $\mathbf{u}_k$ and $\mathbf{u}_j$ are the kth and jth columns of U. Now

$$\frac{\partial \mathbf{u}_k'\mathbf{u}_j}{\partial \delta_i} = -H_i'\mathbf{u}_j - H_i'\mathbf{u}_k \qquad \text{(ii)}$$

and

$$\mathbf{u}_k'P\mathbf{u}_j = \sum_r \sum_s \sum_v \sum_w u_{rk}u_{sj}u_{r-1v}u_{s-1w}C_{vw}^{-1},$$

where C_{vw}^{-1} is the (vw)th element of $C^{-1} = (U_{-1}'U_{-1})^{-1}$. We evaluate the derivative with respect to δ_i of each type of element in this summation.

(a) $\partial C_{vw}^{-1}/\partial \delta_i$

Applying Lemma MD we get

$$\frac{\partial C_{vw}^{-1}}{\partial \delta_i} = -\sum_p \sum_q C_{vp}^{-1}\frac{\partial C_{pq}}{\partial \delta_i}C_{qw}^{-1}.$$

At this point it is convenient to introduce the following notation:

1. Let H_i^1 and $\mathbf{u}_q^1$ be the lagged values of H_i and $\mathbf{u}_q$, respectively (in the text we use $H_{i,-1}$ for the former, but here subscripts will otherwise proliferate).
2. Let $A_{i.}$ refer to the ith row of A and $A_{.j}$ refer to the jth column of A.
3. Let $H_{s.}^i$ refer to the sth row of H_i.

Under this notation $C_{pq} = \mathbf{u}_p^{1\prime}\mathbf{u}_q^1$ and

$$\frac{\partial C_{vw}^{-1}}{\partial \delta_i} = 2\sum_q C_{vi}^{-1} H_i^{1\prime}\mathbf{u}_q' C_{qw}^{-1} = 2C_{vi}^{-1} H_i^{1\prime} U_{-1} C_{.w}^{-1}.$$

(b) $\quad \partial u_{s-1w}/\partial\delta_i$

This is nonzero iff $w=i$. Then

$$\frac{\partial u_{s-1i}}{\partial \delta_i} = -H_{s-1.}^{i\prime}.$$

(c) $\quad \partial u_{sj}/\partial\delta_i$

This is nonzero iff $j=i$. In this case

$$\frac{\partial u_{si}}{\partial \delta_i} = -H_{s.}^{i\prime}.$$

It follows that

$$\begin{aligned}\frac{\partial \mathbf{u}_k' P\mathbf{u}_j}{\partial \delta_i} &= 2H_i^{1\prime} U_{-1} \sum_r \sum_s u_{rk} u_{sj} \sum_v u_{r-1v} C_{vi}^{-1} \sum_w u_{s-1w} C_{.w}^{-1} \\ &\quad -2\sum_s u_{sj} H_{s-1.}' \sum_r u_{sk} U_{r-1.} C_{.i}^{-1} \\ &\quad -\sum_r u_{rk} \sum_s H_{s.}^{i\prime} \sum_v u_{r-1v} \sum_w u_{s-1w} C_{vw}^{-1} \qquad (j=1) \\ &\quad -\sum_s u_{sj} \sum_r H_{r.}^{i\prime} \sum_v u_{r-1v} \sum_w u_{s-1w} C_{vw}^{-1} \qquad (k=i) \\ &= 2\mathbf{u}_k' U_{-1} C_{.i}^{-1} H_i^{1\prime} P\mathbf{u}_j - 2H_i^{1\prime}\mathbf{u}_j \mathbf{u}_k' U_{-1} C_{.i}^{-1} \\ &\quad -H_i' P\mathbf{u}_k - H_i' P\mathbf{u}_j, \end{aligned} \qquad \text{(iii)}$$

where the last two terms are obtained when $j=i$ and $k=i$ respectively. From (ii) and (iii) we get

$$\frac{\partial S_{kj}}{\partial \delta_i} = (2\mathbf{u}_k' U_{-1} C_{.i}^{-1} H_i^{1\prime} Q\mathbf{u}_j - H_i' Q\mathbf{u}_k - H_i' Q\mathbf{u}_j)/n, \qquad \text{(iv)}$$

with the same understanding for the last two terms.

Substituting (iv) into (i) gives

$$\mathbf{q}(\delta_i) = -\frac{1}{n}\sum_k \mathbf{u}'_k U_{-1} C_{.i}^{-1} H_i^{1'} Q \sum_j S^{jk}\mathbf{u}_j + \frac{1}{n}\sum_k S^{ik} H_i' Q \mathbf{u}_k,$$

$$= (H_i' QUS_{.i}^{-1} - H_i^{1'} QUS^{-1} U'U_{-1} C_{.i}^{-1})/n.$$

Now $\hat{E} = QE$, $S = \hat{E}'\hat{E}/n$, and $\hat{R}_i = U'U_{-1}C_{.i}^{-1}$.

We therefore end up with

$$\mathbf{q}(\delta_i) = H_i'\hat{E}(\hat{E}'\hat{E})_i^{-1} - H_i^{1'}\hat{E}(\hat{E}'\hat{E})^{-1}\hat{R}_i,$$

as stated in the text.

CHAPTER 5

Nonlinear estimation with instrumental variables

5.1 Introduction

The burgeoning of interest in nonlinear equations and models that has occurred in the last decade or so has been largely contemporaneous with the enhancement of computing power and the availability of convenient and effective algorithms for numerical optimization. Thus whereas students in the fifties and early sixties were preoccupied with linear models or their direct generalizations, the seventies saw the establishment of a better understanding of the estimation theory for nonlinear models. In particular, it was realized that instrumental variables methods could, by the definition of an appropriate minimand, be regarded as a minimization problem and the resulting estimators regarded as fairly natural generalizations of the linear theory, with respect to both limited- and full-information systems. At the same time it became clear that there were limits to this process of generalization – that certain efficiency properties, for instance, did not carry over to the nonlinear context.

In setting out to describe these developments, the first task is to establish some kind of taxonomy of the types of models encountered. One may distinguish between models that are nonlinear only in their parameters, or only in their variables, and models that are nonlinear both in their equations and in their variables. The relevant models are set out, with examples, in Section 5.2. In this section we use the relatively simple context of linear-in-parameter models to establish certain generic kinds of instrument. These distinctions are based on the instrument sets involved. In Section 5.3 we consider, in a limited-information context, the minimand that is involved in the IV approach to essentially nonlinear models, that is, models nonlinear in both parameters and variables. After establishing the asymptotic sampling theory of the resulting estimator, we consider in Section 5.4 the lessons to be learned in the design or choice of instruments. The relative efficiency with respect to maximum-likelihood methods is explored.

System estimation is considered in Sections 5.5 and 5.6. With respect to definitional matters, it is shown that various possible IV estimators, corresponding to distinctions of the kind developed in Section 3.2, may be employed, and conditions are explored under which these methods reduce to a common estimator, the "nonlinear three-stage least-squares" estimator. The relative efficiency of these variants is explored, and use is again made of the artifice of a "best" instrument set. The relationship with the method of full-information maximum likelihood is covered in Section 5.6. It is shown that the maximum-likelihood estimator can itself be regarded as an iterative IV estimator. The relative efficiency properties of the likelihood and operational IV methods is explored in detail. The final section, 5.7, summarizes the findings of the chapter.

5.2 A taxonomy of equations

To describe an equation or a model as nonlinear does not in itself convey much information about the methodological tools that will be needed to estimate its parameters. Some sort of classification scheme is therefore necessary. Without going into too much taxonomic detail, it is useful to maintain distinctions (a) between equations that are linear in their parameters and those that are not and (b) between equations that are, or are not, linear in their variables.

To start with, equations that are linear in the right-hand variables but nonlinear in their parameters pose few problems of principle, at least so far as asymptotic sampling theory is concerned. Consider, for example, the following limited-information model, analyzed intensively in Chapter 4:

$$\mathbf{y}_1 = Y_1\boldsymbol{\beta}_1 + X_1\boldsymbol{\gamma}_1 + \mathbf{u}_1 = H_1\boldsymbol{\delta}_1 + \mathbf{u}_1$$

$$Y_1 = X\Pi_1 + V_1.$$

It will be recalled from Section 4.3 that the Cramer–Rao lower bound for the parameter estimate $\hat{\boldsymbol{\delta}}_1$ is given by

$$R_\delta = \sigma_1^2 \operatorname{plim}\left(\frac{H_1'NH_1}{n}\right)^{-1},$$

where $\sigma_1^2 = \operatorname{Var} u_1$ and $N = X(X'X)^{-1}X'$. Suppose, however, that the parameter vector $\boldsymbol{\delta}_1$ is a vector-valued function of more basic or elementary parameters $\boldsymbol{\theta}$, that is, $\boldsymbol{\delta}_1 = \boldsymbol{\delta}_1(\boldsymbol{\theta})$, where the dimension of $\boldsymbol{\theta}$ is at most equal to that of $\boldsymbol{\delta}_1$. Then under suitable regularity conditions,[1] it can be shown that the Cramer–Rao bound for the elementary parameters $\boldsymbol{\theta}$ is given by

$$R_\theta = \sigma_1^2 \operatorname{plim}\left(\frac{J'H_1'NH_1J}{n}\right)^{-1}, \tag{5.1}$$

where $J = \partial\boldsymbol{\delta}_1/\partial\boldsymbol{\theta}$ is the Jacobian of the mapping from $\boldsymbol{\delta}_1$ to $\boldsymbol{\theta}$. (The regularity conditions referred to above will involve the existence and rank of this Jacobian in addition to properties of the exogenous sequence.) In particular, if $\hat{\boldsymbol{\delta}}_1$ is the two-stage least-squares estimator, in which the instrument set Z is taken to be the full set X of predetermined variables, then the corresponding estimator $\hat{\boldsymbol{\theta}}$ attains the Cramer–Rao lower bound.

On occasion, the step of formally taking the Jacobian is built into the problem. Consider the following example, which arose in Section 4.9 in connection with the limited-information model with a serially correlated error term. According to equation (4.70), we are to fit the equation

$$\mathbf{y}_1 = \rho\mathbf{y}_{1,-1} + (Y_1 - \rho Y_{1,-1})\boldsymbol{\beta}_1 + (X_1 - \rho X_{1,-1})\boldsymbol{\gamma}_1 + \boldsymbol{\epsilon}_1,$$

utilizing an instrument set Z that includes $\mathbf{y}_{1,-1}$, $Y_{1,-1}$, X_1, and $X_{1,-1}$ among its columns. It will be noted that this model is nonlinear in its parameters, although linear in variables. Let $\boldsymbol{\theta}' = (\rho, \boldsymbol{\beta}_1, \boldsymbol{\gamma}_1)$ and write

$$\mathbf{g}(\boldsymbol{\theta}) = \rho\mathbf{y}_{1,-1} + (Y_1 - \rho Y_{1,-1})\boldsymbol{\beta}_1 + (X_1 - \rho X_{1,-1})\boldsymbol{\gamma}_1.$$

The IV minimand is then $\mathbf{g}(\boldsymbol{\theta})'P_z\mathbf{g}(\boldsymbol{\theta})$ and it is easily seen (cf. Section 4.9) that this is the same as the nonlinear least-squares minimand $\hat{\mathbf{g}}(\boldsymbol{\theta})'\hat{\mathbf{g}}(\boldsymbol{\theta})$, where we obtain $\hat{g}$ for g by replacing Y_1 by $\hat{Y}_1 = P_z Y_1$. The asymptotic covariance matrix resulting from the minimum is

$$\sigma^2 \operatorname{plim} n[\hat{G}(\boldsymbol{\theta})'\hat{G}(\boldsymbol{\theta})]^{-1},$$

where $\hat{G}(\boldsymbol{\theta})$ is the data matrix of the Jacobian of $\hat{g}(\boldsymbol{\theta})$ with respect to $\boldsymbol{\theta}$ (for a formal definition and discussion we refer the reader forward to Section 5.4). Taking the derivatives with respect to ρ, $\boldsymbol{\beta}_1$, and $\boldsymbol{\gamma}_1$, the above covariance matrix is

$$\sigma^2 \operatorname{plim} n[(\mathbf{y}_{1,-1} - Y_{1,-1}\boldsymbol{\beta}_1 - X_{1,-1}\boldsymbol{\gamma}_1 \vdots \hat{Y}_1 - \rho Y_{1,-1} \vdots X_1 - \rho X_1)' \\ \times (\mathbf{y}_{1,-1} - Y_{1,-1}\boldsymbol{\beta}_1 - X_{1,-1}\boldsymbol{\gamma}_1 \vdots \hat{Y}_1 - \rho Y_{1,-1} \vdots X_1 - \rho X_1)]^{-1}.$$

This justifies the formula (4.71) of Chapter 4.

Returning to the general context of a functional relationship $\boldsymbol{\delta}_1 = \boldsymbol{\delta}_1(\boldsymbol{\theta})$, some points remain to be sorted out in practice – in particular, the process of solution for the $\boldsymbol{\theta}$ in terms of the $\boldsymbol{\delta}_1$ in the overdetermined case where dim $\boldsymbol{\theta} < \dim \boldsymbol{\delta}_1$. Nevertheless, the general situation is a more or less straightforward extension of OLS sampling theory for nonlinear equations. For this reason we do not dwell any further on the case of pure parameter nonlinearity. We remark, however, that parameter nonlinearity frequently occurs in association with the more essential model nonlinearities of the kind considered below, and it is useful to have the bound (5.1) in such contexts.

Models linear in their parameters

Suppose that, in the equation under consideration, the parameters enter linearly but the right-hand endogenous variables enter nonlinearly. Such an equation, or model, is rather more interesting from the estimation point of view. The following will serve as a paradigm for such equations:

$$y_{it} = \sum_{j=1}^{G_1} \beta_{ij} g_j(\mathbf{y}_t, \mathbf{x}_t) + \sum_{j=1}^{K_1} \gamma_{ij} x_{tj} + u_{it}, \qquad t=1\ldots n, \quad i=1\ldots r. \tag{5.2}$$

We have adopted the framework of a simultaneous nonlinear model. Of course, one need not have such a situation explicitly in mind. The functions $g_j(\mathbf{y}_t, \mathbf{x}_t) = g_{jt}$ are linear or nonlinear functions of unspecified variables y_t, which are *not* assumed to be independent of the error term u_{it}. For obvious reasons we rule out $g_{jt} = y_{it}$.

It will further subsequent discussion to present two simple examples of this sort of model.

Example 1

$$y_{1t} = \beta_1 \exp(y_{2t}) + \gamma_1 x_{1t} + u_{1t} \tag{5.3a}$$

$$y_{2t} = \beta_2 \log y_{1t} + \gamma_2 + \gamma_3 x_{1t} + u_{2t}. \tag{5.3b}$$

It will be noted that the simultaneous model does not have an explicit (closed-form) reduced form in which y_{1t} and y_{2t} are solved as a function of x_{1t} and the disturbances u_{1t} and u_{2t}, or at least one that is valid for all β_2 over the range of interest. In general, exponential and logarithmic elements are frequent sources of nonlinearity.

Example 2

Our second example is drawn from the literature of models of markets in disequilibrium, which itself is part of a wider body of writing on models that exhibit dichotomous behavior or truncated distributions. Let

d = demand, s = supply, and q = transacted quantity of a commodity and p the transacted price. The model is

$$d_t = \beta_1 p_t + \gamma_{10} + \gamma_{11} x_{1t} + u_{1t} \tag{5.4a}$$

$$s_t = \beta_2 p_t + \gamma_{20} + \gamma_{21} x_{2t} + u_{2t} \tag{5.4b}$$

$$q_t = \min(d_t, s_t) \tag{5.4c}$$

$$p_t = p_{t-1} + \lambda(d_t - s_t). \tag{5.4d}$$

Essentially what this model is intended to convey is that price may not move to clear the market, that is, make $d_t = s_t$ at each time point. The quantity actually transacted at a nonclearing price is equal to the lesser of demand or supply. The latter variables (d_t and s_t) are themselves unobservable.

At first sight, this model does not bear much resemblance to the paradigm (5.2) above. However, let us introduce the ramp function $R(\bullet)$ defined by

$$R(x) = 1 \quad \text{if } x > 0$$
$$= 0 \quad \text{otherwise.}$$

The minimum condition (5.4c) may be written as

$$q_t = d_t - (d_t - s_t) R(d_t - s_t).$$

Using equation (5.4d) and the maintained hypothesis $\lambda > 0$, we may restate the model in the form of just two equations:

$$q_t = \beta_1 p_t - \frac{1}{\lambda}(p_t - p_{t-1}) R(p_t - p_{t-1}) + \gamma_{10} + \gamma_{11} x_{1t} + u_{1t} \tag{5.5a}$$

$$q_t = \beta_2 p_t - \frac{1}{\lambda}(p_t - p_{t-1}) R(p_{t-1} - p_t) + \gamma_{20} + \gamma_{21} x_{2t} + u_{2t}. \tag{5.5b}$$

Equations (5.5a, b) are not in fact the most convenient "reparametization" of the disequilibrium model since there are some problems as $\lambda \to 0$, but they will do for our present purposes.

It will be observed that equations (5.5a, b) are linear in their parameters (LIP). The nonlinearity arises through the function $g(p) = (p - p_{t-1}) R(p - p_{t-1})$, which is continuous but not differentiable at the point $p = p_{t-1}$. Figure 5.1 sketches this function, which is piecewise linear.

Although equations (5.5a, b) are nonlinear, we note for future reference that the reduced form for price is linear, of the form

$$p_t = \mu p_{t-1} + \mu\lambda(\gamma_{10} - \gamma_{20}) + \mu\lambda\gamma_{11} x_{1t} - \mu\lambda\gamma_{21} x_{2t} + \mu\lambda(u_{1t} - u_{2t}), \tag{5.6}$$

where $\mu = 1/[1 - \lambda(\beta_1 - \beta_2)]$.

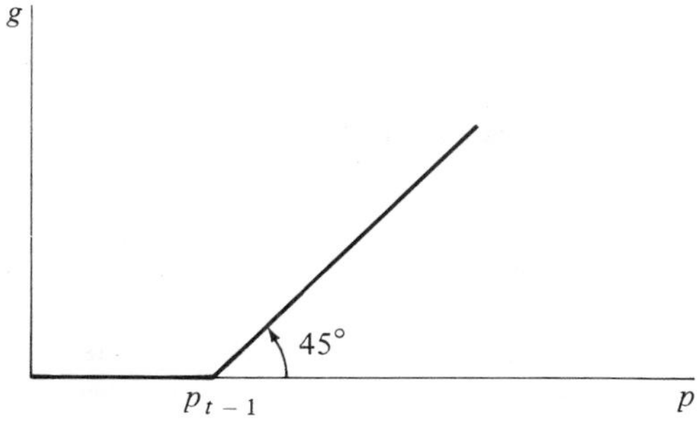

Figure 5.1 The function $g(p)=(p-p_{t-1})R(p-p_{t-1})$.

Essentially nonlinear systems

By an essentially nonlinear equation we shall mean one in which both the right-hand endogenous variables and the parameters enter nonlinearity. Referring back to the model (5.3a, b), if we changed the first equation to

$$y_{1t}=\beta_1 \exp(\beta_3 y_{2t})+\gamma_1 x_{1t}+u_{1t}, \tag{5.7}$$

this would then be essentially nonlinear.

On occasion it may be more convenient to express the equation under consideration in implicit form. For example:

$$y_{1t}^{\beta_1}+y_{2t}^{\beta_2}-\gamma_1 x_{1t}=u_{1t},$$

or in general, an equation of the form

$$f_1(\mathbf{y}_t, \mathbf{x}_t, \boldsymbol{\theta})=u_{1t}, \tag{5.8}$$

where $\boldsymbol{\theta}$ is the vector of parameters. The implicit form can be very useful where a given equation arises (say, from the underlying economic theory) in an essentially symmetric way or where the disturbance is more naturally applied to a functional relationship of the trade-off, or level surface, type. The latter contexts are to be found in such economic areas as consumer demand, production possibility frontiers, and the unemployment–vacancy loci in labor markets.

Notice that we have specified the disturbance term to enter additively. Some models do not satisfy such a requirement. Consider, for instance, the popular Tobit model. Define $y_i^*=\mathbf{x}_i'\boldsymbol{\beta}+\epsilon_i$ as a spherical linear regression model in the dependent variable y_i^*. The latter, however, is not observable. Instead, we observe a variable y_i, which is such that

$$y_i = y_i^* \Leftrightarrow y_i^* > 0$$
$$\quad = 0 \Leftrightarrow y_i^* \leq 0.$$

Or in terms of the ramp function earlier introduced,

$$y_i = y_i^* R(y_i^*) = (\mathbf{x}_i'\boldsymbol{\beta} + \epsilon_i) R(\mathbf{x}_i'\boldsymbol{\beta} + \epsilon_i). \tag{5.9}$$

Now at first sight, this is not of the form (5.8), since the disturbance ϵ_i is not separable from the observables.

However, IV methods of fair efficiency can often be devised for such models. This is done by essentially separating out the observables and unobservables and replacing the unobservables by their expectations in terms of observable quantities. To continue with the simple Tobit example, we may write equation (5.9) in the form

$$y_i = d_i \mathbf{x}_i'\boldsymbol{\beta} + \epsilon_i R(\mathbf{x}_i'\boldsymbol{\beta} + \epsilon_i), \tag{5.10}$$

where $d_i = R(y_i)$ is the binary dummy indicating whether or not y_i is positive. By using the result

$$\int_0^\infty (x-\mu) n(x; \mu, \sigma^2)\, dx = (\sigma/\sqrt{2\pi}) \exp(-\tfrac{1}{2}\mu^2/\sigma^2),$$

where $n(\bullet; \mu, \sigma^2)$ denotes the normal density, we may write equation (5.10) in the form

$$y_i = d_i \mathbf{x}_i'\boldsymbol{\beta} + (\sigma/\sqrt{2\pi}) \exp - \tfrac{1}{2}[\mathbf{x}_i'(\beta/\sigma)]^2 + \xi_i, \tag{5.11}$$

where $\mathcal{E}(\xi_i) = 0$. Equation (5.11) is of the form (5.8), with the disturbance ξ_i separable and additive (although in this particular example, no longer spherical).

It may be of interest to append a few remarks on the fitting of model (5.11). The necessity for IV arises from the correlation of the (observable) binary dummy

$$d_i = R(\mathbf{x}_i'\boldsymbol{\beta} + \epsilon_i)$$

with the disturbance term ξ_i, and one accordingly has to find instruments for the variables $d_i \mathbf{x}_i$. This can be done in various ways on the basis of instrument sets containing elements of $x_i, x_i^2, \ldots$, or else by using such techniques as discriminant and classification analysis (cf. Section 2.6). As it stands, equation (5.11) is nonlinear because of the second term on the right-hand side. Again, one can handle this in various ways. For example, note that

$$d_i = 1 \Leftrightarrow \mathbf{x}_i'(\beta/\sigma) + (\epsilon/\sigma) > 0$$
$$\quad = 0 \Leftrightarrow \mathbf{x}_i'(\beta/\sigma) + (\epsilon/\sigma) \leq 0.$$

A probit analysis can therefore be used to obtain consistent estimates $(\hat{\beta}/\sigma)$, which can be inserted inside the nonlinear term. Following this a simple linear IV can be applied to the equation

$$y_i = d_i \mathbf{x}_i' \beta + (\sigma/\sqrt{2\pi}) \exp -\tfrac{1}{2}[x_i'(\hat{\beta}/\sigma)]^2 + \xi_i$$

to estimate β and σ. Alternatively one can use the theory shortly to be described for a full nonlinear IV calculation based directly on equation (5.11).

Note that the second, nonlinear term in equation (5.11) will be of only small order in magnitude, since it consists in the product of a (hopefully) small disturbance parameter σ with a normal density. Thus an IV fit of equation (5.11), simply ignoring this term, should give a reasonably accurate initial estimate of β, if this is needed to start up a full maximum-likelihood solution.

The Tobit model is of course readily amenable to a full maximum-likelihood solution, and we have used it simply as a convenient example for expositional purposes. The point is that dichotomous or other models may often be converted to the form (5.8) by using a device similar to our suggestion above, entailing the separation out of observable and unobservable variables with replacement of the latter by (unconditional) expectations. An IV calculation can then be applied to yield consistent estimates of the parameters. Approaches previously suggested for such models involve applying ordinary least squares to a transformed equation established by purging the equation disturbance of the influence of the right-hand variables. [See Heckman (1976) and Section 2.6 for examples of this approach.] The present IV formulation may be more robust than such methods, which frequently entail numerically unstable ratios among the regressors [cf. equation (2.24) of Chapter 2].

5.3 LIP equations: limited information

As we shall see, there are several ways in which we may approach the problem of finding acceptable instruments for the estimation of the LIP model (5.2). They have in common the search for admissible and efficient instruments for the random variables $g_{jt} = g_j(\mathbf{y}_t, \mathbf{x}_t)$. As we have stressed in Chapter 2, all IV methods are really also two-stage least-squares methods. This makes rather confusing the terminology current in the literature, which draws a distinction between "nonlinear two-stage least squares" and other methods as though this were based upon some difference of operational substance. We prefer instead to characterize the different methods in terms of the approach taken to the choice of instruments. However, in deference to current usage we shall adhere to the "nonlinear two-stage least squares" label as representing one particular kind of instrument set.

Nonlinear two-stage least squares

The term *nonlinear two-stage least squares* (NL2SLS) usually means an instrument set consisting of the exogenous or predetermined variables X and perhaps polynomials of low order in these variables. To illustrate the method we shall choose the instrument set $Z=X$ and append some later remarks on the question of polynomials. Write

$$Y_1^g=[\mathbf{g}_1(\mathbf{y}_t,\mathbf{x}_t)\ \mathbf{g}_2(\mathbf{y}_t,\mathbf{x}_t)\ \dots\ \mathbf{g}_{G_1}(\mathbf{y}_t,\mathbf{x}_t)],\qquad t=1,\dots,n$$

as the data matrix of observations on the functions g_{jt}. Then the model may be written

$$\mathbf{y}_1=Y_1^g\beta_1+X_1\gamma_1+\mathbf{u}_1=H_1\delta_1+\mathbf{u}_1,$$

where $H_1=[Y_1^g \vdots X_1]$. The IV estimator is then

$$\hat{\delta}_1=(H_1'P_XH_1)^{-1}H_1'P_X\mathbf{y}_1. \tag{5.12}$$

Equivalently, let $\hat{H}_1$ be the fitted values in the regression of H_1 upon X. Since the columns of X include X_1, we have $\hat{H}_1=[\hat{Y}_1^g \vdots X_1]$, and

$$\hat{\delta}_1=(\hat{H}_1'H_1)^{-1}\hat{H}_1'\mathbf{y}_1 \tag{5.13a}$$

$$=(\hat{H}_1'\hat{H}_1)^{-1}\hat{H}_1'\mathbf{y}_1. \tag{5.13b}$$

It will be noted that formulas (5.12) and (5.13) are homologous with the linear case, where now each function g_{jt} is simply treated as a new variable. As with the linear treatment, we note that the fitted values $\hat{H}_1$ themselves constitute an instrument set, which is minimal with respect to the original set X.

Notice, however, that the existence of the NL2SLS estimator requires that $\hat{H}_1'\hat{H}_1$ has full rank. If X is an $n\times K$ matrix of full-column rank that includes X_1 as a submatrix, a necessary condition, for this is the Edgerton (1972) condition

$$K\geq G_1+K_1,$$

where it will be recalled that $G_1=\dim(\beta_1)$ and $K_1=\dim(\gamma_1)$. To prove this, write $\hat{H}$ as

$$\hat{H}_1=X\left[(X'X)^{-1}X'Y_1^g \,\vdots\, \begin{matrix} I_{K_1} \\ \mathbf{O} \end{matrix}\right], \tag{5.14}$$

where I_{K_1} is the $K_1\times K_1$ identity matrix and 0 is the null matrix of order $(K-K_1)\times K_1$. Now $H_1'H_1$ is symmetric of order G_1+K_1 and $\operatorname{rank}(\hat{H}_1'\hat{H})=$

rank$(\hat{H}_1)$. From equation (5.14) we see that rank$(H_1) \leq$ rank X, and so a necessary condition that $\hat{H}_1'\hat{H}_1$ has full-column rank is

$$K \geq G_1 + K_1.$$

Note the similarity between the Edgerton condition and the order condition for identifiability of a linear equation (see Section 4.6). However, for nonlinear equations of the sort studied here, the Edgerton condition is not a necessary condition for identification. Fisher (1966, chap. 5), gives a sufficient condition for a nonlinear equation to be identified, and Edgerton (1972, p. 31), gives a nonlinear model that satisfies Fisher's criterion but violates his condition.

Since the instrument set X is, by assumption, nonstochastic or else includes lagged predetermined variables independent of the current disturbances, the asymptotic theory of the NL2SLS estimator is quite straightforward. Assuming that limiting moment matrices such as plim$(1/n)Y_1^{g'}X$ exist, the asymptotic covariance matrix of the IV estimator $\hat{\delta}$ is

$$\sigma^2 \operatorname{plim}\left[\frac{H_1'X}{n}\left(\frac{X'X}{n}\right)^{-1}\frac{X'H_1}{n}\right].$$

At this point, it is germane to bring up the efficiency question. If one or more of the functions g_j is highly nonlinear, a linear function of the exogenous variables X may be a poor proxy. Considering, for example, the disequilibrium model [equations (5.5a) and (5.5b)], we observed that the reduced form for price p was linear in the predetermined variables. The use of these predetermined variables, which corresponds in this application to the set X, is therefore unexceptionable. However, we are really after a proxy for the variable $g_t = (p_t - p_{t-1})R(p_t - p_{t-1})$. Supposing that p_t can be well approximated in terms of a linear function of the X variables, the same is therefore *not* true of the variable g_t. Looking at Figure 5.1 above, we should want a cubic, at least, in the elements of X.

This suggests that, starting with a set X of predetermined variables (the "primitive" or "elementary" set), one should proceed to add to the instrument set terms of the second, third, or even higher order in the variables of X. The final augmented instrument set Z will then consist of the predetermined variable together with polynomials, suitably chosen to proxy the nonlinearities in the functions g_j, over the relevant range of variation. This procedure was suggested by Kelejian (1971) and Amemiya (1974). The estimators (5.12) and (5.13) are unchanged in form; the projection matrix P_X is simply replaced by the projection matrix P_Z associated with the augmented instrument set. One caveat to be observed in using the strict least-squares formula [equation (5.13b)] is that the approximating polynomials must be the same for all of the variables in H_1. In other words, each element g_{jt} must be regressed on exactly the same instrument set Z. If this is not done, the resulting estimator $\hat{\delta}_1$ is not necessarily consistent. Formula (5.13a), however, is not open to this kind of objection. We refer the reader back to Chapter 2 for a general discussion of this question.

For simple models the NL2SLS technique seems to work well, provided that higher-order polynomials are included among the instruments. The latter proviso is important. Thus Bowden and Turkington (1981) found that for the disequilibrium model the use of the unaugmented set X resulted in a disastrous performance for the NL2SLS estimator, especially if the variation among the predetermined variables is relatively low. The reason appears to be that if variation in p is confined to a smallish neighborhood of a pronounced nonlinearity, the linear instrument is unable to pick up any pattern, so that the fitted values $(\hat{g}_{jt})$ may be constant or even zero. This results in near-singularity of the matrix $\hat{H}$. The use of even a quadratic-augmented instrument set results in a radical improvement in the NL2SLS estimator. A similar if less drastic tendency was noted in respect of the model (5.3) above.

It should by now be apparent that there may be operational problems with the method of NL2SLS. Out of simple risk aversion, one wants to include not only squares and cubes x_i^2, x_i^3 in the predetermined variables but also cross-products such as $x_i x_j$. This can lead to an augmented instrument set of substantial proportions. Asymptotically there is no essential difficulty with this, but one suspects (cf. Section 2.2) that there is a finite sample cost from the implied loss of degrees of freedom in the preliminary regressions forming the minimal instruments $\hat{g}_{jt}$. Computing requirements may also be affected by this expansion of dimensionality. It is therefore important to investigate alternatives to this rather cumbersome procedure. In the remainder of the section we take up this problem.

Internal instruments

Reconsidering the NL2SLS method, we started by regressing the nonlinear function $g_{jt} = g_j(\mathbf{y}_t, \mathbf{x}_t)$ upon the (augmented) set Z of instruments. The resulting fitted values $\hat{g}_{jt}$, collected into a matrix $\hat{H}$, then constituted a minimal instrument set. Suppose, on the other hand, that we started by regressing the endogenous variables $\mathbf{y}_t$ appearing inside the functions $g_j(\mathbf{y}_t, \mathbf{x}_t)$ upon the instrument set Z. The fitted values $\hat{y}_t$ are then substituted inside the functions to obtain as new instruments $g_j(\hat{\mathbf{y}}_t, \mathbf{x}_t)$. The instruments so formed we shall call *internal instruments,* in reference to the substitution of a fitted value *inside* the nonlinear function g_j, rather than fitting (as it were) the function itself.

Once the instruments $g_j(\hat{\mathbf{y}}_t, \mathbf{x}_t)$ are obtained, we can proceed in one of two ways: (a) Since there is evidently a natural pairing of regressors $g_j(\mathbf{y}_t, \mathbf{x}_t)$ with instruments $g_j(\hat{\mathbf{y}}_t, \mathbf{x}_t)$, we can simply define the set of instruments to be used for equation (5.2) as

$$\{Z_{Rt}\} = \{g_1(\hat{\mathbf{y}}_t, \mathbf{x}_t) \ldots g_{G_1}(\hat{\mathbf{y}}_t, \mathbf{x}_t); x_{1t}^1 \ldots x_{K_1 t}^1\},$$

in a notation that should be clear from the context. The estimator is then

$$\hat{\boldsymbol{\delta}}_R = (Z_R' H_1)^{-1} Z_R' \mathbf{y}_1. \tag{5.15}$$

This method is that originally proposed and discussed by Bowden (1978) and Bowden and Turkington (1981).

A potentially more efficient procedure, although more expensive computationally, is to add the internal instruments $g_i(\hat{\mathbf{y}}_t, \mathbf{x}_t)$ to the original instrument set Z to obtain a maximal set $Z_m = \{Z, Z_R\}$. With Z_m now available, one forms a minimal instrument set $\hat{H}_1$ by regressing the columns of H_1 upon those of Z_m. The IV estimator is then

$$\hat{\boldsymbol{\delta}}_m = (\hat{H}_1' H_1)^{-1} \hat{H}_1' \mathbf{y}_1 = (\hat{H}_1' \hat{H}_1)^{-1} \hat{H}_1' \mathbf{y}_1. \tag{5.16}$$

The estimator $\hat{\boldsymbol{\delta}}_m$ will clearly possess superior efficiency. However, the principles involved in the internal instrument methods can be discussed in the more manageable context of the restricted estimator $\hat{\boldsymbol{\delta}}_R$ of equation (5.15). In particular, we shall assume that just one nonlinear function $g(y_{2t}, \mathbf{x}_t)$ of a single endogenous variable y_{2t} appears on the right-hand side of the proposed equation. We shall also assume that the equation to be estimated is embedded in a model in which both y_1 and y_2 are explained in terms of a set of predetermined variables and disturbances.

Thus let us suppose that the equation to be estimated is the first, and that it has the form

$$y_{1t} = g(y_{2t}, \mathbf{x}_t)\beta + \boldsymbol{\gamma}_1' \mathbf{x}_t^1 + u_{1t}, \qquad t = 1, \ldots, n. \tag{5.17}$$

The exogenous variables occurring linearly are denoted by $\mathbf{x}_t^1$. These are not necessarily identical with those collectively denoted by x_t inside the nonlinear function g. We suppose that the random variables $g(y_{2t}, \mathbf{x}_t)$ have bounded means and variances, uniformly in t. We assume also that a reduced-form expression exists for y_{2t}, which we write schematically as $y_{2t} = Y_2(\mathbf{x}_t, \mathbf{u}_t)$, where $\mathbf{u}_t$ is the disturbance vector for the model and $\mathbf{x}_t$ denotes all the exogenous variables. Write $f_t = f(\mathbf{x}_t) = \mathcal{E} Y_2(\mathbf{x}_t, \mathbf{u}_t)$. We assume that the f_t are uniformly bounded in t. It will be understood that both the reduced-form Y_2 and its expectation f will depend on the parameters of the model, but to economize on notation we shall not introduce new symbols for this purpose. Write $\epsilon_t = Y_2(\mathbf{x}_t, \mathbf{u}_t) - f(\mathbf{x}_t)$. Thus

$$y_{2t} = f(\mathbf{x}_t) + \epsilon_t. \tag{5.18}$$

Because of the serial independence assumption on the disturbance terms u_t, the residuals ϵ_t are temporally independent. But since they depend on the exogenous variables, we cannot assume that they are identically distributed. We assume that the variance of y_{2t} exists, so that $\mathcal{E}\epsilon_t^2 < \infty$. Finally, with regard to the predetermined variables, we shall assume that these are composed of strictly exogenous variables, and so the complications caused by the presence of lagged endogenous variables are not formally[2] considered at this stage.

In order to consider in detail the admissibility of the internal instrument, we shall suppose that in stage 1 we regress y_2 on X, the data matrix of all the exogenous variables in the system. The fitted value $\hat{\mathbf{y}}_2 = P_x \mathbf{y}_2$, where $P_x = X(X'X)^{-1}X'$, is the least-squares projection matrix. Define the data matrix $H = [\mathbf{g}(y_2, \mathbf{x}), X_1]$. Our internal instrument estimator is then defined by

$$\hat{\boldsymbol{\delta}} = [\tilde{Z}'H]^{-1}\tilde{Z}'\mathbf{y}_1, \tag{5.19}$$

where $\boldsymbol{\delta}' = (\beta \;\; \gamma_1)$, and the matrix of instruments $\tilde{Z}$ is defined by

$$\tilde{Z} = [\mathbf{g}(\hat{y}_2, \mathbf{x}), X_1].$$

Write $\hat{f}_t$ as the fitted value of f_t in the regression of the mean vector $\mathbf{f}$ of (5.18) on the exogenous variables. That is, if we define e_t as the tth row of the $n \times n$ identity matrix I, $\hat{f}_t = \mathbf{e}_t P_x \mathbf{f}$. Write $g_{x_t} = g(\hat{f}_t, \mathbf{x}_t)$ and denote by g'_{x_t} the partial derivative of $g(\bullet, \mathbf{x}_t)$ evaluated at the point $\hat{f}_t$. It will be necessary to attach a meaning to the limit as $n \to \infty$ of terms $\hat{f}_t$, for fixed t. We shall assume that the limiting regression coefficient $(X'X)^{-1}X'\mathbf{f}$ exists (as $\boldsymbol{\alpha}$, say). Hence if $\mathbf{X}'_{t.}$ denotes the tth row of X, $\tilde{f}_t = \mathbf{X}'_{t.}\boldsymbol{\alpha}$ represents the limiting value of $\hat{f}_t$. We denote by $\tilde{g}_{x_t}$ and $\tilde{g}'_{x_t}$ the values of g and g' evaluated at these limiting values, for example, $\tilde{g}_{x_t} = g(\tilde{f}_t, \mathbf{x}_t)$. The following proposition appears in Bowden and Turkington (1981):

Proposition 5.1:

1. *Suppose the following:*

   (a) *The first and second moments of $g(y_{2t})$ exist and are uniformly bounded in t.*

   (b) *The fourth-order moment of the structural disturbance u_{1t} exists.*

   (c) *The functions $g'(\bullet, \mathbf{x}_t)$ are continuous and $\tilde{g}_{x_t}, \tilde{g}'_{x_t}$ are uniformly bounded in t. As $n \to \infty$, the limits $(1/n)\sum \tilde{g}_{x_t}^2$ and $(1/n)\sum \tilde{g}_{x_t}\mathcal{E}g(y_{2t})$ exist.*

   (d) *The limiting matrix* $\text{plim}(1/n)\tilde{Z}'H$ *is nonsingular.*

Then the internal instrument estimator $\hat{\boldsymbol{\delta}}$ converges in probability to $\boldsymbol{\delta}$.

2. *Suppose in addition:*

(e) *For some* $\zeta > 0$, $\mathcal{E}|\epsilon_t|^{2+\zeta} < M$, *a constant, uniformly in t. Then* $\sqrt{n}(\hat{\boldsymbol{\delta}} - \boldsymbol{\delta})$ *has a limiting normal distribution, with asymptotic covariance matrix*

$$\sigma_1^2\left(\operatorname{plim}\frac{1}{n}\tilde{Z}'H\right)^{-1}\left(\operatorname{plim}\frac{1}{n}\tilde{Z}'\tilde{Z}\right)\left(\operatorname{plim}\frac{1}{n}H'\tilde{Z}\right)^{-1}$$

where $\sigma_1^2 = \mathcal{E}u_{1t}^2$.

Proof[3]*:* Fix n and expand $g(\hat{y}_{2t}, \mathbf{x}_t)$ in exact Taylor series about the point $(\hat{f}_t, \mathbf{x}_t)$. We may then write

$$\frac{1}{n}\mathbf{g}(\hat{y}_2)'\mathbf{u}_1 = \frac{1}{n}\sum_t g_{x_t}u_{1t} + \sum_t (\mathbf{e}_t P_x \boldsymbol{\epsilon}) g'(\bar{f}_t, \mathbf{x}_t) u_{1t},$$

where $\bar{f}_t$ is on the line segment joining $\hat{f}_t$ to $\hat{y}_{2t}$. It is easy to show that the first term on the right side has the same probability limit as $\operatorname{plim}(1/N)\sum \tilde{g}_{x_t}u_{1t}$, which from (c) is zero. The second term may be written

$$\begin{aligned}\frac{1}{n}\sum_t\left(\frac{\boldsymbol{\epsilon}'X}{n}\right)\left(\frac{X'X}{n}\right)^{-1}\mathbf{X}_{t.}\,g'(\bar{f}_t,\mathbf{x}_t)u_{1t}\\ =\left(\frac{\boldsymbol{\epsilon}'X}{n}\right)\left(\frac{X'X}{n}\right)^{-1}\frac{1}{n}\sum_t g'(\bar{f}_t,\mathbf{x}_t)\mathbf{X}_{t.}\,u_{1t},\end{aligned} \tag{5.20}$$

where $\mathbf{X}_{t.}'$ is the tth row of X. Now

$$\begin{aligned}\left|\frac{1}{n}\sum_t g'(\bar{f}_t,\mathbf{x}_t)X_{tj}\mathbf{u}_{1t}\right|\\ \leq\left(\frac{1}{n}\sum_t g'^2(\bar{f}_t,\mathbf{x}_t)\right)^{1/2}\left(\frac{1}{n}\sum_t X_{tj}^2u_{1t}^2\right)^{1/2}.\end{aligned} \tag{5.21}$$

Since the X_{tj} are bounded and the fourth-order moment of u_{1t} exists, it follows from the Khinchine–Kolmogorov convergence theorem that $(1/n)\sum X_{tj}^2 u_{1t}^2$ tends in probability to a constant. Consider now the first term on the right side of (5.21). We may write for $t \leq n$:

$$\hat{y}_{2t} = \hat{f}_t + \mathbf{X}_{t.}'\left(\frac{X'X}{n}\right)^{-1}\left(\frac{X'\boldsymbol{\epsilon}}{n}\right).$$

The term $X'\boldsymbol{\epsilon}/n$ tends in probability to zero, since the ϵ_t are assumed to have finite variance. Since the elements of $\mathbf{X}_{t.}'$ are uniformly bounded, we may write $|\hat{y}_{2t} - \hat{f}_t| < \eta$ (say) $\xrightarrow{p} 0$, uniformly in t. Hence $\hat{y}_{2t} - \hat{f}_t \xrightarrow{p} 0$, uniformly in t. By a similar argument applied to ordinary limits, we may show that $\hat{f}_t - \tilde{f}_t \to 0$, uniformly in t. It follows that $\bar{f}_t - \tilde{f}_t \xrightarrow{p} 0$, uniformly in t, so that $\bar{f}_t$ are uniformly bounded in probability. By assumption (c) and Slutsky's theorem, it follows that the term $(1/n)\sum g'(\bar{f}_t, \mathbf{x}_t)^2$ is bounded in probability. Hence the right side of (5.20) is bounded in probability. Since $X'\epsilon/n \xrightarrow{p} 0$, it follows from (5.20) that $\text{plim}(1/n) \times \mathbf{g}(\hat{y}_2)'\mathbf{u}_1 = 0$. Clearly $(1/n)\sum X_1'\mathbf{u} \xrightarrow{p} \mathbf{0}$. We have therefore shown that $(1/n)\tilde{Z}'\mathbf{u}_1 \xrightarrow{p} \mathbf{0}$. ■

We observe from the above proof that so far as consistency is concerned, it would make little difference if we allowed the set X of primitive instruments to include predetermined variables, provided that the disturbances u_{1t} remained serially independent. One needs simply to show that the sum $(1/n)\sum X_{tj}^2 u_{1t}^2$ tends in probability to a constant and that the vector $(1/n)X'\epsilon$ tends in probability to zero. An interesting violation of the condition 1(c) occurs in dichotomous models. Thus in the disequilibrium model, the function $g(p, p_{t-1}) = (p - p_{t-1})R(p - p_{t-1})$ is not differentiable at the point $p = p_{t-1}$. For such models, however, the differentiability failure typically occurs on a set of zero probability measure, and the above proposition will be unaffected in substance. In summary, the consistency and asymptotic distribution properties of the internal instrument methodology appears to be of fairly general applicability.

Let us turn to the relative performance of this method vis-à-vis the NL2SLS method. The meaning of such a comparison needs to be made more precise. The estimator $\hat{\boldsymbol{\delta}}_m$ defined by equation (5.16) is itself an NL2SLS estimator, in which the instrument set has been enlarged by the addition of the functions $g_j(\hat{\mathbf{y}}_t, \mathbf{x}_t)$. For any given primitive instrument set, therefore, the estimator $\hat{\boldsymbol{\delta}}_m$ will always be superior to the basic 2L2SLS estimator. The comparison has more point if we are to compare the limited internal instrument estimator $\hat{\boldsymbol{\delta}}_R$ of equation (5.15) with the basic NL2SLS estimator, where both utilize the same set (more or less) of primitive instruments. Provided the instruments include polynomials in X of a sufficiently high degree, one would expect the NL2SLS method to perform better. Since the object is to proxy g_{jt}, the least-squares estimate $\hat{g}_{jt}$ will always do this as well as anything, provided one has enough right-hand variables. On the other hand, suppose that the reduced form equations for $\mathbf{y}_t$ (the right-hand endogenous variables) were linear in the elements of X. We would then be in possession of a reasonable approximation $\hat{\mathbf{y}}_t$ for $\mathbf{y}_t$, and by extension one should hope for a reasonable proxy $g(\hat{\mathbf{y}}_t, \mathbf{x}_t)$ for the g_{jt}. In such circumstances, the internal instrument estimator $\hat{\boldsymbol{\delta}}_R$ might be expected to possess superior efficiency. Such surmises are borne out by simulation experiments. In general, the internal instrument methodology works well in most situations and is usually superior to the NL2SLS method if the basic instrument set employed is not augmented with polynomial elements.

The matter of a linear reduced form deserves further comment, since it may seem a more or less accidental phenomenon. On reflection, however, many macro models containing exponential or logarithmic nonlinearities do have a solution that is either linear or log-linear in the exogenous variables. If this is the case, it is plainly worthwhile to try an IV estimator that uses $\hat{y}$ (or $\log \hat{y}$) as an internal variable. One suspects that the internal instrument methodology might be a natural way to approach the estimation of macroeconometric models. The general idea that the nature of the solution to a model should influence the choice of the estimation methodology for its parameters is a rather interesting one that deserves further exploration.

Other instruments

Consider again the representative right-hand function $g(\mathbf{y}_t, \mathbf{x}_t)$. The expectation $g_t^e = \mathcal{E}g(\mathbf{y}_t, \mathbf{x}_t)$, conditional upon the given x_t, will depend only upon the x_t variables. Given that the latter are supposed uncorrelated with the disturbance terms, the same property will be true of the expectations g_t^e. Moreover, one would hope that the expectation g_t^e is closely correlated in the usual asymptotic sense with g_t, even though this might not be true in every context. All this suggests the use of g_t^e as an instrument for g_t. Such a procedure was suggested by Kelejian (1971) and its properties further investigated by Bowden (1978).

Formally, let us suppose that we can write the right-hand function of equation (5.2) as

$$g_{jt} = g_j(\mathbf{y}_t, \mathbf{x}_t) = h_j(\mathbf{x}_t; \boldsymbol{\theta}) + \epsilon_t, \tag{5.22}$$

where $h_{jt} = h_j(\mathbf{x}_t; \boldsymbol{\theta}) = \mathcal{E}g_j(\mathbf{y}_t, \mathbf{x}_t)$. The vector $\boldsymbol{\theta}$ indicates that these expectations will depend upon certain parameters. The suggestion is then to utilize the h_{jt} as instruments for the g_{jt}.

There are, however, some obvious difficulties with the use of this instrument. In the first place, it may be impossible to obtain a closed-form expression for the functions h_j. And even if this were possible, $h_j(\mathbf{x}_t, \boldsymbol{\theta})$ will almost always depend upon basic parameters (such as the β_i, γ_i and the parameters of the disturbance process) that are unknown – and whose determination is indeed the object of the exercise. In certain contexts, however, both these difficulties can be overcome. The functions h_j can be explicitly solved, and though we may not know the parameters $\boldsymbol{\theta}$, it may be possible to devise procedures to consistently estimate this vector. This is not to imply that we have available consistent estimates of the basic parameters (β_i or γ_i), but only of those compound parameters, functions of these basic parameters and limited in number, which go to make up $\boldsymbol{\theta}$.

To see how the process works consider again the disequilibrium model, equations (5.5a, b) and (5.6) above. We recall that this has a reduced form that is linear in the predetermined variables. Let $m_t = \mathcal{E}p_t$ given the predetermined variables p_{t-1}, x_{1t}, and x_{2t}. Let $\sigma_p^2 = \operatorname{Var} p_t = \mathcal{E}[\mu\lambda(u_{1t} - u_{2t})]^2$. Then the expectation of the nonlinear function $g(p_t) = (p_t - p_{t-1})R(p_t - p_{t-1})$, which appears in the equation (5.5) to be estimated, is given by

$$\mathcal{E}(p_t - p_{t-1})R(p_{t-1} - p_t) = m_t[1 - N(m_t; 0, \sigma_p^2)] - \frac{\sigma_p}{\sqrt{2\pi}} e^{-(1/2)(m_t^2/\sigma_p^2)},$$

where $N(x; \mu, \sigma^2)$ denotes the (cumulative) normal distribution function. We see from equation (5.6) that the expectation m_t depends upon the compound parameters $\boldsymbol{\theta}' = [\mu, \mu\lambda(\gamma_{10} - \gamma_{20}), \mu\lambda\gamma_{11}, \mu\lambda\gamma_{21}]$. Consistent estimates of these reduced-form parameters and of σ_p^2 can be obtained from a preliminary regression of p_t upon p_{t-1}, x_{1t}, and x_{2t}. Indeed, the fitted value in this regression, namely $\hat{p}_t$, is then an estimate of m_t, in the sense that if $m_t = m_t(\boldsymbol{\theta})$, then $\hat{p}_t = m_t(\hat{\boldsymbol{\theta}})$. The conditional expectation instrument is then formed as

$$h_t(\hat{\boldsymbol{\theta}}) = \hat{p}_t[1 - N(\hat{p}_t; 0, \hat{\sigma}_p^2)] - \frac{\hat{\sigma}_p}{\sqrt{2\pi}} e^{-(1/2)(\hat{p}_t^2/\hat{\sigma}_p^2)}.$$

It remains to prove as a general proposition that the conditional expectation instrument $h(\mathbf{x}_t, \hat{\boldsymbol{\theta}}_n)$ is admissible and that the resulting estimates $\hat{\boldsymbol{\beta}}$ and $\hat{\boldsymbol{\gamma}}$ are asymptotically normal, with the usual IV limiting covariance matrix. This is quite straightforward, given appropriate regularity assumptions on the predetermined variables and disturbance terms and on the functions h_j and will not therefore be stated as a formal proposition. Considering a representative proposed instrument $h_t(\hat{\boldsymbol{\theta}}_n)$, we may write

$$h_t(\hat{\boldsymbol{\theta}}_n) = h_t(\boldsymbol{\theta}) + (\hat{\boldsymbol{\theta}}_n - \boldsymbol{\theta})h'(\boldsymbol{\theta}_*),$$

where $\boldsymbol{\theta}_*$ is on the line segment joining $\hat{\boldsymbol{\theta}}_n$ and $\boldsymbol{\theta}$. Consider the sum

$$\frac{1}{\sqrt{n}} \sum h_t(\hat{\boldsymbol{\theta}}_n)u_{1t} = \frac{1}{\sqrt{n}} \sum h_t(\boldsymbol{\theta})u_{1t} + \sqrt{n}(\hat{\boldsymbol{\theta}}_n - \boldsymbol{\theta})\frac{1}{n} \sum h_t(\boldsymbol{\theta}_*)u_{1t}. \tag{5.23}$$

If the expectations are bounded and $\lim(1/n) \sum h_t^2(\boldsymbol{\theta})$ exists, then the first term on the right-hand side of equation (5.23) tends to a $N[0, \sigma_1^2 \lim(1/n) \sum h_t^2(\boldsymbol{\theta})]$ variable. If the estimator $\hat{\boldsymbol{\theta}}_n$ has a limiting distribution, then since $(1/n) \sum h_t(\boldsymbol{\theta}_*)u_{1t} \xrightarrow{p} 0$, it follows that the second term on the right-hand side of equation (5.23) tends in distribution to zero. Hence,

$$\frac{1}{\sqrt{n}} \sum h_t(\hat{\boldsymbol{\theta}}_n)u_{1t} \xrightarrow{d} N\left[0, \sigma_1^2 \lim \frac{1}{n} \sum h_t^2(\boldsymbol{\theta})\right]. \tag{5.24}$$

It is immediately apparent that $(1/n)\sum h_t(\hat{\theta}_n)u_{1t} \xrightarrow{p} 0$, so that the instrument and disturbance are asymptotically uncorrelated. Moreover, with the distribution (5.24) established it is easy to show that the resulting IV estimators $\hat{\boldsymbol{\beta}}_j$ and $\hat{\gamma}_j$ have an asymptotic normal distribution, with the standard IV limiting covariance matrix. We leave the details to the reader.

It can in fact be shown that if we simply replace the function $g_j(\mathbf{y}_t, \mathbf{x}_t)$ by the corresponding estimated expectations $h_t(\hat{\theta}_n)$, then a subsequent OLS fit of equation (5.2) will yield consistent estimates of the $\boldsymbol{\beta}_j$ and γ_j. Such estimators, however, do not possess the same limiting distribution as the IV estimators.

One can conceive of alternative instruments to those so far considered. A possible approach in the context of a fully specified simultaneous model is to simulate the model – with or without random disturbances – utilizing an initial "guesstimate" of the model parameters and the historically observed sequence of exogenous variables. The generated values of the endogenous variables and the corresponding functions g_{jt} may then be employed as instruments. Indeed, by replications of such a simulation one can (in theory) estimate the conditional expectations in this way and overcome a lack of a closed-form expression for this purpose. Even if one is not prepared to go this far, it is useful to have alternative sequences of possible instruments to check on the sensitivity of the resulting IV estimates. The idea of stochastic simulation, in particular, as an aid to model estimation is an intriguing one that deserves further work.

5.4 Essentially nonlinear models: limited information

Much of the above discussion on the mechanics of instrument choice applies equally to equations or models that are nonlinear in their parameters as well as variables. For this reason we shall lay primary stress on questions of definition and computation in the case of essentially nonlinear equations, rather than on the actual choice of instruments. Recalling the taxonomic discussion of Section 5.2 above, it will be convenient to write the generic model to be estimated in the following form:

$$y_t = g(\boldsymbol{\theta}; \mathbf{h}_t) + \epsilon_t, \qquad t = 1\ldots n, \tag{5.25}$$

where in this section $\mathbf{h}_t$ is a vector of right-hand variables some of which may be correlated with the i.i.d. disturbance ϵ_t. On occasion we shall simply suppress the h_t variables, writing $g_t(\boldsymbol{\theta})$ in place of $g(\boldsymbol{\theta}, \mathbf{h}_t)$. We shall suppose the parameter vector $\boldsymbol{\theta}$ to have p elements. Thus in an explicitly simultaneous-equations context, the vector $\mathbf{h}_t$ will include both endogenous variables and predetermined variables; we shall in the present section adopt no special terminology to distinguish between endogenous and exogenous variables. As we remarked in Section 5.2, it may on occasion be more natural to write the equation to be estimated in implicit form, as, say,

$$f(\boldsymbol{\theta}; y_t, \mathbf{h}_t) = \epsilon_t. \tag{5.26}$$

The discussion below will be applicable to both (5.25) and (5.26). However, it helps in understanding the various iterative processes that are involved to imagine that the equation to be estimated has a natural dependent variable, and for this reason we shall cast the exposition in terms of the "subject–object" version, equation (5.25).

We conclude this introduction by establishing some notation for future use:

(a) $\boldsymbol{\theta}_0$ = true value of the parameter vector $\boldsymbol{\theta}$, to be estimated.
(b) $\mathbf{e}(\boldsymbol{\theta}) = \mathbf{y} - \mathbf{g}(\boldsymbol{\theta})$, the residual defined at an arbitrary value of $\boldsymbol{\theta}$. If $\boldsymbol{\theta} = \boldsymbol{\theta}_0$, $\mathbf{e}(\boldsymbol{\theta}_0) = \boldsymbol{\epsilon}$.
(c) $\mathbf{q}(\boldsymbol{\theta}) = \partial\phi/\partial\boldsymbol{\theta}(\boldsymbol{\theta})$, gradient vector of ϕ (defined below).
(d) $G(\boldsymbol{\theta}) = G(\boldsymbol{\theta}; H) = n \times p$ data matrix of the first-order derivatives of $\mathbf{g}$ with respect to $\boldsymbol{\theta}$, where H is the data matrix corresponding to the variables in $\mathbf{h}_t$. We have $G(\boldsymbol{\theta}) = \partial\mathbf{g}/\partial\boldsymbol{\theta}'$. The rows of $G(\boldsymbol{\theta})$ we shall denote by $\mathbf{G}_t'(\boldsymbol{\theta}) = \partial g_t/\partial\boldsymbol{\theta}'$.
(e) $G_{\mathrm{II},t}(\boldsymbol{\theta}) = p \times p$ matrix of second-order derivatives (i.e., the Hessian) of g_t with respect to $\boldsymbol{\theta}$. Thus $G_{\mathrm{II},t} = \partial g_t(\boldsymbol{\theta})/\partial\boldsymbol{\theta}\partial\boldsymbol{\theta}'$.
(f) $Q(\boldsymbol{\theta})$ = Hessian of the function $\phi(\boldsymbol{\theta})$; that is, $Q(\boldsymbol{\theta}) = \partial\phi(\boldsymbol{\theta})/\partial\boldsymbol{\theta}\partial\boldsymbol{\theta}'$.

The minimand and stationary solution

Suppose that we have available an $n \times q$ matrix of instruments Z. As we have already seen, the case $q > p$ assumes even greater importance for nonlinear models, so that we shall certainly want to maintain discussion in terms of this contingency. We assume that $\operatorname{plim}(1/n)Z'Z$ exists and is nonsingular.

The nonlinear IV minimand is defined as

$$\phi(\boldsymbol{\theta}) = \frac{1}{n}(\mathbf{y} - \mathbf{g}(\boldsymbol{\theta}))' P_z (\mathbf{y} - \mathbf{g}(\boldsymbol{\theta})) \tag{5.27}$$

where $\mathbf{y}$ and $\mathbf{g}$ are vectors whose representative elements are y_t and $g(\boldsymbol{\theta}, \mathbf{h}_t)$ and $P_z = Z(Z'Z)^{-1}Z'$ is the orthogonal projection matrix associated with the data matrix Z of instruments. Apart from the factor $1/n$, which is there for temporary convenience, this minimand has the same form as that for the linear model (cf. Definition 2.1, Section 2.2).

One would first like to know whether the minimization problem has a unique solution as the sample size $n \to \infty$. This identifiability, or better estimability, requirement is equivalent to the existence of a unique solution for the limiting first-order conditions:

$$\frac{1}{n}G'(\boldsymbol{\theta})P_z[\mathbf{y}-\mathbf{g}(\boldsymbol{\theta})]=\mathbf{0},$$

assuming this limit to exist almost everywhere for $\boldsymbol{\theta}\in\Theta$, a compact set that contains the true value $\boldsymbol{\theta}_0$ as an interior point. We note that such a requirement will evidently depend upon the chosen instrument set Z. It is for this reason that we prefer not to refer to it as an identifiability condition, since the notion of identification depends upon the properties of the joint distribution of y_t and $\mathbf{h}_t$ and is independent of any method of estimation, with the possible exception of the method of maximum likelihood.

Assuming that such an estimability requirement is satisfied does not by itself ensure that the estimator $\hat{\boldsymbol{\theta}}_n$ found as the minimizing value in the IV minimand will converge to $\boldsymbol{\theta}_0$. The usual way of showing almost sure convergence is to prove that all the moment matrices in the minimand tend almost surely to matrices of finite constants uniformly in $\boldsymbol{\theta}$ and that the sequence of minima $\phi(\hat{\boldsymbol{\theta}}_n)$ is bounded, uniformly in $\boldsymbol{\theta}$. The details of this approach require some knowledge of the structure generating y_t and $\mathbf{h}_t$ and indeed $\mathbf{z}_t$, the proposed instrument vector. We refer the reader to Gallant (1977) and our Appendix A3 for a detailed discussion of some of these matters. However, the weaker requirements of convergence in probability require only rather general assumptions on the instruments.

Proposition 5.2: *Suppose that* (i) *the parameter space is compact;* (ii) $(1/n)Z'Z$ *tends to a nonsingular matrix of constants; and* (iii) *the matrix* $(1/n)G(\theta)'Z$ *tends in probability to a matrix of full-column rank, uniformly in* θ.

Then the nonlinear IV estimator $\hat{\boldsymbol{\theta}}$ *tends in probability to the true value* $\boldsymbol{\theta}_0$.

Proof: Expanding $g(\hat{\boldsymbol{\theta}})$ in Taylor series about the true value $\boldsymbol{\theta}_0$ and substituting in the minimand (5.27), we have

$$\phi(\hat{\boldsymbol{\theta}})=\frac{1}{n}[\mathbf{y}-\mathbf{g}(\boldsymbol{\theta}_0)-G(\boldsymbol{\theta}_*)(\hat{\boldsymbol{\theta}}-\boldsymbol{\theta}_0)]'P_z[\mathbf{y}-\mathbf{g}(\boldsymbol{\theta}_0)-G(\boldsymbol{\theta}_*)(\hat{\boldsymbol{\theta}}-\boldsymbol{\theta}_0)],$$

where $\boldsymbol{\theta}_*$ lies on the line joining $\hat{\boldsymbol{\theta}}$ and $\boldsymbol{\theta}_0$. Since $\mathbf{y}-\mathbf{g}(\boldsymbol{\theta}_0)=\boldsymbol{\epsilon}$, it follows that

$$\phi(\boldsymbol{\theta}_0)-\phi(\hat{\boldsymbol{\theta}})=\frac{2}{n}(\hat{\boldsymbol{\theta}}-\boldsymbol{\theta}_0)'G(\boldsymbol{\theta}_*)P_z\boldsymbol{\epsilon}-\frac{1}{n}(\hat{\boldsymbol{\theta}}-\boldsymbol{\theta}_0)'G(\boldsymbol{\theta}_*)'P_zG(\boldsymbol{\theta}_*)(\hat{\boldsymbol{\theta}}-\boldsymbol{\theta}_0).$$

From assumptions (i)–(iii) the first term on the right-hand side tends in probability to zero. Moreover, the limiting matrix $(1/n)G(\boldsymbol{\theta}_*)P_zG(\boldsymbol{\theta}_*)$ is positive definite. Hence since $\phi(\theta_0) \geq \phi(\hat{\theta})$ by definition of $\hat{\theta}$, it can only be that $\hat{\theta} - \theta_0 \xrightarrow{p} \mathbf{0}$. ■

Thus to show weak consistency, one has simply to demonstrate that the proposed instruments are asymptotically correlated with the matrix G of θ derivatives. In practice, of course, this may be difficult, and as with the corresponding nonlinear OLS theory one has sometimes rather to take it on trust that a given global minimum does indeed correspond to a consistent estimate.

Turning now to distributional questions, the stationary solution $\hat{\theta}$ is defined by

$$\frac{1}{n} G'(\hat{\theta}) P_z [\mathbf{y} - \mathbf{g}(\hat{\theta})] = \mathbf{0}. \tag{5.28}$$

Expanding to terms of first order about the true value θ_0, we have

$$\frac{1}{n} G'(\hat{\theta}) P_z [\mathbf{y} - \mathbf{g}(\theta_0) - G(\theta_*)(\hat{\theta} - \theta_0)] = \mathbf{0},$$

where θ_* is on the line segment joining θ_0 and $\hat{\theta}$. It follows that

$$\sqrt{n}(\hat{\theta} - \theta_0) = n[G'(\hat{\theta}) P_z G(\theta_*)]^{-1} \frac{1}{\sqrt{n}} G'(\hat{\theta}) P_z \epsilon,$$

supposing that the inverse exists. If we assume (in terms of the above discussion) that $\hat{\theta}$ converges to θ_0, at least in probability, and also that $(1/\sqrt{n}) Z'\epsilon$ tends in distribution to an $N[\mathbf{0}, \sigma^2 \operatorname{plim}(1/n) Z'Z]$ variable, it is then straightforward to demonstrate the following:

Proposition 5.3: *Suppose that* $\operatorname{plim}(1/n) G'(\theta_0) Z$ *exists and has full rank* p. *Then the vector* $\sqrt{n}(\hat{\theta} - \theta_0)$ *is asymptotically*

$$N(0, \sigma^2 \operatorname{plim} n[G'(\theta_0) P_z G(\theta_0)]^{-1}).$$

The following result corresponds to Theorem 2.7 for the linear context:

Proposition 5.4: *The terminal value of the minimand (5.27) is asymptotically*

$$\frac{1}{n}(\mathbf{y} - \mathbf{g}(\hat{\theta}))' P_z (\mathbf{y} - \mathbf{g}(\hat{\theta})) = \frac{1}{n}(\mathbf{y} - \mathbf{g}(\theta_0))'(P_z - P_m)(\mathbf{y} - g(\theta_0)),$$

where M *is a minimal set of instruments with respect to* Z *and* $G(\theta_0)$.

Proof: Letting $G_0 = G(\theta_0)$, we may write, asymptotically,

$$[\mathbf{y} - \mathbf{g}(\hat{\theta})]' P_z [\mathbf{y} - \mathbf{g}(\hat{\theta})] = [\mathbf{y} - \mathbf{g}(\theta_0) - G_0(\hat{\theta} - \theta_0)]' P_z [\mathbf{y} - \mathbf{g}(\theta_0) - G_0(\hat{\theta} - \theta_0)].$$

Now

$$[\mathbf{y}-\mathbf{g}(\boldsymbol{\theta}_0)-G_0(\hat{\boldsymbol{\theta}}-\boldsymbol{\theta}_0)]'P_z$$
$$=\{\mathbf{y}-\mathbf{g}(\boldsymbol{\theta}_0)-G_0(G_0'P_zG_0)^{-1}G_0'P_z[\mathbf{y}-\mathbf{g}(\boldsymbol{\theta}_0)]\}'P_z$$
$$=[\mathbf{y}-\mathbf{g}(\boldsymbol{\theta}_0)]'[P_z-P_zG_0(G_0'P_zG_0)^{-1}G_0'P_z]'.$$

It will be recognized that

$$P_zG_0(G_0'P_zG_0)^{-1}G_0'P_z=P_m.$$

The result follows from the idempotence of P_z-P_m. ■

The above propositions show that asymptotically, the nonlinear IV theory is to all intents and purposes identical with the linear theory, with $G(\boldsymbol{\theta}_0)=G(\boldsymbol{\theta}_0;H)$ playing the role of the data matrix X. We observe from Proposition 5.4 the futility of attempting to choose an instrument set on the basis of $\min_z \min_\theta \phi(\boldsymbol{\theta})$. That is, we cannot turn the residual sum of squares $\phi(\hat{\boldsymbol{\theta}})$ into a further criterion for the choice of instruments.

It may be also observed that the idea of minimal instruments extends to the nonlinear context. The meaning is essentially an asymptotic one: Given a set Z of instruments, the associated set of minimal instruments has projection matrix

$$P_m=P_zG_0(G_0'P_zG_0)^{-1}G_0P_z=\hat{G}_0(\hat{G}_0'\hat{G}_0)^{-1}\hat{G}_0'.$$

The resulting estimate of $\boldsymbol{\theta}$ is thus equivalent to regressing $\mathbf{y}$ on $\hat{G}_0$ in a second-stage regression. Those familiar with nonlinear ordinary least-squares theory will recognize the similarity. Asymptotically, nonlinear OLS is equivalent to a regression of $\mathbf{y}$ on G_0. Asymptotic nonlinear IV is equivalent to a regression of $\mathbf{y}$ on $\hat{G}_0$, where the latter is obtained from a preliminary regression of G_0 on the instrument set Z.

Attaining the minimum

We turn now to the numerical minimization of the expression (5.27). For the purposes of the ensuing discussion we may omit the factor $1/n$. Differentiating $\phi(\boldsymbol{\theta})$, we obtain

$$q(\boldsymbol{\theta})=-2G'(\boldsymbol{\theta})P_z\mathbf{e},$$

and

$$Q(\boldsymbol{\theta})=-2\sum_t G_{\mathrm{II},t}\tilde{e}_t-2\frac{\partial \mathbf{e}}{\partial \boldsymbol{\theta}}P_zG(\boldsymbol{\theta})$$
$$=-2\sum_t G_{\mathrm{II},t}(\boldsymbol{\theta})\tilde{e}_t+2G'(\boldsymbol{\theta})P_zG(\boldsymbol{\theta}),$$

where $\tilde{e}_t$ is the tth element of the vector $P_z \mathbf{e}$. The latter vector will be recognized as the fitted value in a regression of the residual vector $\mathbf{e}(\theta)$ on the instruments Z. Now if θ is close to the true value θ_0, we should have $e_t \simeq \epsilon_t$ so that $P_z \mathbf{e} \simeq P_z \epsilon$. Since $1/n$ times the latter tends in probability to zero, we should expect that in a neighborhood of θ_0,

$$Q(\theta) \simeq \hat{Q}(\theta) = 2G'(\theta) P_z G(\theta). \tag{5.29}$$

Gradient methods for the iterative minimization of $\phi(\theta)$ are represented by the scheme

$$\theta_{r+1} = \theta_r + \rho_r \mathbf{v}_r,$$

where the direction vector is $\mathbf{v}_r = -R\mathbf{q}(\theta_r)$. Here R is a suitably chosen positive definite matrix, which need not be the same at each step, and ρ is a scalar that determines the step length. The *Gauss–Newton method* employs $R = \hat{Q}^{-1}(\theta_r) = [G'(\theta_r) P_z G(\theta_r)]^{-1}$ at each step. With a unit step length ($\rho = 1$), this is equivalent to solving at each iteration for the minimum of the quadratic function that locally approximates $\phi(\theta)$; one assumes in doing so that $Q(\theta) \simeq \hat{Q}(\theta)$, as defined by equation (5.29). It may also be shown that this method is equivalent to the iterative Gauss–Seidel solution of the first-order equations $q(\theta) = \mathbf{0}$. We refer the reader to Bard (1974) for a full account.

The iterations of the Gauss–Newton method are therefore as follows. Given θ_r, we form $\mathbf{e}_r = \mathbf{y} - \mathbf{g}(\theta_r)$. The new direction is solved as

$$\begin{aligned} \mathbf{v}_r &= -[G'(\theta_r) P_z G(\theta_r)]^{-1} q(\theta_r) \\ &= [G'(\theta_r) P_z G(\theta_r)]^{-1} G(\theta_r)' P_z \mathbf{e}_r. \end{aligned} \tag{5.30}$$

Thus

$$\theta_{r+1} = \theta_r + \rho_r (G_r' P_z G_r)^{-1} G_r' P_z \mathbf{e}_r,$$

where ρ_r is a suitably chosen step length. It is clear that equation (5.30) amounts to applying instrumental variables to the auxiliary regression model

$$\mathbf{e}_r = G_r \mathbf{v}_r + \eta, \tag{5.31}$$

where η is a residual.

In practice, however, we have found that this method has achieved poor results for instrumental variables estimation, and it is worthwhile discussing the matter further. We have seen from our discussion of the stationary solution that it is desirable that Z constitute a good instrument set for $G(\theta; H)$. The first question that arises is: For what value of θ should Z constitute an effective instrument set? Since we should like to think that we end up with a final estimate close to θ_0, this suggests that Z

should be effective for $G(\boldsymbol{\theta}_0; H)$. But suppose that our current iteration $\boldsymbol{\theta}_r$ is some distance from the true value. Then Z may be a poor instrument for $G(\boldsymbol{\theta}_r; H)$.

Of course, we do not know in advance what $\boldsymbol{\theta}_0$ is, so perforce we have to design our instrument set to be effective for $\boldsymbol{\theta}_c$, an initial "guesstimate." But the point is unaffected: Sooner or later, in the course of the iteration, the chosen set of instruments may become a poor set for the current data matrix $G(\boldsymbol{\theta}_r; H)$.

When this happens, as we saw in Section 2.3, one or more of the canonical correlations become small. The result is an unwarrantedly large step in the direction indicated by the associated canonical vectors, often into "nonsense" regions. The point can also be made as follows. Having determined the direction $\mathbf{v}_r = (G_r' P_z G_r)^{-1} G_r' P_z \mathbf{e}_r$ as in equation (5.30), let us consider the value of the minimand along this direction as a function of the step length ρ:

$$\psi(\rho) = \phi(\boldsymbol{\theta}_r + \rho(G_r' P_z G_r)^{-1} G_r' P_z \mathbf{e}_r).$$

The derivative of ψ with respect to ρ evaluated at $\rho = 0$ is

$$\begin{aligned}\psi'(0) &= \left[\mathbf{q}'(\boldsymbol{\theta}_{r+1}) \frac{\partial \boldsymbol{\theta}_{r+1}}{\partial \rho}\right]_{\rho=0} \\ &= -2\mathbf{e}_r' P_z G_r'(G_r' P_z G_r)^{-1} G_r' P_z \mathbf{e}_r < 0.\end{aligned}$$

Thus $\psi'(0)$ may be recognized as -2 times the fitted sum of squares $\mathbf{e}_r' P_m \mathbf{e}_r$ in the IV fit of the auxiliary regression (5.31). Now if Z is a poor instrument set for G_r, then this regression sum of squares will be low relative to $G_r' G_r$. This would lead the computer to infer – wrongly – that the function ψ is rather flat along the direction v_r, leading to a very long step length. Putting the matter this way is valuable because we can see that the variable-step-length methods associated with Box (1957) and Hartley (1961), which rely on the computation of $\psi'(0)$, are not likely to be too effective.

In short, standard Gauss–Newton methods may not perform well with highly nonlinear models estimated by instrumental variables. The solution is to improve the conditioning of the weighting matrix R employed to form the new direction vector. The methods of Levenberg (1944), Marquadt (1963), and Goldfeld, Quandt, and Trotter (1966) adapted to this situation would employ a weighting matrix of the form $R = \hat{Q} + \lambda P$, where λ is a scalar and P a matrix chosen to make R more positive definite. We refer the reader to Bard (1974) for an excellent account of these and other general methods.

However, it is by no means necessary to employ Q or $\hat{Q}$ as the basis for the weighting matrix R. A simpler procedure is to utilize the ordinary least-squares weighting matrix, namely $R^0 = (G_r' G_r)^{-1}$ in place of $(G_r' P_z G_r)^{-1}$. Thus, the iteration is defined by

$$\boldsymbol{\theta}_{r+1} = \boldsymbol{\theta}_r + \rho_r (G_r' G_r)^{-1} G_r' P_z \mathbf{e}_r,$$

where the step length ρ_r may be determined by the method of Box and Hartley. Of course if the OLS problem is itself poorly conditioned, this may not help very much. However, it is worth emphasizing that the consistency arguments depend only upon the properties of $\mathbf{q}(\theta) \propto G' P_z \mathbf{e}$. So far as the iterative process of determining the minimum of expression (5.27) is concerned, we may choose our weighting matrix at will.

The choice of instruments

We have observed that the asymptotic covariance matrix of the nonlinear estimator $\hat{\boldsymbol{\theta}}$ is given by the limit in probability of $\sigma^2 n[G(\boldsymbol{\theta}_0)' P_z G(\boldsymbol{\theta}_0)]^{-1}$. This suggests that we choose our instrument set Z to have a close correlation, in the canonical correlations sense, with the data matrix $G(\boldsymbol{\theta}_0; H)$ of first-order derivatives of the functions $\mathbf{g}(\boldsymbol{\theta}; \mathbf{h}_t)$. Indeed, we can say something a little stronger than this. Since $G(\boldsymbol{\theta}_0)'(I - P_z) G(\boldsymbol{\theta}_0)$ is positive semidefinite, it follows that the covariance matrix has a lower bound, among all possible sets of instruments, which is given by

$$\sigma^2 \operatorname{plim} n[G(\boldsymbol{\theta}_0)' G(\boldsymbol{\theta}_0)]^{-1}. \tag{5.32}$$

If we assume that the functions g are such that probability limits of their derivatives can be replaced by limits of expectations, then the lower bound can be written

$$\sigma^2 \lim n[\bar{G}(\boldsymbol{\theta}_0)' \bar{G}(\boldsymbol{\theta}_0)]^{-1}, \tag{5.33}$$

where $\bar{G}(\boldsymbol{\theta}_0) = \mathcal{E} G(\boldsymbol{\theta}_0)$. This limit is attained by choosing the instrument set $Z = \bar{G}(\boldsymbol{\theta}_0)$. The idea is due to Amemiya (1975), who calls the resultant estimator the "best nonlinear two-stage least-squares" estimator (BNL2S).

The BNL2S estimator is a useful concept for purposes of theoretical efficiency comparisons, and we shall invoke the same or similar concepts at later points in the chapter. For present purposes, we remark that the concept can help us with the problem of instrument choice. In order to break this choice problem down to manageable proportions, let us maintain initially the assumption that, solely for the purpose of discussing instrument efficiency, we know the true value $\boldsymbol{\theta}_0$ of the parameters to be estimated. We imagine also that we have a data matrix Z_0 of "primitive" instruments, in the sense that these variables are exogenous or predetermined. Given such a set Z_0, there are at least three generic ways in which we can proceed to "instrumentalize" $G(\boldsymbol{\theta}_0; H)$:

(i) In some circumstances we may indeed be able to solve for the expectations

$$\bar{G} = \mathcal{E}\frac{\partial g}{\partial \theta'}\bigg]_{\theta=\theta_0}.$$

We refer the reader back to the discussion of Section 5.3 on this. Usually, however, this option is not available.

(ii) We can regress the columns of $G(\theta_0; H)$ upon the elements of Z_0 and polynomials in those elements to any desired degree. The resulting instruments we denote $\hat{G}(\theta_0)$. This corresponds to the strict NL2SLS method of Section 5.3.

(iii) We can regress the elements of H upon the elements of Z_0 or polynomials therein to obtain $\hat{\mathbf{h}}_t$, the fitted values. We then form the matrix $G(\theta_0; \hat{H})$; that is, $\hat{\mathbf{h}}_t$ is substituted for $\mathbf{h}_t$. This is the methodology based upon the internal instruments idea (see Section 5.3 above).

In all cases, once $G(\theta_0; H)$ has been instrumentalized, we may add the result to the original list Z_0 to construct an augmented set Z of instruments, being careful to avoid collinearity problems in doing so.

In practice we do not, of course, know the true value θ_0 for use in instrumentalizing G, and instruments of type (i)–(iii) will have to be formed by employing initial "guesstimates" θ_c.[4] Several points of importance arise in this connection:

(a) If θ_c is too far from θ_0, we may be operating with an imprecise instrument set, which as we saw above creates problems for the IV minimization. One possible way out is to construct a Taylor approximation for $G(\theta_0; H)$. Suppose, for example, that G included a term $e^{\theta_0 h_t}$. Then $e^{\theta_0 h_t} \simeq e^{\theta_c h_t} + (\theta_c - \theta_0) h_t e^{\theta_c h_t}$. This suggests that both $e^{\theta_c h_t}$ and $h_t e^{\theta_c h_t}$ should be instrumentalized as in (i)–(iii) above.

(b) Suppose that we have available a consistent estimator $\hat{\theta}$ for θ_0. The instrumentalization process can be based upon $G(\hat{\theta}, H)$. This immediately suggests the following procedure. Given a guesstimate θ_c, instrumentalize $G(\theta_c, H)$ and create an augmented instrument set Z. Let $\hat{\theta}_1$ be the resulting IV estimator. In a second round we instrumentalize $G(\hat{\theta}_1; H)$. (Clearly this procedure could be repeated, but there is no apparent reason for the resulting process to ever converge.)

(c) If any information exists a priori concerning the elements of θ, it is of importance that this be employed.

A final point concerns the general character of the instrumentalization. It will be apparent that the asymptotic theory, upon which the proposed instrumentalization is based, is essentially a theory based on small variations in θ about the true value θ_0. In such a context, the variations need only be of first order. For small sample sizes, however, higher-order variations may assume greater importance. Thus we might well consider instrumentalizing some or all of the second-order derivatives of the function $g(\theta)$. The case for doing this is reinforced by point (a) above.

It will now be clear that the nonlinear context offers an embarrassment of riches so far as the formation of instruments is concerned and that methods of economization in the choice of instruments may very well be necessary. How far we wish to go in creating alternative instrument sets depends upon the resources available and the alternative estimation procedures that may be possible. If an explicit formulation of a complete model has been worked out, the application of instrumental variables may be a relatively cursory exercise to provide starting-up values for an attempt at a full-maximum-likelihood estimation. Other contexts may be limited-information in nature, and in such instances it is probably worth spending a little time devising instrument sets based upon one's knowledge of the nonlinear functions involved and their derivatives.

The nonlinear limited-information maximum-likelihood estimator

In studying the linear limited-information model we saw in Section 4.3 that several estimators with instrumental variables interpretations achieved the Cramer–Rao lower bound. In particular, we saw that this bound was achieved by the 2SLS estimator, and as the bound is always achieved by the maximum-likelihood estimator (MLE), this implies that the 2SLS estimator is asymptotically as efficient as the LIML estimator. By using a special model, we may demonstrate that this property does not carry over to the nonlinear limited-information model. Following Amemiya (1975), consider the nonlinear simultaneous equation model defined by

$$y_t = g_t(Y_t, \theta) + u_t$$

$$Y_t' = X_t'\Pi + V_t,$$

where y_t and u_t are random variables, Y_t and V_t are (column) random vectors, X_t is a (column) vector of known constants (as exogenous variates), and θ and Π are a vector and matrix of unknown parameters, respectively. In the terminology of simultaneous equations, y_t and Y_t represent the endogenous variables of the model and X_t represents the exogenous variables. We assume that $(u_t \;\, V_t')$ has a multivariate normal distribution with mean $\mathbf{0}$ and covariance matrix

$$\Sigma = \begin{pmatrix} \sigma^2 & \boldsymbol{\phi} \\ \boldsymbol{\phi}' & \Omega \end{pmatrix}.$$

In matrix notation we can write our model as

$$\mathbf{y} = \mathbf{g}(\theta) + \mathbf{u}, \qquad Y = X\Pi + V,$$

where the tth element of $\mathbf{y}$ is y_t and the tth row of Y is Y_t', and so on. As with the linear model, asymptotic efficiency requires us to consider the Cramer–Rao lower bound for a consistent estimator of $\boldsymbol{\theta}$.

Accordingly, let us set up the log-likelihood function for the observations y_t, Y_t. To do this, we can follow through the same type of analysis as given in Section 4.3 to obtain the concentrated likelihood as, apart from a constant,

$$l = -\frac{n}{2}\log\det\Sigma^{-1} - \frac{1}{2}\operatorname{tr}\Sigma^{-1}U'U,$$

where $U = (\mathbf{u}, V)$. After concentrating this function with respect to Σ, we obtain

$$l^{**} = -\frac{n}{2}\log\det S,$$

with $S = U'U/n$, and upon further concentrating l^{**} with respect to Π we arrive at

$$l^* = -\frac{n}{2}(\log\mathbf{u}'\mathbf{u} + \log|Y'M_uY - Y'M_uX(X'M_uX)^{-1}X'M_uY|), \qquad (5.34)$$

where $M_u = I - \mathbf{u}(\mathbf{u}'\mathbf{u})^{-1}\mathbf{u}'$.

The nonlinear limited-information maximum-likelihood estimator of $\boldsymbol{\theta}$, denoted by $\tilde{\boldsymbol{\theta}}$, is the value of $\boldsymbol{\theta}$ that maximizes the expression (5.34). We assume that the regularity properties of the function g and the exogenous variables are such that $\sqrt{n}(\tilde{\boldsymbol{\theta}} - \boldsymbol{\theta})$ has a limiting normal distribution whose covariance matrix represents a Cramer–Rao-type lower bound, namely,

$$\operatorname{plim}\left[\frac{1}{n}\frac{\partial^2 l^*}{\partial\boldsymbol{\theta}\,\partial\boldsymbol{\theta}'}\right]^{-1}.$$

Amemiya (1975) evaluates this bound as

$$V_{\mathrm{LI}} = \operatorname{plim} n[\eta^{-1}A - (\eta^{-1} - \sigma^{-2})B]^{-1} \qquad (5.35)$$

where $\eta = \sigma^2 - \boldsymbol{\phi}'\Omega^{-1}\boldsymbol{\phi}$,
$A = G(\theta_0)'[I - V(V'V)^{-1}V']G(\theta_0)$, and
$B = G(\theta_0)'X(X'X)^{-1}X'G(\theta_0)$.

Earlier, we saw [cf. Equation (5.32) above] that the covariance matrix of any IV estimator had a lower bound given by

$$V_l = \sigma^2 \operatorname{plim} n[G(\boldsymbol{\theta}_0)'G(\boldsymbol{\theta}_0)]^{-1}.$$

We shall now show that $V_l \geq V_{\mathrm{LI}}$, in the sense that the difference $V_l - V_{\mathrm{LI}}$ between the two covariance matrices is positive semidefinite. To do so we shall use the result that if matrices C and D are positive definite, then $C \geq D$ implies $D^{-1} \geq C^{-1}$.

Consider an arbitrary matrix Z of instruments, such that the columns of Z span those of X. Since Z is admissible as an instrument, $\text{plim}(1/n)Z'V=\mathbf{O}$. It follows that the matrix $I-P_v-P_z$ [where $P_v=V(V'V)^{-1}V'$] may be treated asymptotically as idempotent. Hence, writing $G_0=G(\boldsymbol{\theta}_0)$:

$$\begin{aligned}\text{plim}\, n^{-1}A &= \text{plim}\, n^{-1}G_0'(I-P_v)G_0\\ &\geq \text{plim}\, n^{-1}G_0'P_zG_0\\ &\geq \text{plim}\, n^{-1}G_0'P_xG_0\\ &= \text{plim}\, n^{-1}B.\end{aligned} \tag{5.36}$$

Moreover,

$$\text{plim}\, n^{-1}A \geq \text{plim}\, n^{-1}G_0'G_0,$$

and so

$$\text{plim}\, nA^{-1} \leq \text{plim}\, n(G_0'G_0)^{-1}. \tag{5.37}$$

Now from (5.35) and (5.36),

$$\begin{aligned}V_{\text{LI}}^{-1}-\sigma^2\,\text{plim}\, n^{-1}A &= \text{plim}\, n^{-1}[(\zeta^{-1}-\sigma^{-2})(A-B)]\\ &\geq \mathbf{O},\end{aligned}$$

since $\zeta^{-1}\geq\sigma^{-2}$. Hence

$$V_{\text{LI}} \leq \sigma^2\,\text{plim}\, nA^{-1} \leq \sigma^2\,\text{plim}\, n(G_0'G_0)^{-1},$$

from (5.37). Clearly the strict inequality may be expected to hold in some situations. In general, therefore, the LIML estimator for this particular model is more efficient than the family of IV estimators considered hitherto.

5.5 Systems estimation: three-stage least squares

Up to this point, we have considered only one equation in isolation; indeed, in such a limited-information approach one need not even suppose that the equation being considered is part of a larger system. It is now time to turn to an explicitly systems approach according to which specifying and estimating all the equations jointly will increase the precision of estimation of the parameters of any single equation. As with the corresponding discussion in the linear case (see Section 4.4), we consider separately three-stage least-squares analogs and the method of full-information maximum likelihood; the latter is covered in Section 5.6 below.

It will be convenient in the remainder of this chapter to consider a system of equations in the following implicit form:

$$f_i(\mathbf{y}_t, \mathbf{x}_t, \theta_i) = u_{it}, \qquad i = 1, \ldots, r, \tag{5.38}$$

where y_t is an $r \times 1$ vector of endogenous variables, x_t is a $K \times 1$ column vector of exogenous[5] variables, and $\boldsymbol{\theta}_i$ is a vector of unknown parameters. Not all of the elements of $\mathbf{y}_t$ and $\mathbf{x}_t$ need actually appear in the arguments of each f_i. Define the $r \times 1$ vector $\mathbf{u}_t$ as $(u_{1t}\ u_{2t} \ldots u_{rt})'$. Then we assume that the vectors $\mathbf{u}_t$, $t = 1, \ldots, n$, are independently identically normally distributed with mean $\mathbf{0}$ and covariance matrix $\Sigma = \{\sigma_{ij}\}$. In order to be able to form the probability density function of the $\mathbf{y}_t$ terms from that of the $\mathbf{u}_t$ terms we need to assume that the mapping $f_i : \mathbf{y}_t \to \mathbf{u}_t$ is one-to-one from a subset of rth Euclidean space onto the whole of the rth Euclidean space and that the inverse function is also continuous. Finally, we need to assume that partial derivatives appearing in our calculations do in fact exist and are continuous and that $\partial f_t / \partial \mathbf{y}_t'$ and $\Sigma_{t=1}^{n} \mathbf{f}_t \mathbf{f}_t'$ are nonsingular in at least a neighborhood of the true value of $\boldsymbol{\theta}_i$, where $\mathbf{f}_t = (f_{1t} \ldots f_{rt})$ and $f_{it} = f_i(y_{1t} \ldots y_{rt}, x_{1t} \ldots x_{Kt}, \boldsymbol{\theta}_i)$.

As in Chapter 4, we write the system (5.38) in stacked form as

$$\mathbf{f}(\boldsymbol{\theta}) = \mathbf{f}(y, x, \boldsymbol{\theta}) = \mathbf{u}, \tag{5.39}$$

where the first n elements of the supervectors $\mathbf{f}$ or $\mathbf{u}$ correspond to the first equation, the second n to the second equation, and so on. Consider now the IV estimation of the model (5.39). We note that

$$\operatorname{Cov}(\mathbf{u}) = \Sigma \otimes I = \Omega,$$

say, and we observe that Ω is not spherical. The discussion of Chapter 3 on IV analogs in nonspherical contexts is therefore applicable. The IV estimators are defined as the values of $\boldsymbol{\theta}$ that minimize

$$\phi(\boldsymbol{\theta}) = \mathbf{f}(\boldsymbol{\theta})' P \mathbf{f}(\boldsymbol{\theta}), \tag{5.40}$$

for some suitable choice of the matrix P. Suppose that we are given a data matrix $\tilde{Z}$ of instruments of order $nr \times q$, with $q \geq \dim(\boldsymbol{\theta})$. We may recall from Section 3.2 at least two types of estimator corresponding to different choices of P:

(i) The OLS analog:

$$P_1 = \tilde{Z}(\tilde{Z}'\Omega\tilde{Z})^{-1}\tilde{Z}' \tag{5.41a}$$

(ii) The GLS analog:

$$P_2 = \Omega^{-1}\tilde{Z}(\tilde{Z}'\Omega^{-1}\tilde{Z})^{-1}\tilde{Z}'\Omega^{-1}. \tag{5.41b}$$

(iii) A third possible candidate proposed by Amemiya (1977) is

$$P_3 = \Omega^{-1/2}\tilde{Z}(\tilde{Z}'\tilde{Z})^{-1}\tilde{Z}'\Omega^{-1/2}. \tag{5.41c}$$

(A rationale for this estimator has also been presented in Section 3.2.)

In practice, the elements of the covariance matrix are unknown, and one substitutes consistent estimates $\hat{\Omega}=\hat{\Sigma}\otimes I$ obtained from the initial application of a limited-information technique, just as in the linear case. Thus one could utilize for this purpose a prior NL2SLS fit.

A special case of some importance is where we may write

$$\tilde{Z}=I\otimes Z, \tag{5.42}$$

where Z is of order $n\times q$. In this case, it may be verified that versions (i)–(iii) above all reduce to an IV estimator with

$$P=\Sigma^{-1}\otimes P_z, \tag{5.43}$$

where $P_z=Z(Z'Z)^{-1}Z'$. This is the estimator proposed by Jorgenson and Laffont (1974), who called the method "nonlinear three-stage least squares." We shall, however, mean by this term any of the more general estimators (5.41a–c).

Denote by G the data matrix $\partial\mathbf{f}/\partial\boldsymbol{\theta}'$ corresponding to the θ derivatives of the functions f_i, and let G_0 be its value evaluated at the true value $\boldsymbol{\theta}=\boldsymbol{\theta}_0$. Under suitable regularity conditions the IV estimators (5.41) should be consistent and asymptotically normal with limiting covariance matrix

$$\left[\operatorname{plim}\frac{1}{n}G_0'PG_0\right]^{-1}, \tag{5.44}$$

which will be recognized as homologous with the limited-information treatment of Proposition 5.3 above. The question of suitable regularity conditions has been investigated by Jorgenson and Laffont (1974) and Gallant (1977) with respect to the particular case defined by expressions (5.42) and (5.43) above, with Z a nonstochastic matrix of constants and Σ consistently estimated as $\hat{\Sigma}$. We state the Jorgenson–Laffont results formally as follows:

Proposition 5.5: *Suppose that:*

(i) *The data matrix of instrument Z is of full-column rank and that $\lim(1/n)Z'Z=M$, nonsingular;*

(ii) *The parameter space ($\boldsymbol{\theta}\in\Theta$) is compact;*

(iii) $\operatorname{plim}(1/n)X'(\partial f_i/\partial\boldsymbol{\theta}')=S_i$ *uniformly in $\boldsymbol{\theta}$ and*

$$\operatorname{plim}\frac{1}{n}(I\otimes X')\frac{\partial\mathbf{f}}{\partial\boldsymbol{\theta}'}=\begin{bmatrix}S_1\\ \vdots\\ S_G\end{bmatrix}=S$$

has full rank;

(iv) $\operatorname{plim}(1/n)X'(\partial^2 f_i/\partial\theta_j\,\partial\boldsymbol{\theta}')$ *exists, uniformly in $\boldsymbol{\theta}$ for all i, j; and*

(v) $n^{-1/2}(I\otimes X')u$ *tends to a multivariate normal distribution, with mean* $\mathbf{0}$ *and covariance matrix $\Sigma\otimes M$.*

Then

(a) $\hat{\theta}$ *converges in probability to the true value* θ_0; *and*
(b) $\sqrt{n}(\hat{\theta}-\theta_0)$ *converges in distribution to a normal random vector with mean* $\mathbf{0}$ *and covariance matrix*

$$\left[\operatorname{plim}\frac{1}{n}G_0'(\Sigma^{-1}\otimes P_z)G_0\right]^{-1}.$$

We refer the reader to Jorgenson and Laffont (1974) for the proof of this proposition. In the remainder of this section we shall simply assume that the IV estimators of the general class (5.41) are consistent and have the limiting covariance matrix (5.44).

Efficiency properties

In studying the relative efficiency properties of the systems IV estimators, it will be useful to introduce the artifice of a "best" nonlinear three-stage least-squares estimator, a notion originally due to Amemiya (1977).

Definition 5.6: Let $\tilde{Z}_e = \mathcal{E}(G_0)$, the expectation of the Jacobian data matrix, evaluated at the true parameter value. Then the best nonlinear three-stage least-squares (BN3SLS) estimator is defined by the GLS–IV analog, namely the value $\hat{\theta}$ that minimizes expression (5.40) above with

$$P_e = \Omega^{-1}\tilde{Z}_e(\tilde{Z}_e'\Omega^{-1}\tilde{Z}_e)^{-1}\tilde{Z}_e'\Omega^{-1}. \tag{5.45}$$

The usefulness of this notion derives from Proposition 5.8 below, which shows that the BN3SLS estimator provides what is, in a rather loose sense, a lower bound for the variance of the IV estimators (5.41a, b). The following lemma refers to two standard results concerning the comparison of positive (semi)definite matrices:

Lemma 5.7:

(a) *If A and B are two positive definite matrices such that $B-A$ is positive semidefinite, then so is $A^{-1}-B^{-1}$.*
(b) *If A is nonsingular and $B'A^{-1}B$ is also nonsingular, then $A-B(B'A^{-1}B)^{-1}B'$ is positive semidefinite.*

Proposition 5.8: *Suppose that the properties of the sequence of derivatives $g_{\alpha t}^{j} = \partial f_{\alpha t}/\partial\theta_j$ are such that*

$$\operatorname{plim}\frac{1}{n}G_0'\Omega^{-1}\mathcal{E}(G_0) = \lim\frac{1}{n}\mathcal{E}(G_0)'\Omega^{-1}\mathcal{E}(G_0)$$

(so that one can in effect replace limits in probability with ordinary limits of expectation sequences).

Then the BN3SLS estimator is asymptotically superior in efficiency to any of the estimators (5.41), *for any choice of the instrument matrices Z therein.*

Proof: We observe that asymptotic efficiency comparisons are in each case based upon differences of the form

$$\left[\text{plim}\,\frac{1}{n}G_0'PG_0\right]^{-1}-\left[\text{plim}\,\frac{1}{n}G_0'P_eG_0\right]^{-1},$$

where P is defined variously as in equations (5.41a–c). By (a) of Lemma 5.7, it will therefore suffice to show that the differences

$$\Delta=\text{plim}\left(\frac{1}{n}G_0'P_eG_0\right)-\text{plim}\left(\frac{1}{n}G_0'PG_0\right) \tag{5.46}$$

are positive semidefinite. In fact, from equations (5.44) and (5.45), together with the assumption of the proposition, it follows that

$$\text{plim}\,\frac{1}{n}G_0'P_eG_0=\text{plim}\,\frac{1}{n}G_0'\Omega^{-1}G_0.$$

Hence the difference (5.46) becomes

$$\Delta=\text{plim}\,\frac{1}{n}G_0'(\Omega^{-1}-P)G_0,$$

and Δ will be positive semidefinite if the difference $\Omega^{-1}-P$ is. Let us consider the various estimators in turn:

(i) The OLS analog, expression (5.41a):

$$\begin{aligned}\Omega^{-1}-P&=\Omega^{-1}-\tilde{Z}(\tilde{Z}'\Omega\tilde{Z})^{-1}\tilde{Z}'\\&=\Omega^{-1/2}(I-W(W'W)^{-1}W')\Omega^{-1/2},\end{aligned}$$

where $W=\Omega^{-1/2}\tilde{Z}$. Clearly $\Omega^{-1}-P$ is positive semidefinite.

(ii) The GLS analog, expression (5.41b):

$$\begin{aligned}\Omega^{-1}-P&=\Omega^{-1}-\Omega^{-1}\tilde{Z}(\tilde{Z}'\Omega^{-1}\tilde{Z})^{-1}\tilde{Z}'\Omega^{-1}\\&=\Omega^{-1}(\Omega-\tilde{Z}(\tilde{Z}'\Omega^{-1}\tilde{Z})^{-1}\tilde{Z}')\Omega^{-1},\end{aligned}$$

which from (b) of Lemma 5.7 is positive semidefinite.

(iii) Expression (5.41c):

$$\Omega^{-1}-P=\Omega^{-1/2}(I-Z(Z'Z)^{-1}Z')\Omega^{-1/2},$$

which is clearly positive semidefinite. ■

We comment that it will make no essential difference to the above proposition if we replace the covariance matrix $\Omega=\Sigma\otimes I$ by a consistent estimate $\hat{\Omega}$. On the other hand, the instrument $Z_e = \mathcal{E}(G_0)$ is not usually operational, both because analytic or closed-form expressions for the expectations are not usually available and because the expectation will depend upon the unknown parameters $\boldsymbol{\theta}$. We have indeed already remarked on these difficulties in connection with the construction of instruments in limited-information contexts. Nevertheless, the result shows that, asymptotically, an efficient set of instruments will approximate the conditional expectation instrument, which appears in this context as the mathematical expectation of the $\boldsymbol{\theta}$ derivative elements of the function f_i. Thus a knowledge of the functional form of these derivatives should assist in the choice of instruments.

From the theoretical point of view, the notion of a best N3SLS estimator is also useful for further studies of efficiency. Note first that we cannot in general write $\tilde{Z}_e = \mathcal{E}(G_0) = I \otimes Z$ for some Z. It follows that the Jorgenson–Laffont procedure, which utilizes such a decomposition, cannot qualify as a "best" nonlinear three-stage least-squares technique.

An interesting question is whether, and under what conditions, the NL3SLS estimator reduces to a NL2SLS estimator. This point is related in an essential way to whether or not elements of the vector $\boldsymbol{\theta}$ appear in more than one equation. If not, then the matrix G has a diagonal block structure $\text{diag}(\partial \mathbf{f}_\alpha / \partial \boldsymbol{\theta}'_\alpha)$, $\alpha = 1 \dots r$. It is now straightforward to demonstrate that if either (i) $\Sigma = I$ or else if (ii) $Z'(\partial \mathbf{f}_\alpha / \partial \boldsymbol{\theta}_\alpha)$ is nonsingular for all α, then the three-stage least-squares estimator reduces to the corresponding nonlinear two-stage least-squares procedure. These properties correspond to the linear case; condition (ii) is an exact identification condition. On the other hand, suppose that one or more elements of $\boldsymbol{\theta}$ occur in more than one equation. In this case, the matrix $\tilde{G}$ does not have a block diagonal structure and the three-stage technique does not reduce to a two-stage procedure, even if conditions (i) and (ii) above are fulfilled.

A final efficiency comparison is between the best NL3SLS estimator and the method of full-information maximum likelihood. The latter method is considered in detail in Annex A5.1 to this chapter, where the Cramer–Rao lower bound is also established. Assume that elements of $\boldsymbol{\theta}$ do not appear in more than one equation. The α, βth block of the inverse of the asymptotic covariance matrix of the BNL3S estimator is

$$\sigma^{\alpha\beta} \operatorname{plim} n^{-1} \sum_t \frac{\partial f_{\alpha t}}{\partial \boldsymbol{\theta}_\alpha} \frac{\partial f_{\beta t}}{\partial \boldsymbol{\theta}_\beta} = \sigma^{\alpha\beta} F_{\alpha\beta}.$$

Comparing this with equations (A.6)–(A.9) of Annex A5.1, we see that this block is not equal to $-\operatorname{plim}(1/n)\partial^2 l^* / \partial \boldsymbol{\theta}_\alpha \partial \boldsymbol{\theta}'_\beta$. The BNL3S estimator does not then attain the Cramer–Rao lower bound and is generally less efficient, asymptotically, than the MLE.

It may be shown (Amemiya 1977) that the BNL3S estimator is as asymptotically efficient as the MLE only in the case where f_i can be written in the form

$$f_i(\mathbf{y}_t, \mathbf{x}_t, \boldsymbol{\theta}_i) = C_i(\boldsymbol{\theta}_i)' Z_i(\mathbf{y}_t, \mathbf{x}_t) + K_i(\boldsymbol{\theta}_i, \mathbf{x}_t),$$

for some functions K_i and vector-valued functions C_i and Z_i. Thus the only essential parameter nonlinearities allowable are those involving the exogenous variables. On the other hand, the best NL3SLS estimator is more robust with respect to distributional assumptions, in the sense that unlike the likelihood estimator its consistency does not depend in a crucial way upon the assumed normality of the disturbances.

5.6 Full-information maximum likelihood

Let us assume that the disturbances u_{it} are normally distributed with mean zero and covariance matrix Σ. Following a derivation similar to that for the linear case (see Section 4.4) we obtain the log-likelihood function as

$$l = \text{const.} + \frac{n}{2} \log \det \Sigma^{-1} + \sum_t \log|\det J_t| - \frac{1}{2} \sum_{ijt} f_{it} \Sigma^{ij} f_{jt},$$

where J_t is the matrix whose i, jth element is $J_{ijt} = (\partial f_i / \partial y_j)_t$ and $\Sigma^{-1} = \{\sigma^{ij}\}$. Notice that, unlike the linear simultaneous-equation models studied in the previous chapters, the Jacobian, det J_t, is no longer a constant but must be regarded as a function of the observations and parameters.

To concentrate the log-likelihood function we use the result that if $A = \{a_{ij}\}$ is a nonsingular matrix with inverse $A^{-1} = \{a^{ij}\}$, then

$$\partial \log|\det A| / \partial a_{ij} = a^{ji}.$$

Thus,

$$\frac{\partial l}{\partial \sigma^{ij}} = \frac{n}{2} \sigma_{ij} - \frac{1}{2} \sum_t f_{it} f_{jt} = 0,$$

giving

$$\hat{\sigma}_{ij} = \hat{\sigma}_{ji} = \frac{1}{n} \sum_t f_{it} f_{jt},$$

and the concentrated log-likelihood function

$$l^* = \text{const.} - \frac{n}{2} \log \det \hat{\Sigma} + \sum_t \log|\det J_t|, \tag{5.47}$$

where $\hat{\Sigma} = \{\hat{\sigma}_{ij}\}$. To simplify matters we shall assume in what follows that no parameter occurs in more than one equation.

In the annex to this chapter we show that the first-order conditions for the maximization of the log-likelihood function are given by

$$\frac{\partial l^*}{\partial \boldsymbol{\theta}_\alpha} = -\sum_i \hat{\sigma}^{i\alpha}\left(\sum_t f_{it}\frac{\partial f_{\alpha t}}{\partial \boldsymbol{\theta}_\alpha}\right) + \sum_{jt} J_t^{j\alpha}\frac{\partial^2 f_{\alpha t}}{\partial \boldsymbol{\theta}_\alpha \partial y_j}$$
$$= \mathbf{0}, \qquad \alpha = 1, \ldots, r. \tag{5.48}$$

Letting $\mathbf{g}_{\alpha t} = \partial f_{\alpha t}/\partial \boldsymbol{\theta}_\alpha$ and noting that

$$\frac{\partial \mathbf{g}_{\alpha t}}{\partial u_\alpha} = \sum_j J_t^{j\alpha}\frac{\partial \mathbf{g}_{\alpha t}}{\partial y_j},$$

we can write (5.48) as

$$\frac{\partial l^*}{\partial \boldsymbol{\theta}_\alpha} = -\sum_i \hat{\sigma}^{i\alpha}\left(\sum_t f_{it}\mathbf{g}_{\alpha t}\right) + \sum_t \frac{\partial \mathbf{g}_{\alpha t}}{\partial u_\alpha} = \mathbf{0}, \qquad \alpha = 1, \ldots, r. \tag{5.49}$$

The maximum-likelihood estimator $\tilde{\boldsymbol{\theta}}_\alpha$ of $\boldsymbol{\theta}_\alpha$ is defined as a root of this equation.

As in the linear simultaneous-equation model the existence, consistency, and asymptotic efficiency of the MLE requires that the likelihood function l^* satisfy certain regularity conditions. Amemiya (1977) gives such conditions for the nonlinear simultaneous equation model and derives a set of conditions on the functions f_{it} and the derivatives $\mathbf{g}_{\alpha t}$ that are needed to ensure the required regularity conditions. He shows that under these conditions at least one root exists asymptotically to the equation $\partial l^*/\partial \boldsymbol{\theta}_\alpha = \mathbf{0}$, that one of the roots is consistent, and that this root has the usual asymptotic properties. That is, let $\tilde{\boldsymbol{\theta}}_\alpha$ be the consistent root and $\tilde{\boldsymbol{\theta}} = (\tilde{\boldsymbol{\theta}}_1' \, \tilde{\boldsymbol{\theta}}_2' \, \ldots \, \tilde{\boldsymbol{\theta}}_\alpha' \, \ldots \, \hat{\boldsymbol{\theta}}_G')'$. Then $\tilde{\boldsymbol{\theta}} \xrightarrow{p} \boldsymbol{\theta}_0$ and

$$\sqrt{n}(\hat{\boldsymbol{\theta}} - \boldsymbol{\theta}_0) \xrightarrow{d} N(\mathbf{0}, V), \tag{5.50}$$

where

$$V = \left(-\text{plim}\,\frac{1}{n}\frac{\partial^2 l}{\partial \boldsymbol{\theta}\,\partial \boldsymbol{\theta}'}\right)^{-1},$$

evaluated at the true value $\boldsymbol{\theta}_0$. The covariance matrix V may be taken as the Cramer–Rao lower bound. Strictly speaking, it requires a further demonstration that the covariance matrix V does indeed correspond to the classical Cramer–Rao bound. We shall simply assume that the set of regularity conditions imposed by Amemiya is sufficient to ensure this result.

The nature of the limiting covariance matrix (5.49) has been investigated by Jorgenson and Laffont (1974), and their workings are reproduced in Annex A5.1. It turns out that the matrix

$$-\text{plim}\,\frac{1}{n}\,\frac{\partial^2 l^*}{\partial\theta\,\partial\theta'}$$

can be written as the sum of four terms. By computing the limit under special cases, Jorgenson and Laffont were able to interpret these elements in terms of contributions from endogeneity, on the one hand, and the necessity to estimate the covariance matrix Σ, on the other. We refer the reader to the more detailed discussion of the annex to this chapter.

Maximum likelihood as iterative IV

As in the linear case, maximum likelihood has an interpretation as an iterative IV estimator, although as we shall see there is an important difference in respect of their iterative properties. Following Amemiya (1977), let F' be the $r\times n$ matrix whose i,tth element is $f_i(\mathbf{y}_t,\mathbf{x}_t,\boldsymbol{\theta}_i)$ and G'_α be the matrix whose tth column is $\partial f_\alpha(\mathbf{y}_t,\mathbf{x}_t,\boldsymbol{\theta}_\alpha)/\partial\boldsymbol{\theta}_\alpha$. Then we can rewrite the first-order conditions given in (5.49) as

$$\left[n^{-1}\sum_t \frac{\partial g_{\alpha t}}{\partial\mathbf{u}'}\cdot F' - G'_\alpha\right]F(n^{-1}F'F)^{-1}_\alpha = 0, \qquad \alpha=1,\dots,r, \quad (5.51)$$

where the notation $(\quad)^{-1}_\alpha$ signifies the αth column of the inverse of the matrix within the brackets. Define

$$\tilde{G}'_\alpha = G'_\alpha - n^{-1}\sum_t \frac{\partial g_{\alpha t}}{\partial\mathbf{u}'}\cdot F'.$$

Then (5.51) can be written as

$$\tilde{G}'_\alpha F(F'F/n)^{-1}_\alpha = \mathbf{0}.$$

Let $\tilde{G}'$ be the block diagonal matrix with $\tilde{G}'_\alpha$ as the matrix in the α block diagonal position. Noting that

$$\operatorname{vec} F(F'F/n)^{-1} = \begin{pmatrix} F(F'F/n)^{-1}_1 \\ \vdots \\ F(F'F/n)^{-1}_r \end{pmatrix},$$

we can write the expressions (5.51) collectively as

$$\tilde{G}' \operatorname{vec} F(F'F/n)^{-1} = \mathbf{0}.$$

But $\operatorname{vec} F(F'F/n)^{-1} = (\hat{\Sigma}^{-1}\otimes I)\mathbf{f}$, where $\mathbf{f}=\operatorname{vec} F$, and we can write the first-order conditions as

$$\tilde{G}'(\hat{\Sigma}^{-1}\otimes I)\mathbf{f} = \mathbf{0}. \quad (5.52)$$

Given an iteration stage $\boldsymbol{\theta}_k$, expand $f(\boldsymbol{\theta})$ in Taylor series around $\boldsymbol{\theta}_k$:

$$f(\boldsymbol{\theta}_{k+1}) \simeq f(\boldsymbol{\theta}_k) + G_k(\boldsymbol{\theta}_{k+1} - \boldsymbol{\theta}_k), \tag{5.53}$$

where $G_k = G(\boldsymbol{\theta}_k)$ is the block diagonal matrix with G_α in the α block diagonal position. Substituting (5.53) into (5.52) gives

$$\boldsymbol{\theta}_{k+1} \simeq \boldsymbol{\theta}_k - [\tilde{G}'(\hat{\Sigma}^{-1} \otimes I)G]^{-1}\tilde{G}'(\hat{\Sigma}^{-1} \otimes I)\mathbf{f}, \tag{5.54}$$

where G and $\mathbf{f}$ are evaluated at $\boldsymbol{\theta}_k$.

Formula (5.54) is the generalization of the iterative updating procedure (5.30), (5.31) for the limited-information model of Section 5.4. It has a similar interpretation, in terms of an application of an IV–GLS technique to an associated auxiliary regression equation, with $\tilde{G}$ as instrument for G.

The efficiency of iterative MLEs

We have referred on several occasions in the text to second-round estimators in which, starting from an initial consistent estimator $\hat{\boldsymbol{\theta}}_1$, say, a second-round estimator $\hat{\boldsymbol{\theta}}_2$ is obtained, basically by following through a Gauss–Newton iteration with a suitably chosen weighting matrix. The latter is often chosen as the estimated covariance matrix of the gradient of the likelihood function (the method of "scoring"). It is of interest to investigate the performance of this class of techniques in the present context.

Consider, then, the class of gradient methods defined by

$$\hat{\boldsymbol{\theta}}_2 = \hat{\boldsymbol{\theta}}_1 - A \left.\frac{\partial l^*}{\partial \boldsymbol{\theta}}\right|_{\hat{\boldsymbol{\theta}}_1}, \tag{5.55}$$

where $\hat{\boldsymbol{\theta}}_1$ is an initial consistent estimator and A is some matrix that may be stochastic and is preferably positive semidefinite.

Expanding $\partial l^*/\partial \boldsymbol{\theta}|_{\hat{\boldsymbol{\theta}}_1}$ in a Taylor series around $\boldsymbol{\theta}_0$, the true value, allows us to write

$$\sqrt{n}(\hat{\boldsymbol{\theta}}_2 - \boldsymbol{\theta}_0) = -\sqrt{n}A \left.\frac{\partial l^*}{\partial \boldsymbol{\theta}}\right|_{\boldsymbol{\theta}_0} + \left[I - A \left.\frac{\partial^2 l^*}{\partial \boldsymbol{\theta}\, \partial \boldsymbol{\theta}'}\right|_{\boldsymbol{\theta}^*}\right] \sqrt{n}(\hat{\boldsymbol{\theta}}_1 - \boldsymbol{\theta}_0),$$

where $\boldsymbol{\theta}^*$ lies between $\hat{\boldsymbol{\theta}}_1$ and $\boldsymbol{\theta}_0$.

Suppose $\sqrt{n}(\hat{\boldsymbol{\theta}}_1 - \boldsymbol{\theta}_0)$ has a limiting distribution. Then the limiting distribution of the second-round estimator $\hat{\boldsymbol{\theta}}_2$ does not depend on that of the first-round estimator if and only if

$$(\operatorname{plim} nA)^{-1} = \operatorname{plim} n^{-1} \left.\frac{\partial^2 l^*}{\partial \boldsymbol{\theta}\, \partial \boldsymbol{\theta}'}\right|_{\boldsymbol{\theta}^*} = \operatorname{plim} n^{-1} \left.\frac{\partial^2 l^*}{\partial \boldsymbol{\theta}\, \partial \boldsymbol{\theta}'}\right|_{\boldsymbol{\theta}_0}.$$

Moreover, if we make the regularity assumption that $n^{-1/2} \partial l^*/\partial \boldsymbol{\theta}|_{\boldsymbol{\theta}_0}$ tends in distribution to a multivariate normal random vector with mean $\mathbf{0}$ and asymptotic covariance matrix given by the Cramer–Rao lower bound, then the second-round estimator $\hat{\theta}_2$ is a BAN estimator.

So far as the linear simultaneous context is concerned, it may be easily shown that Hausman's iterative procedure [see equation (4.37) of Chapter 4] obeys this property (if we take the estimator at stage r, namely θ_r, to correspond to the required initial consistent estimator). However, Amemiya (1977) showed that a similar property is not true of the nonlinear context. To see this, we note from equation (5.52) above that

$$\partial l^*/\partial \boldsymbol{\theta} = \tilde{G}'(\hat{\Sigma}^{-1} \otimes I)\mathbf{f}.$$

Now the proposed method may be defined in terms of equation (5.54) above with $\boldsymbol{\theta}_k = \boldsymbol{\theta}_1$, the initial consistent estimator, and $\boldsymbol{\theta}_2$ corresponding to $\boldsymbol{\theta}_{k+1}$. Such a technique clearly corresponds to equation (5.55) with

$$A = [\tilde{G}'(\hat{\Sigma}^{-1} \otimes I)G]^{-1}.$$

Considering the α, β block, the iterative MLE is not second-round efficient (to use Amemiya's terminology) if

$$\text{plim}\ \hat{\sigma}^{\alpha\beta} n^{-1} \tilde{G}'_\alpha G_\beta \neq \text{plim}\ n^{-1} \partial^2 l^*/\partial \boldsymbol{\theta}_\alpha\, \partial \boldsymbol{\theta}'_\beta.$$

This indeed turns out to be the case. The proof is rather involved and is reproduced in Annex A5.2. Clearly this lack of "second-round efficiency" will place a greater emphasis upon efficient numerical methods for the attainment of the desired maximum $\tilde{\boldsymbol{\theta}}$. Computational experience is as yet rather limited.

5.7 Summary

We have seen in this chapter that, within limits, there is a fair measure of correspondence between the linear and nonlinear versions of instrumental variables theory. Unlike the linear theory, one cannot in general write down analytically an explicit form for the IV estimator itself. For essentially nonlinear models, the estimator must be obtained numerically as the parameter value that minimizes the IV minimand. The latter, however is of the same form as for the linear theory and can be given the same interpretations. Moreover, the asymptotic sampling theory established in Section 5.4 corresponds very closely to the linear theory, with the matrix of parameter derivatives $G(\boldsymbol{\theta}_0) = (\partial \mathbf{g}/\partial \boldsymbol{\theta})|_{\boldsymbol{\theta}=\boldsymbol{\theta}_0}$ evaluated at the true parameter value, playing the role of X in the linear theory. This enables us to define the notion of a "best" instrument as the expectation of this Jacobian. Since they depend upon knowledge of the true parameter values $\boldsymbol{\theta}_0$, the best instruments are in practice unobtainable. However, the nonlinear context is characterized by a plethora of possible instruments, and indeed classifications are established in Section 5.3 under such headings as polynomial, internal, and expectational instruments. The notion of a theoretical best instrument can help in deciding which of these possible instruments to employ. One limitation of the "best" instrument is that the notion is essentially asymptotic. It is very possibly the case that the polynomial or internal instrument sets have a better finite sampling performance.

When we turn in Section 5.5 to full-information systems (in the sense that the generation of right-hand variables in each equation is explicitly described by the model), one can define different IV estimators. This destination is based upon different choices of the associated minimum-distance matrix P_z and essentially corresponds to the types of estimator described in Section 3.2. Unlike the general situation described in that section, definite efficiency comparisons among the alternative IV estimators can now be made, employing once again the notion of a best instrument as the expectation of the relevant Jacobian. It turns out that of the various possibilities, the GLS analog has superior efficiency properties. Under certain circumstances – basically, that the column vector of the super-matrix of instruments Z contains the union of the spaces spanned by the Jacobian $\mathcal{E}\, G_\alpha(\boldsymbol{\theta}_0)$ for the different equations α – the different IV variants collapse to the same estimator, the "three-stage nonlinear least-squares" estimator.

The relative efficiency properties with respect to the method of maximum likelihood were explored both in a particular limited-information context (Section 5.4) and in the general full-information model (Section 5.6). For both models, it is shown that the relevant fixed-instrument methods do not attain the Cramer–Rao lower bound. In this respect the conclusions differ from the linear context, in which the method of three-stage least squares is asymptotically efficient. Like the linear case, however, the method of full-information maximum likelihood can itself be regarded as an IV method, with the matrix of instruments being updated after each iteration. But as the final "down" in this seesaw of comparisons, the MLE in the nonlinear context does not possess the "second-round efficiency" property, according to which one needs only one further iteration from an initial consistent estimator to achieve asymptotic efficiency.

The net result of this development is that we now have a fairly good understanding of the IV and maximum-likelihood estimation theory and practice for nonlinear systems. In one sense the nonlinear theory is going to be more demanding with respect to model specification, for it opens up the whole subject of alternative functional forms for economic or statistical relationships. In turn, this raises the topic of comparing the fit of models of different functional form, which cannot be nested one inside the other. Such an exploration, although important and worthwhile, is beyond the scope of the present contribution. But the possibility of a range of possible functional forms in other equations of the model, as well as the equation under study, places a burden on the estimation methodology that it shall be relatively robust to specification error. In addition to their convenience and their workhorse role as the generators of initial or ballpark estimates, the IV methods do have the advantage of robustness. For this reason alone they are worth studying.

Annex[6]

A5.1 *The Cramer–Rao lower bound for the nonlinear simultaneous-equation model*

In computing the Cramer–Rao lower bound, use is made of the following matrix differentiation results:

Lemma MD: *Let $A=\{a_{ij}\}$ be a nonsingular matrix with inverse $A^{-1}=\{a^{ij}\}$, whose elements a_{ij} are functions of $\boldsymbol{\theta}$. Then*

$$\frac{\partial \log|\det A|}{\partial a_{ij}}=a^{ji}$$

and

$$\frac{\partial a^{ij}}{\partial \theta}=-\sum_{hm} a^{ih}\frac{\partial a_{hm}}{\partial \theta}a^{mj}.$$

The concentrated log-likelihood function is [cf. equation (5.47)]

$$l^*=\text{const.}-\frac{n}{2}\log\det\hat{\Sigma}+\sum_t \log|\det J_t|.$$

Thus

$$\frac{\partial l^*}{\partial \theta_\alpha}=\sum_{ij}\frac{\partial l^*}{\partial \hat{\sigma}_{ij}}\frac{\partial \hat{\sigma}_{iy}}{\partial \theta_\alpha}+\sum_{ijt}\frac{\partial l^*}{\partial J_{ijt}}\frac{\partial J_{ijt}}{\partial \theta_\alpha}, \tag{A.1}$$

where $\hat{\Sigma}=\{\hat{\sigma}_{ij}\}$. Applying Lemma MD, we have

$$\frac{\partial l^*}{\partial \hat{\sigma}_{ij}}=-\frac{n}{2}\hat{\sigma}^{ij} \quad\text{and}\quad \frac{\partial l^*}{\partial J_{ijt}}=J_t^{ji}, \tag{A.2}$$

where $\hat{\Sigma}^{-1}=\{\hat{\sigma}^{ij}\}$.

As $\hat{\sigma}_{ij}=(1/n)\sum_t f_{it}f_{jt}$, we obtain

$$\frac{\partial \hat{\sigma}_{ij}}{\partial \theta_\alpha}=\frac{1}{n}\sum_t\left(\frac{\partial f_{it}}{\partial \theta_\alpha}f_{jt}+f_{it}\frac{\partial f_{jt}}{\partial \theta_\alpha}\right).$$

But by assumption f_{it} depends only on θ_i but not on θ_j, $i \neq j$. So we use the following simplifications:

$$\frac{\partial \hat{\sigma}_{\alpha\alpha}}{\partial \theta_\alpha} = \frac{2}{n} \sum_t f_{\alpha t} \frac{\partial f_{\alpha t}}{\partial \theta_\alpha}$$

$$\frac{\partial \hat{\sigma}_{i\alpha}}{\partial \theta_\alpha} = \frac{\partial \hat{\sigma}_{\alpha i}}{\partial \theta_\alpha} = \frac{1}{n} \sum_t f_{it} \frac{\partial f_{\alpha t}}{\partial \theta_\alpha}, \qquad i \neq \alpha$$

$$\frac{\partial \hat{\sigma}_{ij}}{\partial \theta_\alpha} = 0 \qquad \text{if } i \neq \alpha \text{ and } j \neq \alpha.$$

Thus,

$$\frac{\partial \hat{\sigma}_{ij}}{\partial \theta_\alpha} = \frac{2}{n} \sum_t f_{it} \frac{\partial f_{\alpha t}}{\partial \theta_\alpha}. \tag{A.3}$$

Now

$$\frac{\partial J_{ijt}}{\partial \theta_\alpha} = \frac{\partial^2 f_{it}}{\partial \theta_\alpha \, \partial y_j},$$

with the simplifications

$$\frac{\partial J_{\alpha jt}}{\partial \theta_\alpha} = \frac{\partial^2 f_{\alpha t}}{\partial \theta_\alpha \, \partial y_j}, \qquad \frac{\partial J_{ijt}}{\partial \theta_\alpha} = 0, \qquad i \neq \alpha. \tag{A.4}$$

Substituting (A.3) and (A.4) into (A.1) gives

$$\frac{\partial l^*}{\partial \theta_\alpha} = -\sum_i \hat{\sigma}^{i\alpha} \left(\sum_t f_{it} \frac{\partial f_{\alpha t}}{\partial \theta_\alpha} \right) + \sum_{jt} J_t^{j\alpha} \frac{\partial^2 f_{\alpha t}}{\partial \theta_\alpha \, \partial y_j}.$$

We now need to evaluate the second-order derivatives

$$\frac{\partial^2 l^*}{\partial \theta_\alpha \, \partial \theta'_\beta} = -\sum_i \left(\sum_t f_{it} \frac{\partial f_{\alpha t}}{\partial \theta_\alpha} \right) \frac{\partial \hat{\sigma}^{i\alpha}}{\partial \theta'_\beta} - \sum_i \hat{\sigma}^{i\alpha} \left(\sum_t \frac{\partial f_{\alpha t}}{\partial \theta_\alpha} \frac{\partial f_{it}}{\partial \theta'_\beta} + f_{it} \frac{\partial^2 f_{\alpha t}}{\partial \theta_\alpha \, \partial \theta'_\beta} \right)$$
$$+ \sum_{jt} \frac{\partial^2 f_{\alpha t}}{\partial \theta_\alpha \, \partial y_j} \frac{\partial J_t^{j\alpha}}{\partial \theta'_\beta} + \sum_{jt} J_t^{j\alpha} \frac{\partial^3 f_{\alpha t}}{\partial \theta_\alpha \, \partial \theta'_\beta \, \partial y_j}. \tag{A.5}$$

Using Lemma MD we have, from (A.3),

$$\frac{\partial \hat{\sigma}^{i\alpha}}{\partial \theta'_\beta} = -\sum_{hm} \hat{\sigma}^{ih} \frac{\partial \hat{\sigma}_{hm}}{\partial \theta'_\beta} \hat{\sigma}^{m\alpha}$$
$$= -\sum_m \hat{\sigma}^{i\beta} \frac{\partial \hat{\sigma}_{\beta m}}{\partial \theta'_\beta} \hat{\sigma}^{m\alpha} - \sum_h \hat{\sigma}^{ih} \frac{\partial \hat{\sigma}_{h\beta}}{\partial \theta'_\beta} \hat{\sigma}^{\beta\alpha}$$
$$= -\sum_m \hat{\sigma}^{i\beta} \hat{\sigma}^{m\alpha} \left(\frac{1}{n} \sum_t f_{mt} \frac{\partial f_{\beta t}}{\partial \theta'_\beta} \right) - \sum_h \hat{\sigma}^{ih} \hat{\sigma}^{\beta\alpha} \left(\frac{1}{n} \sum_t f_{ht} \frac{\partial f_{\beta t}}{\partial \theta'_\beta} \right).$$

Thus the first element of the right-hand side of (A.5) is

$$\frac{1}{n}\sum_{im}\hat{\sigma}^{i\beta}\hat{\sigma}^{m\alpha}\left(\sum_t f_{it}\frac{\partial f_{\alpha t}}{\partial\theta_\alpha}\right)\left(\sum_t f_{mt}\frac{\partial f_{\beta t}}{\partial\theta_\beta'}\right)$$

$$+\frac{1}{n}\sum_{ih}\hat{\sigma}^{ih}\hat{\sigma}^{\beta\alpha}\left(\sum_t f_{it}\frac{\partial f_{\alpha t}}{\partial\theta_\alpha}\right)\left(\sum_t f_{ht}\frac{\partial f_{\beta t}}{\partial\theta_\beta'}\right).$$

Using Lemma MD again, from (A.4),

$$\frac{\partial J_t^{j\alpha}}{\partial\theta_\beta'}=-\sum_{hm}J_t^{jh}\frac{\partial J_{hmt}}{\partial\theta_\beta'}J_t^{m\alpha}=-\sum_m J_t^{j\beta}\frac{\partial^2 f_{\beta t}}{\partial\theta_\beta'\,\partial y_m}J_t^{m\alpha}.$$

The third element on the right-hand side of (A.5) can then be written as

$$-\sum_{jmt}J_t^{j\beta}J_t^{m\alpha}\frac{\partial^2 f_{\alpha t}}{\partial\theta_\alpha\,\partial y_j}\frac{\partial^2 f_{\beta t}}{\partial\theta_\beta'\,\partial y_m}.$$

We can tidy up this term by letting $g_{\alpha t}=\partial f_{\alpha t}/\partial\theta_\alpha$ and noting that

$$\frac{\partial g_{\alpha t}}{\partial u_\beta}=\sum_j J_t^{j\beta}\frac{\partial g_{\alpha t}}{\partial y_j}.$$

Thus the third element on the right-hand side of (A.5) becomes

$$-\sum_t\frac{\partial g_{\alpha t}}{\partial u_\beta}\frac{\partial g_{\beta t}}{\partial u_\alpha'}.$$

The second term on the right-hand side of (A.5) becomes

$$-\hat{\sigma}^{\beta\alpha}\sum_t\frac{\partial f_{\alpha t}}{\partial\theta_\alpha}\frac{\partial f_{\beta t}}{\partial\theta_\beta'}\qquad\text{if }\beta\neq\alpha$$

or

$$-\hat{\sigma}^{\alpha\alpha}\sum_t\frac{\partial f_{\alpha t}}{\partial\theta_\alpha}\frac{\partial f_{\alpha t}}{\partial\theta_\alpha'}-\sum_i\hat{\sigma}^{i\alpha}\sum_t f_{it}\frac{\partial^2 f_{\alpha t}}{\partial\theta_\alpha\,\partial\theta_\alpha'}\qquad\text{if }\beta=\alpha.$$

Amemiya (1977) shows that under suitable assumptions all third-order derivatives can be asymptotically ignored in the computation of the Cramer–Rao lower bound. Hence there is no need to evaluate the last term on the right-hand side of (A.5).

In computing

$$-\text{plim}\,\frac{1}{n}\frac{\partial^2 l^*}{\partial\theta_\alpha\,\partial\theta_\beta}$$

we need to assume the existence of the probability limits of the various expressions appearing in our calculations. In particular, let

$$\begin{aligned}
&\frac{1}{n}\sum_t f_{it}\frac{\partial f_{\alpha t}}{\partial\theta_\alpha} \xrightarrow{p} H_{i\alpha}, && i,\alpha=1,\dots,r\\
&\frac{1}{n}\sum_t f_{it}\frac{\partial^2 f_{\alpha t}}{\partial\theta_\alpha\,\partial\theta'_\alpha} \xrightarrow{p} W_{i\alpha}, && i,\alpha=1,\dots,r\\
&\frac{1}{n}\sum_t \frac{\partial f_{it}}{\partial\theta_i}\frac{\partial f_{jt}}{\partial\theta'_j} \xrightarrow{p} F_{ij}, && i,j=1,\dots,r\\
&\frac{1}{n}\sum_t \frac{\partial g_{\alpha t}}{\partial u_\beta}\frac{\partial g_{\beta t}}{\partial u'_\alpha} \xrightarrow{p} K_{\alpha\beta}.
\end{aligned} \tag{A.6}$$

Moreover, under suitable assumptions the MLEs are consistent and thus $\hat{\sigma}^{ij} \xrightarrow{p} \sigma^{ij}$. Then the plim of $-1/n$ times the first term on the right-hand side of (A.5) is

$$-\sum_{im}\sigma^{i\beta}\sigma^{m\alpha}H_{i\alpha}H'_{m\beta}-\sigma^{\beta\alpha}\sum_{ih}\sigma^{ih}H_{i\alpha}H'_{h\beta}. \tag{A.7}$$

The plim of $-1/n$ times the second term on the right-hand side of (A.5) is

$$\begin{aligned}
&\sigma^{\beta\alpha}F_{\alpha\beta} && \text{if } \beta\neq\alpha\\
&\sigma^{\alpha\alpha}F_{\alpha\alpha}+\sum_i\sigma^{i\alpha}W_{i\alpha} && \text{if } \beta=\alpha.
\end{aligned} \tag{A.8}$$

The plim of $-1/n$ times the third term on the right-hand side of (A.5) is

$$K_{\alpha\beta}. \tag{A.9}$$

Now let $-T_1$ be a partitioned matrix whose α,β block is given by (7), T_2 be a partitioned matrix whose α,β block is given by (8), and T_3 be a partitioned matrix whose α,β block is given by (9). Finally, let T_4 be a block diagonal matrix whose α,α block is given by $\sum_i \sigma^{i\alpha}W_{i\alpha}$. Then clearly,

$$-\text{plim}\,\frac{1}{n}\frac{\partial^2 l^*}{\partial\theta\,\partial\theta'}=-T_1+T_2+T_3+T_4 \tag{A.10}$$

and the Cramer–Rao lower bound is the inverse of this matrix.

Jorgenson and Laffont (1974) interpret the elements T_i as follows:

(a) The term T_2^{-1} would be the Cramer–Rao lower bound if our system of nonlinear equations represented a reduced form, that is, if the equation were of the form

$$y_{it}=f_i(\mathbf{x}_t,\theta)+u_{it}, \qquad i=1,\dots,r. \tag{A.11}$$

(b) The matrices T_3, T_4 represent a modification to

$$-\text{plim}\,\frac{1}{n}\frac{\partial^2 l^*}{\partial\theta\,\partial\theta'}$$

due to the existence of endogenous variables appearing in the right-hand functions of equations like (A.11).

(c) T_1 represents the additional change to the plim due to the fact that Σ is unknown and must be estimated.

A5.2 *Second-round efficiency*

In Section A5.1 we showed that

$$\operatorname{plim} \frac{1}{n} \frac{\partial^2 l^*}{\partial\theta_\alpha \partial\theta'_\beta} = \sum_{im} \sigma^{i\beta}\sigma^{m\alpha} H_{i\alpha} H'_{m\beta} + \sigma^{\alpha\beta} \sum_{ih} \sigma^{ih} H_{i\alpha} H'_{h\beta} - \sigma^{\alpha\beta} F_{\alpha\beta} - K_{\alpha\beta}. \tag{A.12}$$

It is required to show that this is *not* equal to plim $\hat{\sigma}^{\alpha\beta} n^{-1} \tilde{G}'_\alpha G_\beta$. Now,

$$\operatorname{plim} \hat{\sigma}^{\alpha\beta} n^{-1} \hat{G}'_\alpha G_\beta = \sigma^{\alpha\beta} \operatorname{plim} n^{-1} G'_\alpha G_\beta - \sigma^{\alpha\beta} \operatorname{plim} n^{-2} \sum_t \frac{\partial g_{\alpha t}}{\partial u'_t} F' G_\beta, \tag{A.13}$$

where $u_t = (u_{1t}, \ldots, u_{rt})'$.

The first term on the right-hand side of (A.13) clearly equals $\sigma^{\alpha\beta} F_{\alpha\beta}$. We can write the second term on the right-hand side of (A.13) as

$$-\sigma^{\alpha\beta}\left(\operatorname{plim} n^{-1} \sum_t \frac{\partial g_{\alpha t}}{\partial u'_t} \Sigma\right) \Sigma^{-1} \left(\operatorname{plim} n^{-1} \sum_t u_t g_{t\beta}\right). \tag{A.14}$$

Suppose we make the following assumption:

Assumption: The probability limit of n^{-1} times every summation that occurs in the right-hand side of (A.14) is finite and is equal to the limit of n^{-1} times its expectation.

This allows us to apply the following lemma (see Amemiya 1982).

Lemma: *Let $u = (u_1\ u_2\ \ldots\ u_n)'$ have a multivariate normal distribution with mean* **0** *and covariance matrix Σ, where Σ is positive definite. Suppose a function $h(u)$ satisfies the following conditions:*

(a) *$\partial h(u)/\partial u_i$ is continuous;*
(b) *$\mathcal{E}|\partial h/\partial u_i| < \infty$; and*
(c) *$\mathcal{E}|h u_i| < \infty$.*

Then $\mathcal{E}(\partial h/\partial u_i) = \mathcal{E}(h \sum_j \sigma^{ij} u_j)$, where $\Sigma^{-1} = \{\sigma^{ij}\}$.

Using this lemma, we then have

$$\operatorname{plim} n^{-1} \sum_t \frac{\partial g_{\alpha t}}{\partial u'_t} \Sigma = \lim n^{-1} \sum_t \mathcal{E}\left(\frac{\partial g_{\alpha t}}{\partial u'_t}\right) \Sigma = \operatorname{plim} n^{-1} \sum_t g_{\alpha t} u'_t.$$

Thus the second term on the right-hand side of (A.13), under our assumption, is equal to

$$-\sigma^{\alpha\beta}\left(\operatorname{plim} n^{-1}\sum_t g\alpha_t u_t'\right)\Sigma^{-1}\left(\operatorname{plim} n^{-1}\sum_t u_t g_{t\beta}\right) = -\sigma^{\alpha\beta}\sum_{ih}\sigma^{ih}H_{i\alpha}H_{h\beta}'.$$

Substituting back gives

$$\operatorname{plim} \hat{\sigma}^{\alpha\beta} n^{-1}\hat{G}_\alpha' G_\beta = \sigma^{\alpha\beta}F_{\alpha\beta} - \sigma^{\alpha\beta}\sum_{ih}\sigma^{ih}H_{i\alpha}H_{h\beta}'. \tag{A.15}$$

Comparing (A.12) and (A.15), we see that

$$\operatorname{plim} n^{-1}\frac{\partial^2 l^*}{\partial\theta_\alpha\,\partial\theta_\beta'} = -\operatorname{plim}\hat{\sigma}^{\alpha\beta}n^{-1}\hat{G}_\alpha' G_\beta + \sum_{im}\sigma^{i\beta}\sigma^{m\alpha}H_{i\alpha}H_{m\beta}' - K_{\alpha\beta},$$

which obviously establishes the desired inequality.

Appendix: some background notes

With the aim of making the book reasonably self-contained to a reader with a moderate background in probability and statistics, we have collected together some of the most frequently used definitions and results for reference purposes, together with references to more detailed accounts where appropriate. Generally speaking, we have assumed a technical background of the order of advanced undergraduate or beginning graduate econometrics textbooks such as Goldberger (1964), Johnston (1972), or Maddala (1977). The possible exception is in Appendix A3 on stochastic convergence of minima and maxima, where it is hard to accomplish both simplicity of presentation and a reasonable degree of rigor.

A1 Stochastic convergence of estimators

The notions of convergence of estimators $\hat{\theta}_n$ from a sample size n, as $n \to \infty$, are simply particular applications of general ideas of stochastic convergence, applied to an arbitrary set of random variables $\{X_i;\, i=1,2,\dots\}$. The convergence criteria used extensively throughout the book are as follows.

Convergence in probability

Let $X_1, X_2, X_3, \dots, X_n$ be a sequence of random variables. This sequence converges in probability to a constant c if

$$\lim_{n \to \infty} P[|X_n - c| \geq \epsilon] = 0 \qquad \text{for any } \epsilon > 0,$$

and we write $X_n \xrightarrow{p} c$ or $\operatorname{plim} X_n = c$.

This is the weakest mode of convergence commonly employed. Plim $X_n = c$ means that the limiting distribution of X_n is degenerate and its density has the form of a spike of infinite height at $X = c$, that is, the Dirac delta function. A similar definition applies to a sequence of random vectors. If $\mathbf{x}_1, \mathbf{x}_2, \ldots$ are a sequence of $K \times 1$ random vectors, where K does not depend on n, then we say that $\mathbf{x}$ tends in probability to a constant vector $\mathbf{c} = \{c_i\}$ if X_{in} tends in probability to c_i, where $\mathbf{x}_n = \{X_{in}\}$. An estimator $\hat{\theta}_n$ is a (weakly) consistent estimator of θ if $\hat{\theta}_n \xrightarrow{p} \theta$.

Almost sure convergence

A sequence of random variables $\{X_n\}$ converges almost surely to a constant c, written $X_n \xrightarrow{\text{a.s.}} c$ if

$$P\left(\lim_{n \to \infty} X_n = c\right) = 1$$

or equivalently,

$$\lim_{\tau \to \infty} P\left(\bigcup_{n > \tau} |X_n - c| \geq \epsilon\right) = 0 \qquad \text{for every } \epsilon.$$

A similar definition applies to sequences of random vectors.

Almost sure convergence is a stronger mode of convergence than convergence in probability. The former requires that in the limit all the elements of $\{X_n\}$ for $n > \tau$ lie simultaneously in the interval $[c - \epsilon, c + \epsilon]$ with a probability of 1. The latter only requires that single elements of the sequence, taken separately, lie in this interval with a probability of 1. Thus a.s. convergence implies convergence in probability but not vice versa. We say that an estimator $\hat{\theta}_n$ is strongly consistent if $\hat{\theta}_n \xrightarrow{\text{a.s.}} \theta$.

Convergence in distribution

Let $X_1, X_2, \ldots$ be a sequence of random variables with distribution functions $F_1, F_2, \ldots$ respectively. Suppose that $\lim_{n \to \infty} F_n(x) = F(x)$ at all continuity points of the latter and that $F(x)$ is a probability distribution function. Then we say that the random variables X_n converge in distribution and that F is the limiting distribution of X_n; and write $X_n \xrightarrow{d} X$, where X is a random variable having F as its distribution function.

Similarly, let $\mathbf{x}_1, \mathbf{x}_2, \ldots, \mathbf{x}_n$ be a sequence of $K \times 1$ random vectors whose dimension does not depend on n and whose distribution functions are $F_1, F_2, F_3, \ldots, F_n$, respectively. Let $\mathbf{x}$ be a $K \times 1$ random vector with a distribution function F. Then the sequence of random vectors $\mathbf{x}_n$ converge in distribution to $\mathbf{x}$ if $F_n \to F$ as n tends to infinity.

The following propositions are often employed:

Proposition A1.1: *Suppose that* $\{X_t\}$ *and* $\{Y_t\}$ *are sequences of random variables and that* $\operatorname{plim}(X_n - Y_n) = 0$. *If* $Y_n \xrightarrow{d} Y$, *then* X_n *has the same limiting distribution, that is,* $X_n \xrightarrow{d} Y$. *The result holds also for random vectors.*

Proposition A1.2: *Suppose that for every sample size n, the mean and the covariance matrix of* $\hat{\boldsymbol{\theta}}_n$ *exist. Then* $\operatorname{plim} \hat{\boldsymbol{\theta}}_n = \boldsymbol{\theta}$ *if*

$$\lim_{n \to \infty} \mathcal{E}(\hat{\boldsymbol{\theta}}_n) = \boldsymbol{\theta}$$

and

$$\lim_{n \to \infty} V(\hat{\boldsymbol{\theta}}_n) = 0.$$

Proposition A1.3 (Slutsky)**:** *If* $\mathbf{X}_n$ *is a random vector that tends in probability to a constant vector* $\mathbf{a}$ *and if* $f(\mathbf{X})$ *is a real function continuous at* $\mathbf{X} = \mathbf{a}$, *then*

$$f(\mathbf{X}_n) \xrightarrow{p} f(\mathbf{a}).$$

Proposition A1.4: *Let* Y_n *be a random matrix whose dimensions do not depend on n and let* $\mathbf{X}_n$ *be a random vector. If* Y_n *converges in probability to a constant matrix A and if* $\mathbf{X}_n$ *converges in distribution to the random vector* $\mathbf{X}$, *then*

$$Y_n \mathbf{X}_n \xrightarrow{d} A\mathbf{X},$$

as long as the matrices are conformable.

Proposition A1.5: *Let* $\hat{\boldsymbol{\theta}}_n$ *be a K-dimensional statistic* $(\hat{\theta}_{1n} \ldots \hat{\theta}_{kn})$ *such that the limiting distribution of* $\sqrt{n}(\hat{\theta}_{1n} - \theta_1), \ldots, \sqrt{n}(\hat{\theta}_{kn} - \theta_k)$ *is a K variate normal with mean zero and covariance matrix* $\Sigma = \{\sigma_{ij}\}$. *Further, let g be a function of K variables that is totally differentiable. Then the limiting distribution of*

$$\sqrt{n}[g(\hat{\theta}_{1n}, \ldots, \hat{\theta}_{kn}) - g(\theta_1, \ldots, \theta_k)]$$

is normal with mean zero and variance

$$v(\theta) = \sum_i \sum_j \sigma_{ij} \frac{\partial g}{\partial \theta_i} \frac{\partial g}{\partial \theta_j},$$

provided $v(\theta) \neq 0$.

A2 Central limit theorems and BAN estimators

The classical central limit theorems apply to the case of identically, independently distributed random variables. The following is a useful version [see Malinvaud (1970), pp. 250–3]:

Proposition A2.1: *Let* $\hat{\theta}_n = \sum_{t=1}^{n} A_{tn}\epsilon_t$, *where* ϵ_t *are independent identically distributed* $K \times 1$ *random vectors with mean zero and covariance matrix* Ω *and the* A_{tn} *are a sequence of* $K \times K$ *matrices of constants. Suppose:*

(a) $\lim_{n\to\infty} A_{tn} = 0$ *uniformly for all t, and*
(b) $\mathcal{E}(\hat{\theta}_n\ \hat{\theta}_n') = \sum_t A_{tn}\Omega A_{tn}'$ *tends to a positive definite matrix V as n tends to infinity.*

Then $\hat{\theta}_n$ *tends in distribution to a normal random vector with mean* **0** *and covariance matrix V.*

Particularly in cases where the exogenous variables of a model are regarded as fixed variates, situations can arise where sequences involve random variables that are independent but not identically distributed. The following proposition, due to Basmann (1960, pp. 103–4), is employed in Chapter 5:

Proposition A2.2: *Let* $X_n = \sum_{t=1}^{n} x_t$ *be the sum of n random variables that satisfy the following conditions:*

(i) *The* x_t *are independent though not necessarily identically distributed;*
(ii) $\mathcal{E}(x_t) = 0$ *for all t; and*
(iii) $\max_{t\le n} \mathcal{E}(x_t)^{2+\delta} < M$ *for all n, where M is a finite positive number and* $\delta > 0$.

Then if $\lim_{n\to\infty} \operatorname{var} X_n = v$, *a finite positive number,* X_n *is asymptotically normally distributed with mean zero and variance v.*

Let us now turn to a group of properties that concern the optimality of the estimators, as reflected in certain properties of the limiting distribution. Let us assume that $\hat{\theta}_n$ is a consistent estimator of a parameter vector $\boldsymbol{\theta}$. The behavior of $\hat{\theta}_n$ by itself is not of much value for efficiency purposes since, as remarked above, the resulting asymptotic density is degenerate. One is therefore led to consider $\sqrt{n}(\hat{\theta}_n - \theta)$, which may often converge in distribution to a normal random vector with mean zero and covariance matrix V. The latter is called the asymptotic covariance matrix of $\hat{\theta}_n$. Often we will be confronted with two such consistent estimators $\hat{\theta}_1$ and $\hat{\theta}_2$, where we have dropped the subscript n for convenience. Then we decide between these estimators on the grounds of asymptotic efficiency, which we define as follows:

Definition A2.3: Let $\hat{\boldsymbol{\theta}}_1$ and $\hat{\boldsymbol{\theta}}_2$ be two consistent estimators of $\boldsymbol{\theta}$ and suppose that $\sqrt{n}(\hat{\boldsymbol{\theta}}_1-\boldsymbol{\theta}) \xrightarrow{d} N(\mathbf{0}, V_1)$ and $\sqrt{n}(\hat{\boldsymbol{\theta}}_2-\boldsymbol{\theta}) \xrightarrow{d} N(\mathbf{0}, V_2)$. Then $\hat{\boldsymbol{\theta}}_1$ is asymptotically more efficient than $\hat{\boldsymbol{\theta}}_2$ if V_2-V_1 is a positive semidefinite matrix.

Ideally we would like to obtain consistent estimators of $\boldsymbol{\theta}$ that are asymptotically most efficient. To guide us in this we have the following lower bound for the asymptotic covariance matrix of a consistent estimator:

Proposition A2.4 (the asymptotic Cramer–Rao lower bound): *Let* $\mathbf{y}_n$ *be a random sample with likelihood function* $L_n(y;\theta)$, *which is subject to certain regularity conditions. Then*

$$R = -\text{plim}\,\frac{1}{n}\left[\frac{\partial \log L_n(y;\theta)}{\partial\theta\,\partial\theta'}\right]$$

is called (the asymptotic) Fisher information matrix. Let $\hat{\boldsymbol{\theta}}_n$ *be a consistent estimator of* $\boldsymbol{\theta}$ *based on* $\mathbf{y}_n$ *and let* $\sqrt{n}(\hat{\boldsymbol{\theta}}_n-\boldsymbol{\theta}) \xrightarrow{d} N(\mathbf{0}, V)$. *Then* V *exceeds* R^{-1} *by a positive semidefinite matrix.*

Note that the above result is the classical result referring to sampling of independent, identically distributed variables – or equivalently, independent sampling from the same parent distribution. Several sets of regularity conditions have been established in this context, and we refer the reader to Rao (1973, chap. 5) and the extensive bibliography by Norden (1972, 1973). Recently Crowden (1976) has supplied a set of conditions that ensure consistency and asymptotic normality for maximum-likelihood estimators based on generally dependent observations. See also Basawa, Feigen, and Heyde (1976).

Definition A2.5: An estimator $\hat{\boldsymbol{\theta}}_n$ such that $\hat{\boldsymbol{\theta}}_n \xrightarrow{p} \boldsymbol{\theta}$ and $\sqrt{n}(\hat{\boldsymbol{\theta}}_n-\boldsymbol{\theta}) \xrightarrow{d} N(\mathbf{0}, R^{-1})$, where R^{-1} is the Cramer–Rao lower bound, is called a best asymptotically normal (BAN) estimator.

Definition A2.5 is motivated by the classical, independent sampling case. Under suitable regularity conditions the maximum-likelihood estimators (MLEs) are BAN, and this may continue to apply if the classical assumptions are not met – for example, in the case where sampling is from generally dependent observations. In this book we have, following conventional practice, referred to MLEs as obtaining the Cramer–Rao lower bound. In general, however, each case must be justified on its own merits.

A3 Convergence of minima and maxima and related matters

We have seen at various points throughout the book that IV estimators are obtained as solutions to a minimum-distance problem. Likewise, maximum-likelihood estimators correspond to maxima of the likelihood function. It is therefore useful to have criteria that ensure (strong) consistency of the resulting estimator, when viewed as the solutions to an optimization problem.

To start with, the notion of a *Cesàro-summable sequence* is useful.

Definition A3.1 (Gallant 1977)**:** A sequence $\{\nu_t\}$ of points from a Borel set V is said to generate Cesàro-summable sequences with respect to a probability measure υ defined on the Borel subsets V if, for every real-valued continuous function f with $\int |f(\nu)|\, d\upsilon(\nu) < \infty$, the limit is

$$\lim_{n\to\infty} \frac{1}{n} \sum_{t=1}^{n} f(\nu_t) = \int f(\nu)\, d\upsilon(\nu).$$

In other words, the sample sums with respect to any function $f(\bullet)$ tend to the corresponding expectation. The definition itself provides little guidance as to whether a particular sequence is Cesàro-summable. However, it follows from the strong law of large numbers that if the sequence ν_t is a random sample from a probability distribution $F(\nu)$, then ν_t is a Cesàro-summable sequence and the appropriate limit is $\mathcal{E} f(\nu) = \int f(\nu)\, dF(\nu)$. In the case where $x_1 \ldots x_n$ are fixed in repeated samples, one might consider the *empirical distribution function,* defined by

$$F_n(x) = \frac{k}{n},$$

where k is the number of points that are $\leq x$. If we suppose that $F_n(x)$ converges completely to a limiting empirical distribution $F(x)$, then the sequence $x_1, x_2, \ldots$ is Cesàro-summable and the relevant "quasi-expectation" is $\int f(x)\, dF(x)$.

Moreover, we may consider the joint sequence (ν_t, x_t), where either or both ν_t, x_t are random or fixed in repeated realizations, with the probability or empirical distribution functions existing. Then the joint sequence is Cesàro-summable with regard to the product measure, or joint distribution of ν and x. This means in particular that the "tail product" $(1/n) \sum_{t=1}^{n} \nu_t x_t$ converges almost surely to the expectation with regard to the product measure.

Let us, accordingly, assume that ν_t is a vector that may include both random and fixed elements, but is nevertheless Cesàro-summable. The following results are of immediate applicability in respect of maximization or minimization problems:

Proposition A3.2 (Gallant 1977): *Let $f(\nu,\theta)$ be a real-valued continuous function on $V\times\Theta$, where V is a closed set and Θ is compact. Let $\{\nu_t\}$ generate Cesàro-summable sequences with respect to a probability measure v defined on the Borel subsets of V. Let $h(\nu)$ be a real-valued continuous function on V such that*

$$f(\nu,\theta)\leq h(\nu) \qquad \textit{and} \qquad \int h(\nu)\,dv(\nu)<\infty.$$

Then

(i) *The sum $(1/n)\sum_{t=1} f(\nu_t,\theta)$ converges to the integral $\int f(\nu,\theta)\,dv(\nu)$ uniformly for all θ in Θ.*
(ii) *The sum $(1/n)\sum_{t=1}^{n}\sup_\Theta|f(\nu_\epsilon,\theta)|$ is bounded.*

Thus the sum $(1/n)\sum_{t=1}^{n} f(\nu_t,\theta)$ could be interpreted as the log-likelihood function or an IV minimand.

Proposition A3.2 (Amemiya 1973): *Let $Q_n(w,\theta)$ be a measurable function on a measurable space Ω and for each w in Ω, a continuous function of θ in a compact set Θ. Then*

(i) *There exists a measurable function $\hat{\theta}_n(w)$ such that*

$$Q_n(w,\hat{\theta}_n(w))=\sup_{\theta\in\Theta} Q_n(w,\theta), \qquad w\in\Omega.$$

(ii) *If $Q_n(w,\theta)\xrightarrow{\text{a.s.}}\Omega(\theta)$ uniformly for all θ in Θ, then $\hat{\theta}_n(w)$ converges to θ_0 almost surely, where θ_0 is the unique maximum of $Q(\theta)$.*

Again the above definition can be applied to the various optimization problems of maximum-likelihood or instrumental variables, with Q_n as the log-likelihood or minimum-distance function. We satisfy ourselves (perhaps using Proposition A3.2) that the optimand tends almost surely to a limiting expectation and that the latter has a unique maximum at $\theta=\theta_0$ (or a minimum in the case of an IV problem). The existence of a unique limiting maximum or minimum is an identification requirement [see Bowden (1973)] in the case of the likelihood function and an estimability requirement in the context of an IV estimation. If all the above conditions are true, then the estimator exists and converges almost surely to the true parameter value.

Proposition A3.4 (Amemiya 1973): *Let $g_n(w;\theta)$ be a measurable function on a measurable space Ω and for each $w\in\Omega$ a continuous function for θ in a compact set Θ. If $g_n(w;\theta)$ converges almost surely to $g(\theta)$, uniformly in θ, and if $\hat{\theta}_n(w)\xrightarrow{\text{a.s.}}\theta_0$, then $g_n(w;\hat{\theta}_n(w))\xrightarrow{\text{a.s.}} g(\theta_0)$.*

Essentially, this proposition tells us that if a sample-based function of θ is evaluated at the estimated value $\hat{\theta}_n$, and if the sample data consists of Cesàro-summable sequences, then the limiting value corresponds to the expectation of the function, evaluated at the true parameter value.

The above results are evidently both powerful and reasonably general. If our data can be regarded as generated by a stable stochastic model, then the stochastic variables may be regarded as Cesàro-summable. Similar remarks hold with respect to fixed variates such as the exogenous variables of Chapter 4, if they can be regarded as drawings from an empirical distribution function. Notice, however, that we have not covered the question of the asymptotic distribution of the resulting estimates. Rather more stringent requirements may be necessary for us to assert that, for example, the estimators have an asymptotic normal distribution.

The specifications on the exogenous variables that they can be regarded as independent drawings from an empirical distribution function may in some contexts be unduly strong. In time series work, for example, it is common to make use of Grenander's conditions. For a scalar series x_t, these conditions essentially amount to the assumption that the x_t can be regarded as a realization from a stationary stochastic process, so that neighboring values of the x_t can be correlated, with a stable "autocovariance function."

A4 Matrix operations

(a) In the simultaneous stochastic equations work of Chapters 4 and 5 we make extensive use of the Kronecker product of two matrices. We recall the definition

$$A \otimes B = \begin{bmatrix} a_{11}B & a_{12}B & \dots & a_{1n}B \\ \vdots & & & \\ a_{m1}B & a_{m2}B & \dots & A_{mn}B \end{bmatrix}.$$

The following properties are constantly used:

$$\left.\begin{aligned} (A \otimes B)' &= A' \otimes B' \\ (A \otimes B)(C \otimes D) &= AC \otimes BD \\ (A \otimes B)^{-1} &= A^{-1} \otimes B^{-1}, \end{aligned}\right\} \qquad \text{(A4.1)}$$

where in every case it has been assumed that the matrices are conformable or invertible as appropriate. To these we add

$$(A \otimes B)^{-1/2} = A^{-1/2} \otimes B^{-1/2},$$

where A and B are supposed positive definite, of the same order.

[*Proof:* $(A^{-1/2} \otimes B^{-1/2})(A^{-1/2} \otimes B^{-1/2}) = (A \otimes B)^{-1}$ from (A4.1), whence the result.]

(b) The operation of $\text{vec}(A)$ indicates that a supervector is to be constructed by stacking the columns of A one on top of the other, with the first on top. The basic result connecting this operation with the Kronecker product is

$$\text{vec}(PAQ) = (Q' \otimes P) \text{ vec } A.$$

We also have

$$\det(A \otimes B) = |A|^n |B|^m,$$

where A is of order m [*sic*] and B of order n.

$$\text{tr}(A \otimes B) = (\text{tr } A)(\text{tr } B),$$

where tr( ) denotes the trace.

$$\text{tr } ABC = (\text{vec } C')'(B' \otimes I) \text{ vec } A.$$

(c) Notions of vector differentiation will be taken as familiar (e.g., Goldberger 1964, pp. 41–4). We make use of differentiation of the trace of a product of matrices with respect to a given matrix. The two most useful results are

$$\frac{\partial}{\partial X} \text{tr}(AXB) = A'B'$$

$$\frac{\partial}{\partial X} \text{tr}(AX'BX) = B'XA' + BXA.$$

Apart from this, differentiation with respect to a matrix can often be handled by transforming to supervectors by using the vec( ) operation, followed by application of the rules of vector differentiation. Further rules may be found in Dhrymes (1978).

References

Aigner, D. J. (1974). "An Appropriate Econometric Framework for Estimating a Labour Supply Function from the SEO File." *International Economic Review* 15, 59–68.

Amemiya, T. (1966). "On the Use of Principal Components of Independent Variables in Two-Stage Least-Squares Estimation." *International Economic Review* 7, 283–303.

(1973). "Regression Analysis When the Dependent Variable Is Truncated Normal." *Econometrica* 41, 997–1016.

(1974). "The Nonlinear Two-Stage Least-Squares Estimator." *Journal of Econometrics* 2, 105–10.

(1975). "The Nonlinear Limited-Information Maximum-Likelihood Estimator and the Modified Nonlinear Two-Stage Least-Squares Estimator." *Journal of Econometrics* 3, 375–86.

(1977). "The Maximum Likelihood and the Nonlinear Three-Stage Least-Squares Estimator in the General Nonlinear Simultaneous Equations Model." *Econometrica* 45, 955–68.

(1982). "Correction to a Lemma." *Econometrica* 50, 1325–8.

Amemiya, T., and W. A. Fuller (1967). "A Comparative Study of Alternative Estimators in a Distributed Lab Model." *Econometrica* 35, 509–29.

Anderson, T. W. (1958). *An Introduction to Multivariate Statistical Analysis.* New York: Wiley.

Anderson, T. W., and H. Rubin (1949). "Estimation of the Parameters of a Single Equation in a Complete System of Stochastic Equations." *Annals of Mathematical Statistics* 20, 46–63.

(1950). "The Asymptotic Properties of Estimates of the Parameters of a Single Equation in a Complete System of Stochastic Equations." *Annals of Mathematical Statistics* 21, 570–82.

Bard, Y. (1974). *Nonlinear Parameter Estimation.* New York: Academic Press.

Bartlett, M.S. (1949). "Fitting a Straight Line When Both Variables Are Subject to Error." *Biometrics* 5, 207–12.

Basawa, I. V., P. D. Feigen, and C. C. Heyde (1976). "Asymptotic Properties ot Maximum Likelihood Estimators for Stochastic Processes." *Sankhya* 38, 259–70.

Basmann, R. L. (1957). "A General Classical Method of Linear Estimation of Coefficients in a Structural Equation." *Econometrica* 25, 77–83.

(1959). "The Computation of General Classical Estimators of Coefficients in a Structural Equation." *Econometrica* 27, 72–81.

(1960). "On the Asympototic Distribution of Generalized Linear Estimators." *Econometrica* 28, 97–107.

(1961). "A Note on the Exact Finite Frequency Functions of Generalized Classical Linear Estimators in Two Leading Over-Identified Cases." *Journal of the American Statistical Association* 56, 619–36.

(1963). "A Note on the Exact Finite Sample Frequency Functions of Generalized Classical Linear Estimators in a Leading Three Equation Case." *Journal of the American Statistical Association* 58, 161–71.

(1974). "Exact Finite Sample Distributions for Some Econometric Estimators and Test Statistics: A Survey and Appraisal." In M. D. Intriligator and D. A. Kendrick, eds., *Frontiers of Quantitative Economics,* vol. II, ch. 4. Amsterdam: North-Holland.

Bergstrom, A. R. (1962). "The Exact Sampling Distributions of Least-Squares and Maximum Likelihood Estimators of the Marginal Propensity to Consume." *Econometrica* 30, 480–90.

(1966). "Nonrecursive Models as Discrete Approximations to Systems of Stochastic Differential Equations." *Econometrica* 34, 173–82.

Bowden, R. J. (1973). "The Theory of Parametric Identification." *Econometrica* 41, 1069–74.

(1978). *The Econometrics of Disequilibrium.* Amsterdam: North-Holland.

Bowden, R. J., and D. Mazumdar (1983). "Segmentation and Earnings Profiles in LDC's: A Study of the Bombay Labour Market." Discussion Paper no. 40, revised, Development Research Department, World Bank, Washington, D.C.

Bowden, R. J., and D. A. Turkington (1981). "A Comparative Study of Instrumental Variable Estimators for Nonlinear Simultaneous Models." *Journal of the American Statistical Association* 76, 988–95.

Box, G. E. P. (1957). "Use of Statistical Methods in the Elucidation of Basic Mechanisms." *Bulletin of the International Institute of Statistics* 36, 215–25.

Brundy, J. M., and D. W. Jorgenson (1971). "Efficient Estimation of Simultaneous Equations by Instrumental Variables." *Review of Economics and Statistics* 53, 207–24.

Burtless, G., and J. A. Hausman (1978). "The Net Effect of Taxation on Labour Supply: Evaluating the Gory Negative Income Tax Experiment." *Journal of Political Economy* 86, 1103–30.

Byron, R. P. (1978). "On the Derived Reduced Form from Limited Information Maximum Likelihood." Australian National University. Mimeo.

Cooley, W. W., and P. R. Lohnes (1971). *Multivariate Data Analysis.* New York: Wiley.

Court, R. H. (1973). "Efficient Estimation of the Reduced Form from Econometric Models." *Review of Economic Studies* 40, 411–18.

Cox, D. R., and D. V. Hinkley (1974). *Theoretical Statistics.* London: Chapman & Hall.

Crowden, M. J. (1976). "Maximum Likelihood Estimation for Dependent Observations." *Journal of the Royal Statistical Society,* ser. B, 38, 45-53.

Dhrymes, P. J. (1971). *Distributed Lags: Problems of Estimation and Formulation.* San Francisco: Holden-Day.

(1978). *Mathematics for Econometrics.* New York: Springer-Verlag.

Duck, N., M. Parkin, D. Rose, and G. Zis (1976). "The Determination of the Rate of Change of Wages and Prices in the Fixed Exchange Rate World Economy, 1956-1971." In M. Parkin and G. Zis, eds., *Inflation in the World Economy.* Manchester: University Press.

Durbin, J. (1954). "Errors in Variables." *Review of the Institute of International Statistics* 22, 23-31.

Edgerton, D. L. (1972). "Some Properties of Two-Stage Least-Squares as Applied to Nonlinear Models." *International Economic Review* 13, 26-32.

Efron, B. (1975). "Defining the Curvature of a Statistical Problem (with Applications to Second Order Efficiency)." *Annals of Statistics* 3, 1189-242.

Fair, R. C. (1970). "The Estimation of Simultaneous Equation Models with Lagged Endogenous Variables and First Order Serially Correlated Errors." *Econometrica* 38, 507-16.

Feldstein, M. (1974). "Errors in Variables: A Consistent Estimator with Smaller MSE in Finite Samples." *Journal of the American Statistical Association* 69, 990-6.

Fisher, F. M. (1965). "The Choice of Instrumental Variables in the Estimation of Economy-wide Econometric Models." *International Economic Review* 6, 245-75.

(1966). *The Identification Problem in Econometrics.* New York: McGraw-Hill.

Friedman, M. (1957). *A Theory of the Consumption Function.* Princeton: Princeton University Press.

Fuller, W. (1977). "Some Properties of a Modification of the Limited Information Estimator." *Econometrica* 45, 939-54.

Fuller, W., and M. A. Hidiroglou (1978). "Regression Estimation after Correcting for Attenuation." *Journal of the American Statistical Association* 73, 99-104.

Gallant, R. A. (1974). "Seemingly Unrelated Nonlinear Regressions." *Journal of Econometrics* 3, 35-50.

(1977). "Three-Stage Least-Squares Estimation for a System of Simultaneous, Nonlinear, Implicit Equations." *Journal of Econometrics* 5, 71-88.

Geary, R. C. (1949). "Determination of Linear Relations between Systematic Parts of Variables with Errors of Observations, the Variances of Which are Unknown." *Econometrica* 17, 30-58.

Godfrey, G. (1978a). "A Note on the Use of Durbin's h Test When the Equation Is Estimated by Instrumental Variables." *Econometrica* 46, 225-8.

(1978b). "Testing against General Autoregressive and Moving Average Error Models When the Regressors Include Lagged Dependent Variables." *Econometrica* 46, 1293-300.

Goldberger, A. S. (1964). *Econometric Theory.* New York: Wiley.

(1972a). "Structural Equation Methods in the Social Sciences." *Econometrica* 40, 979-1001.

(1972b). "Maximum Likelihood Estimation of Regressions Containing Unobservable Independent Variables." *International Economic Review* 13, 1–15.

Goldfeld, S. M., and R. E. Quandt (1968). "Nonlinear Simultaneous Equations: Estimation and Prediction." *International Economic Review* 9, 113–36.

(1972). *Nonlinear Methods in Econometrics* (in the series *Contributions to Economic Analysis,* no. 77). Amsterdam: North-Holland.

Goldfeld, S. M., R. E. Quandt, and H. F. Trotter (1966). "Maximization by Quadratic Hill Climbing." *Econometrica* 34, 541–51.

Grenander, U., and M. Rosenblatt (1957). *Statistical Analysis of Stationary Time Series.* New York: Wiley.

Haavelmo, T. (1943). "The Statistical Implications of a System of Simultaneous Equations." *Econometrica* 11, 1–12.

Hannan, E. J. (1965). "The Estimation of Relationships Involving Distributed Lags." *Econometrica* 33, 206–24.

(1970). *Multiple Time Series.* New York: Wiley.

Hansen, L. (1982). "Large Sample Properties of Generalized Methods of Moments Estimators." *Econometrica* 50, 1029–54.

Hartley, H. O. (1961). "The Modified Gauss–Newton Method for the Fitting of Nonlinear Regression Functions by Least-Squares." *Technometrics* 3, 269–80.

Hatanaka, M. (1973). "On the Existence and the Approximation Formulae for the Moments of the k-Class Estimators." *Economic Studies Quarterly* 24, 1–15.

(1974). "An Efficient Two-Step Estimator for the Dynamic Adjustment Model with Autoregressive Errors." *Journal of Econometrics* 2, 199–220.

(1978). "On the Efficient Estimation Methods for the Macro-Economic Models, Nonlinear in Variables." *Journal of Econometrics* 8, 323–56.

Hausman, J. A. (1975). "An Instrumental Variable Approach to Full Information Estimates for Linear and Certain Non-linear Econometric Models." *Econometrica* 43, 727–38.

(1978). "Specification Tests in Econometrics." *Econometrica* 46, 1251–70.

(1983). "Specification and Estimation of Simultaneous Equation Models." In Z. Griliches and M. D. Intriligator, eds., *Handbook of Econometrics.* Amsterdam: North-Holland.

Hausman, J. A., and W. B. Taylor (1980). "Identification in Simultaneous Equation Systems with Covariance Restrictions." MIT. Mimeo.

(1981). "A Generalized Specification Test." *Economics Letters* 8, 239–45.

Hausman, J. A., and R. Wise (1978). "A Conditional Probit Model for Quantitative Choice: Discrete Decisions Recognizing Interdependence and Heterogenous Preferences." *Econometrica* 46, 403–26.

Heckman, J. (1976). "The Common Structure of Statistical Models of Truncation; Sample Estimation for Such Models." *Annals of Economic and Social Measurement* 5, 475–92.

Hendry, D. (1971). "Maximum Likelihood Estimation of Systems of Simultaneous Regression Equations with Errors Generated by a Vector Autoregressive Process." *International Economic Review* 12, 257–72.

Hoerl, A. E., and R. W. Kennard (1970a). "Ridge Regression: Biased Estimation of Non-Orthogonal Problems." *Technometrics* 12, 55–67.

(1970b). "Ridge Recession: Application to Non-Orthogonal Problems." *Technometrics* 12, 69–82.

Holly, A. (1982). "A Remark on Hausman's Specification Test." *Econometrica* 50, 749–59.

Johnson, N. L., and S. Kotz (1970). *Continuous Univariate Distributions,* vol. 1. New York: Wiley.

(1972). *Continuous Multivariate Distributions.* New York: Wiley.

Johnston, J. (1963). *Econometric Methods.* 1st ed. New York: McGraw-Hill.

(1972). *Econometric Methods.* 2nd ed. New York: McGraw-Hill.

Jorgenson, D. W., and J. Laffont (1974). "Efficient Estimation of Nonlinear Simultaneous Equations with Additive Disturbances." *Annals of Economic and Social Measurement* 3, 615–40.

Judge, G. G., and M. E. Bock (1978). *The Statistical Implications of Pre-Test and Stein-Rule Estimators in Econometrics.* Amsterdam: North-Holland.

Kakwani, N. C., and R. H. Court (1972). "Reduced Form Coefficient Estimation and Forecasting from a Simultaneous Equation Model." *Australian Journal of Statistics* 14, 143–60.

Kelejian, H. (1971). "Two-Stage Least-Squares and Econometric Systems Linear in Parameters but Nonlinear in Endogenous Variables." *Journal of the American Statistical Association* 66, 373–74.

Kendall, M. G., and A. Stuart (1973). *The Advanced Theory of Statistics,* vol. 2. 2nd ed. New York: Hafner.

Kloek, T., and L. B. M. Mennes (1960). "Simultaneous Equations Estimation Based on Principal Components of Predetermined Variables." *Econometrica* 28, 45–61.

Knight, J. (1977). "On the Existence of Moments of the Partially Restricted Reduced-Form Estimators from a Simultaneous Equation Model." *Journal of Econometrics* 5, 315–21.

Koopmans, T. C., and W. C. Hood (1953). "Estimation of Simultaneous Linear Economic Relationships." In W. C. Hood and T. C. Koopmans, eds., *Studies in Econometric Method.* New York: Wiley.

Kulback, S. (1967). "The Two Concepts of Information." *Journal of the American Statistical Association* 62, 685–6.

Levenberg, K. (1944). "A Method for the Solution of Certain Nonlinear Problems in Least-Squares." *Quarterly Applied Mathematics* 2, 164–8.

Lindley, D. V., and G. M. El-Sayyad (1968). "The Bayesian Estimation of a Linear Functional Relationship." *Journal of the Royal Statistical Society,* ser. B, 30, 190–202.

Liviatan, N. (1963). "Consistent Estimation of Distributed Lags." *International Economic Review* 4, 44–52.

McCarthy, M. D. (1981). "A Note on the Moments of Partially Restricted Reduced Forms." *Journal of Econometrics* 17, 383–7.

McDonald, J. (1977). "The Relationship between Wage Inflation and Excess Demand: New Estimates Using Optimal Extrapolative Expectations." *Economic Record* 53, 490–507.

Maddala, G. S. (1977). *Econometrics.* New York: McGraw-Hill.

Malinvaud, E. (1970). *Statistical Methods of Econometrics.* 2nd ed. Amsterdam: North-Holland.

Mariano, R. S. (1972). "The Existence of Moments of the Ordinary Least-Squares and Two-Stage Least-Squares Estimators." *Econometrica* 40, 643–52.

(1973a). "Approximations to the Distribution Functions of the OLS and 2SLS Estimators in the Case of Two Included Endogenous Variables." *Econometrica* 41, 67–77.

(1973b). "Approximations to the Distribution Functions of Theil's k-Class Estimators." *Econometrica* 41, 715–22.

(1974). "Some Large Concentration Parameter Asymptotics for the k-Class Estimators." Discussion Paper no. 274, Department of Economics, University of Pennsylvania.

(1977). "Finite Sample Properties of Instrumental Variables Estimators of Structural Coefficients." *Econometrica* 45, 487–96.

Mariano, R. S., and T. Sawa (1972). "The Exact Finite Sample Distribution of the LIML Estimator in the Case of Two Included Endogenous Variables." *Journal of the American Statistical Association* 67, 159–63.

Marquardt, D. W. (1963). "An Algorithm for Least-Squares Estimation of Nonlinear Parameters." *SIAM Journal* 11, 431–41.

Mitchell, B. M., and F. M. Fisher (1970). "The Choice of Instrumental Variables in the Estimation of Economy-wide Econometric Models: Some Further Thoughts." *International Economic Review* 11, 226–34.

Nagar, A. L. (1959). "The Bias and Moment Matrix of the General k-Class Estimators of the Parameters in Simultaneous Equations." *Econometrica* 27, 575–95.

Nagar, A. L., and S. N. Sahay (1978). "The Bias and Mean Squared Error of Forecasts from Partially Restricted Reduced Forms." *Journal of Econometrics* 7, 227–43.

Nair, K. R., and M. P. Shrivastava (1942). "On a Simple Method of Curve Fitting." *Sankhya* 6, 121–32.

Narayan, R. (1969). "Computation of Zellner–Theils' Three-Stage Least-Squares Estimates." *Econometrica* 37, 298–306.

Norden, R. H. (1972). "A Survey of Maximum Likelihood Estimation." *International Statistical Review* 40, 329–54.

(1973). "A Survey of Maximum Likelihood Estimation: Part 2." *International Statistical Review* 41, 39–58.

Phillips, P. C. B. (1980). "The Exact Distribution of Instrumental Variables Estimators in an Equation Containing $n+1$ Endogenous Variables." *Econometrica* 48, 861–78.

Rao, C. R. (1973). *Linear Statistical Inference and Its Application.* 2nd ed. New York: Wiley.

Rao, C. R., and S. K. Mitra (1971). *Generalized Inverse of Matrices and Its Applications.* New York: Wiley.

Reiersol, O. (1941). "Confluence Analysis by Means of Lag Moments and Other Methods of Confluence Analysis." *Econometrica* 9, 1–24.

Richardson, D. H. (1968). "The Exact Distribution of a Structural Coefficient Estimator." *Journal of the American Statistical Association* 63, 1214–26.

Richardson, D. H., and R. J. Rohr (1971). "Distribution of a Structural t-statistic for the Case of Two Included Endogenous Variables." *Journal of the American Statistical Association* 66, 375–82.

Richardson, D. H., and D. M. Wu (1971). "A Note on the Comparison of Ordinary and Two-Stage Least-Square Estimates." *Econometrica* 39, 973–82.

Robinson, P. M. (1974). "Identification, Estimation, and Large-Sample Theory for Regression Containing Unobservable Variables." *International Economic Review* 15, 680–92.

Rosen, H. S. (1976). "Taxes in a Labor Supply Model with Joint Wage–Hours Determination." *Econometrica* 44, 485–507.

Rothenberg, T. J. (1973). *Efficient Estimation with A-Priori Information.* Cowles Foundation Monograph 23. New Haven: Yale University Press.

Rothenberg, T. J., and C. T. Leenders (1964). "Efficient Estimation of Simultaneous Equation Systems." *Econometrica* 32, 57–76.

Sargan, J. D. (1958). "The Estimation of Economic Relationships Using Instrumental Variables." *Econometrica* 26, 393–415.

(1961). "The Maximum Likelihood Estimation of Economic Relationships with Autoregressive Residuals." *Econometrica* 29, 414–26.

(1974). "The Finite Sample Distribution of the Instrumental Variables Estimator on Classical Assumptions." London School of Economics. Mimeo.

(1976). "Econometric Estimators and the Edgeworth Approximation." *Econometrica* 44, 421–48.

Sargan, J. D., and W. M. Mikhail (1971). "A General Approximation to the Distribution of Instrumental Variable Estimates." *Econometrica* 39, 131–69.

Savin, N. E. (1973). "System k-Class Estimators." *Econometrica* 41, 1125–36.

Sawa, T. (1969). "The Exact Finite Sampling Distribution of OLS and 2SLS Estimators." *Journal of the American Statistical Association* 64, 923–37.

(1972). "Finite Sample Properties of the k-Class Estimators." *Econometrica* 40, 653–80.

Schmidt, P. (1976). *Econometrics.* New York: Marcel Dekker.

Solari, M. E. (1969). "The Maximum Likelihood Solution of the Problem of Estimating a Linear Functional Relationship." *Journal of the Royal Statistical Society,* ser. B, 31, 372–5.

Sprent, P. (1970). "Comment on the Saddle Point of the Likelihood Surface for a Linear Functional Relationship." *Journal of the Royal Statistical Society,* ser. B, 32, 432–4.

Srivastava, V. K. (1971). "Three-Stage Least-Squares and Generalized Double k-Class Estimators: A Mathematical Relationship." *International Economic Review* 12, 312–16.

Strawderman, W. E. (1978). "Minimax Adaptive Generalized Ridge Regression Estimators." *Journal of the American Statistical Association,* 73, 623–7.

Swamy, P. A. V. B. (1970). "Efficient Inference in a Random Coefficient Regression Model." *Econometrica* 38, 311–23.

(1971). *Statistical Inference in Random Coefficient Regression Models.* New York: Springer-Verlag.

Swamy, P. A. V. B., and J. S. Mehta (1981). "On the Existence of Moments of Partially Restricted Reduced Form Coefficients." *Journal of Econometrics* 14, 183–94.

Theil, H. (1953a). "Repeated Least-Squares Applied to Complete Equation Systems." Central Planning Bureau, The Hague. Mimeo.

(1953b). "Estimation and Simultaneous Correlation in Complete Equation Systems." Central Planning Bureau, The Hague. Mimeo.

(1961). *Economic Forecasts and Policy.* 2nd ed. Amsterdam: North-Holland.

(1971). *Principles of Econometrics.* Amsterdam: North-Holland.

Wald, A. (1940). "The Fitting of Straight Lines If Both Variables Are Subject to Error." *Annals of Mathematical Statistics* 11, 284–300.

Wallis, K. F. (1967). "Lagged Dependent Variables and Serially Correlated Errors: A Reappraisal of Three-Pass Least-Squares." *Review of Economics and Statistics* 51, 555–67.

White, H. (1980a). "Nonlinear Regression in Cross-Section Data." *Econometrica* 48, 721–46.

(1980b). "A Heteroskedasticity-Consistent Covariance Matrix Estimator and a Direct Test for Heteroskedasticity." *Econometrica* 48, 817–38.

(1982). "Instrumental Variable Regression with Independent Observations." *Econometrica* 50, 483–99.

Whittle, P. (1964). *Prediction and Regulation by Linear Least-Squares Methods.* London: English University Press.

Wickens, M. R. (1982). "The Efficient Estimation of Econometric Models with Rational Expectations." *Review of Economic Studies* 49, 55–68.

Working, E. J. (1927). "What Do Statistical Demand Curves Show?" *Quarterly Journal of Economics* 39, 503–45.

Wright, S. (1928). Appendix to *The Tariff on Animal and Vegetable Oils* by P. G. Wright. New York: Macmillan.

(1934). "The Method of Path Coefficients." *Annals of Mathematical Statistics* 5, 161–215.

Wu, D. M. (1973). "Alternative Tests of Independence between Stochastic Regressors and Disturbances." *Econometrica* 40, 733–50.

Zellner, A. (1970). "Estimation of Regression Relationships Containing Independent Variables." *International Economic Review* 11, 441–54.

Notes

1 MOTIVATION

1. Concepts of stochastic convergence are reviewed in Appendix A1.
2. For different applications and some econometric theory we refer the reader to examples such as Zellner (1970), Goldberger (1972b), Aigner (1974), Robinson (1974), and Bowden (1978, chapter 3).
3. We owe this observation to G. S. Maddala (personal conversation with R.J.B.).
4. The minimization can, as usual, be carried out using methods of vector differential calculus. The demonstration that $\hat{\beta}$ is indeed a minimum is straightforward. Write

$$\mathbf{y}=X\beta=y-X\hat{\beta}-X(\beta-\hat{\beta})$$

and the minimand is

$$\phi_w(\beta)=(\mathbf{y}-X\beta)'ZWZ'(\mathbf{y}-X\hat{\beta})+(\beta-\hat{\beta})'X'ZWZ'X'(\beta-\hat{\beta})$$
$$-2(\beta-\hat{\beta})'X'ZWZ'X'(\mathbf{y}-X\hat{\beta}).$$

The last term on the right-hand side is zero, since

$$X'ZWZ'X'(y-X\hat{\beta})=X'ZWZ'X'\mathbf{y}$$
$$-(X'ZWZ'X')(X'ZWZ'X')^{-1}X'ZWZ'X\mathbf{y}=\mathbf{0}.$$

Since the matrix $X'ZWZ'X'$ is at least positive semidefinite, the required result follows.

5. Here and in what follows we shall in the interests of readability frequently use our own notation rather than that of the original authors.
6. To see this, write $m_{ir}-m_{ir}^*=\sum_t(\epsilon_{it}-\bar{\epsilon}_i)z_{rt}/n$. Under our assumptions,

$$\mathcal{E}(m_{ir}-m_{ir}^*)=0 \qquad \text{and} \qquad \operatorname{Var}(m_{ir}-m_{ir}^*)=O(1/n).$$

2 THE SPHERICAL LINEAR MODEL

1. Since both X and Z are in general stochastic, singularities could occur; however, we assume that such singularities occur on a set of measure zero.

2. The reader unfamiliar with the concepts of stochastic convergence used in the theorem and ensuing discussion may like to refer to Appendix A1, which contains a simple glossary of such terms.
3. The k-class estimator in econometrics with $k=1+1/\sqrt{n}$ is one such example; see Schmidt (1976, pp. 103–4).
4. The columns $\mathbf{a}_j$ of A are the solution to the generalized eigenvector equations $[r_j^2 X'X - X'Z(Z'Z)^{-1}Z'X]\mathbf{a}_j = \mathbf{0}$, with the columns of B similarly defined with X and Z interchanged. For a complete review of canonical correlation theory we refer the reader to books on multivariate analysis such as Anderson (1958) or Kendall and Stuart (1973, vol. 2). A practical treatment may be found in Cooley and Lohnes (1971).
5. Expanding in Taylor series about θ_0,

$$\frac{1}{n}\sum f(\hat{\theta}, w_i)u_i = \frac{1}{n}\sum f(\theta_0, w_i)u_i + (\hat{\theta}-\theta)\frac{1}{n}\sum f'(\theta_*, w_i)u_i,$$

   where θ_* is on the line joining θ_0 and $\hat{\theta}$. To show that the left-hand side tends in probability to zero, what is essentially needed is to demonstrate that the sum $(1/n)\sum f'(\theta_*, w_i)u_i$ remains bounded in probability as $n \to \infty$. We refer the reader forward to the proof of Proposition 5.1 in Chapter 5 for a full discussion of a similar problem.
6. In consulting the original source, the reader should be warned that our notation clashes with that of Wu. We have adopted the notational system above because we feel that it is easier to follow and since it relates more effectively to the general notation used in this chapter.
7. For the errors-in-variables model we use i for the representative observation rather than t. This reflects the fact that such models are more often applied to cross-sectional work than to time series.
8. Formulas of the type $[X'X+kA]^{-1}X'\mathbf{y}$, where A is a symmetric, positive definite matrix and k is a scalar, occur in other contexts, notably generalized ridge regression, where k is positive (Hoerl and Kennard 1970a, b; Strawderman 1978), and in the Stein-type estimation considered by Judge and Bock (1978), where k is negative. It would be of interest to explore the connection and resulting analogies between the literatures involved.
9. It may be more than a matter of convenience to restrict k to the interval $(0,1)$. Thus it is known in the simultaneous-equations context that the moments of the (limited-information) k-class estimator do not exist for nonstochastic $k>1$. We refer the reader to Section 4.8 for a discussion of such matters.
10. Thus one could argue that whether $\rho=0$ or $\rho\neq 0$ is not a matter of much intrinsic importance. The issue is whether the estimation and hypothesis testing of β is materially affected. If this line of attack is followed, the Wu-Hausman procedures might be a better way to tackle the problem of serial correlation.

3 INSTRUMENTAL VARIABLES AND NONSPHERICAL DISTURBANCES

1. For the regression $\mathbf{y}=X\beta+\mathbf{u}$, with X a fixed design matrix and $\operatorname{Cov}\mathbf{u} = \sigma^2\Omega$, the Aitken or generalized least-squares estimator is defined by $\hat{\beta} = (X'\Omega^{-1}X)^{-1}X'\Omega^{-1}\mathbf{y}$.

2. Technically, however, the matrix $I-\tilde{P}'\tilde{P}$ is indefinite. Since $\tilde{U}'\tilde{U}=I$, it is easy to show by considering the matrix $\tilde{U}\Lambda^{-2}\tilde{U}'$ that the eigenvalues of $I-\tilde{P}'\tilde{P}$ are $\lambda_j=1-\tilde{r}_j^{-2}$ for $j=1,\ldots,p$; and $\lambda_j=1$ for $j=p+1,\ldots,n$. Those of the first set are always negative.
3. This can be seen by writing

$$y_t=\frac{\beta}{1-\lambda L}w_t+\left(\frac{1-\rho L}{1-\lambda L}\right)\epsilon_t,$$

where L is the lag operator such that (e.g.) $Ly_t=y_{t-1}$. The new disturbance term can be expressed as

$$\epsilon_t+(\lambda+\rho)(\epsilon_{t-1}+\lambda\epsilon_{t-2}+\cdots).$$

It is clear that unless $\beta=0$ and $\lambda=\rho$, the variance of y will exceed that of σ^2.
4. That is, if we write $u_t=B(L)\epsilon_t$ as the moving average representation, the roots of $B(L)=0$ lie outside the unit circle. Hence a representation of the form $A(L)u_t=\epsilon_t$ exists, with $A(L)B(L)=1$.
5. This is not to say that an error structure that is not white noise automatically creates problems of regressor–error correlations.
6. In what follows, we derive results in terms of convergence in probability (weak convergence) rather than the stronger almost sure convergence obtained by White. Apart from expositional advantages in not having to list an extensive set of assumptions, we are able to cast convergence conditions in terms only of the instruments z_{it} and the disturbances u_t, which seems an advantage where the available basic instrument set $\{z_t\}$ may consist of variables that are possibly not independent over t. This said, it is of course desirable to obtain strong convergence if at all possible in the given context.

4 LINEAR SIMULTANEOUS EQUATIONS

1. Such simple models are widely employed in econometric texts. The present version appears in G. S. Maddala (1977).
2. Predetermined variables are lagged values of the endogenous variables plus true exogenous variables. We shall use the terms *predetermined* and *exogenous* interchangeably to refer to both types of variables except where a distinction of importance exists, in which case the usage will be made clear.
3. The vec( ) operator stacks the columns of a matrix one on top of the other. The vec( ) and Kronecker product operations $\otimes$ have a complementary relationship; see Appendix A4 for a discussion and some useful results.
4. Here we use the result (see Rao 1973, p. 32),

$$\begin{vmatrix} A & C \\ B & D \end{vmatrix}=|A|\,|D-BA^{-1}C|.$$

5. This section is based on notes given to a joint Berkeley–Stanford seminar in econometrics and mathematical economics presented by Thomas Rothenberg at Stanford University in November 1978.

5 NONLINEAR ESTIMATION WITH INSTRUMENTAL VARIABLES

1. In addition to the standard regularity conditions on the X variables, it will suffice that (a) $(1/n)J'H_1'X_0$ converges in probability to a constant matrix of

full-column rank, uniformly in $\mathbf{O}$; and (b) $(1/n)(\partial/\partial\theta_j)J'(\theta)H_1'X_0$ converges in probability to a constant matrix, for all j.

2. However, as pointed out below, including predetermined variables among the elements of $\mathbf{x}_t$ should make no difference to the admissibility of the internal instrument, provided of course that the equation disturbances are serially uncorrelated.
3. We shall confine the proof to a demonstration that the proposed instrument $g(\hat{y}_{2t}, \mathbf{x}_t)$ is indeed asymptotically uncorrelated with the disturbance u_{1t}, referring the reader for additional details to Bowden and Turkington (1981). As well as constituting the basic underpinning of the proof, this will facilitate later remarks concerning the applicability of the procedure.
4. Obtaining such initial estimates is a bit of an art form in itself. Often one can linearize the function g by a suitably chosen Taylor expansion in terms of either variables or parameters, followed by a linear IV or OLS estimation. The resulting estimates can be used to recover some at least of the desired parameters $\boldsymbol{\theta}_c$. Our use of the word *guesstimate* refers to the combination of guesswork and prior estimation employed to obtain the initial values.
5. These will in the present section be considered to be true exogenous variables; i.e., they do not include lagged endogenous variables.
6. Because of the heavy notational burden, we shall not use special boldface notation to distinguish vectors from scalars in this annex. Thus, for example, θ_α now refers to a vector containing the parameters of the αth equation. The rest of the notation should be clear from the context.

Index